Intellectual Populism

RHETORIC AND PUBLIC AFFAIRS SERIES

- *Eisenhower's War of Words: Rhetoric and Leadership*, Martin J. Medhurst, editor
- *The Nuclear Freeze Campaign: Rhetoric and Foreign Policy in the Telepolitical Age*, J. Michael Hogan
- *Mansfield and Vietnam: A Study in Rhetorical Adaptation*, Gregory A. Olson
- *Truman and the Hiroshima Cult*, Robert P. Newman
- *Post-Realism: The Rhetorical Turn in International Relations*, Francis A. Beer and Robert Hariman, editors
- *Rhetoric and Political Culture in Nineteenth-Century America*, Thomas W. Benson, editor
- *Frederick Douglass: Freedom's Voice, 1818–1845*, Gregory P. Lampe
- *Angelina Grimké: Rhetoric, Identity, and the Radical Imagination*, Stephen Howard Browne
- *Strategic Deception: Rhetoric, Science, and Politics in Missile Defense Advocacy*, Gordon R. Mitchell
- *Rostow, Kennedy, and the Rhetoric of Foreign Aid*, Kimber Charles Pearce
- *Visions of Poverty: Welfare Policy and Political Imagination*, Robert Asen
- *General Eisenhower: Ideology and Discourse*, Ira Chernus
- *The Reconstruction Desegregation Debate: The Politics of Equality and the Rhetoric of Place, 1870–1875*, Kirt H. Wilson
- *Shared Land/Conflicting Identity: Trajectories of Israeli and Palestinian Symbol Use*, Robert C. Rowland and David A. Frank
- *Darwinism, Design, and Public Education*, John Angus Campbell and Stephen C. Meyer, editors
- *Religious Expression and the American Constitution*, Franklyn S. Haiman
- *Christianity and the Mass Media in America: Toward a Democratic Accommodation*, Quentin J. Schultze
- *Bending Spines: The Propagandas of Nazi Germany and the German Democratic Republic*, Randall L. Bytwerk
- *Malcolm X: Inventing Radical Judgment*, Robert E. Terrill
- *Metaphorical World Politics*, Francis A. Beer and Christ'l De Landtsheer, editors
- *The Lyceum and Public Culture in the Nineteenth-Century United States*, Angela G. Ray
- *The Political Style of Conspiracy: Chase, Sumner, and Lincoln*, Michael William Pfau
- *The Character of Justice: Rhetoric, Law, and Politics in the Supreme Court Confirmation Process*, Trevor Parry-Giles
- *Rhetorical Vectors of Memory in National and International Holocaust Trials*, Marouf A. Hasian Jr.
- *Judging the Supreme Court: Constructions of Motives in* Bush v. Gore, Clarke Rountree
- *Everyday Subversion: From Joking to Revolting in the German Democratic Republic*, Kerry Kathleen Riley
- *In the Wake of Violence: Image and Social Reform*, Cheryl R. Jorgensen-Earp
- *Rhetoric and Democracy: Pedagogical and Political Practices*, Todd F. McDorman and David M. Timmerman, editors
- *Invoking the Invisible Hand: Social Security and the Privatization Debates*, Robert Asen
- *With Faith in the Works of Words: The Beginnings of Reconciliation in South Africa, 1985–1995*, Erik Doxtader
- *Public Address and Moral Judgment: Critical Studies in Ethical Tensions*, Shawn J. Parry-Giles and Trevor Parry-Giles, editors
- *Executing Democracy: Capital Punishment and the Making of America, 1683–1807*, Stephen John Hartnett
- *Enemyship: Democracy and Counter-Revolution in the Early Republic*, Jeremy Engels
- *Spirits of the Cold War: Contesting Worldviews in the Classical Age of American Security Strategy*, Ned O'Gorman
- *Making the Case: Advocacy and Judgment in Public Argument*, Kathryn M. Olson, Michael William Pfau, Benjamin Ponder, and Kirt H. Wilson, editors
- *Executing Democracy: Capital Punishment and the Making of America, 1835–1843*, Stephen John Hartnett
- *William James and the Art of Popular Statement*, Paul Stob
- *On the Frontier of Science: An American Rhetoric of Exploration and Exploitation*, Leah Ceccarelli
- *The Good Neighbor: Franklin D. Roosevelt and the Rhetoric of American Power*, Mary E. Stuckey
- *Creating Conservatism: Postwar Words That Made an American Movement*, Michael J. Lee
- *Intertextuality and the 24-Hour News Cycle: A Day in the Rhetorical Life of Colin Powell's U.N. Address*, John Oddo
- *Superchurch: The Rhetoric and Politics of American Fundamentalism*, Jonathan J. Edwards
- *Rethinking Rhetorical Theory, Criticism, and Pedagogy: The Living Art of Michael C. Leff*, Antonio de Velasco, John Angus Campbell, and David Henry, editors
- *Imagining China: Rhetorics of Nationalism in an Age of Globalization*, Stephen J. Hartnett, Lisa B. Keränen, and Donovan Conley, editors
- *Political Vocabularies: FDR, the Clergy Letters, and the Elements of Political Argument*, Mary E. Stuckey
- *To Become an American: Immigrants and Americanization Campaigns of the Early Twentieth Century*, Leslie A. Hahner
- *The Rhetorical Invention of Diversity: Supreme Court Opinions, Public Argument, and Affirmative Action*, M. Kelly Carr
- *Michael Osborn on Metaphor and Style*, Michael Osborn
- *Debating Women: Gender, Education, and Spaces for Argument, 1835–1945*, Carly S. Woods
- *Strains of Dissent: Popular Music and Everyday Resistance in WWII France, 1940–1945*, Kelly Jakes
- *John F. Kennedy and the Liberal Persuasion*, John M. Murphy
- *National Rhetorics in the Syrian Immigration Crisis: Victims, Frauds, and Floods*, Clarke Rountree and Jouni Tilli, editors
- *The Origins of Bioethics: Remembering When Medicine Went Wrong*, John A. Lynch
- *The Manufacture of Consent: J. Edgar Hoover and the Rhetorical Rise of the FBI*, Stephen M. Underhill
- *Intellectual Populism: Democracy, Inquiry, and the People*, Paul Stob

Intellectual Populism

Democracy, Inquiry, and the People

Paul Stob

Michigan State University Press | *East Lansing*

♾ The paper used in this publication meets the minimum requirements
of ANSI/NISO Z39.48-1992 (R 1997) (Permanence of Paper).

Michigan State University Press
East Lansing, Michigan 48823-5245

LIBRARY OF CONGRESS CATALOGING-IN-PUBLICATION DATA
Names: Stob, Paul, author.
Title: Intellectual populism : democracy, inquiry, and the people / Paul Stob.
Description: East Lansing : Michigan State University Press, 2020. | Series: Rhetoric and public affairs series
| Includes bibliographical references and index.
Identifiers: LCCN 2019028386 | ISBN 9781611863604 (paperback) | ISBN 9781609176358 (PDF)
| ISBN 9781628953978 (ePub) | ISBN 9781628963984 (Kindle)
Subjects: LCSH: Populism—United States—History. | Democracy—United States—History.
| Rhetoric—United States—History. | United States—Intellectual life.
Classification: LCC JC423 .S857 2020 | DDC 320.56/620973—dc23
LC record available at https://lccn.loc.gov/2019028386

Book design by Charlie Sharp, Sharp Designs, East Lansing, MI
Cover design by Erin Kirk New
Cover: Large crowd gathered to hear Booker T. Washington speak, with men standing
on railroad box cars in the background, New Orleans, Louisiana, LC-USZ62-133988,
Library of Congress Prints and Photographs Division Washington, D.C.

green press INITIATIVE

Michigan State University Press is a member of the Green Press Initiative and is
committed to developing and encouraging ecologically responsible publishing
practices. For more information about the Green Press Initiative and the use
of recycled paper in book publishing, please visit *www.greenpressinitiative.org*.

Visit Michigan State University Press at *www.msupress.org*

Contents

Acknowledgments

The process of writing a book is, among other things, a process of accumulating debts to people who make the project far better than it would be otherwise. Even when only a single author's name is on the cover, writing is a collaborative affair. I could not have completed this project without thc insights and assistance of many people and institutions.

Vanderbilt University provided me the time and resources needed to visit several archives, and the College of Arts & Science provided much-needed financial help in completing the book. My colleagues in the Department of Communication Studies provided invaluable feedback on this book's case studies. A faculty fellowship from the Robert Penn Warren Center for the Humanities gave me the chance to share research with colleagues across the university and to discover new, interdisciplinary dimensions to the project. Students in my spring 2019 American

Studies graduate seminar read a draft of the manuscript and helped me strengthen it in many ways.

Colleagues at other universities gave this project the direction it needed. Marty Medhurst is not only an ideal editor but a cherished friend; he shaped the book in an untold number of ways. Mary Stuckey provided incisive, astute feedback and helped me navigate the voluminous literature on American Indian history and discourse. Angela Ray offered suggestions on many aspects of this project and served as an encouraging interlocutor along the way. Steve Lucas was the first person to introduce me to many of the figures in this book, and he will always be an inspiration for my research and writing. The anonymous reviewers for Michigan State University Press helped me grapple with the problems and possibilities of the manuscript. Thanks to the people and institutions who invited me to speak on different parts of this project: Dave Tell and the Department of Communication Studies at the University of Kansas; Dave Gore and the Department of Communication at the University of Minnesota, Duluth; John Murphy and the Department of Communication at the University of Illinois; and Marty Medhurst and the Department of Communication at Baylor University.

A project that depends on extensive archival research can't happen without the support of some incredible archivists and librarians. Thanks to the staff at the Abraham Lincoln Presidential Library; to the good folks at the Mary Baker Eddy Library, which supported this project with a research fellowship; to the archivists at Yale's Beinecke Library; to the many people working behind the scenes at the Library of Congress; to the amazing people at the Tuskegee University Archives; to the staff at the L. Tom Perry Special Collections at Brigham Young University; and to the interlibrary loan staff at Vanderbilt, who always found ways to get me the resources I needed. Although not an archivist or librarian, Tadeusz Lewandowski provided indispensable assistance on navigating the archives of Zitkala-Ša.

Thanks to the staff at Michigan State University Press for their expert editorial guidance and their commitment to this book. Thanks to Ann Weaver for her incredible attention to detail.

My wife, Sarah, and my son, Elliott, along with our two dogs, patiently listened to many ideas and factoids from this project. My mom and dad have always been encouraging, generous, and supportive. This book is dedicated to the memory of Andrew Bandstra and Henry Stob, my grandfathers, who were, and will remain, an inspiration.

Introduction

Populism threatens democracy—or so the current political moment suggests. Now that Donald Trump has assumed the presidency, now that civil society seems patently uncivil, now that white nationalism marches resolutely forward, populism occupies a lamentable place in public culture. And that's just the United States. Populism roils the globe as well. European leaders such as Silvio Berlusconi, Geert Wilders, and Marine Le Pen; Latin American leaders such as Nicolas Maduro, Evo Morales, and Rafael Correa; African leaders such as Yoweri Museveni, Julius Malema, and Raila Odinga; and Asia-Pacific leaders such as Pauline Hanson, Rodrigo Duterte, and Prabowo Subianto—all of them, in their own ways, have disrupted civil society and blasted the existing political order for the purported benefit of "the people," who are really just a narrow constituency of donors and supporters. By propping up their constituency as "the people," these supposed populist leaders circumvent the pluralism and diversity of modern liberal democracy to push their agenda, creating widespread division and thwarting the public good.

Regardless of whether Trump and his ilk are truly "populists"—they may be better understood as "authoritarians" or "autocrats"—the terms "populist" and "populism" have accompanied their rise and, in turn, surged to the fore of political discourse. Writing in *Politico*, Joshua Zeitz denounces the "populist demons Trump has unleashed—revanchist in outlook, conspiratorial in the extreme, given to frequent expressions of white nationalism and antisemitism."[1] Writing in the *Washington Post*, Jennifer Rubin argues that Trump rode "a global wave of right-wing populism—xenophobic, authoritarian, protectionist and (white) nationalistic—into office," resulting in a presidency based on "a gambit, a play for attention and fame, another Trump marketing ploy."[2] Writing for *NBC News*, Evan McMullin summarizes the problem: though some herald populism "as embodying the will of the people, in reality populism—on either ideological side—corrodes the foundations of democracy and destabilizes nations."[3] In word if not in deed, then, populism stands against democracy and the liberal values we have striven to implement across generations.

Political commentators are not alone in sounding the alarm against populism; numerous scholars have also positioned it as a threat to democracy. To contextualize the Trump presidency and the wave of populist revolts overseas, Jan-Werner Müller answers the question "What is populism?" by pointing to antipluralist sentiments propelling the rise of an authoritarian state.[4] In *The Populist Temptation*, Barry Eichengreen argues that populism is not only simplistic but also counterproductive to the kind of economic policies that will actually benefit ordinary people.[5] Similarly, in *The People vs. Democracy: Why Our Freedom Is in Danger & How to Save It*, Yascha Mounk argues that global populist movements undermine democracy by trumpeting the popular will over individual rights.[6] William Galston summarizes this danger in *Anti-pluralism: The Populist Threat to Liberal Democracy*, linking the rise of populism to declining support for democratic institutions, the rule of law, and even the Constitution.[7] Ultimately, Galston states, populism threatens liberal democracy because of its "tribalism, its Manichean outlook, and the constant conflict it entails."[8]

Populism's threat to democracy is a quandary for many scholars. Yet equally problematic, if not more so, is populism's threat to thought—that is, to inquiry and to the existing intellectual order. When "the people" join together to oppose "the elites," as they do in populist uprisings, they often oppose not just established politicians and financiers but also academics, experts, and highly educated members of the privileged class. Galston argues that one of the primary factors of the United States' current populist fervor is the divide separating those with advanced degrees from "the masses":

> As a group, individuals with higher education value science, professional expertise, and relationships across national boundaries. Those without a higher education value these things much less. In themselves, these differences are not a cause for alarm. But difficulties emerge when educational inequalities become markers of social status. Put bluntly, if Americans with more education regard their less educated fellow citizens with disrespect, the inevitable response from the disrespected will be resentment coupled with a desire to take revenge on those who assert superiority. Much of the populist spirit in the United States reflects this dynamic.[9]

To be sure, the educational divide is not the only source of populist resentment; other factors such as employment, globalization, immigration, geography, and cultural values also shape the movement. But if, as Galston continues, highly educated people tend to believe "that they have options in life and that they retain a measure of control over their own fate," while less educated people "are more likely to see themselves as lacking control over their own lives," then populist ire will burn against those who claim expert knowledge of and authority over reality.

Because of this burning ire, many scholars have deemed populism an anti-intellectual movement. Richard Hofstadter was among the first to detail this charge. His *Anti-intellectualism in American Life* drew a line from populist politics in the nineteenth century to a pervasive suspicion of intellectual life in the twentieth century. As American populism grew in strength and confidence, wrote Hofstadter, it averred the truth of "inborn, intuitive, folkish wisdom" along with the "native practical sense of the ordinary man." The result was "a kind of militant popular anti-intellectualism." Populism's reactionary intuition thus impeded proper inquiry, creating a generation that opposed the authority of "the specialist, the expert, the gentleman, and the scholar." This hostility alienated intellectuals from public life for much of the twentieth century.[10]

Although many historians have raised questions about Hofstadter's account—skewed perhaps by the context of McCarthyism in which Hofstadter wrote—other scholars have seen a similar anti-intellectualism in populist politics.[11] Kenneth Minogue, for instance, has criticized American populism for the "intellectual emptiness" it displays by spouting off slogans that mask its inconsistent ideology.[12] Colleen Shogan has argued that several recent U.S. presidents—well before Trump ascended to the office—have used populism's anti-intellectual orientation to build their political base.[13] John Lukacs has argued that populism is overwhelming democracy by pitting reactionary nationalism against intellectual advancement and scholarly expertise.[14] Perhaps Aaron Lecklider has put the point best: "In contemporary American culture, anti-intellectualism represents a form of populism that is at best dangerous, at worst an indicator of Western civilization in its final death throes. Either way, it is not a good look."[15]

According to these and many other accounts, then, populism imperils inquiry at the same time it impedes democracy. Populist fervor threatens the life of the mind, the status of the university, the diversity of American life, and what we think we know about the world. That is why, one might conclude, we now see widespread denial of evolution, flippant dismissal of the severity of climate change, the return of flat-earth theory, a surge of antivaccination efforts, a host of ill-founded conspiracies, and vehement denunciations of universities as out of touch and subversive. These dynamics provide compelling evidence that populism goes hand in hand with anti-intellectualism, at least in public discourse. In turn, the chasm between "intellectuals" and "the masses" threatens to swallow civil society whole.

But maybe it does not have to be that way. Maybe populism need not threaten intellectual culture and democracy. Maybe populist fervor can spur inquiry, bolster education initiatives, and enrich the pluralism, diversity, and collaboration of our communities. Maybe populism can bridge the chasm between "intellectuals" and "the masses." As this book will suggest, populism and intellectualism can work together to enhance our knowledge of the world, to infuse inquiry with a democratic ethos, and to bring ordinary people into deliberations about the most important issues we face. Throughout American history a number of prominent thinkers have used populist discourse in this way, deploying a set of ideas, appeals, and attitudes to animate the intellectual lives of ordinary Americans. Instead of opposing inquiry and democracy, populism has fostered it, constituting what this book characterizes as a populist intellectual tradition. Although populism begins with a spirited sense of conflict and antagonism, even in the realm of ideas, it can build diverse, democratic communities of inquiry that make the pursuit of knowledge responsive to the needs and lives of the people. And it can vest the people with the responsibilities of intellectual engagement.

Intellectual Populism is a book about the way the rhetoric of populism can animate, and has animated, a distinctive mode of inquiry useful for bringing individuals often excluded from the world of thought into new, democratic communities of inquiry. Although several scholars have already shown that populism need not oppose democracy[16] and that populist politics has often included robust intellectual affairs,[17] this book connects these dynamics to expose a largely overlooked strain of American thought and culture. Many prominent thinkers have used language that infuses populist energy into the pursuit of knowledge, thereby drawing ordinary people into intellectual affairs attuned to the norms and ideals of democratic culture. In that way, *Intellectual Populism* explores not how populist political movements have contributed to intellectual affairs but how intellectuals—thinkers, writers, orators, scientists, philosophers, educators—have used populist rhetoric to propel a distinctive tradition of inquiry. This book, therefore, asserts and builds on an analogy: the appeals that have constituted the populist political tradition have also constituted a populist intellectual tradition. To be clear, there is not necessarily a historical connection between political populism and intellectual populism. That is to say, the intellectual figures and groups discussed in this book were not political populists in the way that the People's Party of the 1890s, Huey Long in the 1930s, George Wallace in the 1960s, and Donald Trump in the 2010s have been deemed populists. Rather, the language of populism, which I will detail below, has animated a distinctive intellectual tradition that pits "the people" against "the establishment" in an effort to revitalize and reclaim the world of thought.

In its most basic form, "intellectual populism" refers to a mode of symbolic engagement—a way of speaking, writing, and carrying oneself in the public arena—that calls ordinary people together in a project of resisting the intellectual status quo and reclaiming the pursuit of knowledge for pluralistic, democratic, productive ends. In this mode of engagement, the status quo refers to the figures, forces, and institutions that comprise the world of inquiry—professors, academics, research universities, funding agencies, specialized forums, and spaces considered off limits to people without training in a particular field. These figures, forces, and institutions comprise the establishment—real or imagined—against which "the people" align in a battle over the pursuit of knowledge. However, "the people" is never as inclusive as the label suggests; it is too often skewed according to race, class, gender, geography, and similar dimensions. Yet it is a powerful, useful term, especially in the United States, because many individuals respond to the idea that they are part of "the people"—that they are "ordinary" individuals, not the elites.[18] Recognizing the suasory potential of this term, intellectual populists hail "the people" and denounce the status quo to enliven the world of thought with new and diverse voices. Together in community and opposed to the establishment, ordinary people are empowered to debate such topics as the nature of reality, the nature of being, the conditions of right and wrong, the elements of good and bad, and the meaning of life. Where inquiry seems exclusionary, aloof, and inconsequential, intellectual populists rally the people together for renewed attention to life's big questions.

I first explored these dynamics and coined the term "intellectual populism" in a book about the philosopher and psychologist William James.[19] From early in his career until the year of his death, James traveled the country (and the world) addressing popular audiences about important topics in philosophy, psychology, religion, and similar subjects. His lectures routinely criticized current practices of academic specialists, bemoaning the obtuse arguments of philosophers and the self-importance of psychologists. In James's lectures, out-of-touch academics and the institutions that ensconced them failed to serve the needs of the people. Yet these criticisms were not meant to destroy philosophy, psychology, religion, and the areas of inquiry James held dear. Rather, they were designed to pull popular audiences into those areas to create a stronger, more robust, more democratic intellectual community. James's popular lectures rendered ordinary people as intellectual agents who could contribute to the progress of modern knowledge. His populism was not anti-intellectual; it was a way of bolstering intellectual culture by bringing the people into the world of ideas.

As this book will demonstrate, James was far from the only thinker leading the charge of intellectual populism. Intellectual populism has been an oft-overlooked yet regular part of American thought for some time. Around the turn of the twentieth century, as well as in other epochs, populism was an expansive, flexible style of intellectual engagement, allowing a diverse array of thinkers to cast their work in populist terms and to embolden ordinary people as intellectual agents. These intellectuals seemed to understand what James understood about populist discourse: opposing the established intellectual order is actually a way of strengthening intellectual culture writ large. Speaking against experts and institutions, as intellectual populists do, calls together people frustrated by those experts and institutions. In turn, they can contribute to the same culture of knowledge that the experts and institutions were serving. Intellectual populism opposes the status quo, but only to improve the discussions and deliberations the status quo controls. In other words, denouncing what frustrates people is a good way to energize them to contribute to the areas where their frustration lies. Through shared opposition to the established order, more people can gather for the important work of thinking together.[20]

However, understanding the function of intellectual populism requires careful consideration of several key terms, ideas, and contexts. And the best place to start is with the oft-contested, widely maligned concept of populism.

Populism in Perspective

When commentators charge populism with threatening democracy and with anti-intellectualism, they often refer to a notion emptied of its history, complexity, and contributions. Understanding these dimensions requires that we distinguish between two general versions of populism. The first is Populism, the capitalized version, which refers to a particular movement of advocacy and reform—namely, the People's Party of the 1890s.[21] The second is populism, the lowercase version, which refers to a generalized mode of engagement—a style of agitational discourse that figures on the left and the right have employed throughout history.[22] Both the uppercase and lowercase versions are crucial for understanding the intellectual tradition at the center of this book.

The Populism that emerged as the People's Party began amid economic strife, as marginalized people tried "to fashion an alternative modernity."[23] Exploitative finance, especially in the wake of the panic of 1873, contributed to the creation of a generation of farmers who faced inescapable debt. Moreover, new arrangements for shipping, selling, and connecting markets in different parts of the country shifted economic power to industrial centers and away from the producers of goods in the countryside. Frustration with loss of control over agriculture prices and farm practices soon boiled over, especially in the South, Midwest, and Great Plains.[24] In Lampasas County, Texas, in the mid-1870s, local farmers got together to protect their interests from eastern institutions. Similar collectives soon followed in other parts of Texas and in other states. The leaders of these groups established an umbrella organization, the Farmers' Alliance, which attracted a quarter-million members by the end of the 1880s.[25] The Alliance stressed cooperative economics capable of resisting the modernist forces disrupting their way of life. At the same time, the organization reached out to other farm groups and to industrial workers, including the Knights of Labor, hoping to form a broad coalition capable of resisting the status quo.

To form this broad coalition, members of the Farmers' Alliance built their own ways of sharing ideas and aligning people.[26] Pamphlets, newsletters, and even a network of lecturers spread populist thought across the country. In fact, it was the lecture circuit that best connected the main Alliance with its subsidiaries around the country. Lecturers traversed a national network, propagating ideas and plans for effective resistance.[27] Far from being anti-intellectual, they worked diligently to build new, alternative venues of thought and action that they could control.[28] As Charles Postel summarizes, the Populists of the late nineteenth century created "a remarkable intellectual enterprise. . . . Few political or social movements brought so many men and women into lecture halls, classrooms, camp meetings, and seminars or produced such an array of inexpensive literature."[29]

In the case of the Farmers' Alliance, lectures, pamphlets, and newspapers also helped coordinate political action. Sometimes this political action took place within existing party structures, particularly the Democratic Party. But many farmers and industrial workers believed that the only chance for reform came with the creation of a third party. The most notable and successful was the People's Party, which emerged from a series of conferences held in the early 1890s. As legend has it, on a train ride from Ohio to Kansas, a handful of conference participants batted around possible placards for their movement, eventually settling on "Populist," from the Latin *populus*, or "people."[30] Soon Populist candidates, organized under the banner of the People's Party, swarmed local, state, and national elections. They achieved surprising success in local and state elections in the South and West. While national success was more limited, Populists left their mark. In 1894, Populist candidates collectively received 1.5 million votes, sending seven Populists to the House of Representatives and six to the Senate.[31] Once there, Populists championed the direct election of U.S. senators, which was eventually ratified in the Constitution, securing "complete power of the people over their lawmakers," as one Populist orator declared.[32]

For the purposes of this book, the electoral achievements of the People's Party are less important than the themes that defined Populist politics. Perhaps the most salient of these themes was antimonopolism, or what might better be described as opposition to established forms of concentrated power. "Stand firm against privileged monopolies wherever they occur" was a line that echoed through Populist literature and oratory.[33] As a result, Populists defined themselves, at least in part, by their shared opposition to the economic and political status quo, which served as a common enemy against which farmers and industrial workers, men and women, blacks and whites, northerners and southerners could align. Another prominent theme in Populist politics was the producer ethic, which held that farmers and laborers should retain ownership of what they produced. "Wealth belongs to him who creates it," declared Populist leader Ignatius Donnelly.[34] The goal was to overthrow bankers in the East and to put the common people back in control of agriculture, industry, transportation, finance, and politics. As Donnelly said further, Populism meant returning control of America "to the hands of the 'plain people' with whom it originated."[35] In Populist discourse, the idea of ordinary people established an ideological framework in which countless late nineteenth-century Americans could see themselves.

Another theme of Populist politics was equality. Populists embraced antimonopolism and producerism because they hoped to level the playing field with those in power. They wanted to give farmers, laborers, and other ordinary Americans the chance to compete in the modern economy. Unfortunately, the level playing field they envisioned was never as broad as it should have been, often excluding minorities, immigrants, and other marginalized populations. Nonetheless, the slogan

"Equal rights to all, special privilege to none" became a mainstay of Populist discourse.[36] Another mainstay was religion, specifically Protestantism, which guided Populists' agitation and encouraged Populists to see themselves as modern-day prophets. Populists worked to connect their economic and political grievances with a sense of religious purpose and with the symbols that rendered their work sacred.[37] In positioning their movement as religious, Populists hoped not only to reform society but also to construct a "righteous commonwealth" that would live up to the ideals of Christ and American history.[38] They thus preached of a salvation that was communal and social, as opposed to individual. When Populists created new institutions and frameworks, including agricultural exchanges, cooperative businesses, and nonprofit finance operations, they restructured society according to how they believed the world should be. In time, this restructuring would pave the way for a heaven on earth, for a utopia of flourishing families and powerful producers.[39]

While it would be possible to enumerate other aspects of Populist politics, perhaps the best way to summarize the movement is as simultaneously radical and conservative. From the outside, Populists seemed like radical socialists, threatening to disrupt the economic advancements of modern capitalism. To the Populists themselves, however, their work represented a return to traditional American values; theirs was a conservative project of restoration. "The Populists looked backward with longing to the lost agrarian Eden," writes Hofstadter, "to the republican America of the early years of the nineteenth century in which there were few millionaires and, as they saw it, no beggars, when the laborer had excellent prospects and the farmer had abundance, when statesmen still responded to the mood of the people and there was no such thing as the money power."[40] Despite the supposed radicalism of their proposals, Populists saw themselves as working from time-tested values—liberty, equality, fair play, justice, simplicity, morality, righteousness, and more. Radical conservatism, or conservative radicalism, allowed advocates to support seemingly radical changes while speaking for a hallowed tradition.

Unfortunately, this political stance did not lead to the long-term success the Populists sought. Though they built diverse coalitions of farmers and industrial laborers, northerners and southerners, blacks and whites, urban and rural Americans, they never achieved the consensus, organization, and direction needed for a new political party.[41] Problems in the Populist movement came to a head in 1896 when the People's Party threw its support, after much consternation, behind Democratic presidential candidate William Jennings Bryan. Bryan sounded like a Populist, he had grown up among Populists in the Great Plains, and his candidacy seemed to oppose the capitalist oligarchy that the Populists hated. But Bryan's defeat in the most expensive presidential election in U.S. history proved to be the beginning of the end for the Populists. After the 1896 election, the People's Party dwindled from a force for national political change into a collection of rabble-rousers. The dream of a righteous commonwealth dissolved in a "pivotal defeat for the grand coalition of the industrial classes and a decisive victory for corporate America."[42]

However, while Populism may have petered out, populism—the lowercase version—proved more agile. Opposing centralized power—be it political, economic, cultural, or otherwise—and demanding that ordinary people control their own fates became a familiar mode of political engagement. Ronald Formisano has demonstrated how populism operated across American history, recurring in almost every generation from the American Revolution to the Know-Nothings of the mid-1850s.[43] After the People's Party, populism influenced the democratic establishment via the work of Huey Long and Father Charles Coughlin.[44] Later in the twentieth century, George Wallace relied on populist themes to shore up segregationist support in his home state of Alabama and to make a name for himself across the nation.[45] In the 1990s, billionaire Ross Perot disseminated his populist message via a brilliant media strategy that resulted in the second-most-successful third-party race in the history of U.S. presidential elections.[46]

Yet the story of populism is richer and more expansive than this brief overview of U.S. politics. As a mode of political engagement, populism is ancient and expansive. Adrian Kuzminski has traced it to ancient Greece and the ideas of Phaleas of Chalcedon, who insisted that the state must balance the competing demands of democracy and property. This balance, according to Kuzminski, is the "essence of populism" and proves appealing the world over.[47] Political insurgencies around the globe in recent decades seem to bear this out. Since the early 1990s and the collapse of the Soviet Union, populism has moved from being an international political presence to a structure of governance. In South America, Brazil, Peru, and Argentina have seen populist leaders assume high national offices and embrace neoliberal economic policies to empower "the people." In Europe, France, the Netherlands, and Austria have witnessed populist agitators from the radical Right launch new and emboldened attacks on mainstream political orders, achieving significant success along the way.[48] Then came 2016. With Brexit in the United Kingdom, the election of Donald Trump in the United States, the election of Rodrigo Duterte in the Philippines, the flourishing of antiglobalization economics across the Continent, and more, populism seemed to become a global force, at least insofar as commentators characterized these movements as populist.

Benjamin Moffitt has argued that populism's recent success is due to its operation as a political style that involves a repertoire of "embodied, symbolically mediated performance" that pits the people against elites, adopts "bad manners" to coarsen political discourse, and fosters perceptions of crisis to draw people together.[49] Accordingly, it wends its way into specific situations while leaving its marks. That is why political scientists have, in addition to calling it a style, deemed populism everything from an "ideational" phenomenon to a "political-strategic" phenomenon to a "socio-cultural" phenomenon.[50] As with Moffitt's use of style, these labels underscore the notion that populism is less a matter of content than a framework for speaking, acting, and leading. It is an attitude, an orientation, and a way of relating to others. At its core, populism is a rhetoric.

The Rhetoric of Populism

As a rhetoric, populism offers a tool kit for engaging many kinds of situations—not just political ones. As this book hopes to demonstrate, populism's rhetorical repertoire makes it portable and flexible, enabling thinkers, writers, speakers, and audiences to adopt populist orientations toward the world of ideas. To understand this point, we first need to explore the constitutive elements of populist rhetoric.

Michael Kazin's work has been particularly influential in explicating populism as a rhetoric, calling it a "flexible mode of persuasion." According to Kazin, populism is "a language whose speakers conceive of ordinary people as a noble assemblage not bounded narrowly by class, view their elite opponents as self-serving and undemocratic, and seek to mobilize the former against the latter."[51] In approaching populism discursively, Kazin traces its deployment throughout American history—from Jacksonian democracy in the 1830s to the People's Party of the 1890s to Progressive Era unions to Christian Prohibitionists to Father Charles Coughlin to World War II labor struggles to Cold War conservatism to the New Left of the 1960s to the triumph of the New Right during the Reagan era. Across these disparate contexts, the appeals of populism became familiar and suasory to a host of publics.

According to Kazin, populism has proven so appealing because of its "primal grammar," which consists of four main components. The first component is an affirmation of so-called American values: exceptionalism, equality, individual liberty, the right to rise, and a republic run by the citizenry.[52] These "Americanisms" give populism an idealistic yet revolutionary cast that prepares people to defend transcendent values. The second component of populism's primal grammar is a laudatory portrayal of "the people." In populist discourse the people are the creators, producers, workers, and ordinary folk whose tough-minded, practical knowledge fits them for guarding the nation's ideals. The third component of populism's primal grammar is opposition to elites—those who exploit and oppress "the people" for their own gain. Yet in populist discourse, the people and the elites are counterparts, used to define each other and locked in an antagonistic relationship. The people cannot exist without an "elite other." And while the elite other is often vague and indeterminate, it usually assumes the characteristics of an oligarchy or aristocracy trying to consolidate power in the hands of a few and to subvert the liberty of the masses. The fourth and final component of the populist grammar is the call for a coalition, a movement, a cooperative undertaking in which righteous individuals must actively resist the elitist cabal thwarting their lives and livelihoods. In this military-style resistance, the people move from being an imagined community to being an army with a mission to save the nation and the ordinary individuals who comprise it.[53]

In outlining this flexible mode of persuasion, Kazin opens populism to more than American politics. Populist language gives individuals a way of framing themselves, their neighbors, their community, their enemies, and the ideals they ought to defend. It is a powerfully motivating language, offering people life-or-death reasons to fight the status quo. But it is also optimistic, pointing to a utopia that will emerge once the people assume their rightful place. "Hopeful, expansive, even romantic," writes Kazin, populist discourse abounds in "faith in the abilities of ordinary Americans of all races to run their society."[54] That faith spurs the people into combat with their elite foes, destroying the figures and forces that oppress them and building a divine commonwealth on earth.

Kazin's exploration of populist discourse comports well with what scholars of rhetoric have written of populism. Howard Erlich, for one, has found in the rhetoric of the People's Party evidence of how populist discourse can work across significant divisions.[55] In underscoring the value of the individual and in affirming the "brotherhood of man," he argues, Populist politicians resisted their elite opponents by affirming values that rhetorically transcended racial identity.[56] Ronald Lee has similarly explored the constitutive function of Tom Hayden's economic populism.[57] According to Lee, Hayden foregrounded the importance of participation on the part of ordinary citizens, fostering a sense of agency that purported to revolutionize American politics.[58] Lloyd Rohler, borrowing from Kazin's work, has investigated George Wallace's populist rhetoric.[59] Using the four components of the primal grammar Kazin identified, Rohler shows how Wallace positioned himself as the only leader who could defend ordinary people from nefarious, aloof, incompetent elites.[60]

The most extensive account of populist rhetoric has come from Michael Lee, who explicates populism as a chameleon-like discursive form that spans the work of the People's Party, Huey Long, and George Wallace. According to Lee, the basic populist argument contains four elements. First, the populist argument portrays a "people" as the true keepers of traditional values—the "ordinary, simple, honest, hard-working, God-fearing, and patriotic" individuals who ought to lead the nation. Second, the populist argument constitutes the people in opposition to "the enemy," who wields power to subvert the people's way of life. Third, the populist argument involves a conception of "the system," which is "an amalgamation of numerous sites within the national political and economic order in which power is distributed, governed, and managed." The system is the site of power in which, around which, and against which the people fight. Finally, the populist argument culminates in an "apocalyptic confrontation" that will pave the way for revolution and utopia. Through a revolutionary fight with the enemy and the system, the people can regain control and restore the world to its historic simplicity.[61]

Lee's account of the basic populist argument is further evidence of how mobile, flexible, and adaptive populist discourse can be. Like Kazin's work, Lee's indicates how the basic elements of populist rhetoric can operate in different struggles, different cultures, different times, and different places. Populist rhetoric can even operate in the intellectual realm, shaping the way people conceive of the figures, forums, terms, and direction of inquiry.

But before discussing the rhetoric of intellectual populism, there is one more account of populist discourse that warrants attention. Ernesto Laclau's *On Populist Reason* not only provides a theoretical framework for the emergence of populist discourse but also indicates how diverse thinkers in the late nineteenth and early twentieth centuries could have participated in a broad populist project—even if they were unaware of such participation. For Laclau, the seeds of populism are disparate, particular demands. These demands, though different in detail, mark a group of frustrated individuals whose requests remain unfulfilled. Given the right discursive prompts, these individuals move toward a coalition, forming what Laclau calls an "equivalential chain." Essentially, populist discourse pushes particular demands into a larger oppositional framework, with room enough for various people with different frustrations and wants. Now linked in an equivalential chain, these people stand against an ominous force, group, or institution—the supposed source of frustration and want. Thus individuals unite in an "antagonistic frontier separating the 'people' from power."[62]

Laclau is quick to point out that this "people" is never as broad as it claims to be, but its claim of being broad is one of the most salient aspects of populist identity. In Laclau's framework, the plebs—or underprivileged—insist that they are the "only legitimate *populus*," that they are the real people. Such a claim reinforces the antagonistic frontier, further pushing the plebs toward conflict with their oppressors. The people's identity is further constituted through "empty signifiers," or terms that link heterogeneous demands, thereby inviting more and more individuals into populist subjectivity. Empty signifiers such as justice, liberty, equality, fairness, and the elite have no real content until they are filled with heterogenous demands, thus defining who becomes part of the people and who remains on the outside. As a result, claims Laclau, populism is vague, but vagueness provides its power and longevity. Contrary to those who complain that populism is too indeterminate and widely applicable, Laclau insists that populism's strength is its indeterminacy. Because populist discourse emerges through empty signifiers filled in particular encounters and struggles, it gives people in different times and places a set of rhetorical resources for building coalitions.[63]

The rhetoric of populism thus builds a coalition out of disparate people and groups with their own grievances. Once they are united, these people resolve to reclaim their world. Populist leaders speak in a way that moves individual grievances into larger webs of signification, linking people in an antagonistic frontier that purports to defend ordinary folk against concentrated power. This is the same dynamic that has undergirded the work of some of the nation's greatest thinkers, who cast inquiry as a struggle, contest, and fight between the elites and the masses.[64]

The Rhetoric of Intellectual Populism

As I have outlined above, populism involves a rhetorical repertoire that allows it to move in and out of different political contexts around the globe. It is a flexible discursive practice that enables would-be populist leaders to rally ordinary people around a cause and in opposition to the status quo. As a discursive practice, it does not hinge on particular policies or programs but on a style of symbolic engagement that links individual grievances in an equivalential chain of resistance. In this section I argue that populism's repertoire in the sociopolitical realm has an analogue in the intellectual realm. Like political populism, intellectual populism is a discursive practice distinguished by a series of rhetorical markers that can be adapted to different purposes and situations. Thus, as with political populism, intellectual populism can vary widely in terms of the ideas pursued, but it proceeds through a flexible rhetoric that links ordinary people in common intellectual cause. Given its flexibility, intellectual populism can propel the work of thinkers who are not normally associated with one another, but who deploy similar appeals in the pursuit of knowledge.

At a general level, intellectual populism proceeds through a combination of five appeals: (1) an attack on the figures and institutions that control intellectual culture; (2) an affirmation of ordinary people as the best stewards of modern inquiry; (3) a deployment of "Americanisms" in the realm of thought; (4) a characterization of true inquiry as radically conservative and conservatively radical; and (5) a visualization of a utopian intellectual community on the other side of a populist revolution. While different thinkers emphasize some of these appeals more than others, the appeals on the whole constitute the markers of the distinctive discursive practice that defines the populist intellectual tradition.

ONE: ATTACKING THE ESTABLISHED INSTITUTIONS AND FIGURES OF INTELLECTUAL CULTURE

Intellectual populists center their attacks on powerful institutions and the figures who represent those institutions, much as political populists center their attacks on monopolies, financiers, and other representatives of concentrated power. In the intellectual realm, however, powerful institutions usually take the form of colleges, universities, religious orders, medical establishments, and professional organizations, which claim superior knowledge over a particular field of inquiry. The figures who represent these institutions—experts, specialists, and academics—are also part of the problem. In the field of religious inquiry, for example, ministers and theologians represent churches and denominations, and their work reaffirms particular views of God, heaven, hell, sin, salvation, and more. They instruct the laity on what to believe, how to worship, what is orthodox, what is heretical. To intellectual populists, such instruction amounts to an unwarranted imposition because it discourages ordinary people from thinking about and discovering God in their own way. Rhetorically, knowledge institutions and the experts who speak for them serve as the power-hungry "other" against which individuals can stand as a united, antagonistic frontier. Intellectual populism thus grows out of grievances and dissatisfaction with mainstream inquiry—be it religious, scientific, medical, pedagogical, technological, or otherwise.

TWO: AFFIRMING "THE PEOPLE" AS STEWARDS OF INQUIRY

The second appeal of intellectual populism involves the same lauding of ordinary people that defines the political tradition. The idea is that the people ought to control inquiry in the same way they ought to control governance and society. Because of their position outside the establishment, because they have not been co-opted by a particular ideology or institution, they are in the best position to understand the world around them. Or so populist logic asserts. In the field of ethics, for instance, intellectual populists maintain that people's everyday experience is the best evidence of right and wrong, proper and improper conduct. Because people are in tune with the world, they can see the results of their actions, which give them a sound perspective on what to do and what not to do. Their connection to results through everyday experience is more valuable than any abstract philosophical argument or categorical imperative. Once again, however, the work of this appeal can be misleading. Intellectual populists speak against the ethical establishment not to destroy ethics itself but to strengthen it by bringing ordinary people into renewed deliberations. Assaulting the status quo is ultimately a way to fortify and democratize the intellectual terrain on which the status quo is built.

THREE: DEPLOYING "AMERICANISMS" IN THE PURSUIT OF KNOWLEDGE

The two appeals discussed above are the primary appeals of the populist intellectual tradition, but they are regularly reinforced by a series of related appeals. To that end, the third appeal involves the same Americanisms that pervade the populist political tradition in the United States. Intellectual populists speak extensively of liberty, equality, hard work, justice, fairness, and democracy—only they apply these ideographs to the pursuit of knowledge.[65] When it comes to inquiry, populists proclaim, people must be *free* to follow their interests, they must be treated *equally* in their pursuits, and they must be given the chance to express themselves in a *democratic* marketplace of ideas. Even the most disempowered person can and should use his or her personal experience to discuss the meaning of life. Ultimately, intellectual populists project an arena in which all people can argue their position, speak up for their beliefs, and clash with one another over opposing viewpoints. No one has a special claim to knowledge because of his or her training, advanced degree, or expertise. The unschooled African American has as strong a claim over literature and aesthetics as the upper-class, Ivy League graduate. The working-class immigrant from the slums of New York can philosophize as well as the German-educated, white aristocrat. At the very least, the perception of liberty and equality draws ordinary people into the world of thought.

FOUR: CHARACTERIZING INQUIRY AS RADICAL CONSERVATISM

The fourth appeal of intellectual populism is the appeal of conservatism—that is, a return to tradition, to basic goods, to life as it supposedly once was. But as with political populism, this conservatism is eminently radical, achieved through a progressive restructuring of the status quo. Simplicity, common sense, egalitarianism, democracy, and liberty mark a time in the past before the onslaught of existing knowledge institutions. The goal of populist agitation is to return to such a past by any means necessary. In the medical realm, for example, intellectual populists maintain that modern medicine has obscured the practices of healing that once existed. The spiritual healing depicted in the Bible once saved people from devastating illnesses. Yet modern treatments, doctors, and hospitals have pushed people away from the spiritual healing of primitive Christianity. The goal, then, is to destroy, or at least circumvent, these institutions and to put people in a position to live free, healthy lives. Intellectual populists demand a radical return of power to people who want to experiment with their own healing practices.

FIVE: VISUALIZING A UTOPIAN COMMUNITY OF THOUGHT

The fifth appeal of intellectual populism involves imagining a utopian future that depends on reorienting the way people think. Once people think for themselves, once they inquire in community with fellow citizens, they will be able to create an intellectual heaven on earth. Therefore, intellectual-populist discourse usually culminates with a depiction of a revolutionary thought community that will replace the entrenched status quo. In this community people are intellectually engaged, dedicated to the common good, respectful of the opinions of others, liberal in their views, and living happy, productive lives. Creating this utopian community can be difficult because it requires a revolution. But intellectual populists are unabashed in promising a completely new future for those who join them in reclaiming the world of thought. As subsequent chapters will show, every populist thinker discussed in this book pictured for popular audiences an intellectual utopia that served as a motivating telos. With working-class immigrants, oppressed African Americans, and exploited American Indians, among others, intellectual populists visualized a new day dawning.

These five appeals constitute the discursive markers of intellectual populism. Again, the specific content of these appeals can vary widely depending on context and rhetor. Nevertheless, they recur across contexts and rhetors as ways of drawing people on the margins of inquiry into a new, revitalized community of thought. Yet it would be a mistake to deem intellectual populism only a rhetorical form. When put together, the discursive markers of intellectual populism move in a particular direction and have important consequences for inquiry and society.

As I have suggested, intellectual populism seeks to make the pursuit of knowledge more democratic, bringing new voices and perspectives into an expansive marketplace of ideas. Laura Grattan has recently defended the racial and democratic potential of political populism, which, she argues, "facilitates efforts by unlikely actors to engage each other across differences in their social identities, spaces, and times."[66] Intellectual populism brings the same spirit to the realm of ideas, uniting people across differences to contemplate their collective world. In that way, intellectual populism taps into the deliberative potential of political populism to democratize conversations about truth, beauty, right, wrong, good, bad, heaven, hell, and more.[67]

As a result, intellectual populism entails an unflinching commitment to democratic communication—to making forums of speech, debate, and discourse open to an ever-increasing number of voices. Intellectual populism embraces the communicative ideal of deliberative democracy, which holds that our political procedures depend on "practical communication to produce understanding and regulate public action," and that our intellectual affairs can profit from more democratic deliberations, relying on wide-ranging, disputative discourse to strengthen the character, quality, and usefulness of our ideas.[68] The hope is to implement the "republican-rhetorical aspect of citizenship"—which is based on participation, speaking, listening, and acting—in the pursuit of knowledge.[69] Grassroots cultures of discussion and argumentation are no less crucial for inquiry than they are for politics.[70]

Finally, intellectual populism advances the intersection of education and ordinary democracy. Several scholars have shown how our education systems seem to thrive when shaped by ordinary voices in the community—when citizens come together with "vernacular intelligence" to influence the direction of education.[71] Thus far, this intersection of education and ordinary democracy has largely concerned primary and secondary schooling.[72] Intellectual populism extends this intersection to higher education, adult education, and advanced scholarly conversations. Just as our primary and secondary schools can benefit from the vernacular speech and intelligence of ordinary people, so can our lofty intellectual affairs. The "rough, messy, complicated, intelligent, artful, and effective" speech of ordinary democracy is crucial for a bustling marketplace of ideas at whatever level people pursue those ideas.[73] Or so the intellectual populism discussed in this book will demonstrate.

Looking Back

To explicate intellectual populism, this book will focus on the challenges, efforts, and contributions of various intellectuals at the end of the nineteenth century and beginning of the twentieth century. This period, often referred to as the Gilded Age and Progressive Era (1870–1920 or so), offers a useful vantage point on the problems and possibilities of intellectual populism for a number of reasons. Chief among them is the fact that this time period bears striking resemblance to our own. Rapid social and technological change, staggering wealth concentration in the hands of a few, pervasive demographic and geographic shifts, political corruption and corporate collusion, peculiar realignments in international relations—these are just some of the ways that the Gilded Age and Progressive Era seem all too familiar.[74]

Then, as now, people responded to widespread tumult by rethinking basic assumptions about their lives, livelihoods, societies, and cultures.[75] History is always marked by change, always asking people to rethink basic assumptions. But the rate and nature of change during the second half of the nineteenth century seemed especially ominous, revealing an apparent break with the past that shook many Americans.[76] On the one hand, the nation experienced incredible progress in such areas as manufacturing, communication, technology, and transportation. On the other hand, this rapid progress broke apart the communities of the past, what Robert Wiebe has called "island communities."[77] Many Americans no longer knew where they fit, and they "feared the system would dominate the people."[78]

The threat of "the system" dominating the people, whatever the system might have been, signaled a loss of control, which many people believed they once possessed. Wherever they looked were signs that the proud, self-reliant individuals of the past—however mythic those individuals were—held little sway in the new order. Big business, corporate trusts, wealth accumulation in the hands of the few, cities teeming with unknown faces, the spoils system, skyscrapers, factories, tenement houses—these signs of the times dwarfed "regular folks" trying to earn their keep. The changes wrought by industrialized America upended perceptions about personal power, the way individuals related to one another in community, and the viability of American public culture.[79] In the new century, one's future and the future of one's family depended on forces far outside one's control.[80]

It was often difficult to identify what or who those forces were, but that did not stop many Americans from trying. Immigrants often functioned as the outsiders against whom "true" Americans could align, given that immigrants represented not only urban overcrowding and the associated vices but also increased competition for jobs and economic resources.[81] For others, the robber barons and captains of industry represented malignant forces, even while they inspired a mixture of envy and contempt—much as the superrich do today.[82] But these titans were not the only figures of the new industrial economy to serve as targets of animus. Even run-of-the-mill bankers, financiers, speculators, and politicians could stand in for the new, exploitative power structure. Wherever the "monied classes showed a new brand of arrogance, tampering with the political faith of the people,"[83] grievances against the status quo began to mount. Ultimately, the Gilded Age enabled ordinary Americans to define themselves as "ordinary" because they were not foreigners, heartless industrialists, scheming politicians, or conniving bankers. However accurate or inaccurate these characterizations were, an increasing number of Americans saw themselves on the side of the many, living wholly apart from the few.

These same dynamics were at play in intellectual culture. To many onlookers, the world of thought was spinning out of control along with society writ large. One of the reasons for this perception was what Burton Bledstein has called the "culture of professionalism." According to Bledstein, professionalism remade American life in the late nineteenth century in that it attempted "to define a total coherent system of necessary knowledge within a precise territory, to control the intrinsic relationships of [a given] subject by making it a scholarly as well as an applied science, to root social existence in the inner needs and possibilities of documentable worldly processes."[84] The birth of the modern professions remade work and knowledge, offering "special services" that both constituted and controlled a market for expertise. These markets, in turn, conferred social power on professionals and created a new kind of inequality between those with certified expertise in a particular arena and those without.[85] In the intellectual sphere, legitimacy became integrally linked to control over a specialized territory of knowledge.

Professionalism arose in conjunction with new systems of education and credentialing, best represented in modern research universities. The modern research university, which emerged in the Gilded Age in the United States, placed "science, technology, and an attendant belief in human progress through rational, systematic investigation" at the center of "the national consciousness."[86] Colleges once dedicated to citizen training reorganized themselves into research institutions. In so doing, they mapped the pursuit of knowledge onto increasingly narrow specialties, and the number of academic departments and disciplines skyrocketed. Science divided into natural science and social science, and those categories further divided into such fields as chemistry, physics, and biology on the one hand, and sociology, anthropology, and economics on the other hand. These fields had long existed in one form or another, but now they were guarded by scholars who had been trained specifically in these areas and had little knowledge of the other fields. Through specialized journals, abstruse terminologies, professional associations, and cordoned-off academic spaces, professionals established their authority and legitimacy over a narrow yet deep intellectual terrain.[87] This was especially true in the sciences, which proliferated as the very idea of "science" took on the appearance of objectivity, reliability, replicability, and truth.[88] Science purported to lead to real knowledge and real control over the world, and being scientific meant being able to contribute to the advancement of true understanding.

The new systems of education and credentialing also created powerful new figures in the world of thought: experts. Indeed, it was during the middle decades of the nineteenth century that experts, at least in their modern incarnation, were born.[89] For the first time in history, a substantial number of people could earn a living by selling knowledge-based advice and services. Experts oversaw a limited intellectual domain, but they controlled who had access to the specialized space, who had authority to speak over it, and who could build upon it. Speaking authoritatively about health and the body, for instance, required a medical degree. Nonspecialists often tried to speak on matters of health, but their views were suspect, and the culture of professionalism demanded that they defer to the authority and insights of the specialist. Thus "specific formal training and anonymous certificates" came to represent academic and intellectual power, which were increasingly conflated.[90] To contribute to the advancement of knowledge in a particular field, one needed the proper series of letters after one's name—PhD, MD, JD, MDiv, and so on.

In many ways, the experts, specialists, and academics associated with modern research universities became an intellectual aristocracy. It was an aristocracy defined not by wealth and birth but by specialization along technical lines, which created the same kind of social stratification that existed in the old world.[91] Because of their authority and positions of privilege, experts had a trump card to play in matters of inquiry and public debate.[92] What they said about a particular subject was supposedly right, objective, true, and backed by evidence. Specialized training and a series of letters after their name gave them the authority and prestige once conferred by noble birth. However, such authority and prestige seemed out of place in a nation supposedly ruled by the people. To many onlookers, professionalism seemed an undemocratic extension of the old world, which America had purportedly left behind.[93]

All told, the changes in and around modern intellectual culture pushed professionals and the laity further apart. At least that was the feeling. Education, training, credentials, discourses, and worldviews created high intellectual barriers that compartmentalized knowledge and marked in-groups and out-groups. "Through a special understanding of a segment of the universe," explains Bledstein, "the professional person released nature's potential and rearranged reality on grounds which were neither artificial, arbitrary, faddish, convenient, nor at the mercy of popular whim." Conversely, "Laymen were neither prepared to comprehend the mystery of the tasks which professionals performed, nor—more ominously—were they equipped to pass judgment upon special skills and technical competence."[94] Doctors, scientists, theologians, professors, and lawyers amassed, because of their training and certification, "monopolies of competence" that displaced and disempowered those who lacked specialized training and certification.[95]

Given the massive structural realignment of inquiry in the post–Civil

War decades, it is unsurprising that a number of alternative intellectual movements emerged. If academic experts were going to cordon themselves off in specialized spaces and dictate answers to life's big questions, there was plenty of room, and a pressing need, for popular education. Popular education involved ordinary people getting together for enlightenment in a variety of contexts, including settlement houses, civic associations, social-gospel organizations, religious revivals, and amateur science collectives.[96] A prime example was the Chautauqua movement, which promoted "self-culture" and offered a blend of education, entertainment, and edification to those whom the complexities of modern society had displaced.[97] Forums for inquiry such as Chautauqua lacked the intellectual respectability of academic arenas; few would have said that cutting-edge research happened in popular education venues. But intellectual respectability was not foremost in the minds of the people who felt enriched and enlivened by joining with others to think about their interconnected world. Amid the rise of professionalism, popular education strove to reaffirm the sovereignty of ordinary people, not only serving their intellectual well-being but also teaching them to be critical thinkers, discerning listeners, and responsible citizens.[98]

In one sense, intellectual populism in the Gilded Age and Progressive Era was a popular education movement, especially with its democratic ethos and commitment to empowering ordinary people as intellectual actors. Yet intellectual populism was distinctive in several crucial ways, including its oppositional stance, its frustrated cry for relief, and its aim of abolishing or circumventing the status quo to achieve a new utopia of thought. As we shall see, intellectual populists decried academic professionals for usurping the people's right to think for themselves. They pledged to destroy, or at least leave behind, the structures and figures of established institutions. Empowering the people was a priority for intellectual populists, as it was for those engaged in popular education. But intellectual populists couched their efforts in a life-or-death discourse that pitted them in a struggle against evil. They called on their followers to storm the ramparts of inquiry and to retake what was rightfully theirs. With angry cries, with rollicking gatherings, with resolute opposition, intellectual-populist leaders and groups banded together to reclaim an intellectual holy land.

Before turning to the leaders and groups featured in this book, it is necessary to explain one other crucial aspect of intellectual populism in the Gilded Age and Progressive Era. In particular, it is necessary to underscore *where* intellectual populism generated its combative cries for coalition. While essays and books, newspapers and periodicals were important for populist inquiry, the lecture stage represented the most significant space for riling the masses. The platforms of lecture halls, opera houses, auditoriums, churches, and similar venues reinforced intellectual populism's oppositional stance, largely because of what had happened to lecture culture during the nineteenth century.

Public lecturing was a part of inquiry in America since at least the Revolution.[99] In the antebellum era, public lecturing became an industry, instantiated in the lyceum movement of the 1820s, which started as a form of education for tradesmen. Its main purpose, writes Carl Bode, "was to provide practical scientific instruction for workmen, and to have as a result a more intelligent worker as well as a better product. The main methods were the use of lecture-demonstration courses organized by public-spirited citizens and the assembling of local libraries of technical books."[100] As the lyceum movement spread, American thinkers and writers began to see the potential of lecture culture for their own work. Ralph Waldo Emerson, for instance, made public lecturing a vocation and the premier pathway to the pursuit of knowledge. Lecturing spread new and exciting ideas to audiences across the country and, in turn, legitimized the lecturer as a leading thinker. In the 1830s, 1840s, and 1850s, new ideas were not simply deployed on the lecture stage but developed in conjunction with general audiences who demanded expansive insights instead of pedantic trifling.[101] Along the way, inquiry assumed a proud civic character; the life of the mind was integrally linked to "the people" writ large.

Because of the proud civic character of lecture culture, the pursuit of knowledge in the decades prior to the Civil War was closely connected to oratory and rhetoric. Eloquence and insight went hand in hand. In the popular imagination, ideas were sharper, better, and stronger to the extent that they inspired diverse audiences. Inquiry was bound to what James Perrin Warren has called "the culture of eloquence."[102] In this culture, the biggest thinkers of the day were also some of the most celebrated speakers and writers. In addition to Emerson, Henry David Thoreau, Frederick Douglass, Oliver Wendell Holmes Sr., Margaret Fuller, and Louis Agassiz, to name a few, produced American thought through their engagement with popular audiences. As the primary site for intellectual progress, the lecture hall forced aspiring thinkers to appreciate, serve, edify, and entertain ordinary Americans. To be intellectual, one had to be rhetorically adept.

Because of the close connection between lectures and intellectual practice, popular audiences had remarkable agency in the culture of eloquence. They played an active role in the creation of knowledge because they authorized thinkers to continue their work, inviting to town only those who could animate collective discussions and blend entertainment with edification.[103] In that way, ordinary Americans helped produce the nation's leading thinkers, and they came to expect that all great thinkers would also be "complete orators"—interested less in "personal achievement" than in "the public responsibility of citizenship."[104] Together, the people and leading thinkers collaborated in the unfolding of understanding.[105]

It is easy to romanticize this time in American intellectual history. However, the democratic ideals that animated lecture culture were never as democratic as they could have been; they were too often tied to white males and New England elitism. The audiences that ventured into lecture halls were never as inclusive as they should or could have been.[106] Nevertheless, perceptions matter, and both popular lecturers and the audiences they engaged believed that they were participating in truly democratic thought. The lecturer, declared Edward Channing in 1856, was "one of the multitude, deliberating with them upon common interests, which are well understood and valued by all."[107] To the extent that people believed they were participating in the advancement of knowledge, the changes wrought by the culture of professionalism in the post–Civil War decades seemed all the more disempowering.

As the culture of professionalism took root in the second half of the nineteenth century, the locus of knowledge production shifted out of popular lecture halls and into laboratories, research universities, specialized journals, and expert symposia. When people considered where ideas moved forward, they thought less of the lecture stage than of the halls of academia. Insight was tied to academic spaces, not to public forums.[108] At the same time, intellectual leaders no longer needed to be effective orators; they no longer depended on popular audiences for their intellectual livelihoods because of their specialized forums for specialized knowledge. Being an effective orator was not a detriment, but it was not a requirement. Professional inquiry was more valuable than popular interaction. One's colleagues, those who shared professional training and credentials, were the primary audience for one's research.[109]

This is not to say that popular lectures by scholars vanished in the post–Civil War decades. But it is to say that the role of the lecture hall was less to produce knowledge than to transmit it. Specialists, academics, and professionals lectured as a way of disseminating insights they had already secured. In the culture of professionalism, discussions among specialists produced insight; lecturing was a way of propagating ideas to nonacademic audiences.[110] No longer agents in the shape, character, and direction of thought, "the people" became receivers of what experts created.

At the same time, popular lecturing became increasingly associated with entertainment. Education, edification, and entertainment had long been interconnected in nineteenth-century lecture culture,[111] but as professionalism ascended, so did the entertainment function of lecturing.[112] The long-term shift, as Angela Ray notes, was from popular education and practical knowledge to commercial entertainment.[113] As entertainers became the public face of the lecture hall, specialists, academics, and experts had even less reason to approach lectures as sites of intellectual progress. To professionals, the vaudeville-like spectacle of many late nineteenth-century lectures did not abide by the rigorous methods of the research university.[114] Popular lectures were, at best, marginal in intellectual affairs.

But such marginalization opened a space for alternatives, even resistance. As popular lectures were pushed to the periphery of intellectual culture, they became forums in which intellectual populists could rally the dispossessed, push back against the status quo, and create alternative intellectual orders. For populist thinkers and the publics they empowered, communal auditoriums served as places where "the people" could gather as an antagonistic frontier. Oratorical interactions with ordinary Americans allowed intellectual populists to articulate positions and ideas in which an array of individuals could identify their own grievances. Through the lecture hall, the people could emerge as an ideologically linked collective—a counterpublic to the intellectual status quo.[115]

Looking Ahead

To trace the discourse and dynamics of intellectual populism, this book explores the work of different thinkers and groups in the Gilded Age and Progressive Era. As I have suggested, these thinkers and groups would not have thought of themselves as part of the same tradition, nor would they have labeled themselves political populists. Yet they joined together not through personal connections and political affiliations but through the way they drew "the people" into the world of ideas. They shared a repertoire of appeals, strategies, and orientations that aligned ordinary people against the status quo, not to destroy intellectual culture but to democratize and strengthen it. The following five chapters unfold more or less chronologically, according to when the featured intellectual was most active. At the same time, each chapter builds on what came before to reveal different dynamics of populist intellectual engagement, from the importance of conflict to the role of space to the redirection of prejudice.

Chapter 1 explores the work of Robert Ingersoll, the "Great Agnostic" of the Gilded Age who eloquently ridiculed America's religious establishment and, in the process, built a religiously diverse and engaged movement. At the end of the nineteenth century, there was perhaps no better exemplar of intellectual populist rhetoric than Ingersoll. There was also no more engaging model of how populist appeals assault established structures at one level while animating the intellectual lives of ordinary people at another level. Ingersoll made a name for himself by criticizing religion, but his critiques stirred important religious conversations across the country. He helped people participate in religious culture by lambasting a status quo that seemed hollow instead of hallowed.

Chapter 2 explores the work of Mary Baker Eddy, the "discoverer" of Christian Science, who built a powerful movement in opposition to the medical establishment and who sent a group of lecturers across the country to spread a populist gospel. Eddy's movement was based on the promise of healing—healing people, communities, and societies. As modern medicine transformed and professionalized health and well-being, it also pushed individuals away from directing their own health and well-being. This was especially true in the field of women's health. Christian Science tried to change that by calling individuals into new, resistive, even brazen communities of healing.

Chapter 3 explores the work of Thomas Davidson, an acerbic philosopher who built a number of intellectual communities during the Gilded Age and Progressive Era. Davidson never felt at home among academic philosophers, even though he was considered one of the world's leading scholars of ancient thought. But he did feel at home as a freelancer, roaming the nation, building connections with different groups, and creating new venues for individuals to develop their own philosophical lives. Shortly before his death in 1900, Davidson found what he had been looking for his whole life in the form of abstract, graduate-level philosophizing with working-class immigrants on the Lower East Side of New York. More than any other intellectual in this book, Davidson understood the need to construct appropriate spaces for populist resistance.

Chapter 4 explores the work of Booker T. Washington, the undeniably eloquent but woefully misunderstood race leader. Although Washington is often considered the practical foil to the intellectual W. E. B. DuBois, he was a populist thinker dedicated to restructuring the way knowledge was pursued, produced, and practiced among minorities and the lower class. Washington institutionalized the intellectual populist spirit in and around the Tuskegee Institute, which empowered African Americans in the rural South for generations. Tuskegee did not always succeed, but it nonetheless signaled how populist rhetoric could serve as an organizing principle for an oppressed people fighting for survival.

Chapter 5 explores the work of Zitkala-Ša, also known as Gertrude Bonnin, a member of the Sioux nation who seized upon and remade perceptions of American Indians—a term this book uses interchangeably with Native Americans and indigenous people[116]—at a pivotal time of pan-Indian organizing. Eloquent and strategic in her efforts, Zitkala-Ša used her speeches, lectures, and public performances to oppose the white power structure and to draw other Indians into new intellectual pursuits. She became adept at shaping public perceptions to suit her purposes, which at various times included creating community centers on western reservations, strengthening the first pan-Indian organization run by Indians themselves, and creating an association that put Indian women at the forefront of the push for equal rights.

The conclusion draws together the themes of these case studies to show how we in the twenty-first century might deploy intellectual populism for a stronger, more diverse, more inclusive culture of inquiry. Amid the turbulence, animosity, resentment, and opposition of the twenty-first century, we would do well to understand how people and groups in the past have managed to join together for collective contemplation of common problems. If we can harness the antagonistic energy of the current political moment, we might be able to direct that energy in practical, democratic directions. Indeed, we scoff at populism to our own peril. Simply dismissing it as "anti-intellectual" or "uninformed" only emboldens those who attract others through populist appeals. It would be much better for scholars and intellectuals to investigate and redirect populist energy toward pluralistic, unifying ends. If an educational divide fuels our political discord, perhaps a populist approach to education, to inquiry, to thought is precisely what we need to move society forward. Perhaps the remedy for populist frustration is populist intellectualism.

CHAPTER ONE

Robert Ingersoll's Religious Resistance

The cops were ready to close in. The clergymen were ready to write it all down. The audience had no idea what was afoot.

A massive crowd had descended on the Hoboken Theatre in Hoboken, New Jersey. Theatergoers were eager to listen to the man widely considered the greatest orator in the world. Incidentally, he was also considered a heretic, an infidel, a blasphemer. For decades he had been delivering public lectures that ridiculed God, the Bible, and revealed religion. Given that blasphemy was then a crime in New Jersey, the cops and clergy were ready to catch him in the act of blaspheming and to put him behind bars. Two Hoboken detectives in the audience waited for the signal from two Protestant clergymen, H. T. Beatty and Herbert Campbell, who sat with notebooks and fountain pens in hand, ready to write down the heretic's sacrilege.

What the cops and the clergy did not know was that the orator had been tipped off. Well before the date of the lecture, he had heard whispers about Hoboken's mayor, police chief, and prominent clergy scheming to prevent him from speaking. But they had consulted the city attorney and concluded that they could not block the infamous infidel from speaking; the best they could do was wait until he blasphemed and arrest him on the spot. Abreast of the situation, the orator mounted the platform in the Hoboken Theatre and decided to have some fun with the crowd. He unleashed his characteristic ridicule, but attributed his statements to other infidels. "Mind you it's contrary to the act of the Legislature for me to express any opinion about these things," he announced after roasting the Holy Bible, "and I can only tell you what other people say, and you can decide for yourself. I don't think that there's any law against making up your mind. Oh, I'd tell you some things if it wasn't for that act of the Legislature." The crowd began to catch on, laughing every time the orator stopped his criticism just shy of violating the blasphemy law. "Mind you," the speaker continued, "I don't say that the Scriptures are not inspired. On the contrary, I admit that they are in New Jersey. That's in accordance with the statutes, and I'm not foolish enough to fight any statute. You see, if the Legislature of New Jersey says a thing, that ends it with me." The more the orator jested, the more the audience howled. He then turned his criticism directly to the clergy: "They're a pretty mean lot of men, by the way. Now, they know I'm going to the penitentiary of God, and that I'm going to roast and blister and burn all through eternity. But these sanctified swine are not satisfied with that. They want to see me in the penitentiary here." The audience doubled over in laughter and applause.

All the while, the clergymen wrote furious notes and the cops continued to wait for the signal to move in. But as the lecture continued, something surprising happened. Slowly but surely, the cops and clergy began to snicker, then chortle, then laugh as the eloquent infidel played with Bible stories and theological creeds. Even though the speaker ridiculed what they held sacred, they became part of the mass of laughing bodies. As the *New York Sun* reported, "They howled and creamed with delight. The ministers lost their dignity and joined in the jollification. The detectives just doubled up." When the lecture concluded after

10:00 p.m., noted the *Sun*, "the detectives and the ministers went out ahead of the other people. What reports they are going to make is not known. But they laughed, and they probably won't want to prosecute the Colonel."[1] The paper's prediction was correct. Hoboken authorities never brought blasphemy charges against Colonel Robert Green Ingersoll, the greatest orator of the day and America's most scorned critic of revealed religion.

Ingersoll's performance in Hoboken took place on February 24, 1895, close to the end of his career. But what happened that day had been happening for decades. Since the early 1870s, he had proven able to draw massive crowds, to speak with wit and humor, to captivate listeners with his eloquence, and to stake a claim as perhaps the greatest intellectual performer of the day. Most remarkable was his ability to connect with those who opposed him, those who held sacred the very ideas he ridiculed. Across the nation, in bustling cities and sleepy towns alike, Ingersoll addressed people who believed wholeheartedly in that which he profaned. Yet they loved his challenges to their faith, and they routinely left the lecture hall feeling energized and alive. After an 1877 lecture in Pittsburgh, for example, Alexander Clark, editor of the weekly Christian publication *Methodist Recorder*, sent Ingersoll a letter of thanks for championing the "ideas of magnified manhood," which "took hold of me." Clark went on to note that he differed from Ingersoll "widely on some foundational principles," but also that he stood "on the ground of 'fair play,'" which "the New Testament allows me." He concluded the letter by insisting that he and Ingersoll would likely meet someday in heaven: "I expect to see you in a better life and in an unending world of liberty and love."[2] Countless other lecture-goers sent the Great Agnostic similar notes. One attendee thanked Ingersoll for his views, even though they disagreed on important matters. But, the correspondent continued, "In these days every man should be allowed to think as he chooses." He also insisted that he and Ingersoll could worship together, for "the religion of morality and the worship of the beautiful in nature . . . is a form of God worship."[3] Another correspondent reported to Ingersoll that everyone around him at a recent lecture, including a Quaker and a Methodist, was enthralled with Ingersoll's oratory. The writer's wife, in fact, remarked that she wished that religious believers were as Christlike as Ingersoll.[4]

Ingersoll's oratory prompted such responses in part because of his intellectual populism. His lectures were a model of how intellectual populists could criticize the status quo while strengthening the terrain on which the status quo was built. On the public stage, he ridiculed, rebuffed, and rebuked religious institutions and the experts who represented them—priests, ministers, theologians, and the like—while drawing ordinary Americans into conversations and deliberations that fortified and expanded religious culture. The critiques he offered, the audiences he rallied, the opposition he faced, and the eloquence he proffered produced a democratic coalition of intellectual agents dedicated to exploring the most important religious questions of the day. To borrow Ernesto Laclau's terminology, Ingersoll's lectures fostered an "equivalential chain" that linked the grievances of the religiously devout with the decidedly atheistic and those in between.[5]

This is a much different role for Ingersoll than commentators have recognized. Reading Ingersoll's work nowadays, it is easy to conclude that he led an antireligious, areligious, or secularist movement. Susan Jacoby, for instance, has called Ingersoll "a secular intellectual bridge into the twentieth century" and an "antireligious orator" with an "antireligious stance."[6] But this characterization overlooks what Ingersoll's lectures did on the ground in conjunction with popular audiences. As this chapter will show, Ingersoll was far from an antireligious orator; his intellectual populism actually enlivened, diversified, and democratized religious culture. His appeals criticized the religious status quo not to tear it down but to open it up and return it to ordinary Americans. Consequently, Ingersoll's lectures illustrate the generative role of conflict in populist coalition building and ordinary democracy. For Ingersoll, as for other populists, coalitions emerge through conflict, disputation, and verbal battle. As this chapter will detail and as subsequent chapters will elaborate, these rhetorical clashes draw populist communities together and goad them to retake control of their intellectual lives. The more perspectives one can bring into the agon of debate and the more participants one can connect, the stronger will be the resulting intellectual culture.

Ingersoll, Oratory, and Religious Inquiry

When Americans packed into auditoriums to hear Ingersoll lecture, they gathered to hear not only the nation's most visible critic of revealed religion but also a cultural icon. Ingersoll's success on the lecture circuit was linked in no small part to his ethos as a Civil War veteran, a celebrated lawyer, a leader in Republican politics, a well-known connoisseur of the arts, and a wordsmith of the highest order.[7] He was an odd duck in the transforming world of the Gilded Age, which likely contributed to his visibility. Ingersoll was an elite corporate lawyer and a pillar of the Republican Party. He was also a democratic humanist who worked for racial justice alongside his friend Frederick Douglass. At the same time, he supported the economic reforms of Henry George and maintained a close friendship with the labor leader and socialist Eugene Debs. Ingersoll's biography, no less than his oratory, cut across common divisions of the Gilded Age.

Ingersoll's father was an itinerant preacher and an associate of the great revivalist Charles Finney. Although Ingersoll later begrudged his boyhood Sundays in church, he spoke highly of his father and his father's commitment to social justice. The Ingersoll family moved often but eventually settled in rural Peoria, Illinois—the city that became Ingersoll's hub of operation for over a quarter century. After the nation plunged into civil war, Ingersoll raised and led the Eleventh Illinois Cavalry. His service earned him the title of colonel, which became central to his image in postwar decades. In fact, Ingersoll's service in the Civil War became intertwined with legends of his eloquence. An oft-told and likely apocryphal story involved Ingersoll and his small band of Union troops fighting twenty-five hundred rebels led by Confederate general Nathan Bedford Forrest in the Battle of Lexington, Tennessee.

The confederates overwhelmed Ingersoll and his men, took them prisoner, and confined them in a nearby store. A few days later, the prisoners and guards were joking together, playing poker, telling stories, and trying to pass the time. For added entertainment, they asked Ingersoll to deliver a speech. He obliged and took his position atop a nearby crate. Speaking to Confederate and Union soldiers alike, he told the group how reluctantly the North had taken up arms, and he explained that enslaved people and poor whites actually had much in common. The speech apparently captivated its auditors, and, seeing its effect on the audience, Forrest spoke up. "Here Ingersoll," said the famous general, "stop that speech and I'll exchange you for a government mule." Ingersoll was subsequently released on parole. The tale, repeated in newspapers across the country after Ingersoll had achieved oratorical celebrity, was likely a creative reimagining of the past, but it pointed to the aura that surrounded America's silver-tongued wordsmith during the second half of the nineteenth century.[8]

Back in Peoria after the war, Ingersoll launched a successful law practice, which led to a stint as attorney general of Illinois, the only political office he ever held. Soon, however, his reputation and ambition outgrew Illinois, and he moved his law practice first to Washington, DC, and then to New York City. In both locales he served as lead counsel on a number of high-profile cases. For instance, he defended brothers Stephen and John Dorsey from government corruption charges in the widely followed Star Route trials. He represented a group opposing Jay Gould's monopolistic practices. He defended the outspoken C. B. Reynolds from blasphemy charges in New Jersey. And he represented the family of a wealthy industrialist in a contentious will dispute. According to reports from the courtrooms in which he spoke, Ingersoll's oratory was as spellbinding before judges and juries as it was before lecture audiences. After a speech during the first Star Route trial, for example, the *Washington Evening Critic* reported that "Many an eye was wet with tears, not a few belonging to the male sex. [Ingersoll's] closing words were listened to with a silence almost painful, and at the end the bailiffs found it difficult to suppress the applause."[9]

But skill in the courtroom was only one factor in Ingersoll's reputation. Far more important was his work stumping for the Republican Party. Strange as it may seem today, the most prominent critic of revealed religion in the Gilded Age was also the most sought-after stump speaker for Republican politicians—congressmen, senators, and presidents alike.[10] The defining moment of Ingersoll's political oratory came in 1876 with a nominating speech for James G. Blaine at the Republican National Convention. Conjuring all the imagery he could muster, Ingersoll deemed Blaine an "armed warrior" and a "plumed knight," who marched down the halls of Congress and "threw his shining lance full and fair against the brazen foreheads of the defamers of his country and the maligners of his honor."[11] Pandemonium swept the hall. Even though Blaine failed to receive the Republican presidential nomination, commentators hailed Ingersoll's oration as the best convention speech in history.[12]

It would be a mistake, however, to suggest that the Blaine speech was a turning point in Ingersoll's career.[13] While it spread his name to new parts of the country, he was already regarded as a brilliant, challenging lecturer.[14] From the late 1860s until his death in 1899, Ingersoll lectured in every state in the union except Mississippi and North Carolina.[15] In a given year, he might speak anywhere from one hundred to two hundred times, though his performances usually happened in dedicated tours that lasted weeks or months.[16] It was often grueling work. In one fifteen-day stretch, for example, Ingersoll spoke every day in a different city, most of which were not considered hubs of agnosticism. He began in Janesville, Wisconsin, then hit Madison and Beloit, dropped into the Illinois towns of Freeport and Elgin, swung up to Ann Arbor, headed south into Ohio, where he lectured in Toledo and Delaware, moved onto the Indiana towns of Union City, Elwood, and Anderson, stopped in Pana and Litchfield, Illinois, en route to St. Louis, and concluded in Brazil, Indiana.[17]

Managing a hectic lecture schedule required the work of many hands. Ingersoll employed clerks, assistants, friends, and family to answer the flood of lecture requests and to coordinate his tours. At the height of his career, according to the best estimates, he received three hundred lecture invitations for every one he was able to accept.[18] Ingersoll's brother-in-law, C. P. Farrell, was central to the logistics and publicity of the tours. He coordinated the distribution of pamphlets, books, and lithographs that were hocked at every performance, and he negotiated with theater owners about compensation and revenue. Venues were usually instructed to charge 50 cents for cheap seats and $1.50 for premium seats, although scalpers outside the venue could get $3 or more for sold-out performances in big cities.[19] Ingersoll retained 70 percent of the gross receipts for a lecture, and theater owners kept the remaining 30 percent. However, Ingersoll furnished several hundred lithographs for sale at the venue and supplied posters for public display and advertisements for local newspapers.[20] Usually the operation ran like clockwork and led to impressive profits for everyone involved. Ingersoll could net over $1,200 per lecture (over $30,000 in today's values), and his annual income from lecturing alone often climbed to well over $50,000 ($1.25 million today).[21] The noted lecture promoter James Redpath, who helped manage Ingersoll's activities for several years, once remarked that Ingersoll "was the best card in America, no other man could draw such audiences. . . . His last house in San Francisco, I am told, had more money in it than any lecture ever yielded since lecturing began."[22]

Such operational success was crucial to building a populist coalition around the nation, for as Ingersoll traveled and lectured, he left behind crowds of people energized to ponder the world's deepest religious questions. He also left behind spatters of controversy. Ingersoll often reported on these controversies to his wife, Eva, when she was unable to accompany him on the road. From Utica he told Eva about local preachers doing "all they could to prevent people attending" his lecture. Several preachers even used their sermons to advise "their people to keep away. . . . They abused me as though I had recently stolen a horse." But he reassured her: "Don't allow these things to make you unhappy. I care nothing for them. They simply show the impotence of hatred. In a few years this storm will have blown over. It cannot last long. Church members visited me this morning and thanked me for my lecture. I never had a more enthusiastic audience."[23] From Louisville he explained that

"Several preachers in Indiana have given notice that they will answer me. Two are going to try it in this city next Sunday, and a professor of geology at some college in this state gives notice that he is going to show that there is no conflict between science and Moses. I am expected to catch hell in Cincinnati next Sunday. The preachers have got to combine and make war on all new thought even to hold out for a few years."[24] Taken together, these comments reveal the layers of influence Ingersoll's oratory often had. Preachers, the leading figures of the religious establishment, fought Ingersoll as though they were fighting one of Satan's minions. Even some professors—figures of academic professionalism—entered the fray against the devil's imp. Yet church members—the ordinary people in the pews—showed up at Ingersoll's hotel to thank him for his lecture. They felt alive and appreciative, thanks to the rotund orator who set their minds ablaze.

Opposition from local clergy and support from ordinary townsfolk only enhanced Ingersoll's visibility and influence. Lecture performances were a regular spectacle, exactly as Ingersoll wanted. Spectacle, denunciations, arguments, crowds, energy, and oratory—these were the markers of an engaged public. Even when his opponents assailed him as a P. T. Barnum–like entertainer whose lectures were calculated only to return a high profit,[25] he relished the controversy. A typical lecture stop for Ingersoll proceeded as follows. An advertisement for his lecture in a local newspaper was reinforced by editorial coverage elsewhere in the paper.[26] Some commentators then responded gutturally to Ingersoll's impending arrival, insisting that his blasphemy should not be tolerated.[27] Local ministers demanded that their congregations stay away from his performance, and Ingersoll thanked the ministers for advance publicity.[28] On the day of the lecture, religious organizations demonstrated outside the auditorium, distributing Bibles and pamphlets to lecture-goers as scalpers hocked overpriced tickets.[29] Ingersoll then delivered his lecture to great acclaim and made his way to the train station, where reporters hounded him for opinions on religion, society, culture, economics, and politics.[30] Over the following days and weeks, clergy responded with their own sermons and lectures, denouncing the "apostle of modern infidelity" for attracting a "large multitude" and reaping "rich reward for a single night's service in the employ of evil."[31] Finally, local papers published lengthy discussions about the value (or lack thereof) of what the community had experienced.[32]

Religious controversy and circus-like spectacle combined to make Ingersoll the "apostle of modern infidelity." But he was not alone in this regard. One of the reasons Ingersoll was able to speak and act as he did was because of the changes then underway in American religious culture. As Susan Jacoby has detailed, Ingersoll was part of a "golden age of free-thought," which extended from about 1875 to 1915.[33] "Free thought" was an ill-defined movement at best because it lacked specific goals, formal organization, or much collaboration on the part of proponents. The movement also ranged widely, with self-proclaimed advocates tackling such topics as free speech, free press, free inquiry, woman suffrage, birth control, penal reform, public education, and more. But because these topics proved interesting to a significant portion of the population, free-thought speakers and writers could make a decent living discussing their ideas. Soon, free-thought periodicals sprang up across the country. The *Truth Seeker*, for example, began in Peoria, Illinois, before moving to New York City. The *Blue Grass Blade* was published in Lexington, Kentucky. Ottawa, Kansas, was home to both the *Free-Thought Ideal* and the *Free-Thought Vindicator*. Down the road in Topeka one could find *Lucifer, the Light-Bearer*. And Waco, Texas, was home to the ever-combative *Iconoclast*. By the end of the 1880s, words such as *secularist* and *agnostic* were more than pejorative; they were proud self-descriptors for free-thought advocates.[34]

As free-thought spread around the nation, it often ran into staunch opposition from entrenched religious authorities, and the consequences could be deadly. Case in point was the clash between William Cowper Brann, publisher of the *Iconoclast*, and several Baptist stalwarts associated with Baylor University. After Brann began publishing his periodical and a prominent local judge, George Bruce Gerald, began defending his right to do so, a handful of ministers, lawmen, and Baylor students pledged to murder Brann, or at least tar and feather him. The conflict came to a head in 1897, one year after an Ingersoll lecture tour across

Texas, when two Baptist brothers ambushed Judge Gerald in the Waco town square. Gunfire erupted, with Judge Gerald getting the best of the two assailants. A few months later, another Baptist assailant ambushed Brann. The two men exchanged gunfire, and both were killed. After that, the conservative Baptist establishment in Waco dug in even further, preparing the way for robust fundamentalism to take hold in the ensuing decades.[35]

The clash in Waco between free-thought advocates and the religious establishment was an extreme example of the possible consequences of religious conflict. But the sentiments that ignited the factions were widespread—and no doubt overblown. To figures of the religious establishment, especially orthodox ministers, the rise of free thought portended damnable religious decline in America. To free-thought advocates, the push of infidelity portended a new day of secularism and intellectual liberty. Both factions soon discovered that a major secular uprising was not to be, for the rise of the free-thought movement corresponded with an *increasingly* religious nation.[36] In the post–Civil War era, "Christian idioms and ideologies touched all parts of American society and life."[37] Even America's visual culture became increasingly religious.[38] For a nation trying desperately to recover from the horrors of war, religion provided significant common ground. Too often this ground was racially divided, as appeals to Protestant Christianity helped white Americans to see past North-South divisions while simultaneously justifying separation from black Americans.[39] Yet black Americans, particularly formerly enslaved people, were busy building scores of Protestant churches.[40] Then there were the religious revivals sweeping the nation. Dwight Moody and, later, Billy Sunday enflamed the faith of tens of thousands,[41] and both found time to spar with Ingersoll in the press.[42]

Nor was Protestant Christianity the only religious tradition on the rise. As immigration flowed, so did religious diversity; new sacred symbols and rituals flooded the country along with the immigrants. Waves of Catholics from Ireland and elsewhere were followed by waves of Jews from Germany and Eastern Europe. Asian immigrants brought Confucianism and Buddhism. Theosophy and other new-thought movements rolled in from across distant seas. And at the World's Parliament of Religions in Chicago in 1893, Americans were able to see and hear about faiths around the globe from representatives of those faiths. Religious pluralism had planted its foot firmly on American soil. While such pluralism made plenty of people nervous, leading to various hate and nativist countermovements, it pushed religious issues to the forefront of public culture. "The multiplicity of cultural patterns," summarize Edwin Gaustad and Leigh Schmidt, "gave religion new opportunities for colorful display, even as it heightened anxieties regarding national unity and religious direction."[43] These new colorful displays included the rollicking rebukes of the Great Agnostic and the audiences who paid a good price to join in the jollification.

As religious pluralism came to America and as even Protestantism diversified, new questions about ancient traditions altered the religious landscape. Most often, these questions posed difficult challenges to religious conservatism because people felt free, on an unprecedented scale in the United States, to question and debate what previous generations had largely accepted. But again, the result was not so much secularism as it was "a larger and different kind of religious constituency."[44] The changes in and around Protestant theology were perhaps the best indication of how the nation's religious constituency shifted, expanded, and diversified at the time. In fact, the rise of so-called liberal theology proved crucial for Ingersoll's populist appeals. Liberal theologians and ministers primed the intellectual pump for Ingersoll's assault on revealed religion.

In the United States, liberal theology was closely linked to, among other developments, the rise of German higher criticism. As Peter Thuesen summarizes, "Whereas evolutionary theory attacked biblical history on natural-scientific grounds, higher criticism attacked it on literary-historical grounds, pointing to textual inconsistencies that raised such questions as whether Moses really wrote the Pentateuch, whether Jesus was really born in Bethlehem, or—and this question strained both methodology and soteriology—whether Jesus really rose from the dead."[45] The emerging historical consciousness associated with German higher criticism called for a critique of orthodoxy that many Americans, including many Protestant ministers, found liberating. Horace Bushnell, David Swing, Theodore Munger, Henry Ward Beecher, and others saw historical inquiry as a way of returning theology to proper biblical considerations, thereby avoiding the cruft of dogma that had arisen in Protestantism since the Reformation.[46] When Ingersoll critiqued orthodoxy and the Bible itself from a textual, historical perspective, he echoed key themes and methods in modern liberal theology.

There were other important similarities between Ingersoll and the liberal theologians. For example, liberal Protestants emphasized Christian ethics and social reform over staid doctrine. Although Ingersoll frequently assaulted the ethics of orthodox Christianity, he spoke adamantly about national improvement, kindness and charity, helping the poor, enriching one's community, moral purity, love, marriage, and family. In fact, Ingersoll often found himself at odds with other freethought advocates who scoffed at traditional marriage and embraced the idea of free love. Ever the Victorian, the Great Agnostic insisted that the traditional family structure was the true temple and that the fireside of home was the best altar at which to worship.[47] His emphasis on family, moral purity, and love made it difficult for many Americans to oppose his conduct, even if they opposed his religious views. Despite the broadsides of ministers who spread rumors that Ingersoll was a drunk, a gambler, a philanderer, and a cruel husband and father, Ingersoll eventually emerged as the symbol of how morality and religion could be separated—how a person could live a morally upright life without religious belief.[48]

The increasingly religious character of American society during the Gilded Age and Progressive Era offered a series of signifiers in which Ingersoll and many other citizens could align their views. Liberal Christians who believed that reforming society started at home could celebrate Ingersoll as an example of ethical living despite his lack of religious conviction. In placing ethics above creed and church, Ingersoll occupied an expansive, modernist common ground on which liberal believers could join him. David Swing, for example, one of the great liberal ministers of the nineteenth century, rebuked the "great vices" of modern America and the pragmatic failure of "creedal religion."[49] These were points Ingersoll himself could have made, and many commentators at the time viewed Swing and Ingersoll as working in tandem.[50] The spirit of their ethical appeals and their common aversion to religious institutions linked the two men in a larger religious transition.

Yet it would be a mistake to position Ingersoll's lectures as a mere extension of the religious changes afoot. As we shall see, Ingersoll differed from liberal theologians and ministers in significant ways, and he often delighted in turning their critiques of creedal religion back on them. Nevertheless, the similarities between Ingersoll and liberal Protestants revealed the widespread desire for engaging discussions of new religious ideas. In particular, those "ordinary believers who had been left bewildered, even if relieved, by the loss of traditional doctrines" could find in Ingersoll's work the same novelty they experienced in liberal Protestantism, revivalism, and the free-thought movement.[51] Ingersoll's message in lecture halls across the country articulated a set of frustrations and desires that many Americans—believers and agnostics alike—could see as their own.

Ingersoll's Populist Performance of Thought

The best window into Ingersoll's intellectual populism is the texts of his lectures, but as with many public lectures at the time, authentication can be challenging. The problem of textual authenticity is particularly acute in Ingersoll's case given the number of times he spoke. He delivered individual lectures dozens, sometimes hundreds, of times over a span of decades. What he said early in the life of a lecture might differ significantly from what he said a dozen years later. What's more, portions of some lectures occasionally made their way into other lectures, and depending on situational constraints, Ingersoll sometimes delivered only particular sections of larger lectures.[52]

One source of Ingersoll lecture texts is the "authorized" twelve-volume *Works of Robert G. Ingersoll*, published in 1901. Before his death in

1899, Ingersoll himself worked on preparing the collection, but in the process he thoroughly revised the texts.[53] As a result, the collection offers the spirit of his performances, but it is not a reliable record of what he said. Another source of lecture texts is the Robert Green Ingersoll Papers at the Library of Congress. Once again, this source offers an incomplete record of Ingersoll's work on the public stage, documenting only a portion of the lectures he delivered. However, the collection does provide a valuable glimpse into Ingersoll's preparation and delivery habits. When working on a new lecture, Ingersoll usually composed the text in longhand, and the Ingersoll Papers contain several longhand drafts showing the care with which he crafted his sentences.[54] After writing out a lecture by hand, Ingersoll often gave it to C. P. Farrell to create a typeset version, which he had in his coat pocket when lecturing.[55] Farrell also used the typeset copy to create a bound version of the text for sale at Ingersoll's performances. On occasion, after Ingersoll had grown comfortable with the content of a particular lecture, Farrell created a bullet-point outline of the full-sentence manuscript, and the bullet-point outline helped jog Ingersoll's memory at the lectern. Interestingly, Ingersoll seldom needed to reference his notes—full sentence, bullet point, or otherwise. The reason was his photographic memory. Many contemporaries noted Ingersoll's ability to memorize hundreds of pages of minute detail in a brief period of time.[56] This ability to memorize was partly responsible for his success on the lecture stage, allowing him to internalize exact phrases, punch lines, and declarations, which he delivered for maximal effect.

Because official collections offer a limited glimpse into what Ingersoll actually said on stage, we are left with two general sources of Ingersoll texts. Fortunately, these sources offer, at times, a verbatim record of his words to particular audiences on particular occasions. First are the nation's newspapers, which eagerly reprinted lengthy, and sometimes complete, transcripts of Ingersoll's performances. The words of the Pagan Pope, many editors seemed to believe, could sell newspapers, so they often hired stenographers to record what he said and the reactions of the crowd (e.g., "applause," "laughter," "great sensation"). Second, because

Ingersoll's lectures were such a draw, several fly-by-night publishers offered "unauthorized" collections of his talks. These usually involved reproductions of newspaper coverage, with or without attribution of the original source, to turn a quick profit. Some of these unauthorized collections even lacked the name and location of the publisher, simply stating "Published for the trade." Regardless, they offer rich transcripts complete with indications of applause and laughter, accounts of Ingersoll's gestures, and orally stylized syntax.

In analyzing Ingersoll's intellectual populism, then, I rely on the most complete record available for each lecture. Often these records come from the unauthorized collections; occasionally they come from newspapers. In some instances, I rely on Ingersoll's lecture notes because the notes are the most complete text available. Taken together, these sources provide a well-rounded picture of Ingersoll's appeals, including the turn that occupies the core of intellectual-populist discourse—namely, criticizing the established order to strengthen that which the order is trying to serve. Criticizing the religious order of the day was Ingersoll's way of enlivening religious inquiry, rendering ordinary Americans agents in the pursuit of religious knowledge.

The following analysis will explore how Ingersoll accomplished this turn while articulating the five appeals of the intellectual-populist tradition: (1) attacking the established institutions and figures of intellectual culture; (2) affirming "the people" as the true stewards of inquiry; (3) deploying "Americanisms" in the pursuit of knowledge; (4) characterizing inquiry as radical conservatism; and (5) visualizing a utopian community of thought. As I pointed out in the introduction of this book, however, these appeals combine in different ways for different rhetors. In Ingersoll's case, we can best gauge his combination of appeals by considering how he opposed the religious status quo, how he drew ordinary people into religious inquiry, and how he modeled populist thought for audiences across the country.

OPPOSING THE RELIGIOUS STATUS QUO

In developing the antagonistic tone of populist discourse, Ingersoll focused his ire on religious institutions and their representatives—ministers, priests, theologians, and scholars. These institutions and representatives, he argued, had accumulated undue intellectual power and were wielding it to keep ordinary people from thinking for themselves. In claiming almost exclusive authority over questions of God, sin, salvation, and morality and in formulating strict creeds, doctrines, rituals, and orthodox viewpoints, the religious status quo worked not for truth but to perpetuate religious authorities' power. Of course, whether or not religious institutions and their representatives were ever as oppressive and exploitative as Ingersoll insisted was less important than the fact that his indictments rang true for droves of lecture-goers. These figures and forces constituted the nefarious power structure against which ordinary people could align.

Consider a few of Ingersoll's anti-institutional appeals. In "Individuality," he portrayed the church in much the same way a political populist might portray a monopoly—namely, as "the great robber" that had "rifled not only the pockets but the brains of the world."[57] The church, he continued, "filled the world with hypocrites and zealots, and upon the cross of its own Christ it crucified the individuality of man."[58] He advanced a similar critique in "The Gods," only he positioned reason in the role of savior: "The whole power of the church has been brought to bear against philosophers and scientists in order to compel a denial of the authority of demonstration, and to induce some Judas to betray Reason, one of the saviors of mankind."[59] Because "the church hated to see the people wearing out their brains in thinking upon" sacred subjects, he said in "Heretics and Heresies," it created a creed so that "all men might know just what to believe," and "whatever might be lacking in evidence might be made up in force."[60] In "The Ghosts," he explained exactly what such forced belief looked like:

> In the name and by the authority of the ghosts, men enslaved their fellow-men; they trampled upon the rights of women and children. In

> the name and by the authority of ghosts, they bought and sold each other. They filled heaven with tyrants and the earth with slaves. They filled the present with intolerance and the future with horror. In the name and by the authority of the ghosts, they declared superstition to be the real religion. In the name and by the authority of the ghosts, they imprisoned the human mind; they polluted the conscience; they subverted justice, and they sainted hypocrisy.[61]

Whatever form Ingersoll's anti-institutional appeals took, his lectures depicted an insidious force that thwarted and controlled people who hungered for knowledge. The great battle at the end of the nineteenth century, according to Ingersoll, was between religious institutions and the minds and bodies of ordinary Americans.

But ordinary Americans faced more than insidious institutions; they also faced scheming representatives of those institutions. Extending populist opposition of elites to the experts of religious orders, Ingersoll routinely chided clergy, theologians, and the religious aristocracy. "I have just as much at stake in the way of soul," he declared in "Some Reasons Why," "as any doctor of divinity that ever lived, and more than some I have met."[62] In another lecture he chastised the nineteenth-century church—"presided over by professors, by presidents of colleges, and by theologians"—for indoctrinating the world with scientifically false ideas.[63] "Standing as I do in the presence of the Unknown," he announced elsewhere, "I have the same right to guess as though I had been through five theological seminaries. I have as much interest in the great absorbing questions of origin and destiny as though I had D.D., L.L.D. at the end of my name."[64] In the culture of professionalism, letters of academic certification signaled an authority against which ordinary Americans could align. These aristocrats of the mind, these experts who believed their connection to academic institutions and narrow methods of inquiry elevated them above the masses, were an ideal foil for populist agitation.

To increase the stakes of the opposition between ordinary Americans and aristocrats of the mind, Ingersoll often cast religious power in the same terms by which he positioned political power. Because Americans knew how to throw off political tyranny, perhaps they could throw off the yoke of religious tyranny. He thus pressed together kings and priests as two sides of the same tyrannical coin. "To attack the Kings was treason," he explained in "The Great Infidels," and "to dispute the priests blasphemy. The sword and the cross have always been allies, they defended each other. The throne and altar are twins—vultures born of the same egg."[65] Given that kings and priests were kindred beasts, Ingersoll hoped the American people would ask a question about the latter similar to that which they had asked about the former: "By what right does a crowned robber make me work for him? . . . By what right does a robed priest rob me?"[66] The robed priest was a stock figure in Ingersoll's lectures, effectively playing upon widespread Protestant suspicions in the Gilded Age. "Wicked industry supported pious idleness," he announced in "What Must We Do to Be Saved?" "The hut gave to the cathedral, and frightened poverty gave even its rags to buy a robe for hypocrisy. . . . Priests have invented a crime called 'blasphemy,' and behind that crime hypocrisy has crouched for thousands of years."[67]

Gilded cathedrals and robed priests were commonplace images in nineteenth-century anti-Catholic rhetoric. The good Protestants who ventured to hear Ingersoll speak, whether they were of the liberal or more orthodox variety, likely would have nodded in agreement with the Great Agnostic's denunciations of Catholic grift and corruption.[68] Moreover, as Elizabeth Fenton has argued, the basic idea of a "right to conscience"—the idea Ingersoll affirmed in countless lectures—drew its force in the nineteenth century from widespread anti-Catholicism.[69] "A foil for political and social freedom," writes Fenton, "Catholicism becomes the impetus for continual renewal of the nation's revolutionary promises and international interests. Thus it operates as the institution against which U.S. liberalism can define itself."[70] It is unsurprising, therefore, to hear Ingersoll's denunciations slide into pleas for "republicanism in the domain of thought as well as in civil government."[71] As he elaborated in "Ghosts," "I glory in the fact that in the New World, in the United States, liberty of conscience was first granted to man. . . . The Declaration of Independence was the first document that retired ghosts from politics. It is the first document that said authority does not come from the clouds."[72]

The key to Ingersoll's anti-Catholic rhetoric, however, was its foray into critiques of the *Protestant* status quo. An anti-institutional agitator above all, Ingersoll recognized that anti-Catholicism—be it latent or overt—could be used to assault other forms of religious power. Accordingly, he regularly drew on the Protestant spirit of the age to critique Protestantism itself. As he saw it, there was little difference between "the prejudiced priest" and "the malicious minister."[73] "The Protestant," he explained in "Individuality," "has vied with the Catholic in denouncing freedom of thought, and while I was taught to hate Catholicism with every drop of my blood, it is only justice to say that in all essential particulars, it is precisely the same as every other religion."[74] In "What Must We Do to Be Saved?" he declared himself opposed to "spider-like priests," but then proceeded to ridicule the Episcopalian Church as "utterly unsuited to a free people"; to critique Methodism and John Wesley for "not believ[ing] in human liberty"; to scorn Presbyterianism and John Calvin for destroying "every human feeling" and filling "the mind with the infinite gloom of predestination and eternal death"; and to denounce the "Evangelical Alliance," which was a composite of all orthodox denominations, for affirming "the right and duty of private judgment in the interpretation of holy scriptures" while simultaneously preaching that "if you interpret wrong you are damned."[75]

Susan Griffin has persuasively argued that anti-Catholic narratives in the late nineteenth century routinely functioned as indictments of Protestant culture. Because anti-Catholic discourse had become familiar, writers could use it as a subtle and "flexible medium of cultural critique."[76] As a result, Ingersoll's use of Protestant claims to confront Protestantism was not unique. However, many critics of Protestantism, most notably Mark Twain, launched their challenges through humorous verbal jousting. Ingersoll approached the matter differently. His proclamations from the lecture stage were often direct and vitriolic, rattling the Catholic and Protestant establishments through quick jabs and powerful hooks. This created the frenetic movements suited to a populist uprising. Ingersoll's verbal barrage set established authorities back on their heels and created an opportunity for "the people" to join him in battle.

DRAWING ORDINARY PEOPLE INTO RELIGIOUS INQUIRY

More people responded to Ingersoll's appeals than to the appeals of any other free-thought leader of the time. None of the other speakers and writers in the "golden age" of free thought had the same following as the Great Agnostic. But why? Scholars of rhetoric have offered several reasons, including Ingersoll's language and delivery, his oratorical and intellectual pacing, and his naturalistic preaching style.[77] Although such reasons offer a partial explanation of Ingersoll's oratory, they do not go far enough in explaining how he was able to maintain visibility and influence for a quarter century while assaulting what many listeners held sacred. To understand this feat, we need to understand his ability to accommodate different people with different perspectives in his lectures. After assaulting existing religious institutions, Ingersoll made rhetorical space for the religious convictions of his listeners, allowing believers to exempt themselves from his larger assault on religious institutions. In short, his ridicule of the status quo marked off a space where ordinary people of diverse perspectives could gather and define themselves *as* ordinary—as free thinkers not beholden to the figures and institutions of religious power.

Time and again, Ingersoll insisted that he opposed institutions, not individuals, thereby inviting religious believers into a populist coalition. "I do not say, and I do not believe," he announced in "Heretics and Heresies," "that Christians are as bad as their creeds. In spite of church and dogma, there have been millions and millions of men and women true to the loftiest and most generous promptings of the human heart. They have been true to their convictions, and with a self-denial and fortitude excelled by none, have labored and suffered for the salvation of men."[78] Those listeners who saw themselves as open-minded individuals, who saw themselves as true to their convictions, who saw themselves as working for the salvation of others—and what late nineteenth-century

American did not see himself or herself that way?—were thus excused from Ingersoll's attacks. "Do not imagine for a moment that I think people who disagree with me are bad people," he explained in "What Must We Do to Be Saved?" "I admit, and I cheerfully admit, that a very large proportion of mankind, and a very large majority, a vast number, are reasonably honest. It is an intellectual question."[79] Even when it came to clergy who tried to stop Ingersoll from lecturing, he clarified the target of his invective: "Against these men I have not the slightest feeling in the world; every man is the product of his own surroundings. . . . I blame the creed, I blame the religion, I blame the superstition that forced them to do so. I do not blame those men."[80] In such statements, Ingersoll's anti-institutional fury turned into a reasonable criticism of the power structures that many Americans recognized as problematic. As free thinkers, the individuals in Ingersoll's audiences could see in the outlines of his rebuke their own complaints about particular clergy, churches, and denominations.

Yet Ingersoll went further, inviting his listeners to identify with his anti-institutionalism. In several lectures he lauded different aspects of Christian history. "I admit," he declared in the conclusion of "The Devil," "that there are many good and beautiful passages in the Old and New Testament; that from the lips of Christ dropped many pearls of kindness—of love."[81] It was not only Christ's pearls of kindness that appealed to Ingersoll; it was also Christ's work as an agitator, as an Ingersollian heretic: "He did what He could to tear down the religion of His day; . . . He held the temple in contempt. I like Him because He held the old Jewish religion in contempt; because He had sense enough to say that doctrine was not true."[82] In "Individuality," he extended this affirmation to church history: "I will not say the church has been an unmitigated evil in all respects. Its history is infamous and glorious. It has delighted in the production of extremes."[83] Even the most devout believer could admit that church history was not a tale of unmitigated love. Along the way, the believer could nod in agreement with the Pagan Pope.

Perhaps the most notable accommodationist strategy in Ingersoll's rhetorical oeuvre was his thoroughgoing Americanism. Populism, at least as it has surfaced in American history, has relied extensively on such ideals as liberty, freedom, equality, justice, self-determination, and individualism. Ingersoll's lectures extended these terms to the pursuit of knowledge. Radical equality, for example, was central to his vision of inquiry because "Each person should be allowed to reach his own conclusions and to speak his honest thought. Every man should be true to himself—true to the inward light. Each man, in the laboratory of his own mind, and for himself alone, should test the so-called facts—the theories of all the world."[84] Elsewhere he declared, "I claim no right that I am not willing to give to every other human being beneath the stars—none whatever. And I will fight to-night for the right of those who disagree with me to express their thoughts just as soon as I will fight for my own rights to express mine."[85] Intellectual equality meant leveling the barriers between the powerful and the marginalized. It meant that "the Pope and Peasant are equal. Each must read for himself—and each ought to honestly and fearlessly give to his fellowmen what he learns."[86]

Other Americanisms followed close on the heels of equality. Time and again he praised the "liberty of thought," or "the right to think and the right to think wrong," as "the means by which we arrive at the truth."[87] He also spoke of "liberty of conscience" as an American birthright given by the great American infidels—"Paine, Franklin, and Jefferson."[88] Along with liberty came individualism and self-determination: "Whoever worships, abdicates. Whoever believes, at the commands of power, tramples his own individuality beneath his feet, and voluntarily robs himself of all that renders man superior to brute."[89] Elsewhere Ingersoll declared that "each human being" ought to be "self-supporting" and "take intelligent thought for the morrow."[90] Several Americanisms came together in the conclusion of "Ghosts": "I believe the American people have brains enough, and nerve enough, and courage enough, to control and govern themselves, without any assistance from dust or ghosts. That is my doctrine, and I am going to do what I can while I live to increase that feeling of independence and manhood of the American people."[91]

Perhaps the best way to understand Ingersoll's deployment of Americanisms is as an ideographic shift. Ideographs, as Michael McGee has explained, function as one-word sums for an orientation—terms that effectively summarize an ideology. According to McGee, ideographs are structured both vertically and horizontally—that is, structured according to a historic symbolic order (vertical) and according to the symbols that cluster with them in the present (horizontal).[92] Thus in the United States, liberty and freedom often travel together, and not far behind come justice, equality, individualism, the rule of law, and similar notions. These words "sum up" the American political orientation. What's more, they gave Ingersoll an opportunity to use people's existing political commitments for religious resistance. The same coalition that gathered around the ideographs of American politics might also gather around them in religious culture. The *Milwaukee Daily Sentinel* seemed to recognize this in 1877 when covering one of Ingersoll's recent lectures in the city. Though some in his audience "were shocked by the sentiments that he uttered," and though the *Sentinel* could not "follow him to the extremes to which [his] sentiment carries him," it was undoubtedly possible to "differ with him widely and still learn from him":

> He hates tyranny, whether it comes in the form of a father brutally beating his child, or a creed that may impair the freedom of human thought. He believes in the widest liberty with a belief that is part of his very existence. . . . It was not his word pictures—dazzling as was their beauty—that [united the audience]; it was the intense human feeling manifested in every word, look and gesture, and uniting him with every one before him. . . . His scathing invectives were not claptrap or wanton abuse, but an expression of his profound sympathy for oppressed humanity and a correlative hatred for the oppressors. Upon the same broad basis his code of ethics is founded, and it isn't a bad code either.[93]

These were the qualities that allowed believers and agnostics alike to gather as "the people" around Ingersoll's appeals. His hatred of tyranny, his love of liberty, his human feeling, his honest expression, and his code of ethics—countless Americans found something with which to identify.

In turn, they formed an equivalential chain ready to resist the established order and to reclaim religious inquiry for the people.

MODELING POPULIST THOUGHT

Benjamin Moffitt has recently argued that political populism hinges, in part, on careful performances by populist leaders. In performing their antipathy toward the status quo, these leaders demonstrate to their followers how "the people" ought to engage in politics. Yet, Moffitt warns, leaders need to be careful that their performances remain attuned to the "ordinariness" of the people. They need to ensure that their abilities are not beyond the capacities of their constituencies but ordinary enough for others to emulate.[94]

Ingersoll's work demonstrated the intellectual extension of this political balancing act. His oratory performed the kind of inquiry his audiences could undertake as ordinary people aligned against the religious status quo. Together in frustration, they could investigate the world as free, liberated sovereigns of their own mind. Because "every one is monarch" over his or her thought, declared Ingersoll, all individuals must "become investigators, not followers; not cringers and crawlers."[95]

To spur populist investigation, Ingersoll routinely called attention to himself as a free inquirer, as someone liberated from the strictures of religious power and ready to live a contemplative, combative life. Ingersoll opened "Ghosts," for example, with long paragraphs about his own place in the thinking world:

> This is my doctrine, and I am going to do what I can while I live to increase that feeling of independence and manhood in the American people. . . . I tell you, the man that tries to make somebody else happy, and who owns his own soul, nobody having a mortgage or deed of trust upon his manhood or liberty—this world is a pretty good world for such a man. I do not care: I am going to say my say, whether I make money or grow poor; no matter whether I get high office or walk along the dusty highway of the common. I am going to say my say, and I had rather be

> a farmer and live on forty acres of land. . . . I had rather live there, and have the freedom of my own brain; I had rather do that than live in a palace of gold, and crawl, a slimy hypocrite, through this world.[96]

The "I" statements portrayed an active subject—a free, proud intellectual populist in touch with the world and able to create a place for himself apart from centers of power. The American people, he suggested, should do the same.

In addition to offering these "I" statements, Ingersoll often placed himself as an actor inside familiar religious narratives, playing with the terms of sacred stories because he was free to do so. Not only did this establish his ethos as a critic of the Bible and the Judeo-Christian tradition, but it signaled the kind of creative power populist thinkers possessed. In "Liberty of Man, Woman, and Child," for example, he placed himself in the Garden of Eden, devouring fruit from the Tree of the Knowledge of Good and Evil: "I would have done it in fifteen minutes, and I know it. There wouldn't have been an apple on that tree half an hour from date, and the limbs could have been full of clubs."[97] In "Orthodoxy," he made himself an interlocutor with Lazarus after Lazarus had come back from beyond the grave: "Where were you when you got the notice to come back? What kind of country is it? What kind of opening there for a young man? How did you like it?"[98] In "Some Reasons Why," Ingersoll placed himself at the pearly gates of heaven hashing out his differences with God: "If I find at the day of judgment that I have been mistaken, I will say so like a man. If God tells me then that he is the author of the Old Testament I will admit that he is worse than I thought he was, and when he comes to pronounce sentences upon me I will say to him: do unto others as you would that others should do unto you."[99] This challenge to God demonstrated to listeners how they could bend the terms of sacred stories back on those stories, thereby rendering themselves creative forces in the unfolding of religious history. Like Ingersoll, they could challenge received wisdom, even sacred wisdom, and create their own understanding of God, the afterlife, and the religious origins of humankind.

Ingersoll's reconfiguration of sacred stories produced a sense of impropriety, which, in turn, generated a palpable rhetorical electricity. Effectively, his tactic amounted to what Kenneth Burke has called "perspective by incongruity," which involves a violation of "*what properly goes with what*," a "constant juxtaposing of incongruous words," and an experimental "wrenching apart" of the "molecular combinations" of language.[100] The purpose of wrenching apart symbol systems is to formulate novel terministic screens—alternatives to the established order and new perspectives on the world. Ingersoll's perspective by incongruity was especially powerful because it trafficked in sacred symbols—symbols categorically "set apart," in Émile Durkheim's formulation.[101] Ingersoll seemed to relish forcing sacred symbols into syntactical relationship with profane symbols. The closer he could bring the sacred and profane in his statements, the more he was able to disrupt religious systems, making the good seem bad, the divine seem devilish, and the virtuous seem vicious.

For instance, Ingersoll often portrayed God not as kind, benevolent, and loving, but as an "infinite fiend" and "the insane keeper of a mad house."[102] The existence of hell, he said, turned God into "the basest and most cruel being in the universe. . . . If the doctrine of eternal damnation is true, let me have my portion in hell, rather than in heaven with a God infamous enough to inflict eternal misery upon any of the sons of men."[103] Toward the end of "Some Mistakes of Moses," he took a more rapid-fire approach to describing the God of the Old Testament, calling him a "false fiend, an unjust judge, a braggart, hypocrite, and tyrant, sincere in hatred, jealous, vain, and revengeful, false in promise, honest in curse, suspicious, ignorant, and changeable, infamous, and hideous."[104] Christian orthodoxy did not fare much better. In Ingersoll's hands, Christianity became a "coiled serpent," equating "the spirit of worship" with "the spirit of tyranny" and welcoming "the smell of innocent blood" as "divine perfume."[105] Ingersoll also insisted that arguments for the truth of Christianity were not real arguments; they were, rather, "iron arguments" of torture, made with the thumbscrew, the collar, the rack, and the "scavenger's daughter." These iron arguments were put forth, Ingersoll announced to underscore the irony of the situation, in "the name of law and order," in "the name of morality," in "the name of religion," and in "the name of God."[106]

Ingersoll's perspective by incongruity not only turned the sacred into the profane but also positioned the profane as the new sacred. In his lectures, infidels were not dangerous or contemptible; they were responsible for "intellectual advance," "the flower of all this world."[107] "Every heretic," he said, "has been, and is, a ray of light."[108] Ingersoll also told listeners about the true religious heroes of the world, at least in his eyes. The "inventors of all the wonderful machines," the men "who have explored the heavens and traced the orbits of the stars," the "great philosophers and naturalists," the "great orators who have swayed the world," and "the captains of industry, the producers, the soldiers who have battled for the right, the vast host of useful men"—these ought to be "our Christs, our apostles and our saints."[109] Perhaps more unnervingly for many in Ingersoll's audiences, the Pagan Pope often praised Satan as a religious hero. If the creation story in Genesis is true, Ingersoll questioned, "ought we not . . . thank the serpent? He was the first schoolmaster, the first advocate of learning, the first enemy of ignorance, the first to whisper in human ears the sacred word liberty."[110] As he put it in another lecture, Christians ought to thank "his Satanic Majesty. He opened for us the gates of paradise and made it possible to obtain eternal life. Without Satan, without Judas, not a single human being could have become an angel of light."[111]

Perspective by incongruity modeled the intellectual freedom ordinary Americans could obtain if they followed Ingersoll's lead. The point was less that God was a monster and Satan a hero than that sacred and profane terms could be broken apart and recombined for novel perspectives. Simply by thinking through the implications of received wisdom, ordinary people could hold the religious establishment to account and could emerge as thinkers in their own right.

Ingersoll similarly modeled intellectual resistance when he engaged his listeners in a kind of live, collective biblical criticism. The Great Agnostic had his own method for reading the Bible, and it was a method practically anyone could do on his or her own. This method was what we might call "plain reading." Flexible and accessible, plain reading gave those outside, or on the margins, of the culture of professionalism a way to pronounce upon the most pressing religious debates of the day. According to the plain reading method, the best way to understand and critique religious claims was to pick up a text, read it, and evaluate it according to commonsense standards. Plain reading required no theological training, no mastery of Greek or Latin, no understanding of biblical exegesis and hermeneutics, and no concern for the problems of translation. Regardless of one's social, economic, or educational position—save for literacy—one could evaluate sacred texts as effectively as (and often more effectively than) any trained theologian.[112] Yet even the illiterate could, by paying fifty cents for a lecture ticket, join Ingersoll in a collective plain reading. While this methodology may have been intellectually problematic in several regards—texts are seldom as straightforward as the plain-reading method suggests—its appeal stemmed from the way it displaced institutional power, wrenched the locus of judgment from existing authorities, and gave it to those in Ingersoll's audiences.

"Some Mistakes of Moses" offered an extended lesson in the plain-reading method. On stage, Ingersoll quoted lengthy passages from scripture and moved carefully through the books of the Old Testament. Reading aloud with the audience, he questioned the story of Adam and Eve, the Fall, the flood, the arithmetic associated with the animals on Noah's ark, Methuselah's age, the Tower of Babel, Jewish laws, the Israelites in captivity, the plagues, the exodus, and more. In almost every confrontation with these stories, Ingersoll bent passages and interpretations in a way that created an alternative perspective—a perspective ordinary Americans could reach on their own simply by picking up the Bible and reading it. When they did, they would see a "god who multiplied the agonies of woman, increased the weary toil of man, and in his anger drowned a world." This was the same God "whose altars reeked with human blood, who butchered babes, violated maidens, enslaved men, and filled the earth with cruelty and crime."[113] The Bible, he lamented with a kind of Victorian sensibility, contained many pages "too unfit to read, many stories not calculated, in my judgment, to improve the morals of mankind. If there is a God, it certainly is blasphemous to attribute to him the authorship of pages too obscene to be read in the presence of men and women."[114]

Ingersoll also structured "What Must We Do to Be Saved?" according to the plain-reading method. In that lecture, he moved through each of the four Christian Gospels to uncover the requirements for salvation. He then engaged the creeds and doctrines of various Christian denominations. In analyzing what he read (and what he quoted for the audience), he disregarded the insights of secondary literature, theological commentaries, intertextual references, and Greek and Latin dictionaries. He confined himself, as anyone could, to the words on the page. "I made up my mind," he explained, "to see what I had to do in order to save my soul according to the Testament, and thereupon I read it. I read the gospels, Matthew, Mark, Luke, and John, and found that the church had been deceiving me. I found that the clergy did not understand their own books; that they had been building upon passages that had been interpolated; upon passages that were entirely untrue."[115] He discovered this deception, the lecture suggested, just by picking up the Bible and reading it.

In reading the four Gospels, Ingersoll found several passages that inspired him. The Sermon on the Mount was particularly praiseworthy.[116] But as he finished reading the Gospel of Matthew, he noticed something amiss. According to Ingersoll's plain reading, Christ did not say, "'You must believe in me—that I am the only begotten son of the living God.' He did not say: 'You must be born again.' He did not say: 'You must believe the bible.'"[117] Mark and Luke, Ingersoll discovered, also failed to mention these doctrinal building blocks. John was another matter:

> Read Matthew, Mark, and Luke, and then read John, and you will agree with me that the three first gospels teach that if we are kind and forgiving to our fellows, God will be kind and forgiving to us. In John we are told that another man can be good for us, or bad for us, and that the only way to get to heaven is to believe something that we know is

> not so. All these passages about believing in Christ, drinking his blood and eating his flesh are after-thoughts. They were written by the theologians, and in a few years they will be considered unworthy of the lips of Christ.[118]

"You will agree with me" signaled the power of plain reading, a power that undercut what theologians (figures of the establishment) had spent centuries constructing. Simply read the Bible on your own, Ingersoll encouraged, and you will understand everything you need to know. Much in the Gospels could remain, for the "lips of Christ" still had plenty to teach. But the eating of flesh and the drinking of blood would be exposed as institutional impositions on free intellectual practice. "Read [the Bible] as you would any other book," Ingersoll underscored elsewhere. "Think of it as you would any other; get the bandage of reverence from your eyes; drive from your heart the phantom of fear; push from the throne of your brain the cowled form of superstition."[119]

Ingersoll's plain reading of the Bible smacked of Protestantism. It eschewed ecclesiastical authority and put individuals in direct connection with sacred texts, giving them the power to understand and evaluate the purported Word of God. Even though Ingersoll used plain reading for ends that may have troubled some listeners, the methodology itself would have been familiar because "the overwhelming majority of American Christians" at the time held that the Bible should be approached through "commonsensical methods for interpreting it."[120] The problem at the end of the nineteenth century, however, was that these commonsensical methods seemed under attack. Liberal theology, especially the German higher criticism from which it emerged, had wrenched the ability to understand texts from the ordinary Americans Ingersoll engaged. Higher criticism approached the Bible as something that had to be understood in historical context, as something shot through with allegory and symbolism, as something closely connected to other texts from thousands of years ago. As a result, the Bible became "a book for experts, requiring an elaborate training in linguistics and historical disciplines before it could be properly understood; if it needed expert knowledge before it could be read, it was best to leave the Bible to the experts, like so many other things in a world of specialization." In a notable twist, then, the rise of higher criticism meant "the gradual decay of the ordinary Christian's sense that he can read the Bible for himself without an interpreter and discover its unambiguous meaning."[121]

Plain reading offered ordinary people a way of reclaiming their connection to the Bible. The method completely disrupted the religious status quo, or so Ingersoll suggested, and in that way it was eminently radical. Yet it was familiar to the audience and grounded in Protestant history, and in that way it was staunchly conservative. Here, then, was one instantiation of the radical conservatism and conservative radicalism of intellectual populism. In Ingersoll's work, plain reading disrupted the establishment, but it did so for the purpose of returning religious inquiry to the hands of the people from whom it had been wrested in the first place. As with his Victorian sensibilities, affirmations of traditional public morality, and string of Americanisms, his method of biblical criticism offered a radical return to a world that seemed to be slipping away.

When people embrace the radical conservatism of plain reading, when they think for themselves, when ordinary Americans participate in the great religious discussions of the day, then, Ingersoll promised, a new intellectual day would dawn. Ingersoll's lectures frequently culminated with a romantic, almost syrupy, utopian vision of America's intellectual future. Here was the intellectual utopia on the other side of the populist revolution. "Oh, liberty!" he exclaimed at the end of "Liberty of Man, Woman, and Child." "Float not forever in the far horizon! Remain not forever in the dream of the enthusiast and poet and the philanthropist! But come and take up thine abode with the children of men forever!"[122] At the end of "The Gods," his utopian pleading assumed the character of a populist religion, where the people were the new priests: "We are laying the foundations of a grand temple of the future—not the temple of all the gods, but of all the people—wherein, with appropriate rites, will be celebrated the religion of Humanity."[123] At the end of "Individuality," he pictured power vanquished and people freed: "Surely it is worth something to feel that there are no priests, no popes, no parties, no government, no kings, no gods to whom your intellect can be compelled to pay a reluctant homage. . . . Surely it is sublime to think that the brain is a castle, and that within its curious bastions and winding halls, the soul, in spite of all worlds and all beings, is the supreme sovereign of itself."[124] And at the end of "Some Reasons Why," Ingersoll unveiled the "religion of the future," which said "to every man, you have the right to think and investigate for yourself. Liberty is my religion. Everything that is true, every good thought, every beautiful thing, every self-denying action—all these make my Bible. . . . Every violet, every blade of grass, every tree, every mountain crowned with snow, every star that shines, every throb of love, every honest act, all that is good and true combined, make my Bible, and upon that book I stand."[125]

Removing oppressive institutions and empowering ordinary people to think for themselves laid the groundwork for a future of expansive beauty and unrestricted intellectual advancement. Or so Ingersoll suggested. The likelihood of such a future coming to pass was less important than the fact that it was a future countless Americans could support. In the lecture hall, vision and eloquence trumped practicality. Even the most devout could accept Ingersoll's basic plea—that people should be allowed to think for themselves. The religious and nonreligious could, in the Gilded Age, find much to admire in the idea of a populist utopia controlled by salt-of-the-earth Americans. Whatever one ultimately believed about the divine, the cry of liberty could still sway a multitude.

Conclusion

On December 29, 1895—a Sunday—several newspapers across the country, including the *Milwaukee Sentinel* and the *Denver Daily News*, published a sermon that tried to explain why Americans flocked to Ingersoll's lectures.[126] Noting that wherever the Great Agnostic traveled "crowds of people want[ed] to hear" him, Rev. Charles F. Dole of Boston offered a plethora of reasons for Ingersoll's influence. He "strikes from the shoulder and hits hard," the minister mused, which is something Americans relish. He uses "fitting and eloquent language," which makes for captivating performances. He is also witty, and "it is in human nature to like wit and fun." But the real reason Americans flock to hear Ingersoll, the minister claimed, is because he "goes straight for shams and 'humbugs.'" The clergyman elaborated: "We Americans rather like this. It is honest, democratic treatment. If things or men cannot bear the daylight, we have no use for them. If religion must be kept in a dark place, in a closet or a church, and cannot stand out in the sunshine or the market, if it will have no questions asked, it is not the kind of religion that men in America want."[127]

The opinion of only one minister, Dole's words nevertheless pointed to the core of Ingersoll's contribution to intellectual populism. A religious divide separated Dole and the Great Agnostic, yet the two found common ground not in spite of but *through* Ingersoll's assaults on the religious establishment. Ingersoll's lectures prove, Dole revealed later in his sermon, that "religion is really a very big and interesting subject. No one would want to hear about it if it was dead. . . . Mr. Ingersoll knows, and every one ought to know, that there is something real in religion."[128] From Dole's perspective, Ingersoll's lectures did not vanquish religion or dictate answers to the great questions of the universe. Rather, the Pagan Pope advanced the kind of populist combat that enlivened religious inquiry. He brought religious questions into the marketplace of ideas, which strengthened religion by showing what was real in it. In short, critiquing the status quo was an effective way to get ordinary people involved in the pursuit of religious knowledge, and when that happened, the world of thought became more democratic, more pluralistic, and more resilient.

Over the years, Ingersoll received countless letters from people who had come to a similar conclusion. In 1877, for example, a young woman from Stockbridge, Wisconsin, thanked Ingersoll for his intellectual courage, and then concluded: "You have shown yourself superior to the multitude by recognizing the fact that a woman can *think* independent of the priest. And I think I should not mind *pious persecution* if I know I had the sympathy of woman's teacher and the child's champion, Robert

Ingersoll."[129] In 1878, a correspondent who had recently read Ingersoll's book *The Gods and Other Lectures* penned a note of thanks for the "delicious mental food." He went on to explain that even though he was "a young man, unmarried, and poor," he was nevertheless "*rich* in health and muscle" because of Ingersoll's work.[130] Another correspondent thanked Ingersoll for "industriously trying to keep all souls out of hell" and for leaving "God's character good."[131] Yet another correspondent, who had attended a lecture the previous night, praised the "strong, healthful tone" of the talk, "which was inspiring, uplifting, and, if you will permit me to say it, thoroughly *Christian.* For I was delighted to detect in this tone the true ring of a liberal, large-hearted hope for the redemption of man from all that is low and mean and small, and for the ultimate triumph of all that is high and noble in his nature."[132] A preacher of the gospel and editor of the *Southern Kentucky Evangelist* wrote a similar note, thanking the Great Agnostic "for the good you have not only done me but the good you have done to our common country." He concluded, "I had much rather meet you in Heaven than Calvin."[133]

To be sure, not all religious believers thanked Ingersoll so profusely. Over the years he received countless letters attacking him and trying to convert him. Christian groups even held massive prayer vigils to ask God to save the Pagan Pope's soul.[134] Nevertheless, a remarkable number of believers and nonbelievers felt that Ingersoll's lectures had prepared them to participate in intellectual culture and to consider the greatest religious questions of the day. Such was the upshot of Ingersoll's intellectual populism, achieved through his own combination of the five appeals intellectual populists shared. Ingersoll focused his attack on the religious institutions of his day and on the ministers, priests, and theologians who represented those institutions. After articulating grievances against those forces in a way with which many people could identify, he invited ordinary Americans to take control of religious inquiry and to contemplate sacred reality on their own. Once they did, they would recognize their freedom to think, their equality with others, and the importance of liberty in the intellectual realm. This liberty, especially in the context of religion, meant not only a radical restructuring of ecclesiastical power but also a conservative return to ordinary folks contemplating God on their own terms. With radical conservatism instantiated in American religion, the nation would enter a new era of utopian understanding. The way he combined these discursive markers of intellectual populism did not harm religious thought. Rather, it expanded, diversified, and democratized it. After attending an Ingersoll lecture, countless Americans came away with a new vigor, ready to ponder God, the devil, heaven, hell, sin, and salvation—and to do so with people across their community, many of whom held very different religious beliefs. In that way, Ingersoll worked in service of a stronger, freer, healthier religious culture. Maybe the Pagan Pope was, at the end of the day, more pope than pagan.

To be sure, Ingersoll had help with the project of democratizing inquiry in the Gilded Age and Progressive Era. The same kind of opposition he led against religious institutions proved useful for opposing other institutions and for bringing the people together in new ways. As we shall see, Mary Baker Eddy not only founded a new religion but also formed a populist coalition to resist the onslaught of modern medicine. Along the way, she upended what many Americans thought they knew about sin, sickness, and salvation.

CHAPTER TWO

Mary Baker Eddy's Divine Healing Science

Toward the back of every issue of the *Christian Science Journal*, Christian Scientists testify about healing. In the early decades of the church these testimonials were especially valuable in showcasing the promise of the new religion. In September 1901, for instance, C. S. Harris, a Jewish man from Chicago, told readers about attending "a lecture at the Third Church" of Christ, Scientist. Because of this thought-provoking lecture, Harris started attending regular meetings at Third Church, where he learned one of the mandates of Christian Science: "Work out your own salvation." Soon he began to do just that. For thirty years he had been a heavy smoker and drinker, but after studying Christian Science, he reported that both "appetites left me without notice." Moreover, he had long struggled with poor vision. "Oculists, specialists, and professors"—professionals, in other words—all insisted that he "must have an operation." Instead of having an operation, Harris carefully studied *Science and Health with Key to the Scriptures*, the "textbook" of

Christian Science. Soon his vision returned. Another healing took place when he accidentally punctured his thumbnail with a "pair of sharp-pointed tweezers." With blood "spurting all over" his hand, he retrieved the church's "Scientific Statement of Being" from his coat pocket, read it carefully, and "neither saw nor felt any ill effects" from the injury. He concluded, "I did not lose my finger-nail as on similar occasions before knowing of Christian Science."[1]

Harris's claims may have sounded fanciful to some, but such reports of healing were commonplace in the *Christian Science Journal*. Every issue contained similar stories of ordinary people "working their own salvation"—salvation that often began with a Christian Science lecture. Elma Williams, for example, attended a Christian Science lecture and came away "feeling much as I think Paul felt on the road to Damascus." Now, she reported, "Every day gives me fresh proofs of God's goodness."[2] Louise Reich reported a similar Saul-to-Paul conversion. After calling on "many physicians" and "a specialist in Florida," all of whom "gave me no encouragement," Reich attended a Christian Science lecture in Jacksonville. Feeling "at great peace" from the lecture, she then read *Science and Health* on her own. "Many diseases left me almost immediately, among them catarrh of the stomach, dyspepsia, headaches, and many little troubles."[3] David Moir had long suffered as "a man of the world, guided mainly by the lusts and passions of the natural man." After contracting a lust-related problem that was best left unsaid, Moir consulted a physician, who "said I must take medicine for two years, and could give me no hope of a permanent cure." Then he attended a Christian Science lecture, began studying *Science and Health*, and soon experienced "peace and satisfaction beyond anything I had ever hoped for in the old condition."[4]

These testimonials contain the nucleus of Christian Science's appeal. Suffering from various ailments, individuals turned to the medical establishment for help, but they found no remedy. Then they attended a Christian Science lecture. Armed with knowledge accrued in the lecture hall, they began studying Christian Science for themselves, working diligently, carefully, and conscientiously through Mary Baker Eddy's *Science and Health*. Soon, their ailments disappeared. The medical establishment had left them hopeless, with little more than the threat of surgery and a few worthless pills, but Christian Science made them agents in their own healing—indeed, in their own salvation.

One of only a handful of global religions born in the United States, Christian Science used these testimonials to attract tens of thousands of believers in a short time. It began in 1866 when Mary Baker Eddy, suffering and on the brink of death, received a revelation from God. The revelation showed her how to overcome sin and sickness just as Jesus had. To do so, all she had to do was understand and live according to an idea that was simple to say but revolutionary in its implications—the idea that matter was not real. Jesus had realized the unreality of matter and was able to heal people instantly, using the method of Divine Science. Eddy took this world-changing revelation on the road and attracted legions of followers. By 1910, the year of her death, Christian Science claimed around eighty-five thousand members and over eleven hundred churches, with congregations in almost every country.[5] As biographer Gillian Gill writes, Mary Baker Eddy was then "regarded with reverence bordering on adoration by men and women all over the land and in several other countries and was widely hailed in the American press as the most powerful woman in the United States."[6] To be sure, Eddy had legions of detractors, including Mark Twain, who ridiculed her whenever he had the chance.[7] Nevertheless, Christian Science proved to the world "that a woman could pioneer and direct a successful and thriving religious organization composed of both men and women."[8]

Central to the spread of Eddy's revelation and the success of Christian Science was intellectual populism. The previous chapter demonstrated how Ingersoll combated the religious establishment of the Gilded Age not to undercut religion but to draw ordinary people into religious inquiry and thereby strengthen the pursuit of religious knowledge. By diversifying and democratizing conversations about the divine, he revitalized an intellectual terrain that seemed fallow. Ingersoll's anti-institutionalism, hailing of ordinary people, use of Americanisms, radical conservatism, and picture of an intellectual utopia combined on the lecture stage to embolden individuals marginalized by professionalism as intellectual actors. These same appeals, albeit combined in different ways, propelled the early Christian Science church. For Eddy and her followers, however, the nefarious power structure standing in the way of human flourishing was not only religious but also medical. According to Christian Science, the medical and theological establishments of the late nineteenth century deceived people about health and salvation and bound them in sin and sickness. Eddy argued that the principles Jesus had demonstrated two thousand years prior enabled people to reclaim their own well-being, no longer subject to the deceptive dictates of medical authorities.

This populist message emerged in numerous forms and venues—workshops, periodicals, books, interviews, demonstrations, and more. But public lectures were indispensable to Christian Science's spread. Like Ingersoll, Christian Scientists traveled the country riling audiences into populist resistance. Yet Eddy and her followers took their commitment to lecture culture a step further than Ingersoll by institutionalizing the performance of populist discourse. In 1898, to push back against her critics and detractors, Eddy established the Christian Science Board of Lectureship, which sent church-sanctioned lecturers across the country in a strategic campaign to spread a new gospel. With a multipronged discursive push, the early Christian Science church linked audiences across the United States in an antagonistic frontier of ordinary people working their own salvation.

This chapter explores the development and discourse of Christian Science, particularly the Christian Science Board of Lectureship. As I will show, the Board of Lectureship was instrumental in moving ordinary Americans from the periphery of intellectual life to active participants in the realization of Divine Science. Though the medical and theological establishments had displaced nonexperts from the pursuit of knowledge, at least according to Eddy and her followers, Christian Science lecturers called on nonexperts to become part of a logical proof demonstrating Christian Science's ability to heal. In turn, those whom medical professionalism had pushed aside reclaimed their place in a new intellectual order.

To explicate the populist character of Christian Science, this chapter begins with a discussion of a bold sermon by Eddy, "The People's God," which set the new church on a populist trajectory that lasted well into the twentieth century. I then offer a history of Christian Science and the opposition through which it grew, followed by an exploration of the creation and discourse of the Christian Science Board of Lectureship, which made the experiences of ordinary people central to a utopia of the Mind. As we shall see, Christian Science lecturers left an evidentiary void in their arguments, but this void drew audience members into the logic of Divine Science. Accordingly, the discourse of the early Christian Science church offers a prime example of the way intellectual populism not only appeals to ordinary people but also renders them agents in an uprising that will purportedly remake reality.

Summoning "The People's God"

On March 14, 1880, Mary Baker Eddy, then leader of a relatively small religious movement, mounted the platform in Boston's Hawthorne Hall to deliver a sermon titled "The People's God."[9] Years later, after the sermon had been published as a standalone pamphlet, Eddy retitled it "The People's Idea of God," believing that the original title was too brazen. Yet the original title better signaled the populist energy that permeated Eddy's movement to rid the world of sin and sickness. In 1880, Eddy had recently moved her organization from the small town of Lynn, Massachusetts, to Boston. Not only was she hoping for a larger base of operation but she also needed a fresh start, having recently emerged from a bizarre trial in which her husband and a close associate had been accused of conspiring to murder a former student of Eddy's. Though charges were eventually dropped, harsh newspaper coverage and sizable legal debts persuaded her to move on from the birthplace of her church.[10] In Boston, Eddy hoped to preach unfettered of the people's God.

"The People's God" was one of many sermons Eddy delivered to her small flock in the early 1880s. It was notable, however, for being one of only two sermons during this period to be published in pamphlet form. Serving "a missionary as well as homiletic purpose," the sermon helped Eddy stake a claim in the intellectual milieu of Gilded Age Boston.[11] Other alternative healing methods were already vying for public recognition, as we shall see later in this chapter, and mainstream theology and medicine were beginning to look askance at those who traveled new pathways to God and wellness. To shore up her movement, Eddy needed to chart a clear course for the rightness and righteousness of Christian Science.

Christian Science was the right and righteous approach, she explained in "The People's God," because it offered the only real chance to resist the established order. In the sermon's introduction, Eddy foregrounded the "intellectual wrestling and collisions with mortal beliefs" that were necessary to reach "more spiritual latitudes." At such latitudes, "even the pangs of death disappear, . . . and we learn our capabilities for good, which ensures man's continuance and is the true glory of immortality."[12] This was the struggle to which all people were called. Intellectual wrestling with mortal beliefs necessitated combat with established belief systems. Yet this was not some mundane struggle; it was a struggle to save one's soul, to overcome death itself. Intellectual wrestling, at least in accord with Christian Science principles, was a path to immortality—to a utopia of Mind. Eddy went on to describe the two belief systems that stood in the way of this utopia: first, "the crudest ideals of speculative theology," which have "made monsters of men"; and second, "the ideals of *materia medica*," which have "made helpless invalids and cripples."[13] To elaborate on her critique of speculative theology, Eddy adopted a tone reminiscent of an Ingersoll lecture:

> The eternal roasting amidst noxious vapors; the election of the minority to be saved and the majority to be eternally punished; the wrath of God to be appeased by the sacrifice and torture of his favorite Son—are some of the false beliefs that have produced sin, sickness, and death; and then

> would say, these are natural, and that Christianity and Christ-healing are preternatural; yea, that make a mysterious God and a natural devil.[14]

Ingersoll and Eddy would have disagreed vehemently over the proper course of action once belief in eternal damnation had been vanquished. Yet they began with the same anti-institutional impulse, calling for the destruction of the Calvinist status quo.

To elaborate her critique of modern medicine, Eddy focused on the key terms *materia medica*, *materialism*, and *material man*. "Sin, sickness, and death," she explained, "originated in the belief that spirit materialized into a body, infinity became finity, or man, and the Eternal entered the temporal." These erroneous beliefs created "cold materialisms of dogma and doctrine," "learned quacks," and "scientific guessing"—all of which conspired "unwittingly against the liberty and lives of men." In Eddy's sermon, the figures and institutions of modern medicine were not only unhelpful but also eminently harmful to the realization of true health, even to the natural right of liberty, a key Americanism. Professional medicine needed to be abolished for people to live as they were born to live. As Eddy summarized toward the end of the sermon, "having faith in drugs and hygienic drills, we lose faith in Omnipotence, and give the healing power to matter instead of Spirit."[15]

Denouncing the theological and medical establishments was the first step in Eddy's intellectual populism, positioning her movement as anti-institutional and committed to restructuring the world. The second step was lauding ordinary individuals, who, if they had the chance, could enter a life of completed Being. The key phrase in this regard was one that Eddy borrowed from the apostle Paul: "Work out your own salvation" (Philippians 2:12). In "The People's God," Eddy used the phrase twice, first when she admonished her listeners to "grow out of sin in the way that our Lord has appointed; viz., to work out our own salvation"; and second when she emphasized the unity and simplicity of Christian Science, which allowed Eddy and her followers to "work out our own salvation, after the model of our Father."[16] This populist phrase suggested that once people were free from the institutions that opposed them, they could achieve being in the same way Christ had. The power to overcome sin, sickness, and death was inside everyone, but it required a reorientation of thought and a rejection of complicated theological and medical systems.

Elsewhere in the sermon, Eddy illustrated the power of ordinary people with a rich, artistic metaphor: "We are all sculptors working out our own ideals, and leaving the impress of mind on the body as well as on history and marble, chiseling to higher excellence, or leaving to rot and ruin the mind's ideals." Themes of individual agency and empowerment continued throughout the sermon, as Eddy emphasized everyone's ability to "bring out [divine] qualities of character in our own lives"; as she proclaimed that "We possess our own body and make it harmonious or discordant according to the images that thought reflects upon it"; and as she insisted that silent prayer, which everyone could do, removed "all evidence of any other power than mind," a "truth of Deity" that "destroys discord."[17] In Eddy's formulation, Christian Science was a method for demolishing false systems and for giving people the tools they needed to realize their infinitude.

Other prominent populist themes followed on the heels of Eddy's attempt to shift power from the status quo to the people. Americanisms were key to the kind of participatory inquiry she offered her listeners. Christian Science was egalitarian, she indicated, because it meant that "the feeblest mind, enlightened and spiritualized, can free its body from disease as well as sin." She boasted of the simplicity of her system, especially when compared with modern theology and medicine: "Life is God; but we say that Life is carried on through sanitary methods and speculative theories of matter. Mind is supreme; and yet we make more of matter, and lean upon it for health and life." And she offered her listeners a method of healing and salvation that was both radical and conservative. It was radical in that it upended every aspect of modern science and medicine, revealing matter as an illusion. It was conservative in that it purported to restore what once was, returning humanity to now-forgotten truths. Christian Science was a rediscovery of the spiritual ideals of "the risen Christ, whose *materia medica* and theology were one."[18]

Where the modern world had separated theology and medicine, Christian Science put them back together.

Returning to primitive Christianity was, in the end, the pathway to immortality that Eddy referenced at the beginning of the sermon. "The People's God" thus followed the intellectual-populist framework of visualizing a people's utopia on the other side of combat. By fighting through the destructive deceptions of modern theology and medicine, Eddy said, Christian Scientists could enter the plane of true existence:

> O! Christian scientist, thou of the church of the new-born; awake to a higher and holier love for God and man; put on the whole armor of Truth, rejoice in hope, be patient in tribulation, that ye may go to the bed of anguish, and look upon this dream of life in matter, girt with a higher sense of Omnipotence; and behold once again the power of divine Life and Love to heal and reinstate man in God's own image and likeness, having "one Lord, one faith, one baptism."[19]

This conclusion, which contained the resistive energy of an Ingersoll lecture, invited Eddy's listeners to return home, to overthrow matter, and to vanquish the sin and sickness that theology and medicine perpetuated to imprison spiritual beings. They could interpolate whatever health problems they had in their own lives to the populist framework Eddy articulated.

Given the conciliatory tone and motherly persona of Eddy's later career, it is easy to overlook the brash, oppositional, vitriolic origins of Christian Science.[20] While Eddy no doubt knew how to connect with different people and groups, she also knew how to establish an oppositional force against which individuals could align. This is an important point for understanding her rhetoric. Scholars tend to underscore Eddy's ability to build bridges—no doubt an important part of her success—while overlooking the strategic opposition at the heart of her movement.[21] Eddy's early populist appeals fostered the energy her followers needed to fight and resist insidious institutions. To bring together ordinary people, Eddy helped them recognize their shared antipathy with the status quo.

Such recognition was crucial to the spread of Eddy's movement because it enabled countless Americans in the late nineteenth century to see their frustrations in Eddy's own grievances, especially in her grievances with modern medicine.

Medical Professionalism and the Emergence of Christian Science

In the United States prior to the nineteenth century, women were esteemed as healers. Because medicine was largely confined to the domestic sphere, it fell naturally within the purview of female authority, "part of the domestic economy for which the wife assumed responsibility."[22] This is not to say that America lacked male doctors or professional healers. But physicians were usually jacks-of-all-trades, and whatever esteem they may have held was often due more to their social status than to their occupation.[23] Moreover, many Americans looked askance at medical practices carried out by supposed professionals who could not agree among themselves about the body and how to heal it.[24] As a result, women managed most medical care, especially when it came to childbirth. The midwife, a role reserved almost exclusively for women until the mid-nineteenth century, played a pivotal role in a female community that surrounded the birthing process. Midwives, their daughters, other female family members, an attending woman or apprentice, the expectant mother—all came together with a kind of informal folk wisdom.[25] Though midwives often had a close relationship with a local physician in case the birth went seriously wrong, men were seldom involved directly.[26] The result was a patchwork of relatively skilled, largely self-taught midwives.[27]

Around the mid-nineteenth century, however, the pace of medical professionalization quickened and threatened the sphere of female medical authority. The medical establishment was still incredibly diverse, and it would be for many decades; thus it would be hasty to characterize the establishment as a unified power structure.[28] Yet the changes underway in medical inquiry enabled many Americans, rightly or wrongly, to perceive a new medical force upending traditional health practices. Part of this force was a result of Americans seeking their education abroad. Thousands of American students began studying science in Germany, among other European countries, and many returned to America to practice medicine.[29] The overwhelming majority of these students were men. Armed with the prestige of a German education, they looked aghast at problems that centuries of folk healthcare had created. To address these problems, they began building German-style institutions that could, they believed, effectively disseminate scientific knowledge. During the nineteenth century, medical schools in the United States proliferated rapidly, growing from seven in 1810 to 110 in 1870. At the dawn of the Gilded Age, these institutions churned out nearly twenty-five hundred physicians per year. By 1902, there were a total of 160 medical schools minting six thousand new doctors annually.[30] To be sure, not all of these doctors practiced medicine in the same way; there was widespread division within the medical community at the time.[31] But the existence of professional credentials—the fact that a healer had purportedly been "properly trained"—gave male physicians the aura of respectability at a time when professionalism demanded it.

So did the specialized medical tools that proliferated along with the number of new doctors. As Erwin Ackerknecht explains, "The invention of new instruments, such as the many 'scopes,' provided further incentive for the formation of specialties. These instruments required special training for their proper use and often transformed completely the fields to which they were applied."[32] The creation of specialties and specialized tools was hugely consequential for doctor-patient interactions. If specialized training and medical instruments were necessary for diagnosing, understanding, and treating disease, then the specialist occupied an ideological space between the patient and the patient's body. The patient's own report of symptoms became less reliable than the information the scopes gathered. The stethoscope, ophthalmoscope, laryngoscope, and others—all inventions of the mid-nineteenth century—could gauge the patient's body better than the patient could. The tools and scopes in the doctor bag equipped the physician with a wealth of information that the patient could not access, even though the patient supplied the information. In turn, male doctors transformed personal health troubles into the marks and noises of modern science, effectively standing between people and knowledge about their own health.[33]

To many patients of the nineteenth century, the new specialists were a cause for concern, especially insofar as medical professionalism intersected with ideals of womanhood. Medical etiquette made male-female interactions somewhat taboo, as the idea of a man inspecting the female body threatened Victorian sensibilities and public morality. One male commentator warned other men of the threat that new physicians posed:

> The doctor may be a sober, discreet, oily man, of staid appearance, and a very pattern of propriety; or he may be a vulgar, low-bred person in his leisure consorting with those of similar bent; or he may be a tippling, jovial fellow, who at some roystering party is always called on for "a good song," sure to have as its theme wine, love, and women. . . . Nevertheless, whatever he be, *the very inmost secrets of your wife's person* are known to him, the veil of modesty has been rudely torn aside, and the sanctity of marriage exists but in the name.[34]

Despite such warnings of immodesty in the examination room, the allure of professionalism won the day, and male physicians became the norm.[35] But their ascendency raised additional concerns. When male physicians began to inspect female bodies in large numbers, they found bodies that seemed dreadfully unprepared for life. Women, many doctors concluded, were naturally enfeebled.[36] After adolescence, they seemed to enter a prolonged period of "energy drain," wherein, because of the cycles of their bodies, they eventually became invalids. This energy drain demanded, at least according to the doctors themselves, that doctors guard, regulate, and direct female behavior.[37] So physicians prescribed a combination of bedrest and overeating, hoping that relaxation and consumption would add to the energy reservoir that was draining away. They also recommended leeches, electricity, bloodletting, and small quantities of arsenic.[38] These treatments, they insisted, would preserve the physical, mental, and moral health of Victorian women.

It was not coincidental that Christian Science arose at the same time professional, specialized, male-dominated medicine was reconfiguring American healthcare. It was also not coincidental that Mary Baker Eddy often referred to herself as "Professor of Obstetrics," a title that signaled her interest in taking back the healing process from the experts.[39] But it is important to note that she shared this interest with many other people and groups at the time. Eddy was far from the only activist trying to circumvent the consolidating power of modern medicine. Indeed, Christian Science was one of many so-called mind-cure movements sweeping the nation—although Christian Scientists insisted theirs was not a mind cure movement, at least in terms of theology.[40] Regardless, the prevalence of so-called mind-cure movements indicated widespread dissatisfaction with mainstream medicine—or what people perceived to be mainstream medicine. Eddy and the multitude of others who had become displeased with the direction of healthcare agreed that it was time to experiment with new, alternative, unorthodox therapies.[41]

There is no need to recount all of Mary Baker Eddy's life and discovery of Christian Science. Biographers have done that admirably.[42] However, several aspects of Eddy's upbringing deserve mention to understand her populist efforts later in life. Eddy was a sickly child. Born in 1821, she struggled with health issues for decades. Though she loved school, she was often too ill to attend. To combat the illness, Eddy experimented with almost every available healing method. She visited homeopaths, attended seances, prayed ceaselessly, and took numerous medications, but nothing seemed to work. Then, in the early 1860s, she spent several years studying with Phinneas Quimby, a mental healer prominent in and around Maine.[43] Because of Quimby, Eddy experienced some of the first moments of relief she had felt in a long time, and she came to see mental healing as a viable avenue for health.

Then on February 1, 1866, Eddy "discovered" Christian Science. It happened in the small town of Lynn, Massachusetts, which had recently been hit with wintery weather. Eddy, whose last name at the time was

Patterson, was walking with a group of friends when she fell on a slippery sidewalk. She hit the ground hard and was "severely injured," according to the local paper.[44] Her friends took her to a nearby house, where a popular homeopathic doctor in Lynn found "her injuries to be internal, and of a very serious nature, inducing spasms and intense suffering."[45] Fearing the worst, Eddy's friends moved her to her own home, where a doctor administered morphine to ease the pain. Then came the news that she had broken her spine and had little chance of recovery. At one point a local clergyman paid Eddy a visit and, upon seeing her, told her friends to prepare for the end and to join him in prayer.

After emerging from the morphine fog, Eddy became cognizant of her dire situation. Unable to stand, aching in bed, facing death's door, she did what she had often done over the decades—she turned to her Bible. By chance she opened it to a gospel story of one of Jesus's healings. Carefully, slowly, conscientiously, she read of Jesus's power. Then, as Eddy later reported, "the healing Truth dawned upon my sense" like "the daystar that dawned on the night of material sense."[46] Instantly, her pain and injury vanished. She rose from bed, dressed herself, and sauntered into the next room, where she found family and friends pondering her fate. They were shocked to see her. When the clergyman who had led the group in prayer returned that evening, Eddy met him at the door. He was so startled that he thought her a ghost.[47] But as she understood the incident, "The divine Spirit had wrought a miracle—a miracle which later I found to be in perfect Scientific accord with divine law."[48]

For years after her recovery, Eddy studied the Bible to try to understand what had happened. The conclusion she reached was that God had revealed to her the transcendent truth of Healing, Life, and Love. Here was a new, or a renewed, divine revelation. That Christian Science began with a divine revelation is not surprising. Emergent religions commonly start with the declaration of a new message from God. Yet the character of Eddy's revelation was noteworthy. Most revelations purportedly come from a supernatural source, which means that they resist the laws and operations of the empirical realm.[49] Even outside the Christian tradition, commentators who study revelation describe divine messages that burst the boundaries of reason and demand faith in that which lies beyond human understanding.[50] That was not the character of Eddy's revelation. To her, Christian Science was demonstrable and scientific, able to be proven with clear evidence and replicable results. It was a science that signaled "the certainty with which the method can be applied," producing a system of knowledge that "is infallible, absolute, and exact."[51]

Eddy published her scientific findings in 1875 in the "textbook" of Christian Science: *Science and Health with Key to the Scriptures*. It was, and remains, a dense text, difficult to read and even more difficult to understand. Yet its promise was essentially populist because it purported to bestow perfect health and new life to anyone who studied it properly. "The time for thinkers has come," Eddy declared in the first edition of *Science and Health*, "and the time for revolutions, ecclesiastic and social, must come. . . . The science of man alone can make him harmonious, unfold his utmost possibilities, and establish the perfection of man. To admit God the Principle of all being, and live in accordance with this Principle, is the Science of Life."[52] In essence, Christian Science made physicians and theologians unnecessary.

The publication of *Science and Health* in 1875—and the decades-long process of revision that Eddy undertook shortly thereafter—helped formalize the teachings of the emergent religion. While it is a complex and nuanced belief system, five tenets of Christian Science deserve mention here. First, Christian Science affirms the sovereignty of God—certainly not a unique idea among religions. What is unique, however, is the way Christian Scientists talk about God. As Eddy refined and revised *Science and Health* over the years, she eventually settled on seven synonyms for God: Principle, Mind, Soul, Spirit, Life, Truth, Love.[53] Adept and strategic with capitalization, Eddy crafted a new way to communicate the fullness of her understanding of God. These synonyms pointed, she believed, to a transcendent, all-encompassing power. To Eddy, God was Life itself.

Second, in addition to affirming the sovereignty of God, Christian Scientists follow Christ—also not a peculiar idea. What is distinct about Christ in Christian Science is the term's relationship to Jesus. As

Stephen Gottschalk explains, "In Christian Science, Christ is the divine ideal of manhood, the model of perfect spiritual sonship; while Jesus was a human being who through the extraordinary conditions of his birth completely demonstrated this Christ ideal." Christ, therefore, is not confined to Jesus; Christ is a purely spiritual idea. Yet Jesus is not wholly separable from Christ because Jesus "represented the individualization of the Christ to human consciousness."[54]

The sovereignty of God and the spiritual ideal of Christ are not controversial assertions. But the same cannot be said of the third noteworthy Christian Science tenet—namely, that matter is unreal. The unreality of matter is perhaps the most confusing aspect of the religion to people who encounter it for the first time. After all, the unreality of matter seems immediately confounded by everything at hand. For Christian Scientists, however, the appearance of matter is a misapprehension of the world by what Eddy called "mortal mind" or "carnal mind." The real order of being, she insisted, was not matter but Spirit, and accepting a material order was accepting a false view of the world; it was buying into a widespread deception.[55] In fact, accepting a false view of the world was itself sin. In Christian Science, sin and evil are not due to the devil's influence—there is no personal devil or literal hell in Christian Science. Rather, sin is due to human error, a "mistake about being—pure failure, falsity, negation."[56] Because God never made evil and could never make evil, being both omnipresent and Good, sin is the result of a misapprehension of God's created order. It is a problem not of action but of cognition.

But that does not mean that sin and evil are incapable of wreaking havoc on God's created order. Errors of cognition can be disastrous to Christian Scientists. Case in point is the fourth tenet, one for which Eddy took extensive criticism during her life: "malicious animal magnetism." Malicious animal magnetism, which Christian Scientists sometimes refer to as "mesmerism," is a kind of mental malpractice. Through hypnotic deception, people can be trapped in error, tied to beliefs that prevent their connection to Being. Perhaps most strangely to Americans of the late nineteenth century, Eddy held that malicious animal magnetism could be a tool of "mental assassination."[57] Ne'er-do-wells could focus their malicious thoughts on an enemy, from nearby or from afar, and effectively debilitate that person. Eddy herself claimed to have been the victim of an untold number of mental attacks. She even attributed the death of her third husband, Asa Gilbert Eddy, to mental assassination.[58]

Over time, Eddy de-emphasized her teaching on malicious animal magnetism, largely because of the public backlash against it. She was also concerned that it obscured the promise of the fifth tenet—namely, healing. To be sure, "Christian Science is a religious teaching and only incidentally a healing method."[59] Yet its public appeal, especially in the Gilded Age and Progressive Era, was as a means to both physical and spiritual health. When Eddy and her followers promoted Christian Science to new audiences, they seldom discussed the unreality of matter, but they frequently articulated how Christian Science could help anyone overcome sin and sickness. Divine Science promised healing that was free from drugs, free from surgery, free from the pain of modern medicine. Regardless of the theological status of healing in Christian Science, its public appearance was primarily as a pathway to health.

Perhaps the best way to summarize the belief structure of Christian Science, then, is as a form of pragmatic idealism.[60] Both of these terms can be dangerous due to the philosophical baggage that accompanies them. Yet Christian Science is certainly idealistic in its conception of Spirit and Divine Mind, and it is certainly pragmatic in its affirmation of the demonstrable consequences of healing. As Chapel and Jensen summarize, "Given Eddy's pragmatic epistemology, healings functioned as evidence to support her idealistic ontology. Healings were the practical evidence that noumenal being is perfect and supreme, untouched by the seeming reality of phenomenal existence. And it is the dynamic role healing plays in the synthesis that brings Plato's lofty theory of ideas into direct contact with the cultural pragmatism of the American religious experience."[61] It is not surprising that William James, the popularizer of philosophical pragmatism, defended the right of Christian Scientists to experiment with what worked for them.[62] For Eddy and her followers, empowerment came through the ability to experience matter as unreal.

Christian Science, explains Gottschalk, is "best understood, not as an abstract metaphysical or theological system, but with reference to *what it claims to make possible.*"[63] Christian Science made health possible, it made sin and sickness errors to be brushed aside, and it made a place for everyone who wanted to practice Divine Science.

The Emergence of the Christian Science Board of Lectureship

As the nineteenth century drew to a close, Christian Science attracted followers at a rapid clip. Along the way, it ran into significant opposition. Ministers and theologians were some of the earliest critics, cringing as congregants of mainstream churches gravitated toward Eddy's purported rediscovery of primitive Christianity. As one newspaper summarized in the mid-1880s, "Clergymen of all denominations are seriously considering how to deal with what they regard as the most dangerous innovation that has threatened the Christian Church in this region [Boston] for many years. Scores of the most valued church members are joining the Christian Scientist branch of the metaphysical organization, and it has thus far been impossible to check the defection."[64] To stem the tide, influential ministers across New England wrote scathing tracts and delivered passionate public lectures against Eddy's movement.[65]

Figures in the medical establishment took longer than the theologians to stand against Christian Science, but when they did, they brought bigger weapons and hit harder.[66] Ridicule was central to their assault. The physician Edmund Andrews, for example, underscored the irony of Christian Scientists trying to heal that which they did not believe existed: "It must be very interesting to see a non-existent bone, having only the substantiality of thought, which had been dislocated from a socket which never existed, going back without being touched into that imaginary socket with a thump audible to all the bystanders."[67] While physicians used ridicule to knock Christian Science down a peg, they collaborated with prosecutors and politicians to launch a legal campaign that, they hoped, would stop the religion in its tracks. In the late 1880s, a Christian Science practitioner was tried for manslaughter for the death of one of her patients. Though the practitioner was acquitted, the manslaughter charge emboldened other prosecutors.[68] Most manslaughter cases involving Christian Science resulted in not-guilty verdicts; those that received guilty verdicts were overturned on appeal. Nevertheless, the trials received extensive coverage in the press, and they created the perception that this new religion was not only wrong but dangerous. That was certainly true when it came to the deaths of children who received Christian Science care. When children died, prosecutors sometimes went after parents along with practitioners. To many Americans, parental responsibility and public health were more important than any supposed religious freedom. It was one thing to deny traditional medicine for oneself; it was another to impose that choice on children and the community.[69]

In addition to the largely ineffective manslaughter cases, states responded to the perceived health threat of Christian Science by enacting or strengthening medical licensure laws. One needed to be properly trained and professionally certified, states insisted, to practice healing. By the early twentieth century, thirty-eight states tried to codify some version of this idea, hoping to stop the spread of Christian Science. Eventually, Christian Scientists learned to argue for the legitimacy of their work, and licensure laws slowly "evolved to accommodate religious healing."[70] But in the court of public opinion Christian Science had taken a serious reputational beating.

Eddy knew that she needed to counter negative perceptions if Christian Science were to thrive in the twentieth century. In the early 1880s, she had begun building the institutions that would, she hoped, resist incursions from opposing forces.[71] But it was in 1898 that she launched the first major offensive to change public perceptions.[72] That year she created the Christian Science Publishing Society, the Committee on Publication, the Board of Education, and the weekly newspaper the *Christian Science Sentinel.* She also created the Christian Science Board of Lectureship. Over the next several decades, the Board of Lectureship would occupy the vanguard of Eddy's populist campaign, showing tens of thousands of people that Christian Science was a careful, legitimate intellectual endeavor.

The design of the Board of Lectureship, as the February 1898 issue of the *Christian Science Journal* stated in announcing the organization, was to employ speakers who would "lecture at such places and at such times as the Cause of Christian Science demands."[73] The statement was vague, largely because the board was still working out its role in the movement.[74] But a March 1899 article in the *Christian Science Sentinel* specified the intended audience for the lectures as "those who are strangers to the truth regarding Christian Science, or who are interested enough to listen to a public discussion regarding Christian Science, but who, so far, have not been reached by other methods."[75] Importantly, the lectures were not addressed to Christian Scientists, at least not primarily. Their aim was to prompt a general intellectual discussion with those who had not yet encountered the principles of Divine Science. To further explain the Board of Lectureship, the Mother Church in Boston issued circulars to branch churches about the board's aim and operation. Audiences for Christian Science lectures, the circulars stated, should be "more than three-fourths . . . made up of people who were not Christian Scientists." Accordingly, it was important to hold the lectures in "some public hall, opera house or similar place," thus making the lecture "a matter of general interest." The idea was to avoid, whenever possible, hosting lectures in Christian Science churches; instead, lectures should take place in venues that held other public lectures. "Reaching the public through the rostrum" was the board's central mission.[76]

Perhaps surprisingly, conversion was not central to the board's mission. The aim of the lectures was less to convert people than to advance Christian Science in modern intellectual culture. Edward Kimball, one of the most effective, successful, and compelling lecturers on the board, explained to a Christian Science church in Milwaukee that

> The lectureship is not for the purpose of missionary work which the Manual provides for by the appointment of missionaries. The lectures are mostly delivered in the larger cities where the work is fully organized

> and under way. They are not for the purpose of teaching the students or of presenting the subject anew to the public. Wherever the work of the churches is established, the incidental antagonism and prejudice has been aroused and all kinds of misstatements have been put forth by pulpit, press, and otherwise and these lectures are calculated as an offset and designed to correct the wrong impressions and state some of the facts.[77]

If people converted because of the lectures—and they often did—all the better for the church. Yet lecturers saw themselves less as missionaries spreading a new gospel than as intellectual actors clarifying questions about a movement that claimed to bridge the gap between science and religion. At a time when the division between science and religion seemed to be growing, Christian Science lecturers offered a system of belief and practice that was purportedly in perfect accord with the scientific laws of the universe.[78]

Another objective of the Board of Lectureship was to get Christian Science discourse into local newspapers. Eddy and her lecturers knew that face-to-face exchanges were important, but they could reach many more people through the printed word. As early as April 1898, Edward Kimball explained to branch churches that "One of the particular objects of the lectureship is to get the lecture or a synopsis of it in the secular press, . . . to have someone see the managers of the papers and ascertain how much they will print, so that I can prepare a synopsis in advance, rather than to have a reporter make his own choice of what to present."[79] Another lecturer, Irving Tomlinson, told other board members of the importance of paying "practically as much attention, if not more, to papers and editors as to the lecture itself. I make it a point to visit every editor in every city, [and] have as much of a chat as the situation will allow."[80] In another letter, Tomlinson summarized that the "published lecture is of inestimable value since it is read by three classes of people. First, by those who desired to attend the lecture but for some reason were unable to do so; second, by those who did hear the spoken word of Truth but wish to read and ponder it for further enlightenment; third, by those who, because of a lack of interest in or knowledge of Christian Science, made no effort to attend the lecture."[81]

To make their lectures appealing to editors, members of the Board traveled with different versions of their text—a brief synopsis of approximately one thousand words, a somewhat longer version of perhaps two thousand to four thousand words, and the full text.[82] Sometimes these versions contained headnotes that editors could draw on in their coverage. For example, Irving Tomlinson's thousand-word synopsis of a lecture entitled "Christian Science: A Practical Religion" provided verbiage for editors to use as though they had sent a reporter to the lecture. "Mr. Tomlinson," reported the synopsis, "spoke in a clear and pleasing manner, and throughout his lecture quoted from the Bible and the writings of Mrs. Eddy in support of the statements he made."[83] The synopsis also instructed editors to follow the capitalization found in the text, given how important capitalization was to Christian Science.

Because the Board of Lectureship hoped to flood local markets with Christian Science discourse, the church needed a significant number of lecturers traveling the country. When the Board of Lectureship was established, Eddy appointed five members: Edward Kimball of Chicago, George Tomkins of New York, Carol Norton of New York, William McKenzie of Boston, and Irving Tomlinson of Boston.[84] But the demand for lecturers quickly outstripped the supply, so three months after announcing the first group, Eddy added two more lecturers: Annie Knott of Detroit and Sue Harper Mims of Atlanta. By the end of 1898, the board's first year, four more lecturers had joined: Edward Hammond of Baltimore, Alfred Farlow of Kansas City, Francis Fluno of Oakland, and Abraham Sulcer of Riverside. The geographic distribution of the lecturers was important. For the first few years of the board's operation, lecturers were assigned to cover a specific geographic area. The hope was that geographic boundaries would limit the travel and hardships lecturers had to endure on the road. But as particular lecturers became popular, the Mother Church lifted the geographic restrictions and allowed lecturers to travel to wherever they received an invitation.

The gender makeup of the early Board of Lectureship was also important. From 1898 to 1910, the year of Eddy's death, only three women served on the board; Annie Knott and Sue Harper Mims were appointed in 1898, and Mary Brookins of Minneapolis was appointed in 1903. During that same period, twenty-four men served. One way to explain the gender imbalance is as a result of nascent or overt sexism. That was certainly a factor. The original female lecturers received few invitations compared to the male lecturers, and Eddy found herself consoling the women as audiences adjusted to the idea of female speakers.[85] But sexism does not tell the whole story. Gender imbalance was a strategic choice on Eddy's part. Not only were men more welcomed as lecturers across the country, but they also served as a symbolic counterpoint to the widespread perception that Christian Science was a religion for women. Women made up the majority of Christian Scientists during the first decade of the twentieth century. In 1906, they accounted for 72 percent of church members, and female practitioners outnumbered male practitioners five to one.[86] Well aware of the perceptions surrounding women and Christian Science, Eddy put male lecturers at the forefront of the religion to signal that men could logically, rationally, and studiously support the movement.

Eddy handpicked the lecturers and exercised close control over the board. Together with Edward Kimball, she developed a set of topoi that lecturers had to cover in each presentation: "God, Prayer, The Bible, Salvation, Jesus, Discoverer and Founder of C.S., Christ, healing."[87] The order in which the lecturers handled the topics could vary, but they had to appear in some way. Of particular importance was addressing the "Discoverer and Founder of C.S." Early lecturers struggled with how to speak about Eddy, and they did not always succeed. In 1899, for example, one of the lecturers defended Eddy from sharp attacks by Josephine Woodbury, a fierce critic and former student of Eddy's. In Eddy's mind, the lecturer's defense had been too sharp and gave undue credence to Woodbury's cry for attention. In response, Eddy thanked the lecturer for defending her but asked him not to do it again. She then instructed all lecturers to refer to her as a wise leader and to insist that her "life is above questioning."[88] The goal, Eddy said elsewhere, was to avoid verbal abuses and to relate “a clear, strong word” of her virtues.[89] To ensure that lecturers discussed her and Christian Science properly, Eddy required that lecturers send their texts to the Mother Church for vetting.[90]

The Christian Science Board of Lectureship was a success—at least according to newspaper coverage. Regardless of whether the papers were simply running with the kind of coverage lecturers encouraged, the result was that, in print if not elsewhere, Christian Scientists were expanding the intellectual life of the nation by drawing ordinary Americans into discussions of big ideas. A paper in Portland, Oregon, for example, happily reported that Edward Kimball’s goal was “not to proselyte nor to convert to Christian Science, but rather to correct misconception and give general enlightenment of its doctrine.” To that end, Kimball spoke “with the practical directness of the business man, which has thoroughly appealed, not only to the most intellectual and critical listeners, but to the great rank and file of every-day investigators as well.”[91] Annie Knott’s lecture in St. Paul, a local paper reported, showed that Christian Science “can be rationally explained” and can set aright “people with prejudice springing from misconceptions as to the exact nature of the belief.”[92] A Riverside, California, paper noted that Francis Fluno’s lectures have been “greeted with large audiences constantly increasing in size and interest, drawing further and further from the circle those who wish to learn more of this cult, which is as old as creation but is now presented in a form easily applicable to every day affairs of life.”[93] After Sue Harper Mims lectured in Wausau, Wisconsin, a local paper reprinted the text of her lecture and prefaced it by saying: “It should be read with interest by most of our readers, whether they are in sympathy with the views expressed or not, as a perusal may disabuse their minds of some false notions they may now hold in regard to Christian Science and what it teaches.”[94]

Not all coverage of Christian Science lectures was this glowing.[95] Occasional outbursts or challenges from audience members sometimes derailed a lecturer’s performance and shaped a reporter’s coverage.[96] Yet on the whole, newspapers praised members of the Board of Lectureship for doing what they set out to do—engaging in logical, rigorous, careful inquiry about the great questions of existence. The result was an intellectual community of ordinary people who gathered in a civic space to mull the claims of Eddy and her followers. Of particular importance to this intellectual community was, as I show below, the participatory, populist logic that pervaded Christian Science lectures. Across the nation, lecturers proffered arguments designed to draw audience members into the structure of Eddy's divine, scientific revelation. Once aligned with Eddy, they could disrupt modern medicine and theology, work their own salvation, and create a new utopia of Mind.

Intellectual Populism in Christian Science Lectures

Following the lead of Eddy's sermon "The People's God," members of the Christian Science Board of Lectureship regularly and consistently deployed the five general appeals of intellectual populism. First, lecturers were vehemently anti-institutional, decrying both the medical and theological establishments, as when George Tomkins exclaimed: "There are thousands of God's dear people standing spellbound between the twin rails of theology and medicine today—mesmerized by an ominous rumble in the distance—a fear of death, and the approaching flicker of a false light, . . . which entrances them until escape is almost impossible."[97] Second, lecturers lauded the intellectual power of ordinary people, as when Frank Leonard declared that Christian Science was common sense available to everyone: "It is my sense and your sense; it is a sense that belongs to all of us; and Christian Scientists have nothing that is not yours."[98] Third, lecturers deployed strings of Americanisms to describe their intellectual project, as when Irving Tomlinson concluded: "As the new world flings open all its gates to the oppressed of every nation; as it freely shelters the downtrodden and heavy laden; as it proves a peaceful home for the liberty-loving and the God-fearing; as it lavishes its harvests and pours out its bounties for the honest and consecrated, so this new world of Christian Science welcomes all."[99] Fourth, lecturers portrayed Christian Science as radically conservative and conservatively radical, as when Clarence Eaton insisted: "Inasmuch as the Christian Science church stands for the rehabilitation of primitive Christianity, it of necessity deals with the question of evil on the basis of its unreality, as did the founder of Christianity. And while Christian Science has been severely criticized on this point, we find that on comparing its teaching and that of scholastic theology with the teaching and practice of Christ Jesus, theology suffers most by comparison."[100] Fifth, lecturers regularly visualized an intellectual utopia sitting on the other side of populist uprising, as when Sue Harper Mims praised the religion as "a Science whose laws are the immutable laws of health, holiness, harmony, and immortality; whose results must be, and are, the establishment of the kingdom of God on earth,—the reign of individual and universal righteousness."[101] Using these five appeals, Eddy's cadre of lecturers spread Christian Science's populist gospel around the nation and the world.

While it would be possible to dissect Christian Science discourse into a catalog of examples illustrating the five appeals of intellectual populism, this analysis will focus instead on one particularly salient and powerful part of Christian Science lectures—namely, the creation of a participatory framework through which ordinary people could reclaim their intellectual lives. This participatory framework was the mechanism whereby individuals in lecture halls could assent to Christian Science and, in turn, link themselves with other believers in Eddy's antagonistic frontier. In other words, this analysis will explore the way Christian Science lectures got ordinary people actively involved in and dedicated to the resistance necessary for forming a populist movement.

In the case of Eddy's movement, participation and resistance emerged through a surprising and distinctive rhetorical strategy. As we shall see, members of the Board of Lectureship built their lectures on what can only be described as a gaping evidentiary hole, a void distinguished by a lack of evidence documenting Eddy's method. Everywhere lecturers went, they claimed that their religion was thoroughly, conclusively, provably scientific. They claimed their method was demonstrable in the same way the solution to a basic algebra problem was demonstrable.[102]

However, despite their boast of conclusive proof, lecturers provided almost no evidence to support their claim. For an intellectual movement that declared itself thoroughly scientific, failing to provide persuasive evidence was eminently risky. Then again, the lack of evidence may have ultimately propelled the cause of Christian Science, goading listeners to generate evidence through their personal experience. In turn, they became living proof of Eddy's divine revelation.

The evidentiary void began to emerge when Christian Science lecturers co-opted the language of modern science, thereby establishing a scientific persona and fostering a demand for scientific proof. Speaking in Peoria in 1904, for example, Clarence Buskirk insisted that "to learn anything aright, we must test, apply, and prove as we learn." Christian Science was notable in this regard because it had been tested, applied, and proven; it was built on "correct classifications and precise definitions," which were "essential to every form of systemized knowledge."[103] Speaking in Milwaukee, Hermann Hering couched his lecture in similar language: because "science means exact, systematized, and demonstrable knowledge of facts, laws, and causes," Christian Science is thoroughly scientific, offering "demonstrable knowledge which affords deliverance from evil."[104] Carol Norton also insisted that the basis and operation of Christian Science was "exactness and practicability. As a Science it is logical and in its varied applications demonstrable. This latter fact removes the system from the realm of the so-called inexact sciences."[105] Such claims linked Christian Science to the realm of specialized science and to the intellectual ethos of professionalism, while it remained grounded in the domain of religious inquiry that enthralled Progressive Era audiences.

One of the central terms of modern science, and one of the ideas Christian Scientists drew upon repeatedly in their lectures, was method. The scientific method, lecturers said, was the same systematic, rigorous, replicable method Christian Scientists used to heal. In fact, Christian Science proceeded through a "scientific process for liberating error," thereby divorcing "man from all error by removing the ignorance that makes it."[106] More than a general scientific process, however, Christian

Science operated with mathematical precision. Borrowing an analogy that pervaded Eddy's own speaking and writing, members of the Board of Lectureship insisted that their work was akin to mathematics in that both were universal, objective, exacting, and certain. Anyone could "solve" a "problem" with the Christian Science method in the same way anyone could solve a mathematical problem, so long as he or she understood the math. Thus, as Francis Fluno declared, "Christian Science cannot fail, any more than the Science of Numbers can fail." Whatever problems cropped up around Christian Science, he continued, were due not to the system but to the individual failings of practitioners: "Mathematics never fails, but mathematicians sometimes fail. . . . But who thinks of condemning Mathematics, because some Mathematician has failed?"[107] Or, as Bliss Knapp explained in a lecture,

> A student never prays to have his problem in mathematics work itself out. . . . He has the rule and also the problem, but he must act in obedience to the rule. There must be a mental activity on his part, and as that activity obeys the mathematical rule the correct solution is inevitable. In Christian Science we have this divine law. We are also confronted by the problems of sin and disease. Our next important step is to act, to demonstrate that law, and that which actuates the divine law, that which gives to it a healing effect.[108]

By linking Christian Science to mathematics, lecturers removed the religion from the company of other religions, which were inexact and nebulous by comparison, and placed it among universal science and natural law. More importantly, the mathematics analogy opened the realm of universal science and natural law to audience members. By learning Christian Science, ordinary Americans could achieve the same exactitude as any professionally trained scientist.

The scientific, mathematical, methodological proclamations of Christian Science lecturers greatly raised the stakes of the religion. In fact, lecturers established for their listeners a clear bar by which Christian Science was to be judged. Either Christian Science healing was (or would become) as exacting, systematic, and predicable as solving a math problem, or it failed by its own terms. It was "either science or nothing," insisted Bicknell Young.[109] Christian Science was not to be accepted as a matter of faith; it was to be accepted on the basis of the scientific proof it could produce.

Christian Science lecturers insisted they had such proof, and they never tired of boasting about it to their audiences. "What is Truth?" thundered William McKenzie to a Worcester audience. "That which may be proved! That which I can understand and verify. Today the fact is sought as against the philosophic guess; the demonstration rather than the tradition; the proof in experience rather than the legend." Christian Science was the exacting system that would do away with all guesswork, unverified tradition, and inapplicable legend. "What reason is there for confidence that Christian Science gives the best results as a reformative agency? The fact that in its normal operation we find reappearing the results prophesied by Jesus as inseparable from true believing in his gospel. The evidence of healing is so extensive that everyone can find proof."[110] John Linscott expressed the same scientific certainty to an Atlanta audience in 1901: "Our contention is that there is an absolute science, with an absolute principle, and an absolute rule, and an absolute result in the degree we understand it, and that this law of spirit will act supreme in the intellectual and physical realm of a human being, destroying mental and physical discord, as surely as light dispels darkness."[111] The hubris of absolutism propelled Christian Science as lecturers traveled the country promising nothing less than complete control of health and life.

This hubristic scientific language placed Christian Science discourse atop a logical proof, and it was by this proof that the American people were to judge Christian Science. Put in syllogistic form, the proof was as follows:

- *Major premise*: true science is testable, demonstrable, replicable, available to all, and capable of healing.
- *Minor premise*: Christian Science has been tested, demonstrated,

replicated, made available to all, and has healed the sick and suffering.

- *Conclusion*: therefore, Christian Science is true science.

Deductive, syllogistic arguments work well when the major premise is relatively uncontroversial.[112] Fortunately for the early Christian Scientists, their major premise *was* relatively uncontroversial. Americans of the late nineteenth and early twentieth centuries would have had little difficulty accepting the idea that a true science should be "testable, demonstrable, replicable, and available to all." They would even have had little difficulty accepting the idea that a true science could heal. After all, many Americans considered modern science a panacea that could systematically eliminate the world's problems.[113] So with a widely agreed-upon major premise, the challenge for Christian Science lecturers was to demonstrate the minor premise, from which the conclusion would follow naturally.[114] With proper proof, audiences would have little difficulty accepting the conclusion. Without proper proof, the Christian Science syllogism would fail.

Christian Science lecturers did not deliver proper proof. When it came to supplying evidence for the minor premise, when it came to demonstrating the power of Christian Science, lecturers offered next to nothing. While they addressed the minor premise at the level of assertion, they provided almost no details, specific examples, or instances of healing to support their claims. Clarence Eaton, for example, insisted that Christian Science had "effected the moral, physical, and spiritual regeneration of tens of thousands who have accepted its teaching. Indeed, in this vast army of believers are those who have suffered from every known illness and disease."[115] Bicknell Young similarly spoke of the "numerous cases of healing" that Christian Science principles had accomplished. "Thousands of people have testified to such healing," he declared, "and some of them have done so under oath, in courts of law, and their testimony has not been in the least shaken by cross-examination."[116] George Tomkins put Christian Science healing in more personal terms: "I have witnessed the crippled walking, carrying away their crutches, and those deaf, some over 30 years, hearing. I have been the means of healing many such, some of over 40 years' standing."[117]

Each of these statements—and similar statements in virtually every Christian Science lecture—spoke to the minor premise of the larger argument. But if these statements were supposed to be the rigorous, scientific proof that propelled Eddy's movement, their evidentiary value was slight at best. Lecturers did not offer specific examples, they did not provide exact numbers, and they did not elaborate on their boasts of healing. Given how important the minor premise was, one would expect lecturers to provide some kind of data or documentation—names, dates, places, specific diseases cured, and similar details. Stories of specific people being healed of particular diseases would have gone a long way in illustrating the power of Christian Science. But almost without exception, lecturers asserted the healing capabilities of their system rather than supplying compelling proof.[118] When they did point to a particular person, they pointed to Jesus, whom Christian Scientists claimed as the prototypical practitioner of Divine Science. As for more recent examples of healing, Christian Scientists said little.

Perhaps lecturers said little because they had no persuasive evidence. Perhaps they lacked the names, dates, places, details, and instances that would have bolstered their case. Their critics insisted as much.[119] But such a hypothesis does not hold up on closer inspection. The pages of the *Christian Science Journal* were (and remain) filled with specific cases of healing, filled with testimony from people whose lives were transformed through Divine Science. Highlighting some of these cases would have added weight to the minor premise. Moreover, the back of *Science and Health with Key to the Scriptures* contained a hundred pages of what Mary Baker Eddy called "Fruitage"—letters from people who had experienced the healing effects of Christian Science.[120] Lecturers could have drawn upon these cases, or even upon cases they had personally witnessed. After all, each lecturer was also a Christian Science practitioner, involved at some level in the business of healing.

But the lecturers chose not to provide details that would have supported the minor premise. The result was what can best be described as an evidentiary hole in their argument. Claims of strict logic and undeniable science sat next to assertions that were anything but logical and scientific, creating a void that called out for support. Listeners with an ear for scientific argumentation could have easily picked up on this evidentiary void. By the end of the nineteenth century, the American people had become seasoned veterans of scientific lectures. For decades they had listened to the country's top scientific minds share their research and explain the latest advancements.[121] As longtime consumers of scientific discourse, then, many audiences could have seen the lack of evidence in the face of grand proclamations.

Why, then, did Christian Science lecturers choose not to supply compelling evidence of their claims? Conclusive answers are difficult to come by, but there may have been a rhetorical advantage to creating a void in the larger argument. Establishing the demand for proof but failing to provide such proof invited listeners to fill in the void themselves. This was the crux of the mechanism by which Christian Science lecturers drew ordinary Americans into Eddy's movement and rendered them participants in the antagonistic, populist frontier that could destroy, or at least circumvent, the medical and theological establishments of the day. Because Christian Science was purportedly a method everyone—from the most decorated PhD to the illiterate manual laborer—could practice, it was a pathway to empowering and uniting disparate segments of the lecture-going public. That was how Eddy's populist movement grew. By getting people to participate in the claims of Christian Science, lecturers goaded listeners to become living evidence of the religion, which was more valuable for populist resistance than simply supplying documentation of healing.

Consider the dynamics of the encounter between lecturers and audiences. Those who traveled to the lecture hall were already intrigued by Christian Science and wanted to learn more. It was the lecturer's job, then, to enflame their curiosity and to give them an outlet for it. Excited by the prospect of overcoming sin and sickness, listeners needed something to do with their excitement. Accordingly, in every Christian Science lecture, the lecturer pointed to *Science and Health with Key to the*

Scriptures. By reading *Science and Health* in the hours, days, and weeks after the lecture, audience members could learn the principles of Christian Science healing and could practice those principles in their own lives. They could experience the "fruitage" that established the minor premise of the Christian Science syllogism. Speaking in New Hampshire in 1904, for example, Bicknell Young described the intellectual rigor required for understanding Christian Science. But because of this rigor, he could not provide "demonstrable knowledge of this infinite subject. For that," he continued, "you must seek the pages of its text-book, *Science and Health with Key to the Scriptures*, written by the Discoverer and Founder of Christian Science, Rev. Mary Baker G. Eddy."[122] In this early passing reference, Young introduced *Science and Health* and even foreshadowed the void that would emerge. Later in the lecture, he returned to *Science and Health*, positioning it as the key to the entire enterprise:

> Although the influence of mentality upon disease is now acknowledged, how many understood it prior to the publication of *Science and Health?* The author of that book was the first person to discern the cause of disease correctly since the time of the Master, and to give an adequate and complete analysis of this cause. *Science and Health* is the only book that enables us to give a correct diagnosis of disease, and it is the only book that teaches how to heal meta-physically.[123]

Such promotion of *Science and Health* gave lecture-goers an actionable step for moving further into Christian Science. If they wanted to know more about Divine Science, they now had work to do in the pages of *Science and Health*. This appeal also sold books, which was not a bad thing for the emerging religion. Yet Christian Scientists regularly gave away copies of *Science and Health*, so selling books was by no means a primary objective of the lectures. Instead, lecturers seemed intent on recruiting participants in a populist uprising.

Almost every lecturer adopted the same promotional tactic as Bicknell Young. Septimus Hanna promoted the textbook as "a treatise on healing through the power of God or the Divine Mind. . . . It is a thorough exegesis of the Scriptural method of healing all manner of diseases, and of curing all manner of sin through the understanding of God as all-present, all-powerful, all-wise."[124] Clarence Eaton described *Science and Health* as "the authorized text-book of Christian Science, and the only work published which correctly sets forth its teaching and its demonstration. It does this with much elaboration, and with such clearness of statement that individuals of ordinary mental capacity can, by a systematic study of its content, acquire sufficient understanding of the rule of Christian Science practice as to be able to successfully apply it in the healing of sin and disease."[125] Bliss Knapp took the appeal a step further and promised healing even in the act of reading: "This wonderful treatise on Christian Science presents so accurate an exposition of its Science that thousands of people have been cured of all forms of chronic and acute diseases by the simple reading of that book."[126] By studying *Science and Health*, listeners could join thousands of people who not only experienced healing but also joined Eddy in reclaiming the power to heal from the clutches of modern medicine.

In creating an evidentiary void and promoting *Science and Health*, Christian Science lecturers made a series of bets. They bet that those who came to the lecture hall were interested in learning about Christian Science—a safe bet, considering that few would go to a lecture on a subject in which they were uninterested. They also bet that the logical, scientific style of their discourse would create a demand for evidence of healing. Their assertions of evidence enhanced the demand, but assertions could only go so far. For those who wanted to know more—and it was the lecturers' job to entice audience members into wanting to know more—they offered *Science and Health* as the way to fill the evidentiary void. Interested audience members would, hopefully, begin to study *Science and Health*, and some who studied it would indeed find respite. Those who did not find respite would likely disregard Christian Science and move on with their lives. But those who experienced healing, however large or small, would feel intimately connected to the truth of Eddy's scientific revelation. Their personal experience would leave little doubt that the larger syllogism was true.

The key to the logic of Christian Science, then, was personal experience, which can be a powerful—almost unimpeachable—form of evidence.[127] Although personal experience can introduce argumentative problems of its own,[128] it can animate individuals more than any other kind of proof, especially in the realm of religion. When one undergoes a meaningful religious experience, little can dampen commitment to the reality of that experience. As the philosopher William James stated around the time Eddy's lecturers were traveling the country, "If you have [religious experiences], and have them at all strongly, the probability is that you cannot help regarding them as genuine perceptions of truth, as revelations of a kind of reality which no adverse argument, however unanswerable by you in words, can expel from your belief."[129] Personal experience, as James well understood, leads to the highest form of knowledge possible, at least for the experiencer. Whatever powerful experience the individual undergoes becomes truer, fuller, more absolute than any deductive proof, any rationalist logic chopping, any counterargument.[130] Once lecture-goers turned into readers of *Science and Health*, they entered into a transformative experience that enabled them to identify with and even live by Eddy's system. In turn, they possessed the fullest truth they could possess—and to them it was unimpeachably scientific. As the language of science permeated Christian Science lectures and created a strong evidentiary demand, those who were healed experienced the results of objective, universal, impersonal laws. Thus, both modern science *and* personal experience proved Eddy's revelation.

Because of the role that personal experience played in Christian Science, the intellectual efforts of ordinary individuals authorized the conclusion of the overarching syllogism. Because the American people participated in the minor premise, the truth of Divine Science emerged. Edward Kimball made intellectual participation central to a lecture in Dayton, Ohio. He was not there to proselytize, he told the people of Dayton, but simply to offer ideas that they could pursue on their own: "You don't have to believe anything I say. I simply ask you to put your thought in the way of analysis, simply to investigate, simply to examine—that is all." At the conclusion of the lecture, Kimball invited his listeners to become part of the Christian Science proof:

> There are one million people who declare that by its means they have been extricated from the very depths and brought to see that which means health. . . . I wish that you might once, sometime, know why it is, what is the reason so many people declare that they have been cured of incurable diseases so unspeakable beautifully. I do not ask you to believe anything today. I wish you might sometime want to know enough; you can learn; and what you learn the first day will be a dividend in happiness, the next day another dividend, and before long possibly to your surprise you will find your heaven opening up to you.[131]

Kimball thus offered listeners a pathway not to belief but to inquiry and power. Once ordinary Americans became active investigators, once they grappled with the truth of *Science and Health*, they could take control of their own health and happiness—and do so alongside legions of other Christian Scientists.

Other lecturers similarly emphasized the participatory role of ordinary people. William McKenzie praised Christian Science audiences "as interested seekers after larger knowledge of a truth which has already proved its beneficence."[132] Bliss Knapp called Christian Science an intellectual system "worthy of the prayerful consideration of every man, woman, and child," and he emphasized what its principles could do: "Everyone would enjoy to have the power to do the good that Jesus did; everyone would be glad to understand the divine law well enough to heal and reform men as did the primitive Christians; and when one does understand this law in its spiritual sense, he is indeed a Christian Scientist, as truly as one who understands the mathematical law is a mathematical scientist."[133] Clarence Buskirk likewise called on his listeners to study Christian Science for themselves, given that

> a more complete understanding of its teachings can only be obtained by a careful study of its literature, such as you expect to devote to

> arithmetic, grammar, and their kindred branches of learning. . . . No one has the right to declare that he understands the Christ-method of healing the sick until he has tested, applied, and proven it to be true by his own actual works. The understanding of the process and its practical application go together. The better we understand it, the better we can apply it, and the more we apply it, the more we understand it.[134]

By drawing ordinary Americans into the participatory framework of Eddy's argument, lecturers imbued their religion with a profound sense of agency. As the rise of professionalism left ordinary Americans behind, Christian Science offered them a system of purpose and engagement.

Eddy's movement thus promised resistance and revolution. When the American people entered into the Christian Science syllogism and enacted it in their lives, they would heal the world on a massive scale—or so they believed—and create a utopia of understanding. By studying, learning, and practicing Christian Science, average Americans, who had been pushed out of modern theology and medicine, could reclaim their lives, circumvent the status quo, and bring a new world into being. The idea was a dangerous one, potentially duping lecture-goers into believing that Christian Science could accomplish something it never could accomplish. There was no doubt an air of gullibility that wafted around the encounter between Christian Science lecturers and their audiences. Yet big, largely unrealistic promises are stock in trade for populist leaders.[135] Promises of revolution form the motivational core of populist movements across the political spectrum, even in the realm of ideas. This is why populist discourse often culminates in visions of a utopian future.

And this was why Christian Science lecturers promised their listeners the dawning of a new day—but only if Christian Science succeeded in its revolution against medicine and theology. Lecturers promised that Eddy's movement would establish "a universal brotherhood, equalize the sexes, terminate war between nations, impartially adjust out-of-control civil, political, and social conditions, extirpate criminality and whatever incapacitates, wrongs, or curses mankind."[136] Eddy's movement would also establish a Love that is "as universal as the sunlight, and tender as the dew on small grass. In light of this Love we see all men the image and likeness of God."[137] A Christian Science utopia would instantiate "the Godly standard wherein what blesses one blesses all. Every promise shall be fulfilled, and the grand work of Christ, as exemplified in Christian Science, be universally accepted."[138] Divine Science would lead the way "into the land of Canaan, flowing with milk and honey. The outcome for every honest searcher is already assured. Whoever is willing to set aside false thinking for the true will immediately receive the benefit and eventually earn the crown."[139] This was, to be sure, a world-changing vision of the future—very different from the future implied by the complexities, hardships, confusion, and materialism of industrial America. To those who craved respite from the grind of everyday existence, simply reading *Science and Health* must have sounded like a good idea.

Conclusion

Mary Baker Eddy slipped and fell on the ice and had a revelation from God about the unreality of matter, about the unity of Mind, and about the power to heal. She turned this revelation into the religion of Christian Science and a proud, populist intellectual movement. The movement was a response to establishment theology and medicine, or at least to what Eddy and her followers perceived as established theology and medicine. Theology, they believed, had become staid and uninspiring—a point Robert Ingersoll had also championed. Worse than staid and uninspiring, medicine had become monstrous, pushing surgeries, pills, and falsehoods on a frustrated, sick public. Physicians sold their false bill of goods under the guise of professional expertise and scientific objectivity. Shrouded in the cloak of professionalism, they pushed traditional healers and healing methods to the periphery of healthcare. Their scopes, discourses, tools, and drugs even separated individuals from knowledge of their own bodies. To resist these developments, Eddy offered a rigorous, exacting, objective science that was also in perfect accord with Divine Law. Learning and practicing this science was easy, especially with a copy of *Science and Health*, and its ease opened a world-changing healing method to everyone. In the pages of Eddy's revelation, ordinary Americans could harness a resistive power, could demolish modern theology and medicine, and could bring about a new populist utopia.

Such was the promise of Eddy's revelation. Yet in pursuing this populist uprising, she quickly discovered that the theological and medical forces of the day would not be destroyed without a fight. After significant criticisms and legal challenges, Eddy decided to institutionalize the resistive power of American lecture culture by creating the Christian Science Board of Lectureship. She sent lecturers across the country to lead a campaign against the forces thwarting the health, happiness, and salvation of ordinary people. On the lecture stage, members of the Board of Lectureship constructed a participatory framework, built atop a significant evidentiary void, that invited lecture-goers to practice Christian Science in their own lives and to become living proof of Eddy's revelation. The language of modern science, combined with the promises of complete health and happiness, created a demand for evidence that lecturers practically refused to provide. But their refusal ultimately raised the curiosity of audience members, who could find fulfillment in the pages of *Science and Health*. They could then link with others who had experienced healing and were now prepared to transform the world.

By analyzing the participatory framework of Christian Science lectures, this chapter has offered a window into the way intellectual populism can draw ordinary people into antagonistic frontiers. As Eddy's lecturers demonstrated, inviting people to "discover" the truth of the universe on their own (and with the help of *Science and Health*) served as the mechanism by which individuals could align themselves with others who felt displaced in the culture of professionalism. While Ingersoll's lectures demonstrated that opposing the status quo could strengthen the discussions and pursuits to which the status quo was dedicated, the lectures of early Christian Scientists demonstrated that populist speakers could hail ordinary people as intellectual agents—in this case, as intellectual agents poised to fill an evidentiary void in a new system of truth. Both around the turn of the twentieth century and today, intellectual populism depends on ordinary people becoming thinkers, workers, and participants in the great debates of the era. No mere receivers of wisdom from on high, populist audiences must feel invested in and empowered to decide pressing intellectual issues through their own efforts. Without this sense of empowerment, a populist intellectual movement can never flourish against the forces of the established order. Democratizing the world of ideas requires that ordinary people have purchase in the machinations of inquiry.

Eddy and her lecturers helped to democratize medicine and theology, but as with many democratizing efforts, their work was never as democratic as it could have been. Audiences for Christian Science lectures were largely white, middle and upper class, and in a position to join with their ilk in the leisure time of the lecture hall. Yet in the Gilded Age and Progressive Era, the appeals of intellectual populism were not confined to these audiences. The work of Thomas Davidson—an abrasive, brilliant, freelance philosopher—shows how intellectual populism can animate people far removed from the demographics of Christian Science lectures. For Davidson, populist appeals were useful not only for rebuffing professional philosophy but also for empowering a community of working-class immigrants on the Lower East Side of New York. Amid the tenements, Davidson spoke a populist language that turned exploited laborers into analytic philosophers.

CHAPTER THREE

Thomas Davidson's Push for Philosophical Community

At the time, it was the most crowded neighborhood on the planet.[1] Newly arrived immigrants from Eastern Europe crowded into small, stuffy tenement rooms, hoping to eke out a meager living. But the neighborhood was not built to accommodate the ever-increasing number of bodies, and the result was a public-health nightmare. One settlement worker described the squalid conditions she witnessed daily:

> Every window opens into a room crowded with scantily clothed, dull-faced men and women sewing upon heavy woolen coats and trousers. They pant for air, the perspiration that drops from their foreheads is like life-blood, but they toil on steadily, wearily, except when now and again one, crazed by heat, hangs himself to a door-jamb.[2]

This was New York's Lower East Side at the end of the nineteenth century.

It was emblematic of industrialism's human toll—people crammed into small spaces, desperate for work, under constant threat of disease and violence, unable to meet the basic needs of personal, let alone familial, survival. "On a single block in New York's East Side," writes one historian, "39 tenements provided housing space for 2,871 persons. There was not a single bath in the entire block, and only 40 of the apartments had hot water. The tenements in New York's Lower East Side had one of the highest mortality rates in the world. Thousands died from a variety of common diseases such as typhoid, diphtheria, and tuberculosis."[3]

In this overcrowded, disease-filled, tenement-lined neighborhood, the sometimes-congenial, often-arrogant, but undeniably brilliant philosopher Thomas Davidson delivered a series of public lectures in 1898. The venue for the lectures was a cooperative settlement known as the Educational Alliance, and it put Davidson in touch with a group of people whose existence was worlds away from his own. Most of them were first- or second-generation Jewish immigrants who toiled upward of twelve hours per day in sweatshops, factories, and tenement rooms. They were not the typical audience for abstract, philosophical discussions. Nevertheless, on December 7, 1898, Davidson mounted the rostrum, laid his manuscript on the lectern, and offered a bold salutation to his 250 listeners: "Fellow Workmen!"[4]

For Davidson to lump himself in with "workmen" was not only inaccurate but also potentially offensive. They toiled in sweatshops and tenements; he wrote analytic philosophy. Yet his aim was not to represent his actual station in life but to imagine with those before him a future of cooperative intellectual labor. In a few months, this future would come to pass, resulting in one of the most striking educational experiments of the Progressive Era—the Breadwinners' College. This "college" would help poor, Jewish immigrants exercise their intellectual muscle and, at the same time, transform the Lower East Side into a place of philosophy, rhetoric, populism, and spiritual development.

The Breadwinners' College represented the culmination of Davidson's thirty-year career as an intellectual community builder. On both sides of the Atlantic he created spaces where people could gather, eat, sleep, work, play, and think together. More importantly, in these spaces people could push back against the intellectual status quo, especially academic philosophy. His early adventures in fostering alternative philosophical communities included the Aristotelean Society, the Fellowship of the New Life, the Fabian Society, and the Concord School of Philosophy. Later in his career Davidson created the Glenmore Institute, which served as a philosophical retreat for middle- and upper-class northeasterners who wanted to participate in rigorous inquiry while living in a rustic camp in the Adirondack Mountains. Then came the Breadwinners' College, which represented a dramatic shift in Davidson's community-building efforts. He found new energy and purpose by turning to the educational needs and challenges of working-class immigrants. In conjunction with the downtrodden on the Lower East Side, Davidson discovered the dynamics for a populist uprising that he had been trying to foment for decades.

Intellectual populism is a discursive effort to align individuals against established modes of inquiry to resist, combat, or circumvent the intellectual status quo. As the previous chapters have shown, the discourse of intellectual populism allows individuals to sublimate their particular grievances into a larger chain, joining others in a unified front against the established order. This happened with Robert Ingersoll's audiences, as believers, nonbelievers, and those in between came to see their particular problems with organized religion as part of the anti-institutionalism Ingersoll so eloquently proffered. This also happened with the early Christian Science church, as Mary Baker Eddy and her lecturers drew ordinary people into a movement against medical professionalism and for the healing power of Divine Science. In both cases, the formation of a populist frontier happened in a lecture hall and in the "imagined community" that resulted from discourse circulating across geographic spaces.[5] Through populist appeals, lecture-goers in one town united imaginatively with lecture-goers in another town, and together they constituted a community undefined by geographic coordinates. Thomas Davidson's work demonstrates a different aspect of populist coalition building. Specifically, his efforts show the importance of space and place relative to intellectual-populist speech. While Davidson forged imagined communities through his lectures, essays, and books, he also built *actual* communities—purposefully constructed spaces for inquiry that he believed necessary for intellectual transformation.

The story of Davidson's populist community-building efforts, then, is the story of his experimentation with different combinations of people, places, ideas, and discourses. Bringing together various groups in different locations, Davidson hoped to find the most effective way of reorienting modern thought after academic professionalism had confused it. In the end, he found what he was looking for on the Lower East Side of New York. Among the tenements, Davidson forged a novel juxtaposition of philosophical speech and industrial space, expanding the borders of philosophical inquiry to include new voices, new debates, and new participants in the world of thought. On the Lower East Side, Davidson grasped Doreen Massey's apt insight about space: "Social change and spatial change are integral to each other."[6] To foment a populist countermovement in the world of philosophy, Davidson discovered that he needed to create a community attuned to the rhythms of Progressive Era America.

Space, Rhetoric, and the Geography of Knowledge

The intersection of space and speech extends back at least as far as ancient Greece. The Athenians knew that space was functionally and conceptually central to the movement of language. The Agora, for instance, was a space designed to facilitate public deliberation.[7] But space was also a useful stylistic tool. When the ancients spoke and wrote, they often used spatial imagery, merging space and speech in ways that could animate audiences. As Jane Sutton has contended, classical tropes actually create space "by simulating bodies moving in a variety of ways" and by allowing audiences to imagine new spaces for collective action.[8]

Contemporary scholars of rhetoric have built on Athenian insights by showing how space functions rhetorically—that is, how space can serve as a kind of speech. Museums, statues, art installations, and maps, for instance, organize spaces and bodies in ways that send messages and shape perceptions.[9] Similarly, commemorative ceremonies bring people together, often around material objects, to sacralize the past and to direct the present and future.[10] Even cemeteries organize space in ways that suggest particular interpretations of the dead, the past, and the world beyond.[11] It would be a mistake, however, to suggest that space necessarily precedes speech. Rather, space is both the ground for and the product of discursive interactions. Space creates and is created by rhetoric—or, as Roxanne Mountford puts it, "spaces are *productive* of meaning as well as endowed with meaning."[12] To understand the intersection of space and rhetoric, then, one needs to understand how space and rhetoric are in constant negotiation, altering perceptions about meaning and location, making and remaking each other to address the needs of particular moments.[13]

"Rhetorical space" is one way that scholars have characterized these dynamics, foregrounding the intersection of messages, symbols, embodiment, structure, and ideology.[14] Yet the dynamics extend far beyond particular spaces, combining to shape entire regions.[15] Like particular rhetorical spaces, regions both suggest locations and burst the bounds of those locations, taken up in and altered by the discourses that pervade them. Case in point is Dave Tell's work on "Kansas." In investigating the meanings of Kansas through reception of Truman Capote's *In Cold Blood*, Tell maintains that "senses of place and senses of region require affective ties that bind together the materiality of topography with the much less tangible realm of cultural politics."[16] Furthermore, by placing a piece of land "in a broader network of institutions and ideologies," regions become meaningful, varied, and productive.[17]

While regions shift and change according to circumstances, they nevertheless call attention to themselves. Talking about a region, even when contesting a dominant interpretation, prompts people to think about that region, reinscribing its existence and the appearance of solidity. Debates about "Kansas" or "Appalachia," for instance, effectively call attention to "Kansas" and "Appalachia." The same is true of most rhetorical spaces. Our terms for particular areas, however large or small, serve as an "active interface" through which public discourse moves, cutting through our lives and giving us the opportunity to engage our environment.[18] In the act of speaking about space, we take up, alter, and reinscribe particular spaces for our purposes and the purposes of our communities.[19]

The reinscription of space is important for understanding Thomas Davidson's community-building efforts because of the philosophical character of the communities he tried to build. Philosophy is always produced in spaces—classrooms, campuses, meeting rooms, journal pages—but it often denies its spatiality. Truth, after all, is supposed to transcend particular places, to rise above its origins and to apply broadly, even universally, whether one is in a classroom in the United States or on a mountain in India. The same is true of scientific inquiry. While science depends on labs, equipment, and proper spatial configurations, its insights often claim a universal status beyond labs, equipment, and configurations.

In recent decades, scholars in a variety of disciplines have investigated the spatial dimensions of inquiry, pushing the intersection of space and speech squarely into the pursuit of philosophical and scientific truth. The result has been increased attention to what is now known as "the geography of knowledge."[20] Mapping knowledge geographically is an attempt to show how ideas are linked indelibly to locales. In terms of generation, movement, and reception, ideas depend on the spaces in which and through which they operate. The "spatial turn" in intellectual history, explains Diarmid Finnegan, maintains that inquiry "depends on the manufacture and management of different spaces—real or imagined—to accomplish its objectives and establish its credentials."[21] While such a claim may seem self-evident, it troubles fields of inquiry that attempt to reach a transcendent, universal purview. Even though science and philosophy often claim an epistemological status that belies their origin, scientific and philosophical ideas are "placed"—bound to laboratories, auditoriums, classrooms, libraries, offices, pieces of paper, and all the subjective and intersubjective meanings associated with them.[22]

The goal of the geography of knowledge, then, is to understand the way space conditions ideas. Where we pursue knowledge is closely connected to the knowledge we achieve and advance because the sites we occupy shape what we can do and say as well as what we cannot do and say. In addition, sites of inquiry shape who can and cannot participate with us.[23] Only certain people can enter the spaces of academia and contribute to scholarly journals. Yet the knowledge produced in academia and scholarly journals often assumes a universal veneer, even though, as David Livingston has argued, the appearance of universality is itself the product of spatial configuration.[24] Labs, tools, procedures, methods, measurements, and findings are configured so that research can be replicated across different sites and thus appear universal.

While geography conditions inquiry, then, it is no less true that inquiry conditions geography. Scientific practices—and the practices of every form of inquiry—constitute boundaries of legitimacy, marking off what counts as knowledge, who can participate in the creation of knowledge, where knowledge emerges, and which methods make knowledge possible.[25] Thomas Gieryn has explained this phenomenon as the "boundary work" in which scientists pursue knowledge to defend the spheres of authority that have served their projects. For Gieryn, boundary work means attributing particular qualities and methods to scientists and scientific claims to distinguish among real science, pseudoscience, and some lesser forms of inquiry. With these boundaries, science proceeds through a sociological map that marks people and places as legitimate in a community of inquirers. The map also marks the character and quality of the knowledge produced.[26]

In Davidson's day, the sociological maps of science and philosophy were not as fully charted as they later became. But the rise of professionalism in the Gilded Age and Progressive Era signaled to Davidson and others that massive intellectual realignments were underway. Although structural changes to American universities had only recently begun and would continue well into the twentieth century, Davidson could see academic powers consolidating their hold on philosophy. From early in his career, Davidson rebuffed these trends and charted communities according to maps of people and places that bucked the boundaries of philosophical professionalism. Foreseeing what the academic geography of knowledge would do to philosophy, he experimented with different combinations of space and speech to build communities capable of returning philosophy to the hands of ordinary people. Most of the communities he created would not last. Most would prove too romantic and too far removed from what America was becoming at the dawn of the twentieth century. It was only when Davidson attuned the relationship of space and speech to the rhythms of industrial America that he found the populist configuration for which he had long been searching.

Searching for Community

Born in 1840 in a rural area outside of Aberdeen, Scotland, Davidson grew up in challenging circumstances. Little is known about his early life, but it is clear that he was born into a poor, fatherless family. He may have been an illegitimate child.[27] Nevertheless, he distinguished himself academically and earned a scholarship to King's College, Aberdeen. There he proved adept at learning languages, and in time he would master over ten tongues, including German, Italian, Latin, and Greek as well as Hebrew, Arabic, and Sanskrit.[28] His ability to learn languages would contribute to his reputation in some circles as one of the most learned people on the planet.[29] With a command of language, a photographic memory, and a hunger for knowledge, Davidson developed a broad cultural outlook at a time when ethnocentrism reigned. He was cosmopolitan beyond the transatlantic sense of cosmopolitanism prominent in his day.[30] Propelled by a desire to know the world and to experience human diversity, he traversed Western civilization to find what he thought of as the spiritual core of humanity. And because that spiritual core was well-nigh impossible to find, if it even existed, he traveled on, a wanderer who was at home everywhere and nowhere.[31]

Davidson's wandering was possible in large part because of his unorthodox career and his ability to raise money for his intellectual endeavors. He never married and never fathered children, which enabled him to roam wherever his whims and finances took him. After graduating from the University of Aberdeen, he taught classics and ancient languages sporadically across Scotland and England.[32] He then crossed the Atlantic to teach in Toronto, before heading to Boston, where he joined the noted Radical Club and associated with the likes of Bronson Alcott, Ralph Waldo Emerson, William Lloyd Garrison, Wendell Philips, and Henry James Sr.[33] But even in the presence of these luminaries, Davidson grew restless and soon headed to St. Louis, where he taught Greek in the local public-school system. More interested in philosophic debates than in teaching schoolchildren, he joined a club dedicated to explicating the intricacies of Absolute Idealism. The St. Louis Philosophical Society was effectively a discussion group for Hegelians, with whom Davidson "never in any degree sympathized."[34] Yet he loved having a sounding board for ideas. Debate in community was key to the club's operation, and Davidson took that lesson with him to subsequent endeavors.[35] While in St. Louis, Davidson also developed a close friendship with a young lawyer named Joseph Pulitzer.[36] Pulitzer viewed Davidson as an intellectual guru, and they soon became roommates, which allowed them to philosophize "into the early morning hours on all aspects of western culture."[37] In time, Pulitzer repaid these enlightening discussions by bankrolling many of Davidson's efforts. When Davidson needed money to travel the world or to build a new community, he turned to his wealthy friend. After Pulitzer purchased the *New York World* in 1883, he even arranged to pay Davidson a monthly stipend for his intellectual musings, which the paper published only on occasion.[38]

After St. Louis, Davidson continued to wander, searching for a community of thinkers who pursued knowledge in the way he believed necessary for true intellectual progress. Such wandering was necessary, he insisted, because academic philosophy, the kind many of the St. Louis Hegelians practiced, was woefully disconnected from the needs and conditions of life. In fact, it was partly because of his time in St. Louis that Davidson viewed colleges and universities as the great status quo against which he would align his populist efforts. At least that was what he explained in a sweeping 1894 essay titled "The Ideal Training of an American Boy," published in *The Forum.* The primary purpose of the essay was to argue for "well-arranged, practical knowledge of men and things" and "the education of the citizen and of the man as such." Davidson also used the essay to excoriate American colleges and universities for keeping people ignorant in the service of the wealthy and powerful. The pitiful truth, he insisted, was that "our universities do not turn out men of broad general culture"; rather, they produce people with narrow visions and selfish desires, thereby perpetuating the status quo. Davidson then listed "all the drawbacks of our colleges; their want to definite unitary aim and ideal; their half-medieval, half-professional curricula; the dry, uninspiring formalism and useless erudition of much of the teaching; the easy philistinism or dreary pessimism of many of the older teachers; the pert, callow Germanism of many of the younger ones; the boyishness of many of the students; their smug foppishness and stupid devotion to half-brutal games and half-silly girls." Davidson's indictment of "Germanism" was particularly telling because it pointed to the turbulence specialization had wrought. He went so far as to declare that modern sciences, which were proliferating in American universities because of Germany's influence, "have comparatively little education value," for they do not develop spirit and soul—the things that truly matter. In closing, Davidson hoped that the "free, self-directing man, the man ready and able to act intelligently, nobly, and strongly in all the affairs of life," learns to rely not on outward institutions but on "his own righteous will."[39] In response to the empty husks of inquiry that colleges and universities had become, Davidson placed his faith in ordinary people to reclaim education and to put it to work enriching individuals, souls, and societies.

Because of the hollowness of university education, Davidson refused to settle down in a traditional academic position—even though he had opportunities to do so.[40] He wandered across oceans to find educational spaces that fostered the soul and spirit in addition to the mind. After St. Louis he went back to Boston, where he befriended William James and introduced James to his future wife. He then crossed the Atlantic and traveled to Greece, where he studied architecture. He went to Rome, where he discussed theology for hours on end with the pope. He went to the north of Italy for two years to live and study in a monastery.[41] Eventually he settled in London, where he witnessed, more than ever before, the horrors of industrial society. He was shocked at industrial London, but he was also convinced that philosophy could address the situation. So he rented space in Chelsea for what he called "The Fellowship of the New Life," which not only tested his ideal of proper education but also forced him to confront the challenges of space and speech for intellectual populism.[42]

The year was 1881, and while Davidson did not yet know what this "new life" entailed, he had a grand vision for the group: "the cultivation of a perfect character in each and all," which required "the subordination of material things to spiritual things."[43] In time, after material things had been successfully subordinated, the Fellowship could "live in community, with a view to bringing about the necessary conditions of education."[44] Davidson knew this utopian community was distant, but he also knew how to get there, providing followers with twelve rules for directing their lives. These rules included such principles as regularity, free and open communication, acute criticism, enthusiastic conscience, and courteousness, as well as "absolute truthfulness, simplicity, and chastity, in thought, word, and deed."[45] In case the rules were unclear, Davidson also provided a twenty-four-part creed that addressed religious, political, social, familial, and personal conduct. When they followed the rules and put the creed into action, Fellowship members would show the world a righteous, philosophical, self-sustaining community—and they would do so apart from academia.[46]

This kind of utopian dreaming was not unique in the nineteenth century.[47] But in some ways Davidson was decades late, and his vision was disconnected from the realities of industrial-era London. His ideal community may have been intellectually populist, but it was not politically revolutionary enough for participants. By the early 1880s, many Londoners, including those interested in Davidson's ideas, thought a community based on the "subordination of material things to spiritual things" was unworkable, if not delusional. The time had come, they believed, for political agitation and socialist reform. In 1884, a group of Fellowship supporters formed a new organization: the Fabian Society.[48] The Fabian Society proved far more influential than the Fellowship of the New Life, in large part because of the members it attracted—the poet Edward Carpenter, the sociologist Havelock Ellis, and the writers George Bernard Shaw, H. G. Wells, and Virginia Woolf, among others. To be sure, the Fellowship and the Fabian Society were not mutually exclusive, as many people belonged to both groups. But the Fabian Society operated with intense political energy, which Davidson found worrisome. To him, socialism should only be "ethical and individual rather than economic and political."[49] He warned Fabians not to be "carried away by the temporary reform wave of socialism. You are in the surge, not on the rock—the Rock of Ages." But surges can be powerful, and soon the Fellowship was "settling down into a kind of quietism."[50] London, Davidson realized, was not the right place to build his intellectual utopia.

But maybe New York was. In 1884, Davidson journeyed back across the Atlantic and settled there to organize a new branch of the Fellowship. Fully in control of this branch—he decreed that "each branch shall regulate its own affairs"[51]—he considered how best to manage the group, including how the Fellowship related to space. The first section of the Fellowship's printed constitution specified that "its Domicile shall be wherever any number of persons shall meet and organize themselves in its Spirit." Given Davidson's history of wandering, he understood domiciles as emergent, based on dynamic relationships and mediated by Spirit. He added that the Fellowship "does not identify itself with any particular schemes, and meets solely for lectures, discussions, readings and social intercourse."[52] Wherever members associated discursively, connecting through speech and writing, was the Fellowship's dwelling place. This was an early indication in Davidson's work of the mutually productive relationship between the location of inquiry and the character of thought.

Yet the Fellowship was not as abstract as the beginning of the constitution suggested. Cognizant of the need for actual space, Davidson created an Executive Committee that was charged with the "renting of rooms, letting out of printing, care of library, arrangement of lectures, discussions and social meetings." Throughout his career, Davidson emphasized the importance of finding the right rooms for thinking, discussing, lecturing, debating, and reading. Proper spaces, he knew, enabled people to "endeavor to know well, to love well, and to do well." But proper spaces required proper people, whom Davidson hailed in the organization's constitution. Members of the Fellowship, he said, should be "neither dogmatists, skeptics, nor agnostics, but reverent students of the world of nature and of mind, seeking to supplement their own experience and conclusions with the experience and conclusions of the serious men and women of all time."[53] These were the kind of people needed to sustain the Fellowship's discursive domicile.

In a subsequent public letter about the Fellowship, Davidson gave the organization a decidedly populist direction. In response to the isolation of modern life, the Fellowship promised "a new social order and a new education; an order in which each shall feel the burdens of all, and all of each; an education which shall aim at producing perfect characters, rich in insight, in love, in energy, scorning selfishness, impurity and wrong." With the promise of a populist utopia ahead of them, Davidson and his associates resolved to live a noble life and "to make the redemption of humanity from ignorance, selfishness and vice the end of all their efforts, and ready to search out and communicate the means whereby this may be done." Communication was central; members of the Fellowship had to make their principles "clear to others; to interest other people in them and to form little societies for the study of the highest things, for religious sympathy, for mutual aid."[54] With the Fellowship of the New Life, Davidson beckoned individuals ready to produce the spaces and conversations capable of restructuring education and the social order. Inquiry in community, and apart from the established educational institutions of the day, would lead the group to truth.

If only restructuring education and the social order were that easy. Davidson deemed the Fellowship an organization with a discursive domicile—a space and place that shifted according to member discussions and that rented rooms on an as-needed basis. But this meant that the Fellowship had nowhere to call its own, no structure for sustained communal inquiry, no stability amid the turbulence of industrial city life. The pursuit of knowledge in the Fellowship was nomadic, settling only temporarily and according to availability. Davidson and his compatriots evinced a desire for a resistive intellectual community, but they did not build a lasting, material foundation. The result was predictable. In both the United States and the United Kingdom, the Fellowship languished for about a decade, and then disbanded.

It did not help that Davidson continued to wander and to look for new communities. But that was his nature. Eventually he came upon an exciting community that could better handle the intersection of people, places, ideas, and discourses needed for the late nineteenth century. He found this community in Concord, Massachusetts, on the back corner of Bronson Alcott's property.

Community, Inquiry, and the Retreat to Nature

What Davidson found on Bronson Alcott's property was the Concord School of Philosophy, which was only a "school" in the romantic sense of the term. It was more a meeting place, in a rural, back-to-nature setting, for some of the greatest American minds of the nineteenth century. Bruce Kuklick has called the Concord School "the last gasp of non-professional philosophy in the Transcendentalist style."[55] The statement is more or less accurate depending on how one characterizes the philosophical style of Davidson's own back-to-nature efforts. Though it would be a mistake to call Davidson a philosophical transcendentalist, his interest in building rural, romantic thought communities was a direct extension of what he experienced in Concord.

Beginning in the summer of 1879, philosophers, authors, editors, and critics began to meet annually on Alcott's property, known as Orchard House.[56] At first, the group met in the parlor of Orchard House, but Alcott soon built a modest, stuffy, wooden structure on the back corner of his lot. Dedicated to communal contemplation, the Concord School viewed itself as radically egalitarian, at least from an intellectual point of view. "No preliminary examinations are required," announced a circular for the opening of the school, "and no limitation of age, sex, or residence in Concord will be prescribed."[57] Davidson leaped at the chance to get involved, and he was even able to lecture at the school's first gathering in 1879. Speaking on Greek architecture, he brought with him a series of impressive visual aids—illustrations on glass slides projected via an apparatus known as the "magic lantern."[58] Despite the oppressive August heat, the gathering was a smashing success, reminding visitors of Concord intellectualism in its heyday, thirty or so years prior.

From 1880 to 1883, Davidson was unable to participate in the Concord School due to excursions in Europe. But other luminaries were, including Ralph Waldo Emerson, Franklin Sanborn, Thomas Wentworth Higginson, Julia Ward Howe, William James, and Elizabeth Peabody, among others. After returning from overseas, Davidson rejoined the school and spoke every year from 1884 to 1887, addressing such topics as human immortality, ontology, Dante's teachers, Aristotle's politics, and Plato and irony.[59] Known for impressive visual aids and picturesque language, his lectures were usually—but not always—well received. In 1884, Davidson suggested that the idea of man's immortality actually lessened God's immortality. William Torrey Harris, one of Davidson's old associates from his St. Louis days and a driving force behind the Concord School, found this suggestion unacceptable. Harris rose early the next day, penned an angry reply to Davidson, and delivered a two-hour rebuttal that the audience deemed Harris's best work.[60]

Despite the Concord School's success, it did not—and maybe could not—outlive its founder. When Bronson Alcott passed away in early 1888, everyone knew the school had to end as well. June 16 of that year was the day of Alcott's memorial service and the day the Concord School closed its doors.[61] But Davidson had seen the school's potential and wanted to try it himself. In 1887, even before Concord closed down formally, Davidson and a small group of associates gathered for two weeks on Orange Mountain in St. Cloud, New Jersey.[62] The gathering was dedicated to a topic about which Davidson knew more than perhaps anyone on the planet: Ancient Philosophy and Art. Such a grand topic necessitated a grand space. As he explained in a circular for the meeting, "the summit of Orange Mountain, about 600 feet above the sea-level," is the perfect place for discussion of this weighty subject matter. For Davidson, altitude corresponded with intellectual ascension. The higher one went, the grander one's thoughts became. He explained:

> St. Cloud enjoys every advantage of situation, air and water. It is cool, entirely free from malaria, and highly recommended as a resort for invalids. It is surrounded by woods and fields and offers an almost endless variety of walks, drives and views. Teachers and other persons suffering from nervous exhaustion and similar complaints can obtain the best of medical advice and treatment in St. Cloud. Mr. Davidson's Aristotelian library will be at the service of students during the season of the lectures.[63]

In promoting the Orange Mountain gathering, Davidson articulated a new configuration of space and speech. His ideal of education was no longer nomadic and based on a shifting discursive domicile. Instead, inquiry was tied to the scenery and terrain of a particular mountain—an elevated space removed from the congestion of the city and conducive to robust communal contemplation. Together on Orange Mountain, privileged New Englanders could escape to nature, avoid malaria, exercise the body and mind, and read Aristotle. Away from the sights and sounds of the city, the air and the ideas would be cleaner and clearer.

The St. Cloud gathering was a success, but the space proved too small for everyone who wanted to participate, especially once the Concord School shut down. So in 1888 Davidson moved the gathering to Farmington, Connecticut, where he hoped the confluence of space and speech would reach even higher. The "quaint, old, shady New England town" of Farmington, he explained in a circular, stood "on the western slope of a considerable eminence, . . . affording beautiful and extensive views in many directions." It was a perfect place for investigating

Philosophy and Art, the subject of that year's lectures. In an environment where the climate "is salubrious, the heat moderate, and the region almost free from mosquitoes," people could exercise their philosophical muscles.[64]

As in St. Cloud, the gathering in Farmington was a hit, leading to subsequent meetings in 1889 and 1890. The topic for both years was Philosophy and Ethics. Once again wedding space and speech in his promotional materials, Davidson explained that exploring Philosophy and Ethics would entail a voyage through the rivers of time:

> Beginning at the two sources of this Philosophy in Greek Speculation and Hebrew Moral Inspiration, [the lectures] will follow the streams emanating from these to their confluence in Alexandrine and Christian Thought. Thence it will follow the still distinct currents until they mingle in Patristic Thought, which is deeply affected by Platonism. Lastly, it will follow Christian Thought down to and through the Scholastic Period, in which the influence of Aristotle becomes paramount, and Spiritual Thought receives its highest expression, speculative, mystical and poetical.[65]

Davidson's characterization of Farmington used spatial, natural imagery—streams, currents, confluence, paramount heights—to signal intellectual progression. Ultimately, the group's voyage would culminate in Spiritual Thought—the most advanced kind of thought in Davidson's schema. From new spiritual heights, participants could survey the philosophical landscape as well as the "beautiful and extensive views" of Connecticut.[66]

The success of St. Cloud and Farmington underscored more than ever the market for speculative philosophy in natural, communal spaces. But Davidson did not own the land in Farmington, which meant that he could not configure the space as he saw fit. Convinced that he needed to purchase property for a permanent community, he turned to his wealthy friend Joseph Pulitzer, who donated $1,800 for Davidson to buy 167 acres on the east hill of Mt. Hurricane in the Adirondack Mountains.[67] This acreage became the site of the Glenmore Summer School for the Culture Sciences, otherwise known as the Glenmore Institute. To Davidson, Glenmore represented simplicity in space, thought, and conversation, and it was only through simplicity that people could advance spiritually.[68] "A seminary for the new creed," the institute spread the gospel of "plain living and high thinking." Away from crowded, complex, gritty cities, Glenmore participants could debate "man's spiritual nature," disciplining themselves "in simplicity, kindliness, thoughtfulness, helpfulness, regularity, and promptness."[69]

The geography of Glenmore was meant to facilitate plain living and high thinking. In the early years, the space was rustic—and purposefully so. There was a quaint farmhouse on the property, and its parlor served as the lecture hall, dining room, and sitting room.[70] Attendees, who came largely from New York, New England, and the Midwest but also from as far away as Texas, camped in personal tents or in a large communal tent. Some even slept in a barn, making "pillows of the balsam needles" and experimenting in primitive "cooking and washing."[71] Whenever possible, residents bathed in the brook that cut across the property. They also performed daily chores, including clearing trees, stumps, and brush to have more space for activities. But it was not all work. Davidson ensured that every afternoon afforded time to nap and exercise—hiking, swimming, boating, and exploring the mountains. For only three dollars for the full course of lectures, two dollars per week for room, and six dollars for board, Glenmore attendees could ascend to natural, intellectual, and spiritual heights.[72]

As Glenmore's popularity grew, so did the need for space. In response, Davidson began constructing appropriately rustic buildings, including a few small cottages, a dining hall with bedrooms upstairs, and a dedicated lecture hall. The lecture hall was especially significant. Built on "a clearing on a steep hill looking out over the valley to the western mountains," the lecture hall promoted glorious thoughts to match the magnificent vistas.[73] High on the mountainside, away from the voracious machines of industrial America, Davidson and his followers created a space for broad philosophical inquiry. As one participant described, "Like all the other buildings it was of wood. It contained a spacious room having a large open fireplace. . . . On two sides of the building there was a wide piazza, where hammocks could be swung. From here, later on, we often watched the sunset clouds or the aurora borealis."[74] In the Gilded Age and Progressive Era, as an increasing number of Americans flocked to cities, leaving behind what Robert Weibe has called "island communities," Glenmore's lecture hall offered a romantic return to what once was.[75] Removal was Glenmore's mode of intellectual resistance.

The geography of knowledge that defined Glenmore was centered around the lecture hall. Most attendees slept in buildings or camping areas down the mountain, and to reach the hall, they had to walk up a dedicated path, which was marked by a cheeky sign reading, "The Ascent of Man." The sign at the top of the path heading down read, "The Descent of Man." Glenmore attendees passed these spatial and intellectual puns whenever they gathered for lectures and discussions. But the situation was different for Davidson. In the spring of 1893, he built a cottage higher up the mountain from the lecture hall. To join the others, he descended from the heights of his abode. To the extent that altitude signaled natural and intellectual accomplishment, Davidson was part of the group, yet more advanced than others. Whenever a visitor arrived at Glenmore for the summer, a servant blew a horn and Davidson descended "the hundred and twenty foot declivity, from his abode in higher regions."[76] From such heights, he led others to spiritual thought—or so Glenmore's geography suggested.

Glenmore attendees assembled for lectures two or three times a day except on Saturdays and Sundays, when there was only one lecture or, sometimes, none at all. Surrounded by the beauty of the Adirondacks, they listened to some of the most influential American thinkers of the late nineteenth century. The summer of 1893, for example, featured lectures by William T. Harris, who at the time was U.S. commissioner of education; John Dewey, who, despite many disagreements with Davidson, eventually bought the property adjacent to Glenmore; Josiah Royce, whose absolute idealism seemed a perfect fit for the surrounding mountain peaks; James Seth, a Scottish philosopher who found a kindred spirit in Davidson; and Rev. Sam Smith, who ran the aptly named People's Church in St. Paul, Minnesota.[77] While the majority of lecturers at Glenmore were men, women also spoke. In 1892, for example, Rosa Knorr offered lessons in conversational German. The following year, Mary Foster spoke on botany and sketching. The year after that, Jane Slocum lectured on "social economics."[78]

Davidson was ever-present at the lectures, always directing discussions toward spiritual heights and pushing inquiry away from the reality down the mountain. While Davidson was known as a "delightful" lecturer, he was considered an "even more charming" conversationalist. "A strong personal magnetism," recalled Mary Foster, "enabled him to become a welcome vehicle for the conveyance of truth and the disclosure of wisdom."[79] Foster also noted that Davidson hoped "to impart the instruction of which he felt that the educated classes stood so greatly in need; and he wished to do this in healthy and beautiful surroundings, under simple conditions of life." Put differently, intellectual advancement, even for the already-educated classes—*especially* for the already-educated classes—depended on spaces and discourses conducive to spiritual ascent and apart from the education they had received in the nation's colleges and universities. Glenmore was designed to help them leave behind their existing education. Only by correcting the intellectual problems that established institutions created would "completeness and harmony" with one's world be possible.[80]

When Davidson was not directing discussions from the audience, he was doing so from the lectern. People came to Glenmore to listen to lectures on the most recent advancements in the world of thought, and Davidson was happy to oblige. Given how often he lectured, any attempt to account for his discourse writ large will fall short, but it is possible to account for the geography of knowledge that structured his statements. While running Glenmore in the 1890s, Davidson was writing one of his most influential books: *Rousseau, and Education According to Nature*.[81] The book, published in 1898, both criticized Rousseau's thought and justified educational experiments like Glenmore. Over the years,

Davidson delivered several lectures based on material from the book. Unfortunately, the texts from these lectures have not survived, but William Knight's *Memorials of Thomas Davidson*, published a few years after Davidson's death, reprinted excerpts from the Rousseau book based on what Davidson delivered at Glenmore.[82] *Memorials*, therefore, provides the best glimpse available into the geography of knowledge that distinguished Glenmore. It also reveals the limits of Davidson's intellectual populism when stuck on a mountainside removed from industrial America.

According to Davidson, Rousseau's attempt to engage the state of nature was admirable, but also completely wrong. Noting Rousseau's love of "rural simplicity," the "common people," and "natural scenery," Davidson explained that Rousseau "made his language the expression of genuine passion and first-hand experience." It was an important point for an audience assembled on a mountain listening to a philosophy lecture, for it signaled the intersection of language, thought, and space. The problem, however, was that Rousseau pursued this intersection in unfortunate ways, inquiring into man's base nature—only to stop there. "Obtrusive independence, due to absence of moral ties," was the main idea Rousseau offered readers. Davidson deemed it a "spongy, unmanly, and repellent" picture of humanity.[83]

In response to this unmanliness, Davidson set his own philosophy against Rousseau's. Whereas Rousseau believed that "reflection is contrary to nature, and that the man who thinks is a depraved animal," Davidson insisted that thought and nature not only fit together but also perfect each other. Rousseau's conception of a natural education—based on letting nature have its way—was "highly artificial" and made to "exclude its highest manifestations." Davidson saw slavery where Rousseau saw freedom. Davidson saw oppression where Rousseau saw liberty. Davidson saw animality where Rousseau saw humanity. Davidson saw "the exact opposite of the truth, and the subversive of all civilization" where Rousseau saw enlightenment and advancement.[84]

Glenmore was an intellectual community designed to correct Rousseau's corruption of nature. While Davidson never mentioned Glenmore explicitly, it was unlikely that the implication of his comparisons escaped those gathered in a mountainside lecture hall. To the extent that Rousseau's theory confined humanity to "sub-human nature" and, worse still, reiterated "the sum and substance of much popular teaching in all departments of theory and practice to this day,"[85] Glenmore functioned as a response to the status quo in education and philosophy. Glenmore attendees, Davidson suggested, were tracking down knowledge and participating in a community devoted to high thinking and plain living. Glenmore was where philosophical reflection reached intellectual altitudes mirroring the vistas around. "So the problem of life," Davidson revealed, "is not to make man live according to nature, but to make nature live according to man; or in less ambitious phrase, to elevate the 'natural' into the 'spiritual' man; blind instinct into rational freedom."[86] The power of this insight turned on the nexus of people, space, and ideas—specifically, privileged Americans who had retreated from crowded cities to think big thoughts amid natural splendor. Their alignment on the mountainside, and in opposition to the kind of education prominent at the time, would allow them to reclaim inquiry for elevated spiritual purposes.

Turning nature into spirit was the heart of Davidson's project in the Adirondacks. Glenmore was an intellectual community—both literal and imagined—devoted to moving people from their natural state to spiritual heights. Unsurprisingly, this was the view of education that Davidson believed necessary at the end of the nineteenth century:

> The end of education, therefore, can be none other than the complete satisfaction of feeling by an ever-increasing, harmonious, that is, unitary, differentiation of it into a world of sources of satisfaction. This satisfaction will be greater in proportion as the sources are richer and more numerous. Hence, every soul will be consulting for its own satisfaction by doing its best to satisfy every other soul, and to make it as rich as possible. Thus the most perfect egoism will be found to be one with the most perfect altruism, and the law of virtue to be one with the law of blessedness, as in the end it must be, unless all existence be a

> mockery. On this view of the soul, and on this alone, will it be possible to erect an intelligent and coherent structure of education—intellectual, affectional, and moral.[87]

This concluding appeal marked the end of an intellectual, discursive, spiritual, and spatial journey. Davidson had taken his listeners from a consideration of base instincts—that is, Rousseau's conception of nature—to the heights of soul life, a place where souls metonymically operated in communities of thought, reconciling opposites through conversation and building a perfect life. On this utopian vision of education, humanity could "erect" the future, could build an "intelligent and coherent structure of education" like Glenmore. Davidson's lecture thus concluded where his listeners sat: on a mountain in the Adirondacks, surrounded by like-minded inquirers who could dedicate two or more weeks in the summer to developing their souls in harmonious relationship with nature and community. At Glenmore, space, people, ideas, and discourse operated as one.

While this vision of philosophy and education bolstered Glenmore, it was premised on withdrawal—from cities, from neighborhoods, from the rhythms of the Gilded Age and Progressive Era. Its premise was the same sense of luxurious intellectual retreat that today animates the Aspen Institute and exclusive gatherings in Davos. These pursuits of knowledge are based on the ability to remove oneself from familiar settings and to assemble for critiquing that from which one now stands apart. Davidson's promotion of Glenmore showed how distant he was from the realities of American society at the end of the nineteenth century. Well-to-do Americans could easily embrace the soul life Davidson promoted in the Adirondacks. They could afford to escape the city and to live "manly" lives in the mountains, an attractive notion in American culture at the time.[88] But retreat to the Adirondacks positioned them as another intellectual aristocracy. To be sure, Davidson saw Glenmore as egalitarian and populist—a place where people could become thinkers in their own right, apart from the academic institutions that impeded understanding. But in reality, his alternative intellectual community was cordoned off from the hard life that the vast majority of Americans experienced. By and large, the intellectual revolution Davidson hoped to foment was stuck on mountainside, circumscribed by its own naiveté.

However, Davidson's community-building efforts were not done. Glenmore continued to operate after Davidson's death, but it receded in importance once Davidson happened upon an idea for a radically new intellectual experiment. It was a community based not on retreat from cities but on the reconfiguration of industrial space. On the Lower East Side of New York, amid the tenements, Davidson mapped a new geography of knowledge.

Inquiry among the Tenements

In the late 1890s, Davidson was living in an apartment on East Sixteenth Street in Manhattan, overlooking idyllic Stuyvesant Square. He traveled to Glenmore during summer months, but the rest of the year he lived in the city and earned a modest living as a freelance philosopher. Freelancing included writing scholarly books that never sold well; penning articles for periodicals and newspapers, including for his friend Joseph Pulitzer's *New York World*, which paid Davidson for his efforts but rarely printed his abstract philosophical analyses; and delivering lectures across the eastern United States. Given his scholarly reputation and relative success as a lecturer, and given that he lived in the city, it was not surprising that in 1898 he received an invitation to lecture to the New York People's Institute at Cooper Union. Davidson agreed to speak to the group, but only if he could do so in December; beyond that he would not have the time. December seemed acceptable to the director of the People's Institute, but a scheduling conflict at Cooper Union emerged. Organizers needed to find a new venue, and the best space available was on the Lower East Side, at a cooperative settlement called the Educational Alliance.[89]

Although the Educational Alliance was only a dozen blocks from Davidson's apartment, it was a world away. Not only was the Lower

East Side the most crowded neighborhood on the planet, but its residents were unlike those who frequented Glenmore. Most residents were first- and second-generation immigrants, and many of them Eastern European Jews who worked in the garment trade.[90] Some labored in oppressive factories, while others spent their days as "homeworkers," which meant they constructed garments in their tenement rooms. Either way, they were exploited. The typical immigrant labored between fifty-five and sixty hours per week without overtime pay. During the busiest times of year, seventy hours per week was the norm; during the slowest times, many had to go without work. To maximize paychecks when work was available, families often labored together. Fathers, mothers, sons, and daughters might earn a combined income of $300–$400 per year at a time when the minimum needed to sustain a family of four in New York was $800.[91] It was an ironic turn of events for people who had fled oppressive homelands to pursue the American dream. "This was the boasted American freedom and opportunity," remarked one immigrant, "the opportunity to live in those monstrous, dirty caves that shut out the sunshine."[92]

Urban reformers in the Gilded Age and Progressive Era were well aware of the problems in the Lower East Side and similar neighborhoods. Before major national efforts began, municipal reform clubs tried to alleviate the problems in their communities, including through cooperative education, practical programs, and discussions of industrial democracy.[93] Many of these reform clubs recognized the need to support the intellectual lives of workers, immigrants, and the lower class, so they created places of respite from city life, providing access to reading rooms, lending libraries, and meeting spaces.[94] That was certainly true of organizations like the Educational Alliance, which promised to combat the problems of industrial society through mutual support and the reclamation of space in oppressive neighborhoods.[95] The Alliance began in 1889 when Jewish philanthropists funded a five-story building in the heart of the tenement district. Although the settlement served the entire community, its organizers were particularly interested in reaching young adults, who still had time to better themselves and their families.

The Alliance offered networking opportunities and recreation as well as classes on citizenship, hygiene, English, and American history. During the Alliance's first year of operation, several hundred young adults took advantage of its services.[96]

Though the Alliance was a boon for the community, its focus on young adults often exacerbated existing tensions. The older generation in the neighborhood tended to be pious and devout, while the younger generation tended to embrace secular society. The result, as one former resident recalled, was "a struggle between the old and new ideals, resulting in a conflict between older and younger generations fraught with heart-rending consequences."[97] When generational tensions ran high, the Educational Alliance served as a refuge for men and women in their teens and twenties who wanted to distance themselves from their orthodox, immigrant past. As one Alliance participant noted, "The conflict between me and my relatives at large is as the one who ventures to bring a new idea or movement in an old orthodox community."[98] Another participant bemoaned intense "religious feelings" at home, given that her parents were "strictly orthodox Hebrews" who "insist on the observance of every custom."[99] Still another participant lamented his "discouraging" home life, due largely to financial strain and "the matter of religion." Before getting involved at the Educational Alliance, he felt that "life was not worth living. The social, political, and moral surroundings [of the Lower East Side] discouraged me greatly indeed."[100]

Given the realities of the neighborhood, many of Davidson's friends and colleagues thought that lecturing at the Educational Alliance was a bad idea, and they warned him not to do it. "You don't mean to talk philosophically before a lot of people from the sweat-shops," Davidson recalled his friends asking, "most of whom have but recently arrived in the country, and hardly understand English?" Colleagues cautioned that he would face "a very critical audience, made up largely of socialists of the Marxian type, anarchists, single-taxists, and the like, who, at the close of each lecture, would subject me to a rigorous examination and try to draw me into a dispute."[101] Indeed, some of Davidson's listeners *did* mean to heckle him. They planned to confront him, as one audience member later recalled, with the idea that "no substantial improvement of our human lot was possible without a radical change in our economic setup."[102] But Davidson, an experienced lecturer, was able to anticipate these challenges. Instead of arguing for specific plans of action, he decided to focus his lectures on "The Problems which the Nineteenth Century hands over, for Solution, to the Twentieth."[103] He hoped that focusing on the problems would establish common ground with the audience and avoid controversies over specific solutions.

Regardless, the situation was ripe for appeals of intellectual populism. The exploitative power establishment surrounded the residents of the Lower East Side, restricting their lives to menial labor and curtailing their intellectual futures. To Davidson, this was a chance to engage the residents in philosophical inquiry that the status quo denied them. Better yet: this was a chance to bring abstract philosophy in line with the life of labor they knew all too well. As I mentioned at the beginning of this chapter, Davidson began his lectures with the bold salutation, "Fellow Workmen!" That salutation not only linked Davidson and his listeners but also served as a foray into identifying the forces that opposed them all, including the conniving forces that dismissed their ability to inquire. "I am continually told," he said, "that I need not try to make working men listen to the discussion of really serious problems. They care nothing about them, leaving them to bosses and to priests or ministers. They want to be entertained: they want pictures and jokes and stories—a chance to gape, to laugh, and to have a good time."[104] If there was any way of rousing young Jewish workers at the end of the nineteenth century, it was pitting them against bosses, priests, and ministers, who supposedly knew what was best for them and scoffed at their intellectual aptitude. Davidson, however, saw an opportunity for coalition building. In opposition to those who insisted that wage earners could not or would not engage in serious intellectual discussion, he declared:

> Now I, who am a workman, who have worked hard for all I have ever owned, . . . I have found that hardly any other considerable class of men and women take life so earnestly, so soberly, so truly as working

> men and working women. They have a more natural life; they are closer to its sober facts than any other class. If I was asked to find acceptance for any great truth, a practical truth, a truth bearing on the interests of humanity, I should bring it, by preference, before the working class, sure that there I should find less prejudice . . . than in any other class.

Though somewhat pandering, Davidson's affirmation of the intellectual character of workingmen and workingwomen invited the audience into an antagonistic frontier aligned against those who marginalized them in the pursuit of knowledge. He hailed his listeners as individuals properly positioned to engage the great truths of life—specifically because they were close to the sober facts of reality and less prejudiced than others. In contemplative community and apart from philosophical aristocrats of the day, they could build an intellectual movement close to the rhythms of industrial America. Importantly, this movement was to be based not on vocational training or civics or hygiene—as were many movements to help immigrants at the time—but on rigorous inquiry. "Then you see," he told the audience, "we need food for our bodies, training for our souls, regulation for social intercourse, and a theory of our own nature that shall convince us that we shall live forever, and show us under what conditions we can live with most satisfaction. . . . Only under such conditions is life really worthy and desirable." To people suffering in tenements and sweatshops, Davidson's vision of immortality through philosophy likely seemed unattainable. So, for the remainder of the lecture series, he sought to explain how it was attainable, even in—especially in—the most densely populated neighborhood on the planet.

Davidson grouped the problems that the nineteenth century handed off to the twentieth under three headings: economic problems, educational and moral problems, and philosophical and religious problems. What cut across these subject areas was an abiding concern for space and labor, both of which were central to the creation of a populist intellectual community. When Davidson discussed labor in the lecture series, he dealt with familiar "labor issues"—the tensions related to bosses, workers, capitalism, and unions so pressing at the time. Yet he was much more interested in discussing a different kind of labor—not factory or tenement work but inquiry itself as labor. Positioning inquiry as labor functioned as the central mechanism by which workers became active in the pursuit of knowledge. Much as Eddy's lecturers created an evidentiary void to render ordinary people intellectual agents, Davidson infused philosophy with the terminology of labor, thereby relating it to the work the audience already performed—work they could continue in the realm of ideas. "We ought to realize," he explained, "that there are problems, problems so deep and difficult that no man can expect to solve them, that they cannot be solved without much earnest study in many directions and a wide experience of men and things." "Earnest study" meant hard work, and solving the problems of the era demanded the participation of laborers. Later Davidson reiterated the point by juxtaposing entertainment with the hard work of thought: "There is no harm in making pictures of a future Eden, if any one likes that sort of amusement; but it is rather unprofitable employment. What we should do is to study, with all our might, present conditions, and then try to do what is possible under these conditions." Through study came strength, in the same way manual labor led to strength (at least ideally). Moreover, study meant resistance, in the same way labor organizing tried to level the industrial battlefield: "I should be very sorry to see you becoming the slaves of authority, even of my own. I believe it is better to think for yourselves, even if you think wrong, than to accept even correct thinking from somebody else." As philosophical laborers, residents of the Lower East Side could control their intellectual futures with a sense of freedom and self-determination—key Americanisms in the populist tradition. Everyone "who fails to think for himself," he explained, was "a slave to other people's opinions." To people who were wage slaves, Davidson offered philosophy as a tool for breaking industrial shackles.

In positioning inquiry as labor, Davidson made philosophy familiar to his listeners. Yet inquiry as labor was also distinct from the kind of labor the audience knew. Labor on the Lower East Side was exploitation.[105] Workers did not keep the fruits of their labor, and they struggled to make ends meet. But as philosophers, they could think for themselves and own their ideas. Inquiry as labor was empowerment, not exploitation. Of course, that required space, both in their schedules and in their neighborhood, and space was always in short supply. Davidson seemed to discover as much during the course of his lectures. In the middle of the series, he outlined a "movement toward popular education" that must begin "with the wage-earners":

> If you desire the higher education which shall make you intellectually, morally, and socially independent, begin now to study with regularity and with system, in the quiet of your own rooms. Let each of you, in some undisturbed corner, have his work-table, his books, and his writing materials, so that, as soon as the days' toil is over, and he has had a little exercise and rest, he may be able to sit down and begin each evening where he left off the evening before.

Davidson's attempt to inspire fell on deaf ears. In fact, it agitated many listeners—as Davidson soon discovered. Still steaming from the suggestion to find a quiet nook, one audience member stood up after the lecture concluded and chastised Davidson: life in tenement houses left no room—literally—for study. Many in the audience slept three or four in one room, and there were no undisturbed corners to be had.[106] That Davidson believed their tenements had space for a desk, books, and writing materials showed how distant he was from their lives. Glenmore was nothing but space for thought; the Lower East Side foreclosed any Glenmore-like spiritual ascent.

Fortunately, Davidson's oblivious statement was only part of his plan for intellectual advancement among the wage earners. Ultimately, he hoped they would "begin to demand more favorable conditions for study—shorter work-hours, college-buildings, libraries, instructors." Here was a key insight that represented an important shift in Davidson's geography of knowledge: intellectual advancement in industrial America would not come by removing people from the nation's industrial centers. Shipping people off to Harvard or Princeton or Glenmore was no solution at all. Instead, intellectual advancement hinged on transforming the spaces that defined industrial America. Ideas demanded buildings and libraries—not in spite of but because of the space constraints of the Lower East Side. "There will gradually arise," he foretold,

> institutions of higher education for the great body of the people, and when these are numerous enough to convince the state that there is among the wage-workers a widespread demand for such education, it will take hold of the whole matter and, with public funds, establish a Breadwinners' College or People's University in every city-ward in every country, village, or township. Then the cause of the higher education of the people will be won, and democracy placed on a firm basis.

The institutions Davidson envisioned were titled in the possessive—the "Breadwinners' College" and the "People's University," both proudly populist names—to signal the proper ownership of ideas and spaces. The new institutions were to be their buildings, their rooms, their forums. Compared to the factories and companies that exploited them, these places would allow laborers to work philosophically and to retain the ideas they produced.

Reconstructing the spaces of industrial America to facilitate inquiry as labor was not just a matter of serving the breadwinners, however; it was also a matter of advancing democracy. In Davidson's presentation, getting the working class involved in the pursuit of knowledge was crucial to the character and quality of democratic deliberation—or ordinary democracy, as I discussed in the introduction to this book. As Davidson presented the matter at the end of his lectures, inquiry as labor strengthened ordinary democracy, which set the nation on a new path of enlightenment. "It is time," he declared, "for the three classes of the people"—specifically, the wage earners, philanthropists, and scholars—"to unite to found Breadwinners' Colleges." Unity for education was "one of the chief tasks of the twentieth century" and necessary for "the safety of our whole nation and its democratic institutions. A democracy cannot long be sustained by an ignorant demos."

True to populist form, Americanisms and a utopian vision of the future pervaded the conclusion to the lecture series. By imagining inquiry as labor and by constructing spaces that would facilitate such labor, America could realize its "truly religious purpose of developing the bodies and enlightening the souls" of the populace. This would not happen in places like Glenmore because America no longer looked like Glenmore; it looked like the Lower East Side. Fusing people, space, ideas, and discourse in the nation's industrial centers was the true pathway to the spiritual heights Davidson had long envisioned.

Organizing a Populist Community

The third lecture in Davidson's series at the Educational Alliance dealt with education. Skeptical of Davidson's thoughts on the topic, a young man in the audience, Julius Fein, stood up after the lecture and posed a question: "It is all very well to talk about education for the breadwinners; but how can people like us, who work nine or ten hours a day, who come home tired, who have no convenience there for study, few books, and no one to guide or instruct us, obtain any liberal education?"[107] Thunderous applause followed the question, indicating exactly where Davidson's romantic philosophy collided with life on the Lower East Side. But instead of shrinking from the challenge, Davidson responded in a way that changed his life:

> That is just the chief educational problem which the nineteenth century hands over to the twentieth. Of course you do not expect me to solve it. But one thing I can do for you of a practical sort. I cannot procure for you shorter hours, or make you less tired at night; I cannot supply you with home conveniences for study or with books; but one thing I can and will do, if you care to have me. If you will organize a club of people who are really in earnest, and who will work with all their might, I will devote one evening a week to it.[108]

So began the Breadwinners' College.

Davidson effectively stumbled into broad educational initiatives already underway in the Lower East Side, especially the work of municipal reform clubs to alleviate the problems of the city. Yet the Breadwinners' College marked a distinctive collaboration between a freelance philosopher and a group of working-class immigrants who did not want the typical settlement-house lectures but instead wanted the challenge of abstract philosophy. On January 7, 1899, he began his weekly visits to the Lower East Side. The director of the Educational Alliance provided a meeting room where interested students could assemble every Saturday evening until the end of April. Davidson dubbed the group "A Class in History and Sociology," and interest among neighborhood residents ran high. Almost sixty people attended the first meeting, and they ranged in age from sixteen to fifty-eight.[109] Davidson quickly made clear that this was not going to be another Glenmore. In fact, he "had no intention of teaching them anything"; his only aim was "to direct them to the sources of truth and in the methods of correct thinking. The teaching they would have to do themselves."[110] On the Lower East Side, Davidson did not descend from spiritual heights to impart truth; instead, he empowered others as teachers.

Empowering others did not mean that Davidson was hands-off. He put together a rough curriculum to guide group discussion and to afford a "bird's-eye view of the scene and course of human evolution." The curriculum included biographies of noted thinkers (e.g., Aristotle, Bacon, Kant, Emerson, George Eliot); definitions of key terms (e.g., society, institution, person, duty, religion, nature); maps of world geography (e.g., Egypt, Babylonia, Persia, Palestine, Greece, the Roman Empire); races of people and religious traditions (e.g., Turanians, Semites, Aryans, Barbarism, Buddhism, Christianity, Islam); and texts for recitation (e.g., Portia's "Eulogy of Mercy" from *The Merchant of Venice*, Tennyson's "Love Thou Thy Land" and "In Memoriam," Lowell's "The Present Crisis," Psalm 19, and Emerson's "Days"). The scope of the curriculum meant that students had to work extensively on their own, reading dense philosophical prose after working ten or twelve hours a day. They also had to craft and deliver original essays, reflecting on key issues and sharing their thoughts with the class. After one student delivered his or her reflections, the rest of the group critiqued the author's work, engaging in a Socratic exchange designed to strengthen the audience, the speaker, and the ideas. Despite these demands, or perhaps because of them, the class size grew steadily, which Davidson believed evinced a "burning desire for knowledge" among the wage earners.[111]

Who were these wage earners interested in joining the acerbic Davidson for abstract philosophical inquiry? Surviving records provide some insight.[112] One participant was M. H. Newman, a twenty-two-year-old from Russia who worked ten-hour days in a sweatshop. He learned from Davidson that the purpose of education is to open people's eyes so that "they should see for themselves where the precious stones are lying." Another was Jacob Greenberg, a seventeen-year-old from Poland who worked fourteen-hour days and lived with his family in a tenement "not well adapted for studying purposes." Yet according to Greenberg, Davidson showed "that I was the man to better these conditions." Still another was S. P. Frank, a thirty-four-year-old from Poland who often worked seventeen-hour days and lived with his parents in poverty, yet who joined Davidson to "put into practice the ideal life." One of many female participants was Jennie Louronogy, a nineteen-year-old from Russia who immigrated to the United States when she was ten. Her family was poor but "intellectual," and like Frank, she joined Davidson to "live up to the true ideal of life." Another female participant was Mary Ryshpan, a twenty-year-old born and raised on the Lower East Side. Her orthodox Jewish family pushed her to become a dressmaker, fearing that education would encourage her to abandon Judaism. But she disregarded their advice and found in Davidson her intellectual salvation: "The interchange of thought with that large, rich soul grew to be the keenest joy I had ever experienced. Subsequently it caused my horizon to be somewhat broadened. He opened to me a world of literature, science, and art and philosophy that I had known only very vaguely before. He strengthened my desire to serve Humanity."[113]

Despite their challenging home lives, despite their oppressive work conditions, despite the economic problems, language barriers, and educational deficits they faced, Davidson's students found purpose in the class. Class meetings became so important that students pledged to continue them during the summer months when Davidson was away at Glenmore. Inspired by their teacher's guidance, they led discussions and continued with extensive reading, critical writing, and forthright cross-examination. Davidson even arranged for some of his scholar friends to visit the class, deliver a lecture, and engage in discussion.[114] What's more, students often sent their essays to Davidson for comments and feedback. He felt himself becoming "practically superfluous" as a teacher—and he loved it.[115]

However superfluous he may have been as a teacher, Davidson remained the group's guiding spirit, directing their efforts from afar. At least once a week, he wrote a letter to the entire class, providing advice, answering questions, and following up on their work. He wrote letters to individual students as well, but his correspondence with the class exhibited some of the most populist discourse of his career. Davidson became a kind of apostle in his letters, writing epistles to a body of believers he had formed but could not stay with forever. As an apostolic figure, he directed the community when it strayed, reminded followers of their purpose, and encouraged them to live out their intellectual faith.

The tone of Davidson's letters to students was indeed spiritual and apostolic, as he emphasized the unseen reality that united them in community. In his first letter to the class, dated May 4, 1899, Davidson commented that even though he had gone to Glenmore for the summer, he would still be present when they met: "From eight to ten on the evening of the 6th I shall be with you every moment." On May 9, he followed up: "I am happy to know that you had a good meeting on Saturday night. I was with you every moment." Through this ongoing, mystical connection to the group, Davidson inspired students as "heroes, saints, and prophets" in the mold of Isaiah and other Old Testament figures. But he reminded them that heroic sainthood did not come easy. True inquiry, he explained, required both "scientific insight and apostolic fervor"; only then would they be "inspired by God." Reinforcing the biblical tone of his letters, Davidson gave students twenty commandments for realizing "the greatest of blessings" in their lives. These commandments included such spiritual directives as "Be on earth what good people hope to be in heaven" and "Remember that heaven itself can be nothing but the intimacy of pure and noble souls." By operating as an *ekklesia*—a body of believers following the guidance of an apostle—those on the Lower East Side could write a "new Torah" and become "a living Providence to each other."[116]

The apostolic tone was fitting given the audience and situation. The students were Jewish immigrants whose families fretted over the spiritual welfare of the younger generation. Davidson tried to put the younger generation back on a spiritual track—albeit a different one from the older generation. In so doing, he turned his religious tone in a populist direction, casting the efforts of the group as both conservative and radical. The breadwinners were conservative in their dedication to moral living and spiritual advancement, but they were radical in their push for revolution, agitation for change, and combat with the status quo. By turning displaced Jewish immigrants into intellectual leaders, Davidson's students reaffirmed spiritual purpose and upended established institutions.

The conservative-radicalism of the community also came through in Davidson's deployment of the labor discourse he had originally used in the 1898 lectures at the Educational Alliance. Reinscribing philosophy as a kind of labor agitation, he praised students as "earnest workers" who strive "to be simple, upright, pure, heroic men and women, rich in knowledge, in sympathy, and in wise helpfulness." He told them to "labor then for justice," which meant "being just ourselves." He asked them to "tell me about your work, and send me your essays and exercises." Again, Davidson emphasized labor and work, but as conservative terms of radical liberation. Unlike the exploitative work of the Lower East Side, intellectual work was part of their "eternal career." With eyes turned toward eternity, Davidson said, we should "devote ourselves, body and soul, to welldoing; and, though we may not immediately see the fruit of our labors, the fruit is sure to ripen in the days to come."[117]

This conservative-radical community was a provocative alternative to the conservatism and radicalism the audience knew. The Breadwinners' College was religious, but not in the way that the elder, orthodox Jews were religious. It was radical, but not in the way of the socialists then striving for political and economic change on the Lower East Side. In fact, Davidson took pains to distance the radicalism of his community from the radical socialism that tempted many breadwinners. He did not want socialism to do to this class what it had done to the Fellowship of the New Life and the Fabian Society. "I do not find it possible to be a socialist myself," Davidson wrote, "but many of my friends are, and I believe that the socialist movement has done much good in arousing the world to a sense of injustice due to present social arrangements." However, he cautioned, socialism is ultimately materialistic, providing "only for man's material needs, important as these are. . . . Human nature demands more than food, clothing, and shelter, no matter how rich and elaborate these may be." What is ultimately needed is spiritual progress based in "practical work" and "a new view of the world and of man's relation to it—a view based upon the most comprehensive science and philosophy."[118]

Even though Davidson discouraged his class from pursuing socialism, he understood their desire for uplift, which he offered in the form of intellectual agency. In response to a student who had asked him where true knowledge could be found, Davidson replied: "The fact is, you cannot find such knowledge anywhere. You must think it out for yourselves under proper guidance."[119] Proper guidance was crucial, but Davidson recognized that guidance sometimes flirted with tyranny, and he hoped to correct any misconceptions students may have had about his role in the class: "I am not, in the least, anxious to impose my opinions upon you. I wish to give, here and there, a hint, and allow you to follow it up yourselves. If you come to my conclusions I shall be pleased; if you don't, I shall be pleased also."[120] In determining truth, residents of the Lower East Side were free and emboldened in a way they decidedly were not while laboring during the day.

Yet these portents of intellectual agency would come to nothing without space—a lesson Davidson had learned from a tongue lashing during his 1898 lectures at the Educational Alliance. Accordingly, his letters during the summer of 1899 were filled with concerns about the relationship between space and speech. On June 28, he informed students about discussions with the Educational Alliance for additional "rooms and appliances." This was particularly important given that "the club is increasing in numbers." In mid-July, he was able to report that the class's success had persuaded Alliance trustees to grant students use of "the Fifth Street house" and "a certain sum of money." The house would provide space for "conversation and mutual help." "I sincerely hope," Davidson opined, "we shall be able to have a rounded culture-course, calculated to make you all feel at home in the world."[121]

Davidson realized that the issues of space were not limited to securing rooms. He also fretted about the Lower East Side itself, which stood in stark contrast to his retreat in the Adirondacks. "I wish I could tell you how beautiful these mountains are and what peace reigns here," he wrote at the conclusion of his May 4 letter. "But you must come and see for yourselves."[122] Making good on his word, Davidson arranged for a handful of students to visit Glenmore that summer, including his prize pupil Morris Cohen.[123] But removing students from the Lower East Side was not the ultimate answer; the answer was to transform the neighborhood itself. "One of you spoke of the East Side as a 'hell,'" Davidson wrote on May 23. "If that be true, then each of you has a hell in his world. Are you willing to have that? Think how much more glorious your lives would be if the East Side were a heaven?" Easier said than done, of course, but the question had less to do with actual possibilities than with inspiration and agency. "You know the needs and conditions of the East Side better than I do. One thing is certain—you can all be in your own lives models of kindness, helpfulness, and strength. You can each be a living light in a dark place. You can overcome evil with good, and make the evil ashamed of itself."[124]

This was the community-building realization that industrial America needed. Constructing a populist coalition did not mean removing people from their environment. A true alternative community, one that would not simply recreate privilege in another location, needed a geography of knowledge based on the spaces that distinguished the Progressive Era. Taking a few poor immigrants out of the Lower East Side would do nothing to change the neighborhood itself. "I have no doubt there is many an hour when you feel that your lives are cramped," Davidson wrote on May 31, "and that you have not the opportunities for self-development that you ought to have. That is a right and worthy feeling." But, he continued:

> I have felt it many a time, for there is not one among you whose circumstances are more adverse or unpromising than mine were in boyhood and youth. I have had to fight single-handed for everything: for livelihood, for education, for culture, yea, for moral life. My sympathies, therefore, go out to you in all your toils, struggles, and aspirations. I am one of you, and am proud to be one of you.[125]

Davidson was so proud that he pledged to move to the neighborhood and to "find a quiet place, write my books, and see you often. We might, I think, form a little society of which Isaiah or Plato would not be ashamed—a society which should be known for its high moral aspirations and its good works—a kind of divine commonwealth of which each member should try to live a divine life."[126] This divine commonwealth, this utopian community of thought, would transform the planet's most densely populated neighborhood and the nation itself. Among the tenements, he and the breadwinners could seize intellectual power.

Conclusion

After the summer of 1899, Davidson reunited with the class on the Lower East Side. The number of students had grown dramatically over the summer, thanks in part to Davidson's motivational prowess.[127] But with growth came another space crunch. Davidson worked closely with the brass at the Educational Alliance to secure more rooms. The largest rooms in the Alliance allowed for robust discussions, but they didn't meet all of the group's intellectual needs. With the help of a $600 donation from the Alliance and contributions from several wealthy patrons, Davidson rented a house in the neighborhood that provided discussion rooms, study rooms, reading rooms, and a lending library.[128] The breadwinners thus had something of an "undisturbed corner" for inquiry right in the Lower East Side.

With extra space secured, Davidson once again traveled to Glenmore during the summer of 1900. It was the last summer of his life. Even though his health was failing, he used his remaining strength to stay in touch with the class. On May 30, Davidson penned what was perhaps the most artful, inspirational, and populist paragraph of his long career. Given its significance, I quote it at length:

> That a Breadwinners' College is greatly needed on the East Side no one, I suppose, doubts. The question is, Is there ability and enthusiasm enough among you to carry one on? My own belief is that there is; but you know best. There is certainly a glorious opportunity offered you to do the most beneficent work for your fellow-men—work whose influence would be far-reaching and eternal. Many of you, I know, are eager for such work and are asking where it can be found. Here it is, almost thrust in your faces. Of all philanthropic work, education is the noblest and most effective. It is that which best diffuses truth and righteousness, the lack of which is the cause of nearly all human ills. But it is no light work, and I can well understand your desiring to think twice before undertaking it. The word "college" seems to frighten some of you, and makes you begin to think of examinations and degrees, and all the other formalities of our present institutions. There is no need for such dread. You will never be expected to enter the lists against colleges which do this. It is just because our present colleges are so unsatisfactory, so unsuited to the great body of American people, that colleges of a new sort, Breadwinners' Colleges, are necessary. We want to educate the breadwinners better than our present college men are educated. We want to make them better men and women in all the relations of life—pure, high-minded, public-spirited, generous, cultured.

> The day has come when the toiling millions who have so long been denied their share in the treasures of art, science, culture, and freedom, won by the men and women of past ages, must come to their inheritance; and they can do so only through education. We are engaged in a new movement, one of the most momentous that the world has ever known—the spiritual elevation of the vast majority of mankind. . . . Are you going to take a leading part in this glorious movement, or are you not? . . . Think of it! Think how full of interest and joy your lives would be if you felt that you had taken the first great step in the emancipation of the millions of toilers that now groan in ignorance! A little knot of earnest Jews has turned the world upside down before now. Why may not the same thing—nay, a far better thing—happen in your day, and among you?[129]

This was the culmination of Davidson's intellectual populism and community-building efforts. In this single section of a single letter, Davidson denounced established institutions (colleges and universities) as out-of-touch and ineffective. He hailed ordinary people (breadwinners and toilers) as the true stewards of inquiry. He spoke of this intellectual movement through various Americanisms (hard work, empowerment, emancipation, and freedom). He affirmed radical conservatism via a return to the great intellectual values of the past (art, science, and culture), but only through a far-reaching reconfiguration of the present. And he pictured a glorious utopia of enlightenment for millions of breadwinners on the other side of a populist uprising. Intellectual populism undergirded the Breadwinners' College, which Davidson hoped to replicate in cities, towns, and industrial districts around the nation.

The irony was that Davidson wrote these words from Glenmore. This perfect articulation of Davidson's intellectual populism came from a position physically removed from the community he worked to empower. But perhaps that was as it should have been. Davidson was leading his Jewish people out of the Egypt of ignorance. Like Moses, he would not reach the Promised Land. Before he could move to the Lower East Side as he had promised, he died from surgical complications, on September

14, 1900. But standing on the mountaintop of populist progress, he caught a glimpse of his long sought-after utopia. By transforming the spaces of the Lower East Side, "the people" could link their grievances and unite to circumvent the experts of academia.

In the years after Davidson's death, the Breadwinners' College continued its work. Students even formed the Thomas Davidson Society to honor their late teacher and to further his imagined utopia. But like all utopias, this one petered out. At the beginning of World War I, the classes and programs of the Breadwinners' College folded into the Educational Alliance.[130]

However, the legacy of Davidson's community-building efforts does not hinge on the success or failure of the Breadwinners' College. Davidson's fundamental contribution to intellectual populism was his reconfiguration of speech and space—his grasp of the way words and ideas relate to the geography in which they emerge and through which they move. The Breadwinners' College was ultimately a novel juxtaposition of philosophical speech and industrial space, and that novelty was its power. Davidson's students certainly loved it. Expanding the borders of philosophical conversations to include the dispossessed of the Lower East Side meant new voices and new critiques, new participants and new relationships, new neighborhoods and new networks. Opposing the philosophical status quo strengthened, diversified, and expanded the pursuit of philosophy writ large. And all of that happened because Davidson realized that populist resistance was inexorably tied to space. Empowering the people needed to happen in the spaces that defined their lives.

CHAPTER FOUR

Booker T. Washington's Reclamation of Work

What really stood out about rural Alabama were the naked kids. And they were not just little kids—they were boys of thirteen and fourteen running around naked. The issue was less their nudity than that they "seemed not to mind their condition in the least." Not all of them were naked, but those with clothing had garments "so black and greasy that it did not resemble cloth." Clothed or not, they were poor and uneducated. Yet they understood their predicament and were "desirous of improving."[1]

That was Booker T. Washington's observation of the Alabama countryside shortly after moving there in 1881. He had been there only a month when he sent these observations to the *Southern Workman*, the monthly publication of the Hampton Institute in Virginia. A former student and teacher at Hampton, Washington had contributed regularly to the publication, and he was now ready to report on the prospects of opening a Hampton-like institution in rural Alabama. The prospects were strong, he wrote to readers of the *Southern Workman*, because the people of Alabama so desperately wanted to improve. To help them improve, Washington put his new institution "on a labor basis, so that earnest students can help themselves and at the same time learn the true dignity of labor."[2] Learning the dignity of labor was necessary, he believed, because labor had been degraded and forced upon African Americans during their enslavement. Tuskegee, a school that would alter the direction of black higher education for decades to come, would remake labor as something empowering, something that put individuals, communities, and the race on solid ground as the nineteenth century lurched to a close.

Washington's letter to the *Southern Workman*, written in July 1881, offered one of the earliest articulations of an idea that would form the cornerstone of his efforts at racial uplift. Not only would he build Tuskegee on the "dignity of labor," but he would also preach about it to audiences across the country, from early in his career until the year of his death. In 1882, for instance, at a meeting of teachers in Selma, Alabama, he spoke of instructing students on "the dignity of labor" so they could adjust to "the real business of life."[3] In 1915, the year he passed away, he insisted that race relations in the South were ultimately "a labor problem" and that to combat the problem, "people must be taught a love for labor, must be taught the dignity of labor and at the same time given proper methods in the direction of skill."[4]

Washington did not coin the phrase "the dignity of labor"; it was a staple of nineteenth-century public discourse, especially in industrial contexts.[5] But he put the phrase to strategic use for racial politics, setting it to work in different ways for different audiences—black and white alike. "The dignity of labor" attracted wealthy northern philanthropists by picturing a southern workforce that shared the values of industriousness and self-help that they affirmed. It suggested to southern whites that the masses of African Americans in their midst would remain menial laborers, supposedly serving the interests of the white establishment. To African Americans, however, particularly those in the rural South, the "dignity of labor" served as a rallying cry, an idea around which they could gather to take control of their lives. Washington called on African Americans to work, and to work hard, but also to work intelligently and efficiently. Work would help them accumulate the land, wealth, and resources strong black communities needed.

In championing the dignity of labor throughout his career, Washington deployed a flexible and disruptive rhetoric of work, which proceeded along two main fronts. First, he spoke extensively about work in his public address, and he did so in a way that empowered African Americans in the rural South as intellectual agents. Second, he created an institution—the Tuskegee Institute—that taught work as, among other things, a rhetorical process. To Washington, work was rhetorical because it communicated, influenced, and persuaded as effectively as words. When African Americans in the rural South worked with dignity, they could persuade European Americans of their strength and value. Yet working with dignity was not just about shaping the perceptions of whites; it was also about empowering blacks to live the lives they wanted, to prosper and advance themselves, their communities, and future generations. Washington relied on this double movement—changing white perceptions and empowering black communities—to combat the racist status quo that had long exploited, marginalized, and dehumanized African Americans.

The purpose of this chapter is to trace the rhetoric of work throughout Washington's career and to show how he extended intellectual populism into the rural South. Political populism had deep roots in the South, even among such African American groups as the Colored Farmer's Alliance.[6] Yet Washington's discourse and leadership offer a clear window into how the appeals of intellectual populism could transform the meaning of work for generations of former slaves and their descendants. When Washington discussed work, he positioned it as a form of inquiry, elevating it into an intellectual practice that contributed to the advancement of knowledge, truth, right, wrong, good, bad, and more. In that way, his intellectual populism was the converse of Thomas Davidson's. Davidson pushed inquiry down into a form of labor continuous with what members of the Breadwinners' College already knew.

Washington pushed labor up into a form of inquiry designed to elevate African Americans in the rural South. Like the other rhetors discussed in this book, Washington deployed the basic appeals of the populist intellectual tradition. But in his case, the appeals proceeded through a rhetoric of work suited to the project of resisting white domination. Elevating work to a form of intellectual practice enabled Washington to resist white domination through a language that seemed unobjectionable to white America. He called on African Americans to be workers—something whites of the North and South could support. But he called on them to be more than *mere* workers—an idea behind which African Americans could rally.

Washington's Predicament

Washington's legacy may be the most disputed of any race leader in American history. To some, especially during his lifetime, he was the heir to Frederick Douglass and a Moses-like figure for African Americans in the South. To others, he was a race traitor, or at least someone willing to relinquish true racial advancement for the sake of economic expediency. That was famously the view of W. E. B. DuBois, who charged Washington with extolling "the old attitude of adjustment and submission" while preaching "a gospel of Work and Money to such an extent as apparently almost completely to overshadow the higher aims of life."[7] Although DuBois's criticism was the minority viewpoint during Washington's life, it became widely accepted as the twentieth century progressed. During the 1950s, 1960s, and 1970s, as Pero Dagbovie explains, historians effectively dismantled what remained of Washington's positive reputation. Today, Washington's legacy is mired in the belief that he accommodated and compromised with the Jim Crow South.[8]

Not every scholar agrees. David Jackson and Robert Norrell have each argued that, far from being an accommodationist, Washington worked smartly and strategically within the violent realities of rural Alabama.[9] To survive in the South, he navigated the complex, dangerous terrain of norms, laws, intimidation, and murder that pervaded the region. "With ruthless efficiency," explains Kirt Wilson, "violence communicated and performed the message that one's white neighbors would not accept you as an equal partner in the South's systems of power."[10] Washington's goal was not only to survive but also to thrive amid these systems of power. Black thriving, in turn, could upend white domination in the place Washington and millions of other African Americans called home.

It was a monumental challenge. Today, the Gilded Age and Progressive Era are known as the nadir period of race relations because the political and legal structures of the time hindered a strong civil rights movement. "With racial violence and racist invective against the Negro scaling new heights throughout the nation," writes Mia Bay of these years, "the black future in America looked grimmer than it had since the end of slavery."[11] This is not to say that the nadir period lacked powerful black voices. W. E. B. DuBois, Ida B. Wells, T. Thomas Fortune, Reverdy Ransom, Mary Church Terrell, and William L. Bulkley, among others, offered incisive critiques of American society. Yet these activists shared something important that did not extend to Washington. In general, prominent race leaders at the time lived in, were able to move to, or were forced to move to the urban North. Many of the great activists of the period were born in the South or in rural areas and moved to northern cities to conduct their campaigns. Fortune grew up in the rural Florida panhandle, for instance, before making his way to New York City. Wells grew up in rural Mississippi, moved to Memphis, was effectively exiled from the South, and relocated to Chicago. Ransom grew up in rural Ohio but lived his adult life in Chicago. Terrell grew up in Memphis and ultimately settled in Washington, DC. Bulkley grew up in Greenville, South Carolina, before moving to New York City. Washington, in contrast, pledged to remain in the South and to find a way to resist white domination.

Pledging to remain in the South put Washington in a bind not only because of white opposition but also because of the direction in which racial politics were headed. As race leaders and countless others moved north to escape the horrors of the South, perceptions of proper blackness shifted north as well. As Riché Richardson argues, migration to the urban North fostered "urban-centered paradigms for defining blackness," in which black political activism became closely associated with northern urban communities.[12] At the very least, perceptions of the vanguard of black leadership turned northward along with prominent race leaders. This, in turn, exacerbated already widespread perceptions of southerners, including "lazy and listless, . . . diseased or lethargic Southern bodies."[13] When combined with the new, proud, urban blackness, black southerners, especially men, came to seem either "counterrevolutionary and passive" or "pathological and deviant." Many commentators, even some black commentators, positioned "black men in the U.S. South as emasculated and unmanly."[14] Ultimately, a "cultural feminization of black men" developed during the nineteenth century. Southern black men, especially former slaves, came to represent "the preconceived limitations of black men themselves and their inability to live up to the ideals of (white) American manhood."[15]

Black migration north and the urban-centered paradigm for defining blackness pushed southern African Americans to the margins of the struggle for civil rights. On top of that, national perceptions of progress were focused on industry in the North. Northern cities in the late nineteenth and early twentieth centuries were considered the centers of the new American economy. Many Americans still idealized the rhythms of rural life, but it was in the urban North that one really tested one's mettle and proved one's ability to succeed.[16] Growth, progress, industry, wealth, and power emanated from the urban North because that was where America was headed. In contrast to the "defeated South," the nation's future was tied more or less directly to the industrial centers above the Mason-Dixon Line.[17] Thus not only blackness but also work became associated with northern urban communities. To be fully black and to make real contributions, one needed to be in a northern city, where true labor and learning, inquiry and expression, advocacy and advancement took place.

Washington saw the matter differently. He saw it from the perspective of those with whom he lived—poor African Americans in the rural

South. If they were to have a place in the new century, they needed to have a role in labor, inquiry, and civil rights. Washington devoted his work to giving them such a role. Far from trying to accommodate the Jim Crow South, Washington worked strategically to bring those African Americans who remained in the South into an intellectual populist constituency.

Spreading the Gospel of Work

Washington's biographers have told the story of his journey from slavery to Tuskegee.[18] A crucial theme of that story is the intersection of labor and learning. Born into slavery in 1856, Washington was forced to work almost immediately, but he seized whatever educational opportunities came across his path. He worked around the home of his owner, James Burroughs, and his work included carrying the schoolbooks of one of Burroughs's daughters. This afforded him an early glimpse into formal schooling. Shortly after emancipation, he and his family moved to West Virginia, where he worked alongside his stepfather in the salt mines and learned to read and write basic figures related to barreling the salt. He also worked in the home of Mrs. Viola Ruffner, who taught him unflagging dedication to cleanliness and to literacy and even helped him start his own personal library in a small dry-goods box.

Eventually Washington matriculated to a school for newly freed slaves known as the Hampton Institute. The institute's curriculum offered students the usual academic subjects—literacy, algebra, physiology, botany, Bible, music, history, oral and written rhetoric—but it required that they labor for their education. Instead of paying tuition, most students worked the school grounds—sowing and reaping on the farm, constructing and maintaining buildings, cooking and cleaning, and packaging and selling goods in nearby markets. Washington worked as a janitor while learning the careful process of "scientific agriculture."[19] After graduating from Hampton, he spent a few years teaching school, including at Hampton, and then received an offer to start a school in

Tuskegee, Alabama. Staying with what he knew, he made labor and learning the school's cornerstone, as I will discuss later in the chapter.

In addition to labor and learning, the art of rhetoric played a key role in Washington's maturation. From an early age, he seemed to understand the way suasory speaking and writing could advance himself and his community. He learned pronunciation, syntax, and delivery while working for Viola Ruffner. At Hampton he took formal classes in rhetoric and elocution, he studied the speeches of famous leaders, he participated in the school's debating society, and he was chosen as graduation speaker for his class. As an elementary school teacher in Malden, West Virginia, where he had returned after graduating from Hampton, he started a new debating society with the students, and he delivered numerous public arguments to black voters about why Charleston should become the capital of West Virginia.[20]

Given his extensive rhetorical education, it is not surprising that Washington became a preeminent orator. But it is surprising that oratorical skill has become a black mark on his legacy. As Andrew King explains, "Washington has been faulted for communicating his vision too seductively, and for helping to legitimize the old racial etiquette of deference, a style of courtship still common in many areas of the South."[21] Even scholars of rhetoric purport that Washington's eloquence covered the unfortunate compromise of his leadership.[22] Yet this line of criticism overlooks what went into Washington's public address. To understand that, and to understand the resistive coalition he created across the South, we need to understand the careful coordination that structured and surrounded almost every speech he delivered. What appeared to placate southern racism was actually a strategic masking of his push for black empowerment. His words were designed not to acquiesce but to infiltrate and upend racist, exclusionary, violent southern (and northern) culture. So strategic were his efforts that we might even revisit Washington's reputation as the "Wizard of Tuskegee." A better sobriquet, at least when it comes to his oratory, would be "General." General Washington's success had less to do with magic than with leading a small army in a campaign to foster a populist revolution.

After starting Tuskegee, Washington was on the road for about half of every year. This meant leaving Tuskegee with lieutenants he could trust. His chief lieutenants were Emmett Scott, his personal secretary and closest confidant; John Washington, his brother and director of many vocational training operations at Tuskegee; and Margaret Murray Washington, his third wife, "Lady Principal" of Tuskegee, and campus coordinator while he was away. Sometimes these lieutenants traveled with Washington, especially Emmett Scott and Margaret Washington. But when Washington was on the road and they were at the school, they ensured his continual influence, informing him of issues on campus, of decisions that needed to be made, of resources the school required. Whenever he needed to weigh in—about a student making poor choices, about a teacher making poorer choices, about the work that needed to get done—he shot off letters, telegrams, and postcards from trains, hotels, and the homes of friends, all to ensure that Tuskegee continued to operate as it should.[23] Often, these letters, telegrams, and postcards came down to one thing: work harder and smarter.[24]

While trusted lieutenants ran Tuskegee in his absence, Washington also traveled with a small battalion. This battalion included Charles Fearing, one of Washington's secretaries; Warren Logan, treasurer of Tuskegee; John H. Palmer, registrar; and Richard Leroy Stokes, another secretary. Washington's chief lieutenant on the road was Nathan Hunt, traveling secretary and stenographer. Present at countless orations, Hunt used a portable typewriter to keep an accurate, though often excerpted, record of what Washington said. He seldom transcribed every word of Washington's speeches, often leaving out thanks to local organizers, oft-told anecdotes, and pleas for donations. He did, however, record the main ideas, recognizing that Washington's work was of historic importance.

The small battalion that traveled with Washington supported the General in other ways as well. Hunt and the other traveling secretaries constantly corresponded with lieutenants at Tuskegee to ensure that Washington's speaking engagements ran smoothly. This included having supplies—reinforcements of paper, envelopes, postcards, and letterhead—shipped to the hotel or post office at which the army would arrive next.[25] In addition, because Washington's commitments could quickly change while on the road, the traveling battalion regularly sent messages to Tuskegee to coordinate the campaign. "Mr. Washington is to speak in Boston, March 21st for the Paint and Oil Club," wrote Charles Fearing to Emmett Scott on January 8, 1912. "He can leave Boston that same night, and can leave New York the morning of March 22nd for Bloomsburg, Pa., and can speak that same night for Prof. Albert. He can leave Bloomsburg the morning of March 23rd. He has nothing scheduled after March 21st until April 5th at which time he is to be at Selma, Alabama."[26] Six weeks later, Washington's calendar had filled up even more. During March, April, and May 1912, he spoke in nine cities in New York, six cities in Pennsylvania, and six cities in Ohio.[27]

But the number of cities Washington visited during a particular speaking tour conveys only part of the campaign. He often spoke on multiple occasions in a single day, sometimes in different cities. His typical schedule meant arriving in a town shortly before a speech, delivering the address, and then heading back to the train station so he and his staff could move to the next locale. The details of one speaking tour in Michigan provide a glimpse into the highly structured, coordinated efforts of Washington's oratory. On Monday, October 14, Washington left Detroit at 8:25 a.m., arrived in Ypsilanti at 9:05, and spoke at the State Normal School at 10:30. After lunch with the president of the school, Washington departed at 1:35 p.m. and arrived in Ann Arbor at 2:45. He spoke before a meeting of several Ann Arbor churches at 4:00, and then left Ann Arbor at 5:57, arriving in Jackson at 7:15. He addressed a meeting of several Jackson churches that night, and he stayed at a hotel there. The following day he traveled to Kalamazoo and delivered two speeches, one in the morning and one at 8:00 p.m. On Wednesday, October 16, he left Kalamazoo at 7:25 a.m. and arrived in Lansing at 12:38 p.m. At 2:00 he spoke to a group of local businessmen in the auditorium of the YMCA. Then at 3:30 he boarded a train for Grand Rapids, where he arrived at 5:20. He spoke to a meeting of several downtown churches at 8:00, followed by an address to local African Americans at 9:50. Then it was on to Alma and Saginaw the next day, followed by Grand Haven and Muskegon the day after, along with a stop in Pontiac on Saturday, October 19. On Sunday, October 20, he spoke at four different locations in Detroit—First Presbyterian Church at 10:30 a.m., the YMCA at 3:30 p.m., Woodward Avenue Presbyterian Church at 7:30, and a black church at 9:50.[28]

Not only were the campaigns carefully coordinated, but individual stops were also structured for maximal effect. Advance publicity of a Washington oration was sometimes handled by Tuskegee, sometimes by the local venue or sponsoring organization, and sometimes by a combination thereof. Regardless of who handled it, the publicity boasted of a historic event, with Washington's name boldly printed for easy identification. One broadside declared, "The First Opportunity For the People of Jacksonville to hear Booker T. Washington, the Greatest Negro in America, at Park Opera House, Sunday, Jan 2, '98, at 8:30 O'clock P. M." Below a photo of Washington and a letter of endorsement from Grover Cleveland, the flyer insisted that "None of Our Citizens, white or colored, can afford to miss hearing this Great Man."[29] Bethel Church issued a broadside promising something "Never Heard Nor Seen Before"—an "able lecture from Prof. B. T. Washington, on May 19, 1902, in the Opera House." Attendees would also be able—for only ten cents—to gaze at a "barrel cake just as large as a flour barrel. Having seven candle sticks around it. Oh! what a beautiful sight it will be."[30] Another broadside publicized an appearance by "The Most distinguished Man of his Race, The Most Popular Orator in America, Booker T. Washington." The cost of attending the event was twenty-five cents for general admission and fifty cents for reserved seats, with upward of "four thousand people" expected. It was to be the "Greatest Meeting of the Races ever held in the South."[31]

Such was the pomp and circumstance of a Washington appearance—feverish publicity, prominent citizens in attendance, introductory remarks, music, and, finally, a lecture from Washington. After the lecture, listeners could make a donation to Tuskegee using the handy "form of bequest" included with every program.[32] All of it was conducted with a precision designed to rally listeners around Washington's populist program.

By almost any measure, these campaigns succeeded. After an 1899 address in New Orleans, for instance, the *Daily Picayune* praised the way Washington drew his audience into the speech: "Slow and deliberate in the incipiency of his discourse, he gradually warms up and quickens his utterance and, in the midst of his discussions, becomes a pleasing raconteur, illustrating his convincing arguments with apt anecdotes."[33] After a 1901 address in Spartanburg, South Carolina, arranged by the white president of a local bank, *The Freeman* celebrated the fact that blacks and whites in the city filled the auditorium together, with more than five hundred people of both races turned away at the door. In fact, "The ovation tendered this representative of the race was one such as has been tendered no lecturer who has ever come to Spartanburg."[34] After a 1906 address in Kansas, the *Topeka Plaindealer* marveled that "every inch of space was occupied" in the pavilion for the speech, with countless people turned away. The "solution Washington urges with such adroitness, with such dramatic fervor and yet with such simple and convincing earnestness," wrote the paper, makes it "almost impossible for one who hears him to doubt that Dr. Washington's method will succeed."[35]

From the great cities along the Atlantic to the hamlets of New England to the flourishing industrial areas of the Midwest to the towns of the Mountain West to the sprawling Pacific coast—and, of course, throughout the scorching South—Washington told the story of Tuskegee in a remarkably consistent, compelling way. It was, as we shall see, a populist story told through the rhetoric of work.

Washington's Rhetoric of Work on the Road

Washington's rhetoric elevated the idea of work to something more than menial labor, something greater, something loftier. He preached of work that wedded brains, souls, hands, and arms into a resistive force. At the same time, he wove discussions of work with appeals to dignity, freedom, intelligence, strength, and pride. Such appeals helped counteract the kinds of work African Americans had been forced to undertake during their enslavement. As Washington often insisted, there was a big difference between "working" and "being worked."[36] This notion of "working" formed the centerpiece of the intellectual populism he proffered, which we can grasp by analyzing three dimensions of his speeches: the way he hailed "the people," the way he identified the status quo, and the way he called for the empowerment of African Americans in the rural South.

HAILING THE PEOPLE

Populist discourse encourages "the people" to come together, not because "the people" is a preexisting group but because disparate individuals identify as "ordinary people" and can unite with those of a like mind.[37] In touring the country on behalf of Tuskegee, Washington spoke to individuals who recognized their shared, marginalized position in the white-controlled world. If they could see themselves as "the people," as heirs to the American experience, they could stake their claim in the nation's future.

In hailing the people, Washington regularly insisted that he worked on behalf of the masses. As he explained to an audience in Washington, DC, in 1905, he did not need to concern himself with "the exceptional man," for the exceptional man could make his own way in the world. Instead, "I concern myself about the masses"[38]—whom he elsewhere called "the masses of the people in the Black Belt of the South."[39] These individuals, he insisted in an 1893 address to the New York Congregational Club, were the same people who suffered under slavery and now faced "industrial, mental, and moral slavery."[40] Hoping to lead them out of the new slavery, this Moses of the Progressive Era explained that the "masses of people" thrive in "an out-of-door life, an agricultural life," the kind of life he was trying to cultivate in the rural South.[41] That was why the masses needed to join him at Tuskegee—an institution, he declared in Atlanta in 1908, that had "kept in mind the actual needs and condition of the masses of the Negro people. We have tried as best we could to study their condition and their needs and then adapt our educational system and efforts to meeting and improving these conditions."[42] Speaking to, for, and with the masses of the Black Belt of the South, Washington beckoned oppressed individuals who yearned for a life of peace, prosperity, and freedom.

The Black Belt of the South was appealing to Washington because it afforded African Americans the space—literally—to create what they needed to thrive. He firmly believed that the land, resources, and opportunities of the South enabled African Americans to produce the goods, the wealth, and the communities that would secure their future. In populist vernacular, the South offered the masses the chance to reclaim their status as producers of the nation's wealth; only this time, unlike during slavery, they could retain the fruits of their labor. One of the central ideas of the political populist tradition, "producerism" asserts that people who make the goods and produce surplus wealth ought to control society.[43] Washington spoke continually of producerism, although he couched it in educational, intellectual terms. At a high school in Springfield, Massachusetts, on March 17, 1899, he declared:

> It seems to me that there never was a time in the history of our country when those interested in education should more earnestly consider to what extent the mere acquiring of the ability to read and write, the mere acquiring of a knowledge of literature and science makes men producers, lovers of labor, independent, honest, unselfish, and above all supremely good. Call education by what name you please and if it does not bring about these results among the masses it falls short of its highest end. The science, the art, the literature, that fails to reach down and bring the humblest up to the enjoyment of the fullest blessings of our government is weak, no matter how costly the buildings or apparatus used, or how modern the methods of instruction employed.[44]

It was a bold, sweeping statement about education, the masses, and the production of knowledge. Yet it was careful and strategic. Washington limited his critique of "academic" subjects to "the mere acquiring" of knowledge, which meant that he hoped all inquiry would ultimately reach down "among the masses." This was not a challenge to academia per se; it was a condemnation of an intellectual classism that failed to help "the people" become "producers, lovers of labor, independent, honest, unselfish, and above all supremely good." With this formulation, Washington identified the masses as the mechanism by which education reached its "highest end," correcting the unfortunate shortcomings of academic professionalism.

Similar producer appeals followed Washington throughout his career. Because "no race can be lifted till its mind is awakened and strengthened," he declared in a 1900 address to a Farmer's Improvement Society, those fortunate enough to receive an education should "find employment in the cities or scatter to the four winds of the earth in agricultural communities where they can make an honorable living and where their services are needed."[45] In other words, educated African Americans should join the masses and become producers, contributing to the intellectual character of large cities and small towns. That is why, he declared in a speech in 1902, he would rather see a college graduate work as a farmer and "become a first hand producer of wealth" than see that person "become a parasite, living upon the wealth of another person, seeking uncertain and unsatisfactory livelihood in temporary and questionable positions."[46] In 1906 he called for "an intelligent and skillful producing class" among African Americans,[47] and in 1909 he insisted that every educated person ought to "put his knowledge and his skill into practical effect" in the best place for "actual work"—the South.[48]

Washington's appeals to the masses, to the producers of wealth, invited African Americans, who had long constituted the laboring force of the South, to recognize their place in the drama of the Progressive Era. The South could be theirs, leaving industrialists, labor unions, and immigrants to battle over control of the urban North. Whatever grievances African Americans had about American society, the Black Belt of the South afforded them the chance to join with like-minded people in a project of improvement and transformation. In the very places where work was once enforced through slavery, Washington promised a merger of inquiry and labor that put African Americans on more solid ground. Linked together in the rural South, they could become a populist force for racial uplift.

While Washington centered his appeals to "the people" on African Americans, he carved out an important role for white Americans as well. After all, when he spoke, he was usually raising money for Tuskegee, which meant addressing whites and blacks. "My friends of the white race," he announced in February 1900, "we are one in this country. The question of the highest citizenship and the complete education of all concerns eight millions of my people and sixty millions of yours. We rise as you rise; when we fall you fall; when we are strong you are strong; when we are weak you are weak; there is no power that can separate our destiny."[49] In this mutual rise or fall, whites had a clear role. Their job was to support education for African Americans, specifically Tuskegee, given that education was the fulcrum of progress. Almost every speech Washington delivered on his speaking tours included a plea "for current expenses," which could "be given in the form of annual scholarships or portions of scholarships. $50 pays for the education of a student for a year. $200 enables a student to finish the four year's course. Students pay their own board, partly in cash and partly in labor. Even $1 will help us."[50] Encouraging a donation was both a fund-raising appeal and a subtle gesture toward white comfort. Whites could contribute to racial progress by donating money to a school in the rural South, which would allow them to remain separate and comfortable in their northern abodes.

Appeals for money like this can sound crass, even accommodationist, but that may have been the point. Washington invited African Americans to join him in the rural South, and at the same time he suggested that whites could donate money and remain separate from the black communities he was building. In other words, he wanted to redistribute white wealth to blacks in the South, who could use it to buy land, to start their own businesses, to educate themselves and their children, and to pass on what they cultivated to future generations. In contrast, blacks in the North were limited to working for white-owned businesses and renting white-owned apartments, or purchasing homes with the help of white-owned banks. Washington hoped to end the economic scourge on his race, and he believed that white wealth was the best way to do so. By donating to Tuskegee, whites could pat themselves on the back, satisfied that they had contributed to better race relations, while Washington could use their money to unite and empower "the masses" of the Black Belt.

To be sure, Washington did not limit the responsibility of whites to monetary donations. That was certainly central to his speeches—he was a fund-raiser, after all—but the relationship between whites and blacks went beyond writing and cashing checks. Whites also had a role to play in the way they treated African Americans and had a responsibility to work for equality under the law. "Every white man in America," Washington said to a mixed-race audience in 1900, "should make an especial effort to deal justly and generously with the black race. In doing this you will not only help the Negro, but you will help yourselves."[51] In Virginia, he made his commitment to justice even clearer: "The white people can help us by seeing that the Negro everywhere gets absolute justice in the courts, that throughout the South we get rid of the crime of lynching human beings, and that every man charged with a crime has an opportunity to come before a court of justice where his guilt or innocence can be proved."[52] Washington's demand for equality and justice—key Americanisms—was just as strong as his plea for funds.

At the same time, his demand for equality and justice was part of a larger discursive movement in which he beckoned the black masses to the rural South, told whites to donate money, and then demanded equality under the law—demanded that whites treat blacks fairly. Such a progression allowed him to promote black empowerment in a way that made his demands for legal and political equality seem reasonable and proper. In short, the appearance of accommodation facilitated the appeal for justice in America. Even when it came to political rights—the right to vote, for instance—Washington was clear about where he stood:

> In regard to the ballot I repeat here what I often said in the South: As to my position, I do not approve of the Negro's giving up anything

> that is fundamental and that is guaranteed by the Constitution of the United States. It is not best for him to relinquish any rights; as would his doing so be best for the Southern white man. Every law placed in the Constitution of the United States was placed there to encourage and stimulate the highest citizenship. If the Negro is not stimulated and encouraged by just national and state laws to become the highest type of citizen, the result will be worse for the Southern white man than for the Negro.[53]

With this delicate turn of phrase, Washington turned an appeal for political rights into something close to a threat—pointing to a future that "will be worse" for whites than for blacks. If African Americans were not given what they were due under the law, he said with an imperative tone, then the situation would be bad for those who denied their rights. The syntax of if-then—preceded by praise for the Constitution and citizenship—portended a grim future for the power structure of the South. Yet that was only implied. On the face of the statement, Washington simply demanded fair play. This strategic formulation called the black masses together, gave whites an idea they could celebrate (the rule of law), and at the same time threatened the established order.

IDENTIFYING THE STATUS QUO

Key to building a populist constituency is opposing a power establishment. Indeed, individuals come to see themselves as part of "the people" because they can tie their grievances to an elite cabal that works against them. Like any populist leader, Washington spoke against the status quo, but he had to frame the opposition carefully. Because of the realities of racism and the patronage of wealthy philanthropists, he could not denounce white society writ large. Philanthropists would stop giving money, and racists might kill him. Thus even though Washington wanted to overturn the institutions that oppressed his people, he needed to identify an opposition that would secure his movement for the long term. What he identified as the status quo, then, was simple and inspired—education, or rather the established educational practices that were being forced on African Americans.

Blacks were systematically excluded from taking part in American academic structures. That changed slightly after the Civil War, and a small number of African Americans matriculated to the nation's top schools. DuBois and a few others of impressive mental acumen attended schools such as Harvard, but they were the exception. Formal education was still largely closed to the masses. In the North, schools for African Americans had been in operation since before the Civil War, but a lack of resources made educational progress a constant struggle.[54] The situation was worse in the South, where most African Americans received a haphazard education at best, largely because there was no reliable infrastructure in place to educate a newly emancipated population. There was a fairly substantive network of educational forums that African Americans had developed during and after slavery.[55] But white northerners believed this somewhat ad hoc network was not enough. As a result, during Reconstruction, many northerners flocked south and created schools that closely resembled the institutions of the North.[56] Progress remained a constant struggle, and the curriculum of these schools was ill fitting at best. Reformers taught newly freed slaves the basics of reading, writing, and arithmetic through the giants of the Western, white world. The classics, they believed, were the best way to bring poor African Americans into "civilization."[57]

Washington thought this approach to education a monstrous folly. Education, he believed, should be tied to the realities of life for the people being educated. Imposing a model of white education on a population of African Americans in the rural South was a "grave error," he insisted. Traditional pedagogical models tried "to take a Negro boy from a farming community and educate him in almost every subject in heaven and upon earth, educate him into sympathy with everything that has no bearing upon the life of the community to which he should return."[58] As he lamented in another speech, "Boys have been taken from the farms and educated in law, theology, Hebrew and Greek—educated in everything else but the very subject they should know most about."[59]

In still another speech, he lamented that there were people in the South "who could converse intelligently on Grecian history, who had studied geometry, could analyze the most complex sentences in grammar," and yet knew nothing about agriculture, health, industriousness, and the dignity of labor.[60]

Glancing over these statements, it is tempting to conclude that Washington wanted to limit African Americans in the rural South to job training, keeping them from higher intellectual pursuits. But Washington was careful to explain what he advocated: "I favor the highest and most thorough development of the Negro's mind. No race can accomplish anything until its mind is awakened. But the weak point in the past has been, in too many cases, that there has been no connection between the Negro's educated brain and the opportunity or manner of earning his daily living. There has been almost no thought of connecting the educated brain with the educated hand."[61] As he emphasized in Fort Worth, Texas, in 1898: "Industrial education does not mean that the Negro is to be limited in his mental development. The Negro, like other people, should secure all the mental development possible, but it is especially essential for a people in the present condition of the masses of the Negroes in the South to apply their education in the direction of industrial life."[62] He made the point even stronger at a black church in Washington, DC, in 1904: "I don't care where you get it, you should GET THE BEST MENTAL EQUIPMENT" possible, whether that be "in high school, in university, in college or industrial or manual training school."[63]

The urgency of these statements had everything to do with the way critics frequently mischaracterized Washington's position. Many northern urban race leaders charged Washington with opposing higher education for African Americans. Washington clarified that he opposed higher education divorced from practicalities. In that way, he was not far from other education reformers at the time, including William James and John Dewey, who spoke strongly against a "classroom" disconnected from the realities of the "street."[64] Washington made the same point, but relative to African Americans in the rural South. Opposing disconnected academics meant opposing white educational power structures. It also meant developing models of inquiry and labor that served the needs of black communities, thereby bringing "the mental strength of the masses" to bear upon "the every day, practical affairs of life, upon something that is needed to be done and something that they are permitted to do in the community where they reside."[65] As white America continued to educate black youth according to antiquated standards and practices, Washington suggested, black America could bridge labor and learning in a way that laid the economic foundation for the twentieth century.

That was one reason Washington urged African Americans to stay in the South. Although the South was home to vicious racists and horrific violence, the North was not much different. Violence was everywhere at the time. What's more, in the North, especially the urban centers, blacks remained under white control. The North meant rent, not ownership; it meant prison, not work for oneself. That was why Washington often spoke against city life at the same time he spoke against the educational status quo.[66] As he saw it, northern cities were a lot like established colleges and universities—they severed people from the needs, opportunities, and realities of their communities. Before the national conference of African Methodist Episcopal churches in 1900, for instance, he described the tragedy of the young man who receives an education and "fails to return to his father's farm," instead taking up "his abode in the city" and falling "into the temptation of trying to live by his wits, without honest productive employment." In large cities this temptation created an "idle class of our people that linger about the side walks, bar rooms, and dens of sin and misery."[67] Such denunciations of city life grew louder as the years went by. In 1906 he called cities "unhealthy and immoral environments."[68] In 1909 he condemned cities for enabling people to loaf "around the street corners" and to patronize "dens of sin and misery."[69] In 1912 he lamented that the black man living in the urban North was, "for the most part, not only ignorant but degraded. He has a weakened body and an injured soul."[70]

The cities and the educational status quo—Washington targeted both because of the kind of intellectual community he hoped to foster in the rural South. Apart from white-controlled institutions was the open land of places like Alabama, which gave blacks the chance to secure the wealth that would empower the race. As the masses grew stronger, Washington maintained, they would become capable of resisting the white establishment that ruled industry and education.

STRATEGIZING EMPOWERMENT

In place of the educational status quo Washington wanted to establish industrial education, which he advocated with all the arguments one might expect. He insisted that industrial education nurtured character and morality, hard work and frugality, honesty and accountability. It prepared African Americans to flourish as free people. These ideas pervaded Washington's oratory, calling blacks across the country to join him in a strong, cooperative, prosperous community. That community was Tuskegee. Later in this chapter I will detail the work of Tuskegee itself. For now, we need only to consider how he talked about the institution inexorably tied to his life and leadership.

In promoting Tuskegee, Washington merged the language of industrial education and the language of inquiry, which elevated the idea of labor into something far beyond menial. "At Tuskegee," he explained to an audience in Alabama in 1899, "it has been our aim to give the students intelligence, Christian character, to teach them how to make a living by becoming skilled in some industry—to do a common thing in an uncommon way—and to teach them the beauty, dignity, and civilizing power that there is in intelligent labor."[71] "Intelligence" and "intelligent labor" pushed back against the criticism that Washington promoted "menial labor" at the expense of higher affairs. In fact, he explained to an Atlanta audience in 1908, Tuskegee's advantage was blending intelligence with labor, inquiry with work, producing "results" for a world "interested in results." He continued, tying his institution to the results orientation of the Progressive Era: "Sometimes at the Tuskegee Institute in achieving these results we use the class room; sometimes a farm twenty miles from the class room; sometimes a county fair in a distant county; sometimes we use a text book on arithmetic, sometimes a trowel; sometimes a text book in grammar, or an acre of land planted in turnips."[72] Tacking back and forth between "academics" and "labor," Washington highlighted Tuskegee's balanced pedagogy, even working to erase the supposed line between the two. Tuskegee taught people a trade, a skill, how to make a living, and it taught them the same academic subjects they could learn at any college.

Like his hailing of ordinary people, Washington's presentation of Tuskegee was crafted for whites and blacks. To white audiences, he upheld labor and academics in a way that echoed the themes of industriousness, self-help, and hard work—Americanisms dominant in mainstream culture. Accordingly, the great industrialists of the North, the titans of the Gilded Age and Progressive Era, could rest assured that their donations went to worthwhile ends. But to black audiences, Washington promised individual prosperity and communal advancement. Academics and labor would not only help an individual start a farm, but also subsequently enrich a family, bolster a community, and strengthen a society. Washington often made this progression explicit, as in a 1902 speech in Boston:

> Since 1881 the Tuskegee Normal and Industrial Institute has been one of the forces where we have been trying in an humble way to bring about the readjustment of conditions in the South. We are trying to use our organization at Tuskegee of 1400 students, nearly 100 teachers and the instruction given in industrial and academic and religious branches as a means towards fitting thoughts of young men and women to earn their own living through the industries that are open to them in every part of the South, and to make of themselves such useful members of the community where they live that the white people will feel that the education of man or women is of real and potent value in helping forward the interests of the community.[73]

Educating individuals, sending them into American communities, rebuilding those communities, transforming the nation—these were central to Tuskegee's work, at least in Washington's telling. Yet notice how traditional this view of education was. Education at Tuskegee meant teaching character, hard work, morality, and similar traits to enable people to help their communities and become productive citizens. Far from being a novel pedagogical statement, it was an affirmation of the kind of education white Americans had been afforded for decades before the onslaught of academic professionalism.[74] Of course, this kind of education was novel when offered to African Americans in the rural South. But that was the point: Tuskegee was simultaneously conservative and radical—conservative for the kind of educational traditionalism it promoted, radical when opened to African Americans in the oppressive South. This radical conservatism, one of the primary appeals of intellectual populism, enabled Washington to offer progressive advancement to southern blacks while reassuring whites that Tuskegee promoted traditional values.

To make the populist promise of Tuskegee even clearer, Washington's speeches conjured images of an earlier, supposedly simpler America. He peppered his oratory with the Americanisms central to intellectual-populist discourse. For Washington, the most useful Americanisms involved images of cultivation, farming, agriculture, and the pastoral life. African Americans must "become landowners," Washington insisted.[75] They must work in "the cultivation of the soil, the saving of money, commercial growth, and the skillful and conscientious performances of every duty with which we are entrusted."[76] As he announced elsewhere, there is as much dignity in "tilling a field, in working in the shop or in the kitchen as in teaching school, preaching the gospel or writing poetry."[77] That is why, he explained, "We want a little more of the pioneer spirit, that dogged determination that will make us sacrifice, endure hardships, which will make the poor boy willing to go bareheaded, barefooted and without a coat if necessary, and stand there doggedly until he has wrung success out of the soil."[78] These pastoral images of a romantic past fused Americanisms with radical conservatism. As farmers, hard workers, determined pioneers, and successful agriculturalists, southern blacks carried on the American mythos of the past while they used those values to completely restructure the economics of the South.

Throughout his oratorical career, Washington often told stories of individuals who exemplified the radical conservatism of the American pastoral life. Some of his stories involved notable figures, such as George Washington Carver, Tuskegee's famous scientist, who shocked white farmers in Alabama by producing an order of magnitude more sweet potatoes than any of them. Those white farmers, Washington recounted, "didn't have a bit of prejudice against those sweet potatoes. They forgot all about the color of his skin."[79] In addition to stories of notable figures, Washington often told stories of ordinary black people and what they learned at Tuskegee to empower themselves and their communities. These were known as Washington's "darky" stories, and today they seem either lamentable or racist, especially given the black dialect Washington used to tell them. But it is important to remember that Washington's project was changing people's perceptions. This meant tackling the way whites saw African Americans in the rural South and presenting his people in a new light.

One oft-told "darky" story featured "Uncle Jake," an old black man who lived near Tuskegee. One day, while walking down a public road, Washington ran into Uncle Jake and his family. After Washington asked where they were headed, Uncle Jake reported: "Mr. Washington, I'm gwine to camp meeting." Washington replied that he hoped this camp meeting didn't entail "a whole week singing and eating and shouting"—that is, a week without hard work. But that's exactly what was going to happen: "You see, Mr. Washington, it's like this. It hez been about eight years ago sence I come up to Tuskegee and heered you teach our people 'bout buying land, 'an building decent houses to live in and getting somefin substantial to keep you in a rainy day, and so I got to work and hez been working ever sence that time, me and my family, and we'se bought fifty acres of land, done built a nice house and hez paid the last dollar on that property, and now, Mr. Washington, we'se shortly gwine to camp meeting!"

To underscore what this supposedly ignorant southern black man had accomplished through Tuskegee's help, Washington went into more detail about the scene. Accompanying Uncle Jake was a wagon, which he had repaired and repainted with his own hands. There were also Uncle Jake's daughters, who had attended Tuskegee and now made all their own dresses and hats. There was a basket filled with cornbread, meat, and other food, which Uncle Jake and his wife had cultivated on their land. "We'se all gwine," Uncle Jake insisted to Washington, "even the pig and the corn and the waggin and the gals and all of us is gwine to the camp meeting, and we'se gwine to sing and shout and have a good time—with money in our pockets and religion in our hearts!" The story was crude and simple, Washington admitted, but it was nonetheless a story about opportunities for "thousands of people that we are gradually reaching through these various industrial institutions, gradually teaching them how to begin down at the bottom in this simple, natural manner, and to gradually come up."[80] The story of Uncle Jake was a sly tale of how a supposedly ignorant southern black man had used the resources of Tuskegee to seize the world around him and to secure the lives and livelihoods of his family. Tuskegee taught work, which meant empowerment, which meant the chance to take a weeklong vacation at a religious camp meeting and remain prosperous.

Washington's stories were always crowd-pleasers, but they were also part of a larger argumentative strategy. The strategy was not just to speak about the value of work; it was to show how work itself could be rhetorical. That is to say, Washington maintained that work could persuade people about the value of African Americans. Uncle Jake had worked hard and displayed the fruits of his labor through his wagon, food, and family. But the point went further. As Washington saw the matter, work was just as suasory as, and probably more so than, words and arguments. Work could shape perceptions, facilitate judgments, and encourage action better than any lengthy discourse or impassioned speech. When people worked hard, owned their business, owned their home, and laid a material foundation for their advancement, Washington said at a celebration of Abraham Lincoln's birthday in 1896, "these are the kind of arguments that kill prejudice by the acre."[81] In 1899, he explained that "Object lessons that shall bring the Southern white man into daily, visible, tangible contacts with the benefits of Negro education will go further in the solution of present problems than all the mere abstract argument and theories that can be evolved from the human brain."[82] In 1905, he called on African American listeners to "present year by year to the world, tangible and indisputable evidences of our progress as a people."[83] In 1914, he elaborated on the point: "Instead of giving people opportunity to explain why we failed to build a house"—a comment about the problem of explanatory words—"let us build so many houses that the world will forget about the house that we failed to build. One big, definite fact in the direction of achievement and construction will go farther in securing rights and removing prejudice than many printed pages of defense and explanation."[84] Labor thus did the suasory work that words and pages tried to do, and it was far more successful than any oration could be. The irony was that Washington's point about the suasory power of labor came in the form of suasory words.

Irony aside, Washington told audiences across the country that work spoke through laboring black bodies and the futures they created, through the hands and arms that pushed back against prejudice. But, he reminded listeners time and again, these were the bodies, hands, and arms of learned producers—intellectuals in their own right who thought and worked for themselves and their race. By elevating labor to an intellectual practice, Washington rendered African Americans in the rural South agents in a populist movement to turn inquiry back to the land and the people who cultivated it. When inquiry was so turned, he insisted, a new day would dawn for the empowered black masses. As he stated in Knoxville in 1913: "Work more and more in these directions and neither we nor our children will be dependent upon the uncertainties of seeking for ourselves positions which no man can give nor take from us."[85] In other words, a utopia of freedom, independence, and empowerment sat on the other side of a populist uprising in the Black Belt of the South. This utopia shone as a promise in Washington's speeches, and, as we shall see in the next section, it shone through the creation and operation of Tuskegee itself.

The Rhetoric of Work at Tuskegee

The Tuskegee Institute was alive with labor. Students and teachers labored in the classroom, in the school's fields and shops, and in the surrounding community. It was all part of Washington's overarching vision of the dignity of labor and the rhetoric of work. Tuskegee benefited greatly from Washington's efforts on the public stage, and it also served as proof of the effectiveness of his pedagogy. Just as General Washington was careful, strategic, and deliberate about what he said, he was even more so when it came to running Tuskegee. The institute was Washington's populism in action, empowering ordinary people as intellectual laborers who could resist the status quo and bring a utopia into the South.

When Tuskegee started, it was a small school focused on teacher training for Alabamians. Even then, its curriculum integrated labor and learning. The school offered traditional academic courses, including language study—with special emphasis on oral and written rhetoric—arithmetic, geometry, zoology, botany, history, civics, geography, gymnastics, and vocal music. To enroll at the school, prospective students had to be at least fourteen years old and pass an entrance exam that covered basic reading, writing, and arithmetic. Once enrolled, students had to work on "a farm of one hundred acres on the suburbs of the town. . . . This farm is cultivated so as to supply labor, as far as possible, to those students unable to meet their boarding expenses."[86] Given that the vast majority of students could not afford to pay all their boarding expenses, the farm made labor central to student life. But manual labor was only part of the school's offering. Tuskegee also featured a library with over five hundred books and a reading room featuring "the best periodicals and papers" available. In addition, students could join the literary society, which provided "an opportunity for extemporaneous speaking" and for learning "parliamentary usages."[87] Speech and debate, reading and writing, laboring and learning were central to populist progress.

Although Washington regularly boasted of everything the school had to offer, Tuskegee was seldom the oasis he hoped it would be.

In *Working with the Hands*, a book Washington wrote to explain the operations of his school, he described how even his first class of students balked at the mandated labor. Shortly after the school opened its doors, Washington told the young men that they would come to know the farm not through books but through "work with their hands." Somewhat surprised and put off, the students nevertheless trudged to the job site. There they found Washington himself "present with my coat off, ready to begin digging up stumps and clearing the land." After a few hours of toil, the students realized that "it was not *my* farm they were helping to cultivate, but that it belonged to the school, in which we all had a common interest."[88] In ensuing years students still balked at farm work, especially when the male students realized female students would be watching them (and would later be joining them). But student gripes would not alter Washington's plan to teach "the intelligent use of hands and brains on the farm, not by theorizing, but by practical effort."[89]

Tuskegee's curricular blend of labor and learning quickly expanded. Five years after opening, and after the student body had more than doubled, Tuskegee offered labor opportunities in "farming, brick-making, carpentering, printing, black-smithing, painting, stock and poultry raising, and house-keeping and sewing for girls."[90] In time, female students trained for much more than domestic work, learning to be nurses, small business owners, writers, and teachers. But every career path began with one fundamental: "Work is required of all for the purposes of discipline and instruction, and of teaching the dignity of labor."[91]

By the early twentieth century, after Washington had proven an adept leader and fund-raiser, Tuskegee's curriculum ballooned academically and industrially. The school was no longer just a normal school for training teachers—in 1892 it had changed its name from Tuskegee Normal School to Tuskegee Normal and Industrial Institute. It had become an expansive institution of higher education that instructed students in a broad spectrum of subjects and vocations. The major divisions at Tuskegee included the Academic Department, the Department of Mechanical Industries, the Agricultural Department, Industries for Girls, and the Phelps Bible Training School. In addition, the school established the first hospital for African Americans in Alabama—the School for Hospital and Nurse Training—and it boasted a federally supported Experimental Research Station that spread Tuskegee ideas into surrounding rural counties. Every part of the school integrated inquiry and labor to produce students who could remake the South.[92]

On campus, students learned how seriously the school took the integration of labor and inquiry. A student who entered the academic department and studied literature, for instance, might also work in the machine shop or in the creamery. A student enrolled in a physics course might work in the carpentry shop, and a student in a chemistry course might bake bread as part of his or her work.[93] Just as students from the academic department worked in other divisions, students in the mechanical and agricultural divisions labored academically. A student studying to be a farmer might take a course in English and pen an essay on animal husbandry or dairy work. In *Working with the Hands*, Washington highlighted this approach for students studying carpentry: "Their class-room work in spelling, mathematics, grammar, and English composition comes effectively into play. They find out that a carpenter has small chance of getting ahead unless he can use his head intelligently. . . . He cannot hope to become a good carpenter unless he is also a diligent scholar."[94]

Tuskegee students lived a strict, regimented life, in line with the dictates of the General who ran the institution. Students were separated into two groups—the day-school students and the night-school students. Both groups had to work. When Tuskegee began, students in the day school worked for two hours each day, primarily on the farm, and spent the rest of their time in the classroom. This schedule proved inefficient, however, as transitioning from the farm to the classroom meant too much time wasted during the day. So Washington changed the policy. Instead of two hours per day, students spent four days in the classroom and one day laboring in agricultural and industrial projects. They also labored every other Saturday. For "a long while," Washington later recalled, students referred to the workdays as "lost days."[95] They were never as keen on laboring as Washington was.

The night-school students worked much harder than the day-school students, and they did everything possible to move from the night school to the day school. Night-school students worked every day and, after hours of toil, took classes in the evening. Given how much they worked, their labor was a boon to Tuskegee, which would "otherwise have had to pay out cash to persons not connected with the institution." Although he understood the labor value of the night-school students, Washington viewed them as engaged in the same intellectual project as the day-school students: "In real sound growth and the making of manhood, I question whether the day student has much advantage over the student in the night school. There is an indescribable something about work with the hands that tends to develop a student's mind."[96] Whether day-school or night-school students, they all labored as part of Washington's effort to remake the South.

In addition to laboring, all students were expected to behave like gentlemen and gentlewomen. Cards and dice were strictly prohibited, as were alcohol and tobacco. "Low or profane language," as the school's catalog made clear, subjected "a student to severe discipline. Students are liable to reprimand, confinement, or other punishment." Any kind of courtship between male and female students was off-limits. Moreover, female students were "not permitted to leave the grounds of the Institute unless accompanied by a lady teacher."[97] No similar prohibition applied to male students. Yet all were forbidden from participating in political meetings. Tuskegee would not become—at least outwardly—a politically directed institution. Given that Washington was trying to foment a resistance to white domination without roiling the white establishment, forbidding overt political meetings was an effective way to avoid potentially detrimental attention.

The regimentation of mealtime provides a revealing glimpse into the behavioral code that governed student life. As Washington explained in *Working with the Hands*, "One thousand students assemble three times a day in the main dining-hall. They take their seats without confusion or noise. A line of young men and women face each other at each table, and over them presides a student host and a hostess. The young women are seated first, and then the young men march in. But no conversation is allowed until all are seated and until after a simple grace is chanted by this chorus of a thousand voices." While the description of mealtime suggests a military paternalism on Washington's part, he believed this degree of order and discipline set his school apart. Not only did it teach "self-restraint," "good manners," and "personal responsibility," but it also suggested a student body more advanced than white bodies in the North. "Behavior takes care of itself. It is not long since I read of riotous scenes in the 'commons' of certain Northern universities, in which students were guilty of throwing bread and crockery around the room. This has never happened at Tuskegee and this kind of disorder in our dining-hall is quite beyond my imagination."[98]

Student behavior was itself an argument about what African Americans could be when given the chance. Specifically, they could be just as respectable—and more so, when compared to students at some northern universities—as whites. This was a fairly common argument at the time, advancing what scholars call the "politics of respectability," a term coined by Evelyn Brooks Higginbotham. The politics of respectability promoted "temperance, industriousness, thrift, refined manners, and Victorian sexual morals" as ways of demonstrating that freed African Americans and their descendants were worthy of inclusion in white society.[99] Proponents of respectability politics spoke of self-help and character, hard work and intelligence, personal hygiene and moral accountability primarily to garner "white approval," as Patricia Hill Collins writes.[100] In that way the politics of respectability could be problematic. Because it emphasized moral reform and reconfiguration of self, it eschewed the demand for structural change.[101] Because it urged conformity with the norms of white society, it reified hegemonic values and encouraged African Americans to internalize the oft-skewed perceptions held by white Americans.[102] Thus, while the politics of respectability courted white approval, it carried a distinct message for African Americans: they should act like middle- and upper-class whites, or else they would be censured according to how whites saw them.[103]

In stressing proper behavior, good manners, and character formation,

Tuskegee advanced a politics of respectability.[104] Yet it would be a mistake to align Tuskegee too closely with respectability politics, given that it was directed squarely at structural change. Tuskegee appeared to court white approval—it was well-nigh impossible to survive in the South without white approval—while teaching black southerners to undertake their own projects of betterment. What's more, as the school drew African Americans into white society, it created a space for reconfiguring the norms of that society. When Tuskegee showed southern blacks how to be citizens capable of contributing to modern, industrial society—a significant point, given how modern society had largely bypassed southern blacks—it nurtured people who could contribute to the nation's direction and even alter the nation's purposes.[105] Thus Tuskegee not only advanced a politics of respectability but also took part in what Kirt Wilson has termed the "politics of imitation," in which African Americans mimicked certain aspects of "the dominant culture to obtain a measure of independence and to establish grounds for their inclusion in the body politic." To be sure, imitation had its own limitations, but Wilson argues that it confronted white society while providing blacks some protection from the "hostile tendencies of European Americans." Imitation was a useful political strategy because it gave African Americans a way to enter American politics, moving "from slaves into citizens" and creating "a space from which blacks could resist oppression."[106]

That was why Tuskegee centered on the rhetoric of work—hard work and proper behavior drew African Americans together within the norms of white society so they could affect change, shaping perceptions of and facilitating judgments about black bodies. The ways that students behaved and worked were meant to influence the national conversation about race, citizenship, and worth. No wonder Washington gleefully showed off to visitors what Tuskegee students could do and make:

> The visitor, therefore, who wishes to inspect the Tuskegee Institute is met at the station by a carriage built by the students, pulled by horses raised on the school farms, whose harness was made in a school shop. The driver wears a trim, blue uniform made in the school tailor-shop,

> and shoes made by student class work. The visitor is assigned to a guest room in a dormitory designed, built, and furnished by the students. His bathroom plumbing, the steam heat in his room, and the electric lighting were installed by students. The oak furniture of his room came from the shops. The young woman who takes care of his room is a student working her way through the Institute. After supper, she will change her wearing apparel to a blue uniform dress and a neat straw hat, all made in the school. The steam laundry sends over to know if the visitor wishes some washing done, and girl students send it back, proud of the snowy polish of shirts and collars.[107]

The experience of student labor continued through mealtime, as the visitor consumed food produced, prepared, and served by students. All of it was possible, Washington concluded, because students had learned "the dignity of labor."[108]

Carrying out this impressive display of student labor was no easy task. It required the coordination of thousands of people, and it required lots of space—space for learning, working, living, planning, and more. During Washington's tenure leading Tuskegee, the campus was a place of ceaseless construction, and, as with other efforts at the school, students were central to the building process. They framed the buildings, masoned the bricks, installed the doors and windows, forged the tools needed for construction, sewed the interior fabrics, and worked from plans drawn by African American designers. To facilitate this massive building operation, Tuskegee opened a brickworks, a machine shop, a sawmill and foundry, and a blacksmith shop, turning the institute into something of an "industrial village" that served both the school and the surrounding community. Along the way, as architectural historian Ellen Weiss has explained, Tuskegee recreated the labor and services enslaved people had provided before emancipation.[109] Yet on school grounds, a prosperous black community controlled that labor and those services.

By the final decade of the nineteenth century, Tuskegee's reputation for sturdy architecture had spread across the South. But Robert

Taylor pushed the school's design further, transforming the campus into a world-class landscape. Taylor was the first black graduate of the Massachusetts Institute of Technology and the first black architect in the United States to receive academic certification. Washington lured Taylor to Tuskegee in November 1892, at which point he began to transform the campus. He systematized every aspect of construction with a new architecture curriculum that taught students geometry, drawing, and history. In addition, he brought together students studying to be architects, carpenters, brickmakers, and more. Eventually he coordinated the efforts of over three hundred students spread across several divisions. One of his organization's crowning achievements was the school chapel, completed in 1897. This massive, sacred structure became the center of campus life, housing the school's worship services, commencement ceremonies, international conferences, and agricultural fairs.[110]

Taylor's architectural brilliance helped realize Washington's vision for what his school could be. His landscapes, spatial designs, and classically inspired buildings spoke proudly of race progress and pride. They communicated the deep knowledge African Americans had acquired—of classical architecture, for instance—and had adapted to their situation in rural Alabama. Taylor's buildings were eloquent in their own right, argues Weiss, but they were even more impressive because they grew out of horrific racial conditions to become "monuments of creativity, devotion, and determination in the face of great odds." This message was especially important for white northerners. When white northerners visited the campus, they "would find themselves in a familiar-seeming community even though they had to travel through a dreary and dilapidated land in order to get there."[111]

Partly because northerners had to travel through a dreary, dilapidated land to arrive at the oasis of Tuskegee, Washington set about transforming the school's surroundings. In fact, Tuskegee worked just as hard cultivating the surrounding countryside as it did cultivating the land it owned. At the turn of the twentieth century, there was perhaps no institution in the United States doing a better job of breaking down the barriers that often separated college campuses and the wider community than Tuskegee. The rhetoric of work was not just for those who could earn a degree; it was a rhetoric to transform the entire region.

One way Tuskegee reached the surrounding community was by holding noncurricular events on campus. For instance, the institute held monthly gatherings for local farmers, bringing them together to discuss issues affecting agriculture and their lives in the rural South. Every year the school hosted the Tuskegee Negro Conference, which offered laborers, mostly farmers, the chance to discuss how they could "work out their salvation by the sweat of their brows in tilling the soil of the South," as Washington put it.[112] This Negro Conference included a smaller Woman's Conference, designed for women and led by Margaret Murray Washington, as well as a Worker's Conference, devoted to facilitating discussion among teachers and preachers. All told, hundreds of laborers from across the South met at Tuskegee, often in the chapel, to share ideas and to participate in a populist intellectual community. As Washington explained, the Tuskegee Negro Conference allowed farmers not only to see "what has been done at the school" and to hear "the advice of experts," but more importantly to engage in "the exchange of opinions" and in "comparing experiences in their own field of work."[113]

While this exchange of opinions covered a host of topics, the most pressing issue for attendees of the Negro Conference was debt and ownership.[114] For most of his career, Washington worked to demolish the economic structures of the South that kept black workers in perpetual debt while enriching white financiers. True to populist form, Washington detested economics that propped up owners at the expense of producers, and he created ways for African Americans to keep surplus wealth in their communities, including an organization for finance—the National Negro Business League.[115] The primary focus of his efforts was destroying the crop-lien system, which mortgaged the goods of poor black and white farmers while perpetuating a system of indebtedness from which it was well-nigh impossible to escape. Emmett Scott, Washington's closest adviser and personal secretary, once described the goal of the Negro Conferences as "the transforming of poor, ignorant, debt-accursed, soul-despairing men into property-holding, law-abiding, intelligent, and industrious citizens."[116]

While Tuskegee regularly brought local farmers and laborers to campus, it did far more beyond the campus. Because countless African Americans could not afford to travel to Tuskegee to attend workshops, Tuskegee went to them. Pamphlets, newspapers, and other publications spread Tuskegee's message of intellectual labor across the South. George Washington Carver was an especially influential source of information. As the first African American director of a federal agricultural experiment station, Carver conducted government-sponsored research on soil, crops, animals, and similar subjects.[117] He shared everything he and his team learned through pamphlet-like bulletins written specifically for rural southern farmers. These bulletins covered such topics as "How to Build Up Worn Out Soils," "Cotton Growing on Sandy Upland Soils," "Successful Yields of Small Grain," "Saving the Sweet Potato Crop," and "How to Make Cotton Growing Pay."[118] Running about fifteen pages each, the bulletins appeared several times per year to help farmers navigate the challenges they encountered.

In addition to distributing publications, the effectiveness of which were blunted by low literacy rates, Tuskegee sent people into the community for face-to-face interactions. These interactions proved pivotal for creating intellectual laborers ready for populist resistance. Tuskegee women did crucial work in the community. Often led by Margaret Washington, female students and teachers participated in weekly "Woman's Meetings," which took place Saturday mornings in the Tuskegee town square off campus. Upward of three hundred women participated in workshops on various aspects of domestic work. Their children received separate instruction and care, affording mothers much-needed respite and intellectual engagement. Tuskegee women also performed countless "home visits," traveling to individual homes to instruct residents in more efficient and effective labor.[119]

Yet the most compelling example of Tuskegee's community engagement came via the "Moveable School," or the "Jesup Wagon." The idea for the wagon was simple and brilliant. Recognizing that many rural farmers were unable to travel to campus for events or felt uncomfortable around "educated Negroes,"[120] Washington brought his campus to them. After securing a donation from Morris K. Jesup, a New York philanthropist, to build the wagon, Washington put Tuskegee students to work constructing a school on wheels. Students outfitted the wagon with everything needed to demonstrate effective farming—a plow, planter, cultivator, cotton chopper, cream separator, milk tester, butter churn, and more. George R. Bridgeforth, an assistant to George Washington Carver, was the first operator of the Jesup Wagon. Sometimes Washington himself accompanied Bridgeforth on excursions, along with a student or two. Regardless of who traveled with Bridgeforth, the Jesup Wagon undertook a kind of covert educational mission, which usually proceeded as follows: Bridgeforth drove the wagon to a rural area in Alabama and found a farmer working on his land. He then asked the farmer about his work and challenged him to a contest to see who could work more efficiently and effectively. Taking up the challenge, the farmer plowed in his usual way for several minutes. After that, Bridgeforth or one of his helpers plowed the Tuskegee way, using the tools and ideas of the movable school. Then they compared results. Inevitably the Tuskegee way won. Bridgeforth then spent hours working with the farmer on improving his labor. Others went inside the home to help wives and mothers run their kitchens more healthfully and economically.[121]

But the Jesup Wagon's agro-missionary work did not end there. After several demonstrations in a particular area, Bridgeforth often parked the wagon at some central point and hosted an "open-air meeting for farmers."[122] Attendance at these open-air meetings was sizable, bringing together blacks and whites who wanted to learn about Tuskegee's methods. Before throngs of listeners and learners, Bridgeforth and his team showed off exemplary produce, and local farmers spoke at the gatherings about their challenges and needs. Along the way, these meetings often adopted the tone of a religious revival. There was a public confession, as farmers talked about their failures with crops and finances as well as the state of indebtedness that imprisoned them. There was then absolution and redemption through the blessings of the Jesup Wagon. These meetings were done, Washington wrote, "in Sunday School fashion," as farmers were put through a "catechism" of farming based on "the gospel of Tuskegee."[123] Together, black and white Americans in rural Alabama assembled for anointment from a mobile school.

Over the years the Jesup Wagon became so popular that Bridgeforth and his team took their revivals to parts of the South only accessible by train. Given the supplies on the wagon, rail travel was difficult and often unreliable, so Tuskegee eventually persuaded the state of Alabama to apportion funds for a motorized truck that could reach distant parts of the South. Dubbed the Knapp Agricultural Truck in honor of Seaman A. Knapp, a pioneer in agricultural extension work, this new movable school carried more supplies and equipment, allowed for more demonstrations, and prompted larger revivals.[124] With the Knapp truck and the earlier Jesup Wagon, Washington found a way to miniaturize his institute and to spread his vision of labor and learning to every corner of the rural South. In turn, he hailed more and more people into his populist constituency.

The movable school, the experimental research station, the farmers' institutes, the work required of students—all of these spread the same message that Washington offered in countless speeches around the country. That message was designed to convert the masses to the Tuskegee gospel, an eminently populist gospel that empowered individuals in collective resistance against the status quo. Those who learned to work and inquire the Tuskegee way were positioned to spread the ideas further, persuading others via the rhetoric of work to join them as intellectual laborers. Individuals could change families, who could change communities, who could change the South, the race, the nation, and the future. Or so Washington promised. No longer exploitation and alienation, no longer the result of the evils of slavery, work meant black ownership, control, and salvation. When African Americans worked hard, worked intelligently, and worked for themselves, they could upend the structures of the white establishment that oppressed them for centuries. Ultimately, that was the difference between "working" and "being worked."

Conclusion

Washington's rhetoric of work transformed labor into something more meaningful than it had been for many African Americans. In his hands, work became not exploitation and degradation but a proud process of creation, opportunity, and ownership. It was a conservative view based on hard work and determination, but it was radical when applied to a population recently freed from slavery. This conservative radicalism became institutionalized at Tuskegee, a school premised on the idea that those who made things with their hands ought to direct the nation's education and modes of inquiry. The world of thought, Tuskegee suggested, should not rest in the hands of the white establishment, in the nation's existing colleges and universities, or in the cities teeming with sin and vice. The world of thought properly belonged to those who worked the fields and factories, especially in the rural South. To move inquiry forward, the nation needed to recognize work as the enlightened intellectual practice it was.

The populist utopia Washington envisioned never came to pass. Racism and Jim Crow did not vanish as Washington suggested they would. Yet Washington's populism had a lasting influence on countless people and communities, as the General sent an army into the world to demonstrate the dignity of labor. After Washington passed away in 1915, Robert Moton became president of Tuskegee. Moton continued what Washington had started, but he showed a keen interest in assessing whether Tuskegee made a tangible difference in people's lives. To that end, in the early 1920s he sent J. H. Palmer, a longtime Tuskegee staff member, around the country to interview Tuskegee alumni and to take stock of their work. Over several years, Palmer produced three lengthy volumes of alumni profiles, which offer valuable insights into how former students lived Tuskegee's legacy.[125] Perhaps most striking about the alumni profiles is the proud record of labor, ownership, and dignity they present. To be sure, Tuskegee staff crafted the profiles to present Tuskegee in the best possible light, but even if they merely reinforced the idea of the dignity of labor that Washington so often preached, they illustrated the upshot of Washington's intellectual populism on actual lives and communities. And they illustrated this legacy in more than words. Every profile also contained a photograph or two of Tuskegee alums in clean, properly tailored suits and dresses. They stood smiling outside their homes, their business, and their automobiles—all of which they owned. They assembled with their students outside the schools they ran. They proudly draped arms around family members—spouses, children, and parents—all of whom benefited because Tuskegee taught people how to work diligently and intelligently.

According to one profile, Ora F. Porter, Tuskegee class of '05, worked as a nurse in private practice in Bowling Green, Kentucky. Her success allowed her to care for her aging mother. According to another profile, Fred D. Peck, a former Tuskegee blacksmith student residing in Chicago, owned his own blacksmith and auto-repair business. He also owned his own home. Oceola Jones, another former student residing in Chicago, studied brickmaking at Tuskegee and went on to work as a brickmason throughout the Midwest. His success enabled him to purchase a building that housed three separate apartments. He lived with his family in one apartment and rented out the other two. In Richmond, Indiana, the only African American attorney in town was a Tuskegee graduate, Cornelius R. Richardson, class of '05. After completing his law degree at Howard University, he relocated to Richmond, started a private practice, and flourished. He owned a two-story home on a corner lot, in front of which he parked his two-seat automobile.[126]

Tuskegee alumni were just as prosperous and proud in the South as they were in the North. In North Carolina, Asa Herring established a cooperative society with other farmers in the area. He owned his own home and farm in the town of Clinton. Henry Patterson worked for years as a printer, the trade he learned at Tuskegee, before opening his own grocery store. He owned his own home, store, and "other valuable property."[127] Oliver Nestus Freeman was considered "one of the busy men" in the town of Wilson, North Carolina, working as a brickmason and general contractor. Along with his wife, also a Tuskegee grad, he built his own "seven room home." Tuskegee alumni enjoyed similar prosperity and ownership in Alabama. In Birmingham, Robert Mabray, class of '95, owned and operated a dry-goods store with a stock valuation at over $15,000. In the small town of Dolomite, outside Birmingham, was Green Timmons, a former student who entered Tuskegee with little ability to read or write. Given the chance, he not only learned to read and write but also learned to work and save. For years he worked as a coal and iron miner, saving enough money to purchase his own plot of land. Every year he donated $10 to Tuskegee, which he felt was "his duty."[128] In Ensley, Alabama, Andrew Belcher, Tuskegee class of '09, worked as a dentist, owning his own practice, his own home, and his own car. In Florence, Alabama, William Belcher and his wife Mattie Hatcher-Belcher, both Tuskegee alums, owned their own home and businesses. William worked as a podiatrist, serving an all-white clientele in Florence's business district, and Mattie worked as a dressmaker. In Bessemer, George Logan owned a shoe repair business; Garrison Mitchell owned a tailoring business; and Nancy Thomas-Banks, Luther Johnson, and James Bickerstaff worked as teachers for the local public schools. All were prosperous, proud, hardworking, and in control of their lives—or so the profiles suggested.[129]

To be sure, these alumni profiles were rosy depictions of life, and they emphasized the themes that Tuskegee wanted to highlight—hard work, ownership, and prosperity. Yet they depicted individuals who heeded Washington's call to resist the status quo by spreading Tuskegee's gospel of intelligent labor to their families, communities, and society. Their lives were a testament to how populist appeals could channel resistive energy in productive directions. These were black people working, not being worked.

If, as this chapter has argued, Washington worked to create a populist community by elevating labor to an intellectual practice, these alumni profiles suggest that he succeeded, at least in part. Students learned to work hard, to work smart, and to use their labor to control their lives. Their lives were a rhetorical phenomenon—a statement about the possibilities of a black intellectual culture. A similar rhetorical phenomenon emanated from the lives of American Indians in the Progressive Era, who, for the first time, were linking their grievances in a broad, proud, pan-Indian movement. At the forefront of this movement was the brilliant, eloquent, populist thinker Zitkala-Ša.

CHAPTER FIVE

Zitkala-Ša's Pan-Indian Intellectual Populism

The little girl scampered across the kitchen, and the devil followed. She had been hiding behind the stove, but the devil found her almost immediately, his glittering yellow eyes fastening upon her. The little girl threw down her toys and tried to reach her mother, who was sitting across the kitchen with a friend. Both the mother and friend watched in silence, sitting motionless, as the devil pursued the little girl. They didn't help. They just leered. Realizing she could not outrun the devil, the little girl used the stove as an obstacle, trying to keep the iron-and-fire appliance between her and the pursuing evil. But the devil was quick, and the little girl was getting tired. In a last-ditch effort to save herself, she bounded toward her mother, who remained silent, unhelpful. As the little girl collapsed at her mother's feet, the devil leaned down to seize her, his claws hungry for tender young flesh.

Then she woke up. It was only a nightmare.

Or was it? The little girl looked around and remembered she was still far from home at the white man's boarding school—separated from her family, her nation, her heritage. What's worse, the white man's school had recently taught her about the existence of this ultimate evil, this force of darkness searching the earth for unrepentant souls. Teachers had even shown her a book of Bible stories with the devil illustrated in vivid detail. Maybe the devil really was after her.

In the morning, the little girl sneaked into the school's library and found the book with the devil's picture inside. Clutching a broken pencil, she scratched out the devil's evil yellow eyes. Harder and harder she scratched, more and more, digging into the paper until the image of the devil was abraded. The page was now just a tattered hole.[1]

The little girl who used a broken pencil to scratch away the devil was Gertrude Simmons. Later in life she went by her married name, Gertrude Bonnin, or by the "Indian" name she adopted, Zitkala-Ša, which meant "Red Bird." She had a lot of names, being a Sioux woman in a white man's world. Even being a "Sioux" woman marked her in the white man's world, given that her people referred to themselves not as Sioux but as Yankton, or *Iháŋkthuŋwaŋ*, a band of Western Dakota people. At eight years old she was snatched from the reservation of her birth for supposed education and advancement at White's Manual Labor Institute in Wabash, Indiana. What she found in Indiana was not her salvation but her nightmare, and when she was old enough to speak out against the injustices of boarding schools for American Indian children, she told the world her story. In the January, February, and March 1900 issues of the *Atlantic Monthly*, Zitkala-Ša explained her early life on a reservation, her encounter with the devil (and much more) at the white man's school, and her attempt to make her way in white society.

Like countless other American Indians—a term this chapter uses interchangeably with "Indians," "Native Americans," and "indigenous people" because of the historical complexities and problems of all the labels[2]—Zitkala-Ša felt disconnected from white society, despite, or because of, her education there. But she also felt disconnected from Indian society.[3] When Zitkala-Ša returned to the Sioux reservation of her birth after years of education in white society, she felt broken and alone, even though her mother and brother still lived there. Her energy was "shattered," her "faith in the Great Spirit" was gone, and she stood on the reservation as "a cold bare pole, . . . planted in a strange earth." It was all because she pursued "the white man's papers"—that is, education.[4] Uprooted from tribal life, outcast in racist white society, Zitkala-Ša was stuck between two worlds and at home in neither.

This feeling of disconnection was common for American Indians educated at boarding schools around the turn of the twentieth century (and beyond). It resulted from what Richard Morris has termed "transformational mimesis," a process that "serves to put someone's cultural identity under erasure involuntarily or without their informed consent in the moment of acculturation by denigrating and calling into question that identity and by insisting that a readily available, 'superior' alternative identity provided by the dominant society furnishes the only means of escape for those who are 'trapped' by their heritage."[5] For American Indian children, education at the white man's boarding school was supposed to help them cast off Indian identity and become little republican, almost-white citizens, embracing the U.S. government as their benevolent father.[6] But neither "transformational mimesis" nor paternal benevolence worked out as planned. Instead of moving American Indians from "red" to "white" culture, these efforts resulted in an ideological chasm, leaving American Indians in a liminal space between Native tradition and the white world.[7]

That liminal space was devastating to generations of American Indians and to Native traditions writ large. Nevertheless, in the Gilded Age and Progressive Era, a group of Native thinkers, including Zitkala-Ša, strived to turn liminality to their advantage. Stuck between white society and the reservation, they drew tribally diverse Indians into an expansive coalition that could secure their place in the modern world. It was the first truly "pan-Indian" movement in U.S. history. Although white reformers had tried to bring Indians together while keeping them under the reformers' dictates, pan-Indianism marked the first push by indigenous people themselves to unify as American Indians. This was their own effort to unite as an antagonistic frontier, linked in an equivalential chain of grievances, and set against the white establishment. If the white establishment was going to treat all Native peoples the same—all of them were "Indians," irrespective of nation and tribe, who needed to shed their "Indianness"—then those Indians would use white perceptions to resist the very forces trying to erase their history.[8] Throughout her career, Zitkala-Ša proved adept at playing with white perceptions, all to the benefit of the populist coalition she sought to create. She performed "Indianness" in different ways for different audiences, but always with the goal of inviting other Indians to join her in reclaiming their intellectual lives.[9]

Zitkala-Ša's populist performance of Indianness centered on education—be that the boarding school experience, community centers on reservations, publications in popular periodicals, or gatherings in lecture halls across the country. Intellectual practice, she believed, was crucial for advancing American Indian causes, so she traveled the country, spoke and wrote for white and Native audiences, studied reservation life, built organizations to support American Indians, and grappled with the U.S. government. Similar to the way Booker T. Washington preached the dignity of labor to empower African Americans in the rural South, Zitkala-Ša performed Indianness to build a network of populist intellectual communities across the United States. And similar to all the intellectuals featured in this book, Zitkala-Ša worked to return power to the people—in this case, Indian people. Her performances invited other American Indians to identify their grievances with hers and to join her in a strong, broad coalition that could secure Native lives in the twentieth century.

Accordingly, this chapter positions Zitkala-Ša's work as an example of intellectual populism in response to the American Indian predicament in the Gilded Age and Progressive Era. As a populist thinker and leader around the turn of the twentieth century, she shared a sensibility and rhetorical tool kit with other intellectuals in this book. At the same time, she occupied the unique position of being an Indian woman. Stereotypes abounded regarding Indians and women in public life, and these stereotypes weighed heavily on Zitkala-Ša. Yet she discovered early that stereotypes contained a painful power that she could turn to her advantage. On the public stage she could tacitly acknowledge the stereotypes about her "to gain the attention of the people who had power over Indian lives," and she could "take the control of performance away from" her opponents.[10] Time and again, Zitkala-Ša seized on people's perceptions—however positive or negative—and used those perceptions to advance the cause of her people.

In the next section I explore the predicament Zitkala-Ša and American Indians of her generation faced. I then situate Zitkala-Ša as a writer and community builder who established a place of resistance for her race, and I explore Zitkala-Ša's work as a celebrated lecturer who played the role of Indian to redirect perceptions of Native lives. Finally, I analyze three key speeches in Zitkala-Ša's career—speeches that demonstrate her ability to upend the perceptions of various audiences to draw disparate individuals into a populist coalition. In "talking back to civilization," to borrow the words of Frederick Hoxie, Zitkala-Ša helped "define, preserve, and even stimulate faith in 'Indianness'" for generations to come.[11]

The Native Predicament

Zitkala-Ša's pan-Indian intellectual populism emerged in conjunction with three pressing issues: land, education, and the myth of the vanishing Indian. There were a host of other factors, but these issues shaped her advocacy and spurred the rise of pan-Indianism writ large.

Land had long been the crux of the conflict between the federal government and American Indians. Despite promises to the contrary, the government colonized Indian lands, even at the level of language, engaging in a "rhetorical colonialism" that brought Indian territory under the control of white discourse.[12] During the founding era, the key term among whites for Indian relations was *separation*—keep whites and reds in their own lands.[13] But then whites pushed westward and trampled the idea of separation. They soon saw Indians not as a threat to whites but as markers of land—the "source of the nation's future," as Mary Stuckey puts it.[14] As a result, the watchword became *assimilation*, with many white politicians hoping that Indians would voluntarily become "farmers and amalgamate with the white population, thus releasing wilderness tracts to white settlement."[15] Whites wanted Indians to merge with the new nation, which really meant giving up their cultures and traditions and becoming like whites. But it soon became clear that assimilation would not happen, so whites then pushed for removal, which the Jackson administration carried out with gobsmacking zeal.[16] Jackson viewed removal as a natural and inevitable part of history's unfolding, believing that if Indians put themselves in the path of this unfolding, they needed to be pushed aside (or worse).[17] Unsurprisingly, this belief led to violent clashes, broken promises, and evil profiteering out West, especially after the Civil War. Finally, many white leaders realized that removal would not do; they needed a new policy. After decades of debate, they conceived of the idea of allotment, which was codified in the General Allotment Act of 1887, otherwise known as the Dawes Act because of the efforts of Indian commissioner Henry Dawes. Although allotment sounds more positive than removal, it was just as much of a naked land grab as the earlier policy.

What allotment added, however, was a closer connection between land and citizenship than ever before. Though land and citizenship had long been linked,[18] the 1887 legislation formally, forcibly extended white society's conception of land and citizenship to American Indians. The Dawes Act took large swathes of tribal land—communally owned land—and subdivided it into individual allotments. As a result, the act effectively destroyed tribal land organization, which further undercut Indian societies already struggling.[19] Of course, that was the point of the policy all along. At one level, individual allotments would supposedly show Native people the benefits of private ownership and the habits of civilized life, moving them away from the savagery of the past and toward the shining star of U.S. citizenship. At another level, allotment would break up tribal lands so that white settlers could seize that land through a combination of payouts, corrupt bargains with local politicians, and violence.

To whites, the Dawes Act seemed the perfect solution to the Indian problem because it codified what Jason Edward Black has called "republican fatherhood." With allotment, American Indians formally became children beholden to a Great White Father in the East. As Black explains, republican fatherhood "allowed the government to teach its Native wards citizenship through the practice of cultivating the soil. Here, the republican father 'guided his children in the choice of occupational calling,' property holding, and standards of morality all through laboring upon the land."[20] Just as children must unlearn the wildness of childhood to become adults, so Indians must leave behind their identities to enjoy the blessings of citizenship. To Zitkala-Ša, this kind of imposition on Indian identity and culture from the great white establishment in the East prepared the ground for a vehement populist response.

While allotment defined the issue of land during the late nineteenth century, it intersected directly with the issue of education. If the goal was to turn Indians into faithful citizens, whites felt the need to watch over that process, unwilling to leave the republican transformation to chance. But education raised a host of questions whites were not ready to answer. What kind of education? Where would it take place? Who would run it? Three education models emerged as answers to these questions. The first model was the day school, which involved Indian children going to school during the day, usually on the reservation, and then returning to their home in the afternoon. Proponents of this model hoped that when children returned home, they would share the blessings of their schooling with tribal elders, spreading republican instruction upward through the generations. It didn't work. Day schools were too close—geographically and ideologically—to tribal life, which meant that Indian traditions persisted. The second model was the on-reservation boarding school. If the day-school model allowed too much contact with Indian tradition, the on-reservation boarding school would keep kids close to family members, but always under the watchful eyes of white teachers. Again, it didn't work, as Indian children remained too connected to tribal life.[21]

In response, the third model completely removed children from the reservation, placing them hundreds of miles from home in off-reservation boarding schools and supposedly severing their connection to Indian heritage. The architect of the off-reservation boarding school model was Richard Henry Pratt, who created, with the help of Congress, the Carlisle School in Carlisle, Pennsylvania. The school officially opened on November 1, 1879, and became the model for dozens of off-reservation boarding schools in the coming years.[22] The off-reservation model served as the primary educational means for white America to fulfill Pratt's dictum to "kill the Indian, and save the man."[23] Many white reformers viewed this model as a smashing success.[24] But to countless Indian children, it was another failure—the most traumatic failure of all—because it destroyed their place in Indian tradition without connecting them to white society. For Zitkala-Ša and countless others, this state of limbo was a key motivation for building a pan-Indian coalition that could retake control of Indian lives.

Both land and education in the late nineteenth and early twentieth centuries were weapons that the white establishment used to destroy American Indians—at least as they existed in the white imagination. Take away tribal land and make Indians free-market, private-property-holding entrepreneurs. Send them to school far from their tribal home and teach them to think like civilized whites. In time, many whites believed, the Indian race would vanish. Thus emerged the myth of the vanishing Indian, which captivated public attention for decades, stretching back to Thomas Jefferson and even earlier.[25] Not everyone applauded the idea—poets had long lamented the vanishing Indian—but many accepted it as a fact in the course of history.[26] The end of the Indian was inevitable and rapidly approaching, which was yet another reason for whites to seize and work their land.[27] The impending end of the Indian was purportedly confirmed when government-backed anthropologists headed out West and proved "scientifically" that Indians would soon disappear.[28]

Despite predictions of extinction, the Native population actually grew after 1900. It had been on the decline in the nineteenth century, but the early twentieth century saw a gradual increase in population that continued for generations.[29] The low point in the Native population during this era was 1890, when the U.S. Bureau of the Census counted around 240,000 American Indians. By the middle of the twentieth century, that number had grown to over 500,000.[30] It was as though predictions of vanishing brought visibility to Indian culture and tradition. It was certainly the case that Indian intellectuals used the upheavals of the Gilded Age and Progressive Era to begin their own movement for recognition. Indeed, as Frederick Hoxie writes, the work of Native intellectuals during this time period "placed America's claim to represent 'civilization' under sharp scrutiny while at the same time emphasizing the positive aspects of Native American cultures. These Native efforts affected popular literature, college and university curricula in anthropology and sociology, and legal scholarship that sought to locate the role of tribal governments in the nation's Constitution."[31]

Zitkala-Ša was at the forefront of these efforts, as we shall see below, but she was not alone. Along with such figures as Charles Eastman and Carlos Montezuma, she participated in a loose-knit coalition of Indian intellectuals who sowed the seeds of what would become the Red Power movement. As Robert Allen Warrior demonstrated in his pivotal book on Indian intellectuals, this was "the first coming together of a generation of Native writers" for "common, or at least similar, political projects." In the end, argues Warrior, their achievements were mixed, largely because they attempted to court white reformers while neglecting to build ties with other oppressed peoples.[32]

While Warrior faults the reform strategy of the first pan-Indian generation, other scholars have found more to admire. In *Citizen Indians*, Lucy Maddox positions Zitkala-Ša alongside other members of the Society of American Indians who lectured, wrote, and organized for Indian progress. Their work, she argues, pushed a four-part platform: inserting the Native perspective and "indigenous intellectual tradition" into the historical record, bridging the divide for Native people between on-reservation and off-reservation life, supporting the "precarious position of Native elders as the carriers of traditional knowledge," and performing "Indianness" for whites.[33] This notion of performing Indianness is central to Kiara Vigil's treatment as well. In *Indigenous Intellectuals*, Vigil analyzes the work of Eastman, Montezuma, Luther Standing Bear, and

Zitkala-Ša, all of whom publicized the plight of American Indians by seizing upon and redirecting white perceptions of Indian culture. Yet Zitkala-Ša had a distinctive place in this group, writes Vigil, because she had to assert "her own ethnic female literary identity, while gesturing toward broader categories (Indian and American) to speak for *and* to large groups of people."[34] In short, she had to perform Indianness, womanhood, and intellectual respectability at the same time.

Jessica Enoch has made a similar point, but she has linked Zitkala-Ša to non-Native thinkers struggling with womanhood and intellectual respectability in other contexts. In *Refiguring Rhetorical Education*, Enoch links Zitkala-Ša's work to the efforts of African American and Hispanic educators to show how women appropriated and adapted the norms of rhetorical culture for their own communities. In the case of Zitkala-Ša, Enoch shows how her early public writings challenged the viability of Native schooling, especially the Carlisle School, while combating the gender role imposed on her. In that way, argues Enoch, Zitkala-Ša exercised a kind of "rhetorical sovereignty" to offer a "more complex narrative that details the devastating effects" of off-reservation boarding schools.[35]

Enoch's work shows how Zitkala-Ša participated in an intellectual movement beyond the Native community. Yet her analysis is limited to Zitkala-Ša's early writings for the *Atlantic Monthly*. As a result, we lack an account of Zitkala-Ša's subsequent advocacy, which shifted rhetorical strategies for different audiences and went so far as to support Carlisle and to work alongside Pratt.[36] It is important, therefore, to understand the sweep of Zitkala-Ša's career, especially the way she performed Indianness differently in various contexts. Building a pan-Indian community, her career suggests, hinged on careful navigation of stereotypical perceptions regarding Indians, women, and inquiry. It also hinged on the symbolic resources of intellectual populism.

Creating Indian Community

Zitkala-Ša's *Atlantic* publications vaulted her into the national spotlight. Newspapers took note of what seemed to be her "rare command of English and much artistic feeling."[37] They deemed her "a striking example of the wonders being accomplished through education in the Indian race,"[38] and "probably the most accomplished young Indian woman to be found anywhere."[39] With this coverage, she had a national platform for public engagement.

It did not hurt that she had moved to Boston, where the *Atlantic* publications made her something of a literary celebrity. In Boston, she could hobnob with great writers and thinkers, and she could pursue her other passion: the violin. At the same time she wrote for popular periodicals, she studied violin and performed for audiences across the country and overseas. She even traveled and performed with the Carlisle School Band—the band from the school she had recently chastised in one of the nation's premier periodicals.[40] Still in her early twenties, she stood before the American people "an esteemed contributor to the *Atlantic Monthly*, a rare violinist, an aggressive member of Boston's literary set."[41]

Then she got sick of it all and decided to go back west. In spring 1901, longing to be among people who looked like her and cared about similar causes, Zitkala-Ša moved to the Devil's Lake Sioux Reservation in North Dakota. She remained involved in literary culture, publishing articles about Indian ideas, lives, and traditions in *Harper's Monthly*, *Everybody's Magazine*, and the *Atlantic*.[42] In addition, she published the book *Old Indian Legends*, which collected many of the stories she had heard as a child.[43] While she continued writing, she also focused on her personal life, reconnecting with a beau she had met years before, Raymond Bonnin. In 1902, they married and began a long life together in the public eye.

Shortly after marriage, Raymond Bonnin accepted a job offer from the Office of Indian Affairs on the Uintah and Ouray Reservation in Utah, home to the Northern Ute Indian tribe. Because both Zitkala-Ša and her husband were Sioux, living and working among the Utes posed significant cultural obstacles. Yet they were determined to make a difference among fellow Indians. While Raymond Bonnin worked at the Office of Indian Affairs, Zitkala-Ša took a job teaching at an on-reservation school—the Uintah Boarding School at Whiterocks, which was modeled on the kind of education offered at Carlisle.[44] At the school, Zitkala-Ša launched a music program and created a children's band that performed on the reservation. She also served the elder Ute population by teaching classes out of her home on basket-weaving, hygiene, and other subjects.

These classes were the beginning of Zitkala-Ša's community-building efforts—not the imagined communities she had hailed through her *Atlantic* publications, but actual groups of people gathering to learn, teach, discuss, and deliberate. The classes were also directed at a populist style of inquiry, as they rebuffed the intellectual norms of white society to create a resistive, alternative community among people often marginalized in the pursuit of knowledge. As this community grew into a thriving hub of Indian intellectual engagement, Zitkala-Ša advanced what Jace Weaver has called "communitism"—or "proactive commitment to Native community" for "the healing of the grief and sense of exile felt by Native communities and the pained individuals in them."[45] In Zitkala-Ša's work, communitism was an intellectual practice, focused on the exchange of ideas, culture, and assistance to bind together those whom the white establishment had displaced.

The growth of this community was remarkable, forcing Zitkala-Ša to confront the same problem Thomas Davidson had confronted at the end of the nineteenth century—the need for space. Given interest across the reservation, the group quickly surpassed the space afforded by her home, where members originally assembled for discussion, reading, lessons, and laughter. Zitkala-Ša explored a number of possible meeting sites, and she was finally able to commandeer an empty warehouse at Fort Duchesne and to turn it into a community center for the whole reservation.[46] In community, Zitkala-Ša and the people on the reservation linked their grievances together in a new pursuit of knowledge.

Participants at the community center undertook a number of projects to improve themselves, to serve their neighbors, and to advance their race through inquiry and conversation. Zitkala-Ša documented these projects in an article for the *American Indian Magazine*, a publication of the Society of American Indians, the preeminent pan-Indian organization at the time. Titling the article "A Year's Experience in Community Service Work among the Ute Tribe of Indians," she not only publicized her work but also inspired groups on other reservations to take up similar efforts. An especially notable aspect of the article was Zitkala-Ša's positioning of community work not as a social service but as an intellectual affair for everyone involved. For instance, she described the storytelling practices of her sewing group by explaining how members engaged one another while they worked: participants shared "funny little stories. . . . With laughter they stitched away upon the article in hand." They also participated in "practical demonstration in domestic science" as "women learned improved methods of preparing food in their own homes" and as "Indian men hauled the wood and cut it up for us."[47] "Practical demonstration in domestic science" positioned Ute women as investigators who could contribute to the advancement of knowledge that was both scientific and useful. Their conversations, ideas, and skills brought participants into a culture of learning that stood apart from white overseers whom the Bureau of Indian Affairs sent to the reservation.

Yet the intellectual character of the community center went further, according to Zitkala-Ša. In describing semiregular community meetings she deployed the language of collective inquiry, positioning Ute men and women as thinkers, speakers, and intellectual agents:

> Our programs were both instructive and social. We spent part of the evening in a study of local conditions. We read papers upon selected subjects. We argued in favor of sending all Indian children to school. We talked also of the innumerable benefits to a tribe that held its annual fairs. We mentioned here the good work started by the Commissioner of Indian Affairs in emphasizing the vital importance to the future race, by the saving of the babies. We encouraged co-operation in this, for it was so unmistakably in the right direction. The evening's discussions were interpreted with music and readings in a lighter vein.[48]

In an old warehouse, Zitkala-Ša and residents of the Ute reservation studied, read, argued, talked, and discussed. They created music and literature. They laughed and they thought. What's more, they took the work started by the commissioner of Indian Affairs and made it their own, recreating the meaning of that work in lighthearted "music and readings" that were distinctly Ute.

All of this happened on a shoestring budget that ultimately served "the uplift of the race."[49] Zitkala-Ša took particular pride in the way her group used its meager resources to help and support tribal elders. She explained, "We have awakened, in the midst of a bewildering transition, to a divine obligation calling us to love, to honor our parents. . . . It is our first duty, it is our great privilege to be permitted to administer with our own hands, this gentle affection to our people. There is no more urgent call upon us."[50] With "our own hands"—language that could have come straight from a speech by Booker T. Washington—Zitkala-Ša and her associates ministered to the elders of the tribe, helping the entire community navigate "a bewildering transition." This was the transition of allotment, of the push for preservation, of industrialism, of widespread migration from rural settings to city life—in short, the transitions of the Progressive Era, which threatened reservation life in painful, disruptive ways. Yet the community center empowered Utes anew, and Zitkala-Ša hoped other reservations would undertake similar projects. Through "practical systematic effort" and "a bit of kindness and true sympathy," she concluded, other tribes could replicate the success of the Ute experience.[51] Just as Washington hoped for a proliferation of Tuskegees across the South, forming a network of populist institutes, Zitkala-Ša hoped for community centers of intellectual resistance across Indian lands.

That did not happen. She wanted it to, and was prepared to replicate the community center by traveling to other reservations and working with different tribes. But at the same time she was pulling people together for collective inquiry, something else was tearing them apart: peyote. During the 1910s, Zitkala-Ša became one of the chief opponents of peyote use, which pitted her against a range of pro-peyote forces, including many in the Society of American Indians.[52] Supporters of peyote argued that the substance was central to Native culture and beliefs. Samuel Lone Bear, for one, traveled to many reservations preaching about the importance of peyote for religious rituals and for health (while also using peyote to seduce and impregnate teenage girls).[53] Zitkala-Ša did not buy it. Growing up in the Dakotas and now living on the Ute reservation, she saw peyote as a foreign drug, not a part of Indian tradition. Although tribes in what is now the American Southwest had been using peyote for hundreds of years, it was not introduced to the Ute people until the 1910s.[54] To fight this invading menace and to secure the intellectual future of her people, which, she believed, peyote threatened just like any hard drug, she turned to the lecture stage.

Traveling to reservations across the West, she spoke on the demoralizing, debilitating use of a drug that, she said, harmed women, families, and communities. In 1916 she published a pamphlet version of her anti-peyote lecture called *The Menace of Peyote.* The pamphlet presented many of the ideas she had affirmed on the lecture stage in the form of talking points Native women could use in their own communities to repel the drug. For instance, she noted that peyote started in the American Southwest but only recently spread to northern tribes. To emphasize the threat it posed, she linked her efforts to the temperance movement, labeling peyote "the twin brother of alcoholic beverages and first cousin to habit forming drugs."[55] Then Zitkala-Ša went after the religious argument for peyote. To denounce the idea that peyote was a sacrament in Indian religion, she insisted that "rituals of the church have been borrowed as a cloak to hide under, and to evade the law of morals and decency." She argued that peyote did not enhance religion but undermined it, resulting in "midnight debaucheries" and "a total abandonment of virtue."[56] It was the argument of a practicing Catholic, the religion to which Zitkala-Ša had converted after returning to western reservations from Boston, but it spoke directly to mothers, wives, sisters, and daughters. Zitkala-Ša concluded the pamphlet by arguing that peyote use threatened nothing less than Indian progress in the modern world: "The human system, disabled with dope, is no receptacle for the jewels of education and civilization. The Indian is no exception."[57] For Zitkala-Ša, building intellectual community required care for one's mind, which, in turn, promoted "civilization," even citizenship, for American Indians.

Though brief, *The Menace of Peyote* is the fullest surviving account of Zitkala-Ša's anti-peyote lectures. Most of her lectures were not preserved, which is unsurprising given the lack of documentation surrounding most Native discourse.[58] Yet the fact that she stood against peyote by lecturing and publishing indicates how important rhetorical engagement was to the populist intellectual communities she wanted to build. To get a fuller sense of her work as a lecturer, however, and to understand how she used the public stage to advance pan-Indian intellectual populism, we need to consider her work in the 1920s speaking under the auspices of the General Federation of Women's Clubs (GFWC). More than any other aspect of her career, Zitkala-Ša's lectures for the GFWC reveal her ability to play with public perceptions in the service of a resistive movement.

Public Lectures, Popular Perceptions

The GFWC was formed in 1890 as a network of organizations promoting women's intellectual engagement. Local clubs sprang up in small towns and large cities to facilitate work in the arts, environmentalism, health, civics, and international affairs. Middle- and upper-class white women comprised most of the clubs, but Zitkala-Ša saw an opportunity for Indians as well, insofar as white women could advance Native causes.[59] Speaking at the 1921 GFWC convention, she "described the pitiful plight of the Indian on his reservation without citizenship. She told of his response to the recent call to arms and pleaded that the women of America turn their attention to the first American and attempt to Americanize the Indian."[60] By the early 1920s, such calls to Americanize immigrants, foreigners, and nonwhites had become commonplace in American society.[61] Yet in the precarious push for Americanization, Zitkala-Ša saw opportunity for her people, especially on the road to citizenship. Many American Indian leaders condemned the push for citizenship as relinquishing their centuries-long fight against white invaders. But Zitkala-Ša made a pragmatic calculation that citizenship could bolster the claims of her people, and she enlisted the GFWC in this effort. Because of her prompting, the GFWC created an Indian Welfare Department and arranged for Zitkala-Ša to lecture to "2,000,000 organized women in the General Federation to work through their fifty state units which include 48 states, the District of Columbia and Alaska federations, for enfranchisement of the Indian people."[62]

Through this arrangement, Zitkala-Ša delivered hundreds of sponsored lectures across the country, and her public visibility grew accordingly. Her project, she later recalled, was "crystalizing public sentiment in favor of Indian citizenship."[63] This involved, among other speaking engagements, a "tour of Southern States" in 1922 and "speaking before men's and women's clubs" across "Iowa, Indiana, Michigan, and Ohio" in 1923. Her theme was always "Indian citizenship and justice."[64] Wherever she went, writes Lewandowski, "she had little trouble charming her hosts and the journalists sent to cover her appearances."[65] Unfortunately, coverage of her appearances seldom included coverage of her arguments. Newspapers routinely covered the fact of her lectures: an Indian woman was speaking to women's clubs. But they often passed over her appeals, save for a mention of the talk's topic. This lack of attention to what she said was common for Indian speakers in the nineteenth century and beyond; little effort was given to recording and preserving Indian discourse.[66] Exacerbating the problem, most of Zitkala-Ša's personal papers were destroyed before they could be preserved in her collection at Brigham Young University.[67] Thus, despite her hundreds of lectures during the 1920s, very few texts survive.

As a result, analyzing Zitkala-Ša's lectures to GFWC groups is not possible. Though she likely advocated the idea that education and intellectual advancement qualified her people for citizenship, the details of her appeals have been lost. But not all aspects of her lectures have been lost, especially the way newspapers framed her performances. While reporters seldom quoted her, they nonetheless described her, characterized her contributions, and positioned her as an Indian leader, as a representative of her people whom white Americans could support. In this way, Zitkala-Ša occupied a position similar to Booker T. Washington's relative to her people and white America. Both were seen as representatives of oppressed races whom white Americans could support by making a donation or by treating fairly in civil society. Also like Washington, Zitkala-Ša saw this position as an opportunity that she could turn to the advantage of her cause and her populist coalition.

Because she received extensive newspaper coverage throughout her career, Zitkala-Ša had learned to shape such coverage to her advantage. Even if the papers would not cover her appeals, she reasoned, she could still use the press to advance her pan-Indian intellectual movement. As Vigil writes, "Bonnin understood, in complicated ways, the how, when, and why of audiences and the possibilities she had for controlling the ways she represented herself to them."[68] The same was true of her control of press coverage. Ingratiating herself with white America was, in her career, a useful way of establishing her ethos as a leader behind whom native peoples could rally in a new push for rights.

To judge from the newspapers, one of the most significant aspects of Zitkala-Ša's lectures during the 1920s was her costume. That newspapers chose to focus on what a woman wore on the public stage is not surprising.[69] Notable, however, was the way Zitkala-Ša used coverage of her costume strategically. Standing before an audience of white women and telling "the trials and misfortunes of her people," said one newspaper account, "Mrs. Bonnin was most attractively garbed in a pretty beaded Native costume of her race."[70] The *Oak Park Oak Leaves* similarly noted that Zitkala-Ša was "garbed in Indian costume,"[71] while a neighboring paper, the *Oak Park Oak Parker*, highlighted that she wore "the picturesque costume of her Native tribe" before the Sunday Evening Club of Maywood.[72] Another paper, the *Anaconda Standard*, highlighted the "various decorative and fantastic designs on the uniforms of Indian regalia she wore."[73] Many newspapers even printed an image of Zitkala-Ša in her lecture costume. "Indian to Address Club," read a headline in the *Canton Sunday News*. Next to a picture of the speaker in her Indian outfit, the paper explained that "Mrs. Bonnin will appear in her Native costume. She has an attractive personality and an exquisitely modulated voice, which with her simplicity and directness is said to make her a fascinating speaker."[74]

Extensive coverage of Zitkala-Ša's regalia was significant for two reasons related to the white audience she addressed and the pan-Indian movement she led. First, her supposedly "Native costume" was not actually a Native costume. A Yankton Sioux by birth and upbringing, Zitkala-Ša did not wear the clothes of a Yankton Sioux—or not *only* the clothes of a Yankton Sioux. Instead, she wore "a tribal melange" that represented what white audiences thought Indians wore.[75] On stage, she performed Indianness to draw in her white female listeners. At times, the costume led to a backlash against her advocacy. After she denounced peyote, for instance, some of her opponents criticized the costume she wore as inauthentic—presumably just as inauthentic as her anti-peyote stance.[76] Yet, and this is the second reason coverage of her regalia was significant, even after criticisms of her costume, Zitkala-Ša did not stop wearing her "tribal melange," nor did she set the record straight. Rather, she highlighted the symbolism of the costume to white audiences. According to coverage of a 1925 lecture, Zitkala-Ša took the time to explain "her beautiful tribal costume with its ornamental beaded bodice-part, the symbols and emblems intricately woven into the blue background (blue being the tribal color of the Sioux), has been handed down in the same design for generation after generation—always the same design."[77] The costume was important to her public performances because, as Davidson and Norris conclude, "she felt it would help further the cause of Indian rights."[78] To put the point differently, wearing the costume was an argument in and of itself—an argument about pan-Indianism for white listeners and on behalf of Indian supporters. For whites, the argument signaled Indians' ability to unify in a movement. To Indian supporters, Zitkala-Ša represented them in common cause. She wore an outfit that allowed people from different tribes to see some of their heritage in her appearance and to stand before white Americans in an imagined front demanding justice and citizenship.

But Zitkala-Ša's costume was not the only "melange" that pervaded coverage of her lecture activities. There was also her lineage, which was as strategically concocted as what she wore. Newspapers routinely described her as "full-blooded"—meaning a "full-blood Sioux Indian" or "full blooded Sioux."[79] She was also an "Indian princess of the Sioux tribe," as the *Atlanta Constitution* wrote.[80] According to the *Los Angeles Times*, this "Indian Princess is Historian; Tells Early Status of Tribal Women."[81] By 1928, apparently, she had risen to the rank of "Queen of Indians," at least according to the *Bismarck Tribune*.[82] On top of being full-blooded and Indian royalty, newspapers regularly reported that Zitkala-Ša was "a relative of the famous Indian Chief Sitting Bull."[83] In some papers, she was "born in a tepee of Yankton Sioux parents who were relatives of Sitting Bull."[84] In other papers, she was a "descendent of Sitting Bull,"[85] or even "a granddaughter of Chief Sitting Bull."[86]

Full-blooded Sioux, Indian princess, descendent of Sitting Bull—none of these things were true, at least not in the way her white audiences believed. Zitkala-Ša's father was white, although he departed when she was young, leaving her mother, and the rest of the community, to raise her. She was not related to a tribal chief or part of an Indian aristocracy that white Americans assumed existed. And she was no blood relation to Sitting Bull; that was a claim "she likely made herself in an attempt at self-promotion."[87] Yet like her "Native costume," these descriptions of her lineage followed her for decades, and she did nothing to correct them. They were too useful, positioning her as an ideal leader—a full-blooded Sioux princess, related to Sitting Bull, who could unite Indians across tribal boundaries to stand against the white establishment. She was not only performing for whites but also representing other American Indians in her performances. True to populist leadership, she was extraordinary enough to stand at the head of the movement but ordinary enough to remain one of the people.[88]

While Zitkala-Ša was purportedly a full-blooded Sioux princess, she was also—rather remarkably—at home in white society. This was key to the way she ingratiated herself in white society to lead a charge for Native citizenship. In 1926, the *Los Angeles Times* told readers that Zitkala-Ša "appears thoroughly Americanized and speaks English with no trace of accent," though "her heart remains with her people, and she has devoted her life to their interests."[89] Around the same time, the *Christian Science Monitor* called Zitkala-Ša "a club woman" and "a member of the League of American Pen Women," whose "writings have appeared in the highest type of American magazines."[90] Twenty years earlier, the *New York Tribune* offered a lengthy profile of Zitkala-Ša and called her "a woman of most uncommon character and attainments, one who would attract marked attention in any society."[91] As a woman supposedly at home in the red and white worlds, she was in a perfect position to push into the rights of white society, which would level the playing field for her people—or so she hoped.

Zitkala-Ša's supposed connection to both red and white worlds was due, according to the papers, to her Indian childhood, to her white-like femininity, and to her eloquence. Yet the papers seemed most taken with her brilliance. She was brilliant not only for being an Indian but also according to the standards of white society. A full-blooded Sioux princess who wore Indian clothes, she was also a "highly intellectual and cultured woman," according to the *Canton Daily News*.[92] The *Oak Park Oak Leaves* deemed her "intellectual and cultured"—someone who "fought her way out" of a primitive Indian upbringing and crashed "thru the doors of education, first opened to her by a missionary school, to a foremost place among musicians, authors, and publicists of today."[93] To promote an upcoming lecture, the *Daily Palo Alto* quoted recent coverage in the *Los Angeles Times:* "Her brilliant mind and wonderful spirit enabled her to make such unusual progress that, in a much shorter time than is usually required by the average American girl, she became an accomplished musician, an eloquent speaker, and able to take her place in the highest education environment."[94] The *Bradford Era* took the point a step further: Zitkala-Ša was not just one of the most brilliant Indian women but "perhaps America's most brilliant woman."[95]

In describing Zitkala-Ša's intellect, newspapers proffered the usual sexist and racist ideas of the day: a woman who was actually smart, an Indian who had gone from primitive savagery to the upper echelons of white culture. Yet the coverage bolstered the significance of Zitkala-Ša's appearances. As the papers suggested, white audiences should hear from this striking specimen—an eloquent Indian who could reveal Native culture in a white voice. At the same time, her Indian followers could rally behind a brilliant advocate who looked like them and who could navigate the trappings of white America. Thus newspapers imposed stereotypes on Zitkala-Ša, which she appropriated, even perpetuated, for the advantage of her movement. Appearing in Native costume, conforming to the audience's conception of an Indian princess, she advocated for the rights of "the people"—her people.

To understand the full, populist character of Zitkala-Ša's public performances, however, we need to explore the tone, texture, and force of what she said. While most of her oral discourse has been lost to history, the texts that have survived reveal a strong, populist rhetoric designed to foster a pan-Indian intellectual community.

Three Key Texts

As newspaper coverage of Zitkala-Ša's lectures showed, she knew how to shape popular perceptions of American Indians to the advantage of her movement. As the following analysis of the three key speeches will show, she also knew how to interact with different audiences in a variety of situations to unite and divide various publics in order to build a strong coalition of "the people." The first speech was delivered in 1896 when Zitkala-Ša was a student at Earlham College in Indiana. Representing Earlham at the Indiana State Oratorical Contest, she spoke in a way that resisted the white establishment, rendered American Indians capable of speaking for themselves, and simultaneously drew white listeners to her side. She delivered the second speech more than twenty years later, after hard-fought battles with the white establishment and after assuming a leadership position in the first pan-Indian organization, the Society of American Indians (SAI). In 1919, as the organization struggled, Zitkala-Ša addressed the SAI's Eighth Annual Convention with the goal of rededicating members to the society's mission while expanding the constituency it served. Zitkala-Ša delivered the third speech in 1928 in Atlantic City before the Indian Rights Association (IRA) and in response to one of the most significant reports on Indian affairs the U.S. government ever issued. Now late in her career, Zitkala-Ša performed Indian inquiry and enacted Indian citizenship as a rebuke to the forces infringing on Indian progress.

PREPARING INTELLECTUAL COMMUNITY IN "SIDE BY SIDE"

The last of six speakers, the only female speaker, and the only Indian speaker at Indiana's State Oratorical Contest, Zitkala-Ša was unaware of the melee that had erupted earlier that evening. That was probably for the best, given that her presence at the contest was a catalyst of the fisticuffs.

It was eight o'clock in the evening on Friday, March 13, 1896, and the Indianapolis Opera House was packed with over a thousand students from six colleges across the state—DePauw, Butler, Hanover, Franklin, Wabash, and Earlham. Students from each school formed their own cheering sections, ready to root for their representative at the celebrated annual contest. It was a raucous crowd, made more volatile by what the Butler delegation had done before the program began. Sneaking into the Opera House earlier that evening, Butler students had hung two furled banners from the balcony. The first said, "Butler on Top." The second, which was the real cause of the melee, had the word "Humility" next to "an overdrawn caricature" labeled "squaw," as *The Earlhamite*, Earlham College's newspaper, reported.[96] Shortly before the contest began, the banners were unfurled, prompting a volley of boos and hisses from the Earlham delegation. Ready for a fight, Butler students rushed the Earlham students, the groups exchanged blows, and two police officers had to break up the melee before the contest could begin—forty-five minutes late.

Zitkala-Ša entered the Opera House after the scuffle had taken place, and she sat in the first row facing the stage, so her back was to the caricature still hanging from the balcony. She wouldn't see the banner until after she delivered her speech. Until then, she sat patiently listening to the other contestants. The student from Wabash spoke on the topic "Christianity Reasonable," which apparently included several digs at Robert Ingersoll. The student from Butler spoke on "Indiana: A Century of Progress," while the student from Hanover addressed "The New Divine Right." The student from DePauw spoke on "The Brotherhood of Man," and the student from Franklin spoke on a topic apparently so unremarkable that the paper did not bother to record it.[97] Then it was time for Zitkala-Ša to speak.

Only twenty years old at the time, Zitkala-Ša may well have been the only American Indian in the room. When she stepped to the lectern and looked out at the audience, she saw a sea of white faces and heard a smattering of heckles.[98] Yet despite the challenging situation—or perhaps because of it—she delivered a speech that ought to be considered a classic of American oratory. While several commentators have dismissed the speech as an accommodationist bow to the white establishment[99]—not unlike the criticisms Washington has received—these dismissals, as Lewandowski insists, pass over "a highly subversive text that resists far more than it conforms."[100] Zitkala-Ša's oration, titled "Side by Side," was a direct challenge to the audience, engaging in the play of perceptions that dominated newspaper coverage of her lectures later in her life. Although Zitkala-Ša's intellectual populism was not fully developed in the speech—largely because her audience was white, not Indian—the basic terms of her pan-Indian populist uprising were already coming together.

"Side by Side" began by celebrating the same ideas previous contestants had addressed, drawing the audience into the text. "The universe is the product of evolution," Zitkala-Ša said in the opening line, and through determined struggle, "nations have risen from the mountain foot of their existence to its summit." Long ago, she continued, the "warlike Saxon" began "his bloody conquest of Britain." Though "fierce and barbarous," he nonetheless struggled for advancement. Out of blood, barbarism, and war rose America—"a nation of free men and free institutions." She then celebrated the nation:

> Among its rivers, mountains, and lakes, in its stately forests and on its broad prairies, like rolling seas of green and gold, millions of toiling sovereigns have established gigantic enterprises, great factories, commercial highways, and have developed fruitful farms and productive mines. The ennobling architecture of its churches, schools, and benevolent institutions; its municipal greatness, keeping pace with social progress; its scholars, statesmen, authors and divines, giving expression and force to the religious and humanitarian zeal of a great people—all these reveal a marvelous progress. Thought is lost in admiration of this matchless scene over which floats in majesty the starry emblem of liberty.[101]

Even now, one can practically see the bright eyes and up-curled lips of audience members. Here was an American Indian—one who had just been mocked and heckled—celebrating white society for an audience of white Americans.

Then Zitkala-Ša smashed it all apart. "But see!" she said, immediately after picturing the "starry emblem of liberty." Look again and watch as "the tide of time rolls back four hundred years." Watch as colonists, explorers, and settlers recede "beyond the trackless sea." Watch as they go back across the Atlantic to the world of their birth. Watch as "America is one great wilderness again." Significantly, the name of the land was still America, and America was still home to Americans: "Over the trees of the primeval forest curls the smoke of the wigwam. The hills resound with the hunter's shout that dies away with the fleeing deer." Then followed images of moccasins and "rainbow beads," of the evening glow of the "council fire," and of the "aged brave" telling his "fantastic legends."[102]

If the audience held stereotypes of Indian life, these were likely them. And according to the American Indian orator, this was Indian life before "the invasion of . . . a paler race." In the time before pale-faced invaders, America was home to "forest children," who prayed to "the Great Spirit" and heard "his voice in the wind." They lived with "reverential awe" at the "common lot of human kind," and they knew the "joyous freedom of the hunt" and "the pipe of peace."[103] In short, before whites came to America, the first Americans already knew God, equality, freedom, and peace. These were the Americanisms of the populist tradition, which Zitkala-Ša now claimed for the first Americans. These ideals—the ideals the audience held sacred and had just heard several white male speakers discuss—were already part of the land before the invasion of the pale race. Zitkala-Ša thus built up white perceptions of progress in order to smash them apart and seize them for American Indians.

In smashing apart white perceptions, "Side by Side" not only appropriated the sacred terms white Americans held dear but also addressed listeners in ways that distanced them from the speaker, creating opposition between Zitkala-Ša and her listeners. After describing the invasion of the pale race, she explained how violence had ravaged peaceful America. "The White Man's bullet," she said, "decimates [the Indian's] tribes and drives him from his home," severing him from "the inheritance of his fathers, their traditions, their graves." If this destruction of life and culture seemed unjust, that was the point, which Zitkala-Ša advanced through a series of rhetorical questions: "Do you wonder still that in his breast he should brood revenge, when ruthlessly driven from the temples where he worshipped? Do you wonder still that he skulked in forest gloom to avenge the desolation of his home?" Zitkala-Ša posed similar questions later in the speech when she asked about vanishing Indians: "If in their stead, we have to-day a race of blighted promise, will you spurn them? You, whose sires have permitted the most debasing influences to surround these forest children, brutalizing their nobler instincts until sin and corruption have well nigh swept them from the Earth?"[104] By bringing up the sins of white fathers and the oppression of her race, Zitkala-Ša pitted speaker and listeners, whites and reds, against each other in a battle over past, present, and future.

After distancing whites and reds, the speech turned the tables on the audience. Whatever charges whites brought against Indians—changes that often justified manifest destiny in the minds of whites—were equally applicable to whites themselves. Take "the charge of cruelty," she announced, which has come only when "the White Man has been the witness and judge." Ironically, cruelty and violence were the white man's stock-in-trade: "Puritan Boston burned witches and hanged Quakers, and the Southern aristocrat beat his slaves and set blood hounds on the track of him who dared aspire to freedom."[105] She did not know it at the time, but this dig at slavery would end up costing her first place in the oratorical contest. Yet in the development of the speech, highlighting white violence was a powerful way to upend the audience's perceptions of American Indians and to further separate speaker from listeners.

The distance between speaker and listeners was only a prelude to the coming crescendo. In the final portion of the speech, Zitkala-Ša brought together the various themes of her oration—disrupting perceptions, reclaiming the sacred terms of America, confronting the audience—while preparing the ground for reconnection. Speaking on behalf of her race, she offered a lesson in metaphysics and ontology: "No legacy of barbarism can efface the divine image in man. No tardiness in entering the paths of progress can destroy his divinely given capabilities. No lot or circumstance, except of his own choosing, can invalidate his claim to a place in the brotherhood of man or release more fortunate, more enlightened people from the obligation of a brother's keeper."[106] To the extent that whites and reds were equal in sin and corruption after the invasion of the palefaces, the divine spark in all meant that everyone could begin to move toward the promised land of freedom, justice, and equality. There was still a utopia at the end of the American experiment—an experiment begun by, and soon to return to, Native peoples. "Poets sing of a coming federation of the world, and we applaud," continued Zitkala-Ša. "Idealists dream that in this commonwealth of all humanity the divine spark in man shall be the only test of citizenship, and we think of their dream as future history." To make the point of equality even clearer, she gave both whites and Indians the label "American." "Aside from the claims of common humanity," she asked her audience, "can you as consistent Americans deny equal opportunities with yourselves to an American people in their struggle to rise from ignorance and degradation? The claims of brotherhood, of the love that is due a neighbor-race, and of tardy justice have not been wholly lost on your hearts and consciences."[107] In this formulation, white Americans owed Americanisms, including justice, to the first Americans. Paying that debt would be a radical, yet eminently conservative, gesture because it was grounded in the traditional values Indians held before the invasion of the pale race.

In the final paragraph of the speech, Zitkala-Ša turned her confrontation toward hope and progress. "We clasp the warm hand of friendship everywhere," she declared, grouping Indians together in a pan-Indian coalition under the pronoun "we":

> We come from mountain fastness, from cheerless plains, from far-off low-wooded streams, seeking the "White Man's ways." Seeking your skill in industry and in art, seeking labor and honest independence, seeking the treasures of knowledge and wisdom, seeking to comprehend the spirit of your laws and the genius of your noble institutions, seeking by a new birthright to unite with yours our claim to a common country, seeking the sovereign's crown that we may stand side by side with you in ascribing royal honor to our nation's flag. America, I love thee. "Thy people shall be my people and thy God my God."[108]

More than any other paragraph in the speech, this concluding paragraph has provided ammunition to commentators who deem "Side by Side" an accommodationist, Booker T. Washington–like acquiescence. However, the passage moves in a subtly powerful way that can be easy to overlook. According to Zitkala-Ša, Indians traveled from the wilderness to learn the "White Man's ways." The quotation marks around the phrase may or may not provide insight into how she delivered the line, but on the page they suggest skepticism, especially when related to what she said earlier. She had already applied the standard Americanisms to Indians themselves, so were the "White Man's ways" really the ways of the white man? Or were they simply what the audience thought of *as* the white man's ways?

In addition, the concluding paragraph began with a sense of deference to whites—"your skill in industry and in art," "treasures of knowledge and wisdom," "the genius of your noble institutions." But it ended by inverting the power dynamic in favor of Indians. Consider the phrase, "seeking by a new birthright to unite with yours our claim to a common country." In this statement, Indians had a claim to a common country, as did whites, but "our claim" stood closer to "a common country" than "yours." What's more, Indians sought "the Sovereign's crown"—not the most democratic image, but one that had long underscored the sovereignty of Indian nations.[109] With that sovereign crown, she declared, "we may stand side by side with you in ascribing royal honor to our nation's flag." Again, royal honor was not a democratic statement, and it was certainly not a statement often applied to the United States. Then again, Zitkala-Ša never mentioned the United States. She only mentioned "America," going so far as to express her love for "thee." But as she made clear earlier, "America" belonged more rightly to Indians than to whites. Of course she loved America; America was what Indians had created.

The final line of the speech was a quotation from Ruth 1:16 in the Old Testament of the Bible. It was uttered by Ruth—a foreigner in a strange land, much like Zitkala-Ša in Indiana. And it was addressed to Naomi—a broken, bitter woman whose life returned to fullness through Ruth's faithfulness. It is easy to miss the import of this quotation. At one level, the line seemed to suggest that Indians would become more white, adopting white ways and even the white God. Yet in the context of the story of Ruth, the line suggested that Indians would be the ones saving whites, not the other way around. The book of Ruth tells the story of a foreigner healing a broken Israelite and becoming central to salvation. By the end of the book, Ruth marries a powerful landowner, and their progeny lead to the birth of Jesus Christ. Ruth, the foreigner, heals brokenness and becomes part of the story of salvation. American Indians, Zitkala-Ša suggested, will do the same.

While it is impossible to know how much the audience at the Indiana State Oratorical Contest read into the speech, a careful reading of the conclusion and the final line fits with Zitkala-Ša's overall strategy of seizing on and disrupting white perceptions in service of a resistive pan-Indian coalition. Though deferential at first blush, the conclusion strengthened the position of Indians in American society. America was theirs, she suggested, and they would work its salvation.

The audience loved the speech, at least according to contemporary accounts. The *Earlhamite*, no doubt a biased source, wrote that "tumultuous applause . . . burst from the audience as she closed," indicating that "she had won their hearts."[110] A less biased source was the *Indianapolis News*, which reported similar praise: "When she finished there was a response of hearty and deep-felt applause which mounted to a cheer coming from every part of the house. The vote of the hearts of the hearers was given to her."[111] The article even described a "slight brushing movement about the eyes" of one of the judges, apparently as he wiped away a tear or two. Despite widespread praise, Zitkala-Ša placed second in the oratorical contest. She received top marks from every judge except the judge from Vanderbilt University, who placed her last in "thought and composition" because of her rebuke of slavery. Sentiments of the old South kept Zitkala-Ša from her rightful victory.[112]

Nonetheless, "Side by Side" set her on a course toward pan-Indian populism. In particular, the speech revealed her inclination to clash with white society in a way that could call Indians to her side for a reclamation of the American ideals that were rightfully theirs. By opposing the white establishment, Zitkala-Ša could hail a community of the people—her people—ready for a radical rupture in society that would put American Indians back in control of their lives.

FOSTERING INTELLECTUAL COMMUNITY IN THE ADDRESS TO THE EIGHTH ANNUAL SAI CONVENTION

Between the time of the Indiana oratorical contest and the Great War, Zitkala-Ša built community centers on Indian reservations, wrote extensively about Indian traditions, and even penned an opera, *The Sun Dance*, which had a limited run in Utah in 1913.[113] Her achievements pushed her to the forefront of the pan-Indian movement and made her a de facto spokesperson for the "Indian" perspective. Of course, the idea that there was an "Indian" perspective was problematic, growing out of white prejudice and ignorance. Yet by the late nineteenth century, many American Indians had come to embrace the idea, not because it was accurate but because it could unite them under "broad goals and . . . universal ideas rather than local problems."[114] If whites were going to see them as a homogenous group, they should join forces and agitate for their rights.

Although white reformers had been working on Indian-rights issues for a long time, American Indians had often been treated more like objects than agents in reform efforts. In 1911 a number of prominent activists formed a national, Indian-led, pan-Indian organization: the Society of American Indians (SAI). Founders of the society included Charles Eastman, Carlos Montezuma, and Thomas Sloan. Laura Cornelius Kellogg was the only woman founder.[115] Zitkala-Ša had been invited, but her work out West on the reservations precluded early involvement. She joined the SAI advisory board in 1914 and started contributing to the organization's conferences, publications, and reform efforts. She even organized a chapter of the SAI on the Utah reservation where she lived and worked. "By early 1916," writes Lewandowski, "Zitkala-Ša was firmly in vanguard of the Native rights movement."[116]

Political and intellectual organizing energized Zitkala-Ša. While the SAI had plenty of problems, including internal divisions over the use of peyote, she believed it offered incredible opportunities for American Indians and for her personally. The SAI leadership agreed, electing her secretary of the organization during its annual conference in 1916. By that time, she had grown frustrated with the challenges of community organizing out West. "Every Indian who has attempted to do real uplift work for the tribes gets stung," she wrote to a friend in early 1917. "No wonder that he quits trying; goes back to the blanket, and sits in the teepee like a boiled owl."[117] Disheartened with problems on the reservation and even willing to use the loaded phrase "back to the blanket," she was ready for a change.[118] In the spring of 1917, she and her family moved to Washington, DC, where, she hoped, she could better contribute to the cause of her people.

Once in Washington, Zitkala-Ša expanded her role in the SAI. At first she clashed with the sitting SAI treasurer, Marie Baldwin, but she eventually ousted Baldwin and became both secretary and treasurer.[119] In 1918 she added another title to her portfolio—editor of the *American Indian Magazine*, the SAI's journal. With Zitkala-Ša at the helm, the journal addressed such causes as cultural preservation, citizenship for Indians, land reform, indigenous religious traditions, and the importance of learning English. Some of these causes were contentious within and across Native communities, but Zitkala-Ša wanted to push the SAI in profitable directions given the nation's broader focus on Americanization during the Progressive Era and after World War I. At the same time, she understood the challenges before her and the organization. The SAI had little money, and Zitkala-Ša performed most of her duties without compensation. Peyote continued to be a divisive issue, and Zitkala-Ša's prominence angered many pro-peyote members. There were also ongoing personality clashes. Zitkala-Ša was a close associate of SAI president Charles Eastman, but he had several rivals, including Thomas Sloan, leader of the pro-peyote faction who wanted to oust Eastman and remake the organization.[120]

Tensions ran especially high in Minneapolis during the eighth annual SAI convention, which took place October 2–4, 1919.[121] A few days before the convention, New York congressman Homer P. Snyder introduced a bill that granted U.S. citizenship to all American Indians who had served honorably in the Great War.[122] Citizenship was an issue Zitkala-Ša had championed for a long time, and she hoped to unite those gathered in Minneapolis around the citizenship proposal. At the same time, Sloan and his allies wanted to take control of the organization, not only because they opposed Eastman but also because they opposed working with the federal government's Bureau of Indian Affairs (BIA) on issues of service and citizenship. Many SAI members wanted to cut all ties with the BIA, while Eastman and Zitkala-Ša hoped to maintain a working relationship. On top of it all, attendance at the SAI annual conference was lower than it had ever been.[123]

Zitkala-Ša spoke early in the conference, on the morning of October

2, which gave her the opportunity to shape the tone of the gathering, to strengthen commitment to the organization, and to heal rifts between factions. Just as important, at least for the purposes of this book, was the opportunity to articulate an intellectual populist message for an audience in desperate need of unity and revitalization. As Zitkala-Ša saw the situation, the soul of the SAI and of pan-Indianism was best found in intellectual engagement. Political, social, and civic changes were important, she argued, but they grew out of Indians thinking together in community. Accordingly, she opened her speech with a call for community—a broad, inclusive community of Indian thinkers. Acknowledging her position as one of the few Indian women in SAI leadership, she thanked her "brothers" for the way "they have spoken of their high regard for an Indian sister"—a high regard, she hoped, they would extend "to all Indian women in this country." In her view, it was only through broader inclusion that the organization would fulfill its purpose: "I hope my brothers that at the next meeting you will invite your wife to come with you and you will invite your sister to come with you because you realize that in the home, in the Indian home, the mother teaches the children these very principles we are talking about." In Zitkala-Ša's invocation, the survival of the SAI hinged on principled instruction in the home; indeed, the entire pan-Indian movement depended on teaching Indian children to think critically. Because women "teach our children as they play about our knees," she explained, "the Indian woman must come to these gatherings, she must listen with her mind open and her heart open that she may gather the truths to take home to our little ones."[124] It was a pseudo-prayer for the future of the SAI, and it tied the movement's soul to practices of teaching, learning, and thinking. Their work was, above all, intellectual—a point Booker T. Washington and Thomas Davidson would have applauded.

At one level, Zitkala-Ša wanted to broaden and strengthen ties among Indians. At another level, she wanted to remind the audience of why they needed to fight—specifically, because of the threat white society posed. This was her clear statement of the established order against which ordinary Indians could align. "Now we are meeting a civilization from a race that came from Europe," she declared in characterizing their foe. Because white society came from Europe, from afar, from somewhere outside America, Indians confronted an invading foreign force. "We have to meet it each day," she insisted. "There is no dodging and it is not easy. It is going to take courage; it is going to test your strength. It is going to test your faith in the Greatest of All." The amplification across these phrases moved the audience toward a test of faith, while leaving God's name enthymematic. The religiously diverse group—including Zitkala-Ša, an ardent Catholic—could fill in the name for the divine on their own. Instead of naming what might divide them, she focused on what could unite them: "It is going to be hard, but let us stand the test, true to the Indian blood. Let us do that. Let us teach our children to be proud of their Indian blood and to stand the test bravely."[125]

The sense of embattled community—of an embattled race—was key to Zitkala-Ša's populist discourse. Foreigners from the East, she explained, had come to control the lives and destinies of Indian people, and the only way to resist them was to band together. In her telling, banding together meant recognizing that "The greatest gift in life is consciousness. Not positions, not the dollar, but that the Almighty Spirit gives us life and we have a rational mind with which to see all the wonders of the universe."[126] With this statement, populist resistance became the push for intellectual community, for careful, critical inquiry. Zitkala-Ša called on her audience to embrace a new, pragmatic kind of inquiry—what she called "the practical way" of thought. "We have had to change from the old style of hunting, have had to leave the old trails," she reminded the crowd. "We have got to learn the new trails—we can do it. We have the power, we can think."[127] Notice the careful phrasing: Zitkala-Ša was not celebrating changes from the "old style"; Indians "had" to change, were forced to change. But now that the threat was all around, they had to learn new methods of inquiry and to think together about resisting their common foe. It was a clarion call to pan-Indian intellectual populism.

Then Zitkala-Ša pushed the idea further. In a series of statements that echoed both Thomas Davidson's and Booker T. Washington's vision of labor and learning, she declared: "Work is honorable as long as men and women are honest. There is no work that is degrading. It is all honorable. I do not need to repeat that, because Indians know it. . . . Work is honorable. We have to work and each day do it to the best of our ability." Like Davidson and Washington, Zitkala-Ša explained that this sort of practical, daily effort was not a matter of menial labor but of concerted contemplation: "God has given you life," she urged, "he has given you minds to think with and hearts that we may be just to all, true to all mankind. Then we are true to God—to ourselves. That means each day the simplest things begin from sunrise to sunset, from sunset to sunrise again." Practical, everyday inquiry should unite American Indians across what divided them, all the while bolstering the "honesty, clean living and intelligence" of the race.[128] For Zitkala-Ša, everyday work marked the practical and intellectual struggle through which ordinary Indians could overturn the status quo.

The pragmatic strand of the speech—the call for practical, everyday thought—grew stronger when Zitkala-Ša turned to the topic of communication. In her formulation, the strength of the intellectual community she envisioned could be measured by the number of voices contributing to it. She thus encouraged ordinary Indians to speak up and to share their grievances, thereby opening their individual problems to the equivalential chain of a populist frontier. "We come to commune with our minds, with our hearts," she said to those in attendance. "Do not sit back because you think that you cannot speak English well. Let us hear from those who do not speak it at all, they can have interpreters. We want to hear from the minds and hearts of our Indian people." In fact, the need for speech was more important than ever: "We seem to have no money, no friends, and *we have no voice in Congress.*" Only by speaking what was in their hearts and minds, by having "faith in the Great Spirit"—another broad reference to the divine that allowed people to fill in their own conception of God—could Indians foster "every day thinking in our homes and wherever we go."[129] When ordinary Indians voiced their personal grievances, they linked with others in an equivalential chain united against the white establishment.

Perhaps a chain is not the right metaphor. Zitkala-Ša had a metaphor of her own that, she believed, captured the kind of populist spirit needed for a strong pan-Indian movement: the "national teepee." The national teepee was an ironic metaphor given that teepees were culturally specific to the tribes of the Great Plains, but it signaled the inclusion of all American Indians, not just SAI officers. Because it was national, it had room for everyone to contribute to the direction of the organization and to deliberate about resisting foreign invaders. "Let us develop our powers by thinking and acting for ourselves," Zitkala-Ša explained. "This is a national teepee. We are all coming here to consult together, and from these various ideas we want to come to a conclusion." Think, speak, debate, make decisions—these were the ideals of all prominent organizations, but they were especially pressing for American Indians, who needed unity to resist the colonialism of white thought. "We are rational human beings," she underscored. "Shall we think or shall somebody think for us?"[130] Thinking for themselves was the basic impetus of Zitkala-Ša's intellectual-populist uprising.

In Zitkala-Ša's speech to the SAI, the national teepee was a metaphor that Indians of various tribes could take back home. "Organize," she insisted at the close of her speech, and "act as a body," so that "we may put our ideas together and choose the best." All Indian men and women "must have a voice"; everyone must "say what is in him, and by exchanging opinions, we are going to grow." She called on Indian women in particular to join the SAI, to participate in SAI discussions, and "to do their part in their own homes. Then they will help us carry on this work as it must be done so that we may succeed."[131] Men, women, children—all Indians—had a place to think and speak in the national teepee. When they did think and speak together, they could repel the paleface force from Europe.

Zitkala-Ša's speech to the 1919 SAI Convention was a powerful, populist statement, but it failed mightily, at least in terms of unifying the immediate audience. The meeting remained contentious, and eventually the pro-peyote forces took control. The new SAI leadership asked Zitkala-Ša to stay on as secretary-treasurer, but she declined, and shortly thereafter she resigned from the organization. She cited poor health as the reason—and she was in poor health at the time—but she also feared for the future of this first national pan-Indian organization.[132] She was right to fear for it. Without the enthusiasm, dedication, and sacrifice of people like Zitkala-Ša, the SAI did not last long. Membership declined quickly in the early 1920s, the organization held its last convention in 1923, and it officially folded later that decade.[133] Zitkala-Ša's plea for SAI unity had been for naught. But she was not ready to give up on populist pan-Indianism. Perhaps the best way to proceed, she reasoned, was to start her own organization.

ENACTING INTELLECTUAL COMMUNITY IN THE 1928 ADDRESS BEFORE THE INDIAN RIGHTS ASSOCIATION

Zitkala-Ša's speech to the SAI crystalized the terms of her intellectual populism. Almost a decade later, she redeployed those terms in an intellectual performance crafted to inspire American Indians the nation over.

What happened in Oklahoma was a big factor in her performance. In the early 1920s, the American Indian Defense Association (AIDA) launched an investigation into reports of greed, graft, corruption, and murder in the state, centered on the gas and oil wealth of the Osage tribe. Other tribes had been victimized as well, but the Osage experienced the most brutality, with sixty people murdered between 1921 and 1925. Corrupt officials, scheming lawyers, and dishonest businessmen conspired to seize Osage allotments and to murder whoever stood in the way.[134] In 1923, the AIDA dispatched Zitkala-Ša, attorney Charles Fabens, and Indian-rights activist Matthew Sniffen to Oklahoma to interview victims and to publish a report of their findings. Their report came out in 1924, with the provocative title: *Oklahoma's Poor Rich Indians: An Orgy of Graft and Exploitation of the Five Civilized Tribes—Legalized Robbery.*[135] Newspapers across the country picked up on the story, pushing Zitkala-Ša's visibility to new peaks. She soon participated in legislative hearings about the corruption and evil in Oklahoma. But officials in that state fought back, derailing congressional oversight efforts and defaming Zitkala-Ša and the AIDA.[136]

Zitkala-Ša was crestfallen with the situation in Oklahoma, but there was one positive development for pan-Indianism in 1924. That summer, partly through Zitkala-Ša's efforts, Congress granted citizenship to American Indians. Some Indian nations, including the Onondaga and the Iroquois, opposed the Indian Citizenship Act because it usurped the sovereignty of their own governments. But Zitkala-Ša saw the bill as the culmination of her advocacy until that point. She and other American Indian leaders—and even non-Indian reformers like Richard Henry Pratt—had pushed for citizenship since the end of the nineteenth century. When it finally arrived in 1924, they celebrated, but then they realized they had a new question on their hands: With citizenship secured, where should they focus their advocacy? Zitkala-Ša's answer came in the form of the National Council of American Indians (NCAI), which she founded on February 27, 1926, as a successor to the SAI. As president of the organization, she was able to enact her belief that "women should lead the fight to redress the crimes of white men."[137]

Two years after Zitkala-Ša created the NCAI, there was another key development in the clash between the U.S. government and American Indians. In February 1928, Lewis Meriam, principal investigator of Indian affairs for the Institute for Government Research, submitted an 847-page report to the Department of the Interior denouncing the government's Indian policy as a catastrophic failure. Inaction in Oklahoma was only part of the problem. The Meriam Report, as it came to be known, chastised decades of federal policy as not only ineffective but also destructive and backward. American Indians had been saying this for a long time, but the Meriam Report was the best indication yet that the federal government knew it oppressed and exploited indigenous people. In time, the report became the main catalyst for a complete overhaul of federal Indian policy via the Indian Reorganization Act of 1934.[138] Zitkala-Ša could take significant credit for many of the changes codified in the 1934 act.[139]

When it was released in 1928, many Indian rights organizations welcomed the Meriam Report, even though they thought it did not go far enough in its specifics. One of the organizations especially grateful for the report was the Indian Rights Association (IRA), the premier white-led reform group, founded in 1882 and eminently controversial among Native peoples.[140] Convinced they could use the report to push for structural change, the IRA organized a conference to strategize about moving forward armed with the Meriam evidence. The conference took place December 14–15, 1928, in Atlantic City, and organizers turned to Zitkala-Ša to deliver a keynote address.

Zitkala-Ša's address to the 1928 IRA conference was one of her most mature statements on and enactments of pan-Indian intellectual populism. It also marked a complex, challenging rhetorical situation. An Indian woman and head of a leading pan-Indian organization, Zitkala-Ša had to speak to and for the Indian perspective—whatever that might ultimately mean—regarding the Meriam Report. Because the subject of the conference was a government report, she also had to speak to government interests and federal officials, who might not be in attendance but who would be listening nonetheless. Because the venue was an IRA conference, she also had to speak to white reformers who had been working for decades on Indian affairs but who often failed to include Indians. White society, federal power, and the Native predicament swirled around Zitkala-Ša's address at the conference, and she recognized the moment as a prime opportunity to carve out a distinct intellectual space for American Indians.

At the very beginning of her address, Zitkala-Ša pointed to the distinct space she occupied as a speaker at the conference. "The opportunity to speak today in a conference discussing the report of the Indian survey made by the Institute for Government Research," she said to open the speech, "is appreciated by this Indian speaker."[141] Beneath this opening statement lurked decades of Indian politics. By mentioning the occasion—"a conference discussing the report"—she nodded to white IRA reformers. By mentioning the topic—a report "made by the Institute for Government Research"—she dredged up the oppressive history of federal policy. At the same time, she identified herself as "this Indian speaker." Not a white reformer, not a government bureaucrat—she was an Indian speaker, a *female* Indian speaker, ready to articulate a new perspective.

Zitkala-Ša also made one thing clear about her past—she "did not learn English in the Government Indian Schools. I attended Earlham College, Richmond, Indiana."[142] It was a small but crucial detail. Given her reputation for eloquence, and given her forthcoming denunciations of government schools, she needed to undercut her opponents' potential counterarguments. If she were the product of a government school and also eloquent in her remarks, then government officials could claim that she was proof government schools were working. But by distancing herself from federal education efforts, she invalidated the counterargument. Ultimately, she was simply "President of the National Council of American Indians, an all-Indian organization based upon citizenship rights granted by Congress June 2, 1924."[143]

She made one final distinction in the introduction that was crucial for the argument she would deploy. After noting the importance of citizenship, the service of Indians in the Great War, and the "American Indian's loyalty to the Government of the United States"—even though "this Government has waged more wars upon its Indian wards than any other nation against its own subordinate peoples"—she distinguished between "Government" and "Servants of the Government."[144] This distinction would propel the rest of the speech, allowing her to claim loyalty to the government while eviscerating certain government actors. Pledging loyalty while holding bureaucrats accountable was what good citizens did. Loyalty to the nation through criticism of the government had been a tenet of Progressive Era reform,[145] and carrying it into the late 1920s enabled Zitkala-Ša to surround her speaking position with the legitimacy of progressive advocacy that defined the IRA. Because she was now a citizen, she was prepared to take on a responsibility of all good progressive citizens: criticizing their government out of loyalty to America.

One of the most striking aspects of Zitkala-Ša's performance of citizenship, at least compared to her other speeches, was her use of evidence. Paragraph after paragraph from the Meriam Report, paragraph after paragraph of statements by government officials, paragraph after paragraph of politicians on the defensive—Zitkala-Ša cited a mountain of evidence that signaled the depth of her civic engagement. Not only was she ready to speak as a citizen, but she had also done her homework, as good citizens should. What's more, this mountain of evidence served a crucial rhetorical function, constructing a pseudo-debate between Zitkala-Ša and government authorities, as though she were speaking directly to her representatives. This Indian child was talking back to her republican father.[146]

Her primary opponent in this mock debate was Michigan congressman Louis Cramton, who, a few days before the IRA conference, denounced on the floor of the U.S. House Zitkala-Ša and other Indian activists. Their grievances, he argued, were baseless, impudent, and disloyal. Now it was Zitkala-Ša's turn to respond. In speaking to the IRA, she quoted Cramton directly, no doubt performing the same faux displeasure he had performed when delivering his original denunciations. The NCAI, Cramton had said and Zitkala-Ša now repeated, issued statements with "the character of propaganda used to poison the judgment of the country against their own Government." He had also said, "I have never seen any evidence of the children suffering from lack of food or from an undesirable character of food. Quite the contrary. It is true that oftentimes children will be seen in these schools who give evidence of lack of proper nutrition, but you must remember where these children have come from—the primitive sort of *homes* they come from to the schools."[147] Quoting Cramton directly made the white establishment clear and present, preparing the ground for a unified opposition.

By reissuing Cramton's words against her and the NCAI, Zitkala-Ša initiated a debate that she planned on winning. As she told listeners, Cramton undercut his own position: After "denying the disgraceful condition of Indian affairs, he contradicts himself. He agrees with me and with the Report of the Institute for Government Research in their first sentence, which says: 'An overwhelming majority of the Indians are poor, even extremely poor.' Mr. Cramton falls into this agreement unwittingly in trying to refute the report that children in Government schools are underfed." She continued: "The 'primitive sort of homes'—that is exactly what I had in mind. The Congressman admits these homes are bad and that food is lacking, and therefore, Indians young and old are hungry and sick."[148] In one breath, Cramton had dismissed Indian grievances about poverty, lack of food, and poor health; in another, he had belittled Indians for living in primitive conditions marked by poverty, lack of food, and poor health. From Zitkala-Ša's perspective, he had given Indians what they needed to unite their frustrations and stand against the white power structure.

The performative character of this moment was striking. Standing before members of the IRA, an Indian woman—now a citizen—was quoting and replying to a white, male, elected official. Her voice was the voice of "the people," the Indian people, pushing back against the establishment of the East. Her primary method for pushing back was an evidentiary one, as she deployed piles of evidence documenting federal oppression of the Indian population. Along the way, she signaled her knowledge of the machinations of government by holding officials accountable through government statements. For instance, Zitkala-Ša discussed the dynamics of reservation life in the months since the publication of the Meriam Report. "Indian Bureau Superintendents in the field have been holding meetings this summer," she explained, offering a glimpse into reservation conditions, "discussing this same report of the Institute for Government Research before us now. Their purpose was to refute and disprove the things contained in it! Subordinate employees have been approached and told they should be 'loyal' to the Government when asked to refute statements in the Report. At peril of losing their jobs, some of them refused to deny the facts."[149] Not only was this proof that agents of the government knew about the conditions on Indian reservations, but it was also evidence that they were distorting the information available to the public and stifling civic debate—a supposed hallmark of American democracy. Zitkala-Ša herself told the IRA audience how she recently stood up to a malevolent government official: "A Superintendent who questioned the accuracy of the Report on the 11 cents per child per day spent for food in Government schools was invited to figure it out, which he did while I looked on. Much to his own surprise, he had to admit the Survey staff of the Institute for Government Research knew their business and their Report was correct." Later in the speech, she went so far as to claim that most officials working on reservations were either "incompetent" or "criminals." In either case, she concluded, "a housecleaning is imperative."[150]

Given the occasion and audience for the speech, and given Indians' relatively new citizenship status, Zitkala-Ša spoke with a newfound sense of freedom. Now legally part of "the people," she confronted agents of the government more freely than ever before, especially before a white audience. In fact, she took it upon herself to speak on behalf of the American people, not just American Indians, broadening her populist constituency to better oppose the forces of the East. While discussing hearings before the Senate Investigating Committee, one of the committees charged with studying Indian affairs, Zitkala-Ša insisted that printed reports of the committee's activities be "made available to the public—the American people. They have a right to know the facts. . . . Let the people know the facts, if this is a Government 'of the people, for the people, by the people.'"[151] Later, she chastised a report on nutrition in Indian schools for failing to

> tell the American public, as a matter of fact, how miserably this endeavor fails to actually supply the necessary milk. This kind of a presentation of Indian matters is not conducive to having Congress make larger appropriations. Congress as a whole is dependent upon the Indian Bureau for its information, just as the American public is. Both Congress and the American people are willfully misled about the actual conditions of Indian want and hopeless destitution.[152]

Whatever particular grievances members of the IRA had about government handling of Indian affairs, they could see their grievances in Zitkala-Ša's call for information, discussion, and democracy. Her populist discourse thus enhanced the ordinary democracy of Indian rights by drawing ordinary Indians together with ordinary whites to hold the government accountable. As she summarized toward the end of the speech, the "atrocious misuses of huge Federal machinery against the Indian wards of the Government are sugar-coated to fool the American public."

Fortunately, "the National Council of American Indians was one of the organizations that dared to defend the rights" of American Indians and, in turn, all Americans.[153]

Zitkala-Ša's speech to the IRA was populist and performative, as it not only pitted the people against the elite power structure but also demonstrated how American Indians could think, inquire, and engage as citizens of the United States. Throughout the speech, Zitkala-Ša brought inquiry to life, enacting a kind of rhetorical criticism that other citizen Indians could undertake. She analyzed government reports, broke them apart, and drew conclusions about their language and ideas. To take just one example, Zitkala-Ša quoted a lengthy paragraph from the Meriam Report, then homed in on the paragraph's concluding line: "It may be seriously questioned whether the Indian Service could do very much better than it does without more adequate appropriations." She found this conclusion problematic because it minimized "the Bureau's actual responsibility by blaming Congress for inadequate appropriations." As she explained, "For more than eleven years I have lived in Washington, D. C., and I have learned through attending Congressional Committee hearings and pending Indian legislation that it is the Indian Bureau that drafts these appropriations bills."[154] A citizen ready to hold her government to account, Zitkala-Ša had read the report, had shown up in Congress to observe deliberations, and was now ready to challenge government agents. Her path to doing so was inquiry—reading, observing, and questioning—and it served the ends of democracy.

But pan-Indian intellectual populism did not just mean reading reports and showing up in Congress; it meant telling stories of "the people." Because of their personal experiences out West, American Indians possessed more compelling evidence than government paper could ever present. To demonstrate as much, Zitkala-Ša relayed her recent experience dealing with healthcare on a reservation:

> This summer I went to see a proud Indian Chief who was sick. Before I reached the hut I heard men and women crying aloud. I stepped into the open door. The Indian was dead. They were washing the body, ready

> for burial. The corpse was only skin and bones. These grief-stricken Indians, with tears streaming down their faces, came to shake hands with me. Utterly hopeless, they cried as only heart-broken humans cry, until I, too, wept with them. The Government doctor arrived. I asked him what disease caused the death of the old Indian. He replied that he had no disease, but simply starved to death.[155]

At the beginning of the anecdote, Zitkala-Ša went to see a proud Indian chief. By the end of the anecdote, the chief had withered to skin and bones, wasted away because of government policies. Told in the first person, the story took listeners onto a reservation to witness the evils of federal oppression and to cry together as "heart-broken humans."

The conclusion of Zitkala-Ša's speech thus signaled how Indians could use personal experience to speak up as citizens. Though government agents would chastise them, though many in white society would oppose them, performing their citizenship was the only way to build a strong, populist pan-Indian coalition. "The sole purpose in making any criticism," she announced late in the speech, "has been with a view that the evils pointed out by me might be corrected."[156] As citizens, American Indians had the ability to demonstrate their loyalty by exposing the evils of the federal government. Finally, they had power *as* the people.

Conclusion

The little girl scampered across the kitchen, and the devil followed. As it turned out, this wasn't just a dream. The devil who chased her not only personified evil but also personified the laws, institutions, policies, attitudes, and actions of white America. But that wasn't the only America. The little girl was part of a red America determined to stand up and beat back the devil. Though she was being chased, the little girl figured out how to get other Indians to join her. Right as the devil tried to sink his claws into her tender young flesh, she learned to slap his hand away and to stand her ground with other Indians aligned by her side.

Unfortunately, the little girl could never get the devil out of her kitchen completely. Zitkala-Ša died in 1938, still fighting the prince of darkness. Until the end of her life, she battled the established power structure in the East—specifically, grappling with the Roosevelt administration over a recent veto of legislation to repay the Ute people for their claim on coal proceeds in Colorado.[157] Yet there had been important victories along the way. She had fought for citizenship and had achieved it. She had fought for resources for western reservations and had received some, including the use of an old army building for a community center. And she had fought government policies that oppressed and exploited her people, and had finally achieved some relief in the form of the Indian Reorganization Act of 1934. These fights were admirable, but they never led to complete victory for her people. The populist Indian uprising she promoted did not happen, and white America continued to exploit and oppress Indian America. Of course, failure to achieve complete victory was typical for intellectual populists. Booker T. Washington failed to make the South safer for African Americans. Thomas Davidson created a learning community that fizzled out after his death, and the Lower East Side remained a place of squalor and exploitation. Mary Baker Eddy created a belief system that now seems peculiar in light of twentieth-century scientific discoveries. And Robert Ingersoll battled a religious establishment that not only survived the assault of free-thought advocates but also created a fundamentalist power structure that continues to this day.

If intellectual populism is judged by the utopia it promises to create, it fails on its own terms. But the work of Zitkala-Ša and the other thinkers in this book suggests that populism should be judged less by results than by the fight itself. Intellectual populism is a mode of engagement, of battle, of calling disparate forces together. Zitkala-Ša could not upend the establishment, but no one could have; no one did. However, through eloquent, full-throated appeals, she brought people together in community centers, in lecture halls, in auditoriums, where they could think about pressing problems and shared hopes. In community, they could achieve a level of understanding they did not have before. Sometimes the act of coming together for inquiry and discussion is important in and of itself, even if it does not lead to the destruction of the status quo. Sometimes it is enough for people to feel empowered in the project of investigating, contemplating, and knowing the world.

Conclusion

The twenty-first century may involve the end of inquiry as we know it. For 150 years in the United States, inquiry has been tied, more or less, to institutions of higher education—that is, research universities, specialized forums, laboratories, and classrooms perpetuated by technical discourse, academic certification, and siloed disciplines. As Chad Wellmon has recently argued, these institutions emerged to organize the information overload wrought by the Enlightenment.[1] Their function was to help people winnow through more information than they had ever encountered, achieving knowledge in specialized areas that, when combined, could advance human understanding overall. But now that access to information has multiplied exponentially thanks to digital technology, universities and the specialized inquiry they promote seem antiquated. We need a new model of inquiry.

Or so numerous commentators have insisted. The past few years have produced a veritable cottage industry of writers pondering the future of knowledge, education, and deliberation. Kevin Carey, for instance, has envisioned a "University of Everywhere"—open to everyone, distributed around the globe via the internet, and personalized by "advances in artificial intelligence and fueled by massive amounts of educational data."[2] When this new university emerges, he writes, "people will form relationships with learning organizations that last decades based on their personal preferences, circumstances, and needs. Unlike today, belonging to a learning organization will not involve massive expenses and crippling amounts of debt."[3] Ryan Craig has seen a similar transformation on the horizon. Viewing education as a road to employment, Craig argues for the "great unbundling" of education and the "rise of competency management platforms" that allow students and algorithms to plot the most efficient path toward employment with a particular company.[4] Adopting a similar blend of technological and economic thinking, Richard DeMillo has not only envisioned but also demanded an intellectual and educational revolution. Because the established university system was designed a hundred years ago and based on "a factory approach to education in which raw materials (students) were sorted by age and ability into batches (classes) to receive uniform doses of content (classes, curricula, and majors)," the time has come to overthrow the bosses on the factory floor and to install new digital managers:

> Artificial intelligence makes it possible to personalize classrooms, even when course content is being distributed to a mass audience. Sophisticated analytic algorithms predict where students are likely to have problems and provide clues to master teachers about how to proceed. Even more important, technological innovation can be used to erase inequalities in circumstances—cognitive ability, social status, or academic knowledge—that plague postsecondary education as it scales to the masses.[5]

These commentators, and a host of others, agree that inquiry is on the precipice of a revolution.[6] Changes are afoot, they say, as technology transforms education to better serve the masses, not the elites.

In many ways, these commentators sound a lot like intellectual populists. Concerned about affordability, utility, access, purpose, and people, they hail a new community of inquirers around the promise of technological change and the hope of a more enlightened future. This new community emerges in response to the established educational order—the research university—which no longer serves the people and may even crush them under a mountain of debt and a cascade of false promises. Because inquiry in the university model is disconnected from the needs of ordinary individuals, lost in a foolhardy search for impersonal objectivity, individuals should band together and reclaim intellectual life for their own purposes.[7] Digital technology offers them the chance to do so, establishing radically distributed communities of thought that can become strong enough to resist, circumvent, and even abolish the status quo. The intellectual revolution afoot, these commentators imagine, will restore power to the people on a scale heretofore unimagined.

Regardless of whether these prophecies of a digital intellectual future are correct, they follow many of the same discursive markers as the intellectual-populist figures analyzed in this book. In the Gilded Age and Progressive Era, as in the twenty-first century, people worried that the intellectual status quo was disconnected from the lives of ordinary people, and they sought ways to unite disparate individuals in new intellectual communities. Robert Ingersoll, Mary Baker Eddy, Thomas Davidson, Booker T. Washington, and Zitkala-Ša were as concerned as commentators today with remaking inquiry to facilitate broad, democratic discussion among the masses. And just as commentators today utilize the places and spaces where people assemble (namely, online venues), the populist thinkers of the turn of the twentieth century utilized the popular spaces of their own time—lecture halls, periodicals, civic centers, churches, and auditoriums. Ingersoll, Eddy, Davidson, Washington, and Zitkala-Ša deployed modes of thought, speech, and engagement that seemed enlivening and empowering to people whom the status quo had marginalized. On the public stage, they linked frustrated individuals in a common project of education, entertainment, and edification, while resisting the intellectual establishment.

The heart of their project, as I have argued, was a distinctive repertoire of appeals. Intellectual populism is above all a set of discursive markers that constitute a tradition of engagement between rhetors and audiences on issues related to the pursuit of knowledge. These markers are flexible, adaptable, and portable, helping people address such topics as religion, health, philosophy, education, and human rights. While the specific content of these markers changes depending on specific situations and particular purposes, the markers themselves facilitate a new approach and orientation to intellectual affairs. As the preceding chapters have illustrated, we can identify intellectual-populist discourse by the combination of five basic appeals. The first appeal involves critiquing and attacking established knowledge institutions and intellectual orders, including universities, religious organizations, medical authorities, and educational authorities. To take one of the preceding chapters as an example, Mary Baker Eddy founded a church on her opposition to mainstream theology and medicine. She was particularly interested in exposing nefarious medical practices based on germ theory, the primacy of matter, and materia medica. As professionalized medicine pushed ordinary people away from the truth—the truth that matter was unreal—and subjected them to bizarre, even horrific, procedures, Eddy declared that she had discovered a method of healing that could rebuff established authorities and put people back in control of their lives. In response to the status quo that had long promised health but had only delivered sickness and sin, Eddy gave people a chance to flourish once again. By following Christian Science, ordinary people could circumvent the false promises of the iniquitous medical establishment and achieve total spiritual health. Again, Eddy's movement is just one example of the kind of anti-institutionalism that animates intellectual-populist discourse. But this sense of embattled opposition provides the energy needed for rousing people to the possibility of an alternative order.

The second appeal of intellectual populism, which is closely related to the first, insists that ordinary people—those outside the established order—ought to control inquiry for their own purposes. Intellectual populism hails "the people" as the true and proper stewards of our collective attempts to know the world. To take another chapter as an example, Thomas Davidson called together the Breadwinners on the Lower East Side of New York as the people, as the true stewards of philosophy. Though they were working-class immigrants—rather, *because* they were working-class immigrants—he engaged them on graduate-level issues in philosophy, convinced that they held the key to enlightenment in the twentieth century. Because colleges and universities educated only the idiot children of the wealthy, Davidson brought together a group of laborers to work hard—after they had already labored a full day in the sweatshops of their neighborhood—on issues of truth, beauty, morality, God, humanity, and more. These salt-of-the-earth workers were to spur human advancement in a new intellectual dispensation. On the Lower East Side and in places like it, declared Davidson, inquiry would return to the hands of the people, and they would remake the world. Building on the anti-institutional energy of the first appeal, hailing the people as stewards of inquiry links disparate individuals in the common project of reclaiming the pursuit of knowledge.

The third appeal of intellectual populism involves the liberal deployment of Americanisms—terms such as liberty, equality, freedom, and justice—adapted to the realm of ideas. Intellectual populists base their projects on the freedom of thinking for oneself; on the equality of intellectual pursuits, regardless of academic training; on the justice of broad, inclusive debate about the most pressing issues of life. In that way, they infuse ordinary democracy into the work of inquiry. To take yet another chapter as an example, Zitkala-Ša realized the power of these Americanisms for her movement to create a pan-Indian intellectual community. After all, American Indians were the first Americans. It was natural and useful, therefore, to encourage equal voices among the tribes, to demand freedom for her people to investigate the world on their own terms, and to fight for justice for individuals who had philosophized about existence long before the palefaces invaded these shores. Because of the power and prominence of Americanisms in American life, Zitkala-Ša worked to reclaim the intellectual soul of the nation for her people. Away from the white establishment and in the hands of ordinary Indians, liberty, justice, freedom, and equality would return to their proper place among the first Americans. In intellectual populism, these terms set the people on a revolutionary course to throw off the yoke of the established order and to turn the pursuit of knowledge into a movement for a new society.

The fourth appeal of intellectual populism involves pronouncements that are simultaneously conservative and radical. They are conservative in that they suggest a return to tradition, to the past, to simpler times; they are radical in that their implementation would upend the status quo. To take still another chapter as an example, Booker T. Washington's rhetoric was replete with conservative-radical proclamations. Farming, labor, soil, industriousness, discipline, self-help, faith, virtue, and honor—these were the appeals of an arch conservative. But applied to poor African Americans in the rural South, they were eminently radical, threatening the white establishment by putting land and wealth in the hands of former slaves. Through instantiation of conservative virtues, African Americans could secure their lives and livelihoods for generations. Washington even built a new institution, Tuskegee, to secure a radically conservative mode of intellectual work for formerly enslaved people and their descendants in the Black Belt of the South. United in the South, they could create the political, economic, social, and philosophical structures required for progress. Building on the Americanisms of the previous appeal, radical-conservatism casts populist revolution as a return to a purportedly proper order where salt-of-the-earth, ordinary people can finally get to work, free from the exploitation of the status quo.

The fifth appeal of intellectual populism involves utopian dreaming—or the promise of a utopian intellectual community. With the status quo vanquished, with ordinary people in control of knowledge, with freedom, liberty, equality, and justice firmly in place, and with a radical return to traditional values, the people can flourish in a grand populist utopia of thought. To take the first chapter of this book as an example, Robert Ingersoll ended nearly every lecture with a rich, thick description of such a utopia. Once the people stopped listening to religious authorities and started thinking for themselves, he declared, they would enter a world of open inquiry, honest debate, and intellectual advancement. Freed from the ghosts, freed from malicious ministers, freed from the iron arguments of the church, the American people would create republicanism in the realm of thought, much as they had instantiated republicanism in politics. With a silver tongue, with some of the most eloquent sentences in American public address, Ingersoll brought a populist utopia into vivid relief to inspire and motivate his audiences to build an intellectual heaven on earth. This final appeal of intellectual populism helps ordinary people visualize the world as it should be and as it will be if they battle the institutions of the established order and fight for the freedom they deserve.

I have exemplified the five basic appeals with references to preceding chapters in no particular order because each chapter illustrates, in its own way, the deployment of all the appeals. That is, the figures featured in this book had their own particular anti-institutionalism, hailing of the people, deployment of Americanisms, promotion of radical-conservatism, and visualization of a utopia. The point is not that each appeal is particular to the aforementioned rhetor but that these appeals combine in different ways and for different purposes to constitute a distinct mode of engaging popular audiences in the realm of ideas. These five appeals were flexible and adaptable to a host of situations that seemed ripe for a resistive force. What stands out about the careers of Ingersoll, Eddy, Davidson, Washington, and Zitkala-Ša was how, despite the marked differences in their backgrounds and projects, they each drew on the intellectual-populist rhetorical tool kit to build distinct communities of inquiry. At a general, structural level, they sounded a lot alike, deploying populist symbols at a time of tremendous institutional transformation. Frustrated with the emerging status quo, capable of articulating their grievances in an eloquent, persuasive manner, and committed to building community with similarly frustrated individuals, the intellectual populists in this book adopted a language that critiqued business as usual while drawing ordinary individuals into the very discussions that the great thinkers of the day controlled. Assaulting the status quo, it turned out, was a good way to energize people for discussing the same issues that the status quo pursued. The electricity of populist discourse was an effective way to address widespread frustration and channel it into productive deliberations about religion, medicine, philosophy, education, human rights, and more. As this book has demonstrated, populist discourse can serve the ends of a pluralistic, democratic community, even in the world of thought.

This idea of energizing through assault, of pluralizing and democratizing through combat, propels intellectual populism. It did so in the Gilded Age and Progressive Era, and it can do so today. As we grapple with waves of populist fervor and intellectual transformation similar to those that swept the turn of the twentieth century, and regardless of what we think about prophecies regarding digital technology and the future of education, we can turn to the insights of the past for help navigating the morass of the present. Below I offer six points about the opportunities of intellectual populism today. I offer them as a scholar interested in advancing the scholarly community writ large. As a professor employed at a research university, I am keenly aware of how portents of upheaval may affect me, my profession, and my community. I am also aware of how populist frustrations have led many people—far too many people—outside the academy to distrust, even resent, academic culture. Such distrust has exacerbated the divide between scholars and nonscholars. But the lessons of intellectual populism can point the way forward. The following six points, then, are meant for members of academic communities committed to overcoming the apparent gulf between experts and the masses.

One: The Importance of Face-to-Face Engagement

Many commentators who foresee the end of the research-university paradigm point to digital technology as the driving force of a new paradigm. Online communication, they insist, will enable people in disparate locations to live intellectually productive lives with people of similar interests around the globe. Digital inquiry is the wave of the future.

That may be true. Yet populist movements should remain dedicated to assembling individuals in physical spaces. While online communication can and should contribute to populist coalitions, physical closeness can influence and motivate people on another level. Gathering in the same space links individuals in distinctive, powerful ways.[8] The preceding case studies reinforce this idea, demonstrating how the energy of assembled bodies helps unify frustrated people around a common cause. To be sure, the world was much different during the Gilded Age and Progressive Era than it is today; populist learning *had* to happen in lecture halls, auditoriums, civic spaces, and the like. Today, digital technology frees us from that necessity. Yet we remain human beings who respond to the electricity of other bodies. When we assemble in the same room, listen to the same messages, laugh at the same lines, and applaud the same declamations, we unite in ways well-nigh impossible through digital means. Online tools can supplement physical closeness, just as newspapers and periodicals supplemented popular lectures around the turn of the twentieth century. But we ought to remain committed to analog gatherings if we are to constitute "the people." This means entering auditoriums and meeting spaces with the people frustrated by the status quo.

The intellectual populists of the Gilded Age and Progressive Era used eloquence to great effect in physical spaces. That was the power of Ingersoll's lecture in Hoboken, New Jersey. The ministers and policemen who showed up to arrest him ended up laughing along with him and becoming part of a mass of bodies. Ingersoll's ability to bend ideas, to play with sacred terms, and to promote shared ideals enabled him to turn opponents into collaborators. As the *New York Sun* summarized Ingersoll's feat, the clergy and the cops in his audience "howled and creamed with delight. The ministers lost their dignity and joined in the jollification. The detectives just doubled up."[9] Had they not been sitting with throngs of others, it is unlikely such jollification would have happened.

Something similar happened with Washington and his audiences. Washington received a lot of criticism from people who read his words, but he received almost universal support from people who gathered together to listen to him. Black and white, rich and poor, male and female—they heard Washington's speeches and declared him a black Moses capable of leading his people to the Promised Land. Even in the sweltering, segregated South, Washington spoke in a way that prompted blacks and whites to unify, at least while in the same space.[10] He "electrified the audience," wrote one paper after a speech in Atlanta, prompting "the fairest women of Georgia" to stand up and cheer. When he finished speaking, a "delirium of applause" erupted from the mixed-race audience, and "a great wave of sound dashed itself against the walls" of the auditorium.[11] In that room, at that time, "the people" came together.

As we try to navigate the current onslaught of populist agitation, as we contemplate the future of inquiry and education, we would do well to remember the opportunities of physical spaces and face-to-face assemblages. If scholars fail to utilize these spaces for thinking together, our opponents will use them to the detriment of our intellectual future.

Two: The Intersection of Space and Community

This point is closely related to the first, but it is distinct in its geographic commitments. Not only are face-to-face interactions important for building populist communities, but *where* those interactions happen shapes the character of these endeavors. It is easy for scholars to think of face-to-face interactions in the form of public lectures and talks, which, more often than not, take place on university campuses. It is easy to reserve a room on one's own campus and offer a public lecture that members of the community can attend. These are important events, but they do little to build populist coalitions. A public lecture on campus invites nonacademics to trudge to the ground that the intellectual status quo occupies (and only if they can find parking). But engaging "the people" should happen in spaces other than those that the established order controls. One of the primary insights of the intellectual populists discussed in this book is that the most effective way of empowering the people is to go to them. This doesn't mean going to them to impress "truth" upon them. It means going to them for mutual enrichment.

Thomas Davidson spent decades looking for the right community, going so far as to build a philosophical retreat on a sprawling plot of land in the Adirondack Mountains. But for much of his career he impressed truth on others rather than serving the intellectual needs of his fellow citizens. That changed when he went to the tenements of New York's Lower East Side. Going *to* the Breadwinners and transforming the spaces of their lives, he discovered, was the only way to effect a radical revolution in philosophy. As he concluded to listeners in the neighborhood, the most pressing intellectual project of the twentieth century was to "establish a Breadwinners' College or People's University in every city-ward in every country, village, or township. Then the cause of the higher education of the people will be won, and democracy placed on a firm basis."[12] Transforming the places and practices of the people, he realized, served the cause of intellectual democracy better than pulling people out of their world.

Mary Baker Eddy's lecturers learned a similar lesson. Touring the country to dispel misconceptions about Christian Science and to empower ordinary people as healers, members of the Board of Lectureship resisted lecturing in Christian Science churches. Instead, they tried to speak in "some public hall, opera house or similar place," thus making the lecture "a matter of general interest."[13] By entering into the same civic spaces that housed non–Christian Science lectures, Eddy's lecturers portrayed their work as an advancement in thought just like any advancement in science, religion, philosophy, and other traditional areas. On the public stage, as opposed to in a Christian Science church, they resolved to "correct the wrong impressions and state some of the facts" of their scientific religion, much as a scientist might lecture on recent advancements in his or her field.[14] That enabled ordinary people in cities and towns around the country to ponder on their own terms the big questions of the day.

For us today, the centrality of location and community in populist movements means going to and serving the people we are trying to reach, not bringing them to us. Face-to-face interactions can be more profitable for coalition building when we go to civic centers, libraries, public auditoriums, neighborhood churches, and nonacademic meeting halls. We should work to empower the people there instead of simply inviting them to our institutions. Populist messages and opportunities need to go on the road, not stay isolated on the carefully manicured lawns of college campuses.

Three: Intellectual Populism as Maker Movement

The rise of digital technology and online forums has coincided with widespread interest in making things—physical things. As many aspects of human life have moved online, people have found renewed delight in the tactile fulfillment of using one's hands to build physical objects. A case in point is Maker Faires, started by *Make* magazine, which take place across the country and promote do-it-yourself projects for real-world problem-solving. Colleges and universities have joined these effects by funding "maker spaces," which give faculty, students, and community partners access to the tools of the maker movement. Together with other makers, people can satisfy urges that online interactions alone cannot.

Booker T. Washington was an early proponent of the maker movement, though he did not know it by that name. Nevertheless, he shared with makers a commitment to empowering people through work with their hands. Washington created the Jesup Wagon to inspire a generation of makers across the rural South. He used the resources of Tuskegee to empower people as "producers, lovers of labor, independent, honest, unselfish, and above all supremely good."[15] People in the Black Belt of the South, he insisted, should "become a first hand producer of wealth," so that they can create, retain, and control the world around them.[16] They can then pass on their wealth to future generations and alter the economic inequalities that imprison African Americans. Committed to the producer ethic of populist resistance, Washington and Tuskegee taught people how to make things—crops, tools, goods, and services—because making things would build, piece by piece, object by object, a new reality for the race.

Zitkala-Ša taught something similar on Indian reservations. Having tasted success among Boston's literati, she moved back West because of the emptiness of high society. Going "back to the blanket," as this movement was known disparagingly,[17] she found meaning in a community center that brought people together to make stuff. They made meals for weary travelers. They made clothes and fabrics for beleaguered Indians. They made a community of young and old, male and female, that gave ordinary people purchase in their world. As she wrote of the community-center sewing group she started on the Ute reservation, "We met one day each week, devoting it to charity work for the aged members of the tribe. Plain, warm garments cut in the loose style they are accustomed to wear, were made for those who could neither see to sew nor buy their clothing ready made, with money they did not have. Sometimes members of the sewing classes helped one another with their necessary sewing. Later they learned very rapidly to crochet little caps, jackets and bootees for their babies."[18] Although focused on sewing, Zitkala-Ša's statement was ultimately about how the process of creation can empower people and communities. Populist resistance depends, she suggested, on small-scale maker projects that link ordinary people in common cause.

Empowering people as makers remains a priority for populist coalition building today. For people to join intellectual pursuits, they need to see themselves as agents in the creation of their world. They need to have purchase in working through shared problems. Too often, scholars fall into the trap of giving ordinary people the "right" answers to life's big questions. Too often, academics seek only to transmit ideas based on specialized, exclusionary inquiry. But such transmission positions ordinary people as receivers of knowledge, not creators of their own worlds, and that leads to further frustration, even resentment. Populism, however, demands empowerment and agency, putting people in a position to think and inquire for themselves. Making objects, making ideas, making communities—these are the hallmarks of a populist intellectual project that bridges the divide between ivory towers and the wider world. To effect an intellectual revolution, scholars should facilitate maker projects of the mind, engaging ordinary people as creators and agents who can work things out on their own.

Four: The Centrality of Religious Inquiry

This point may sound strange compared to the points offered thus far and compared to the dynamics of public culture today. But it is because of these dynamics that religion deserves a special position in populist intellectual movements. Religion occupied a primary place in the discourse of the thinkers discussed in the previous chapters. Bold and attentive to the interests of ordinary people, they recognized that religious issues cut to the heart of life's highest ideals. God, the devil, heaven, hell, good, evil, sin, salvation, service, sacrifice, piety, impiety, communion, community—such topics pervaded the lectures, writings, and discussions of intellectual populists in the Gilded Age and Progressive Era. Such topics should also shape intellectual populism today.

Let me be clear: The point is not that intellectual populism is or should be based on religious belief; specific religious beliefs can quickly impede the project of building coalitions. Rather, the point is that engaging religious issues and employing religious terminology are useful for drawing frustrated individuals into an intellectual movement. As William James explained, "There is, it must be confessed, a curious fascination in hearing deep things talked about, even tho neither we nor the disputants understand them. We get the problematic thrill, we feel the presence of vastness. Let a controversy begin in a smoking-room anywhere, about free-will or God's omniscience, or good and evil, and see how everyone in the place pricks up his ears."[19] Movements thrive in the presence of vastness, and if scholars hope to start a movement to bring ordinary people into intellectual culture, we need to embrace rather than skirt religious ideas and terminology. Too often we abandon religious discussion as inappropriate in secular society. But the moment we do that, we give those who oppose us a chance to pick up religious discourse and use it for their own ends. If we cede discussions of good, evil, heaven, hell, sin, salvation, and more to those outside the academy, we also cede a potentially powerful connection to "the people."

Robert Ingersoll realized as much. Interested in combating the religious status quo, he recognized the value of engaging religious ideas on the public stage. Religious topics, he knew, made for energizing conversations. To animate the people, he ranged widely on religious terrain. He denounced the "the prejudiced priest" and "the malicious minister" and deemed God an "infinite fiend" and "the insane keeper of a mad house." But he also praised Jesus Christ for preaching "many pearls of kindness—of love."[20] He then affirmed the freedom of everyone to inquire for themselves: "Each person should be allowed to reach his own conclusions and to speak his honest thought. Every man should be true to himself—true to the inward light. Each man, in the laboratory of his own mind, and for himself alone, should test the so-called facts—the theories of all the world."[21] For Ingersoll, religion was the best way to get the people involved in the hard work of thought and expression. He thus deployed religious terminology around which both believers and nonbelievers could rally.[22]

The same can be said for Mary Baker Eddy, Thomas Davidson, Booker T. Washington, and Zitkala-Ša. Though they personally held very different religious beliefs, they recognized the importance and power of religious discourse. Eddy and her lecturers turned discussions about God into discussions about Mind, Life, Love, and other synonyms for the divine. Davidson and his Breadwinners pledged themselves to the "spiritual elevation of mankind" and joined together as a "little knot of earnest Jews" ready to turn the world upside down.[23] Washington regularly delivered Sunday evening talks on Tuskegee's campus about God, work, and morality, and he traveled the country preaching a salvific gospel of work.[24] Zitkala-Ša, even though she became a committed Catholic in her twenties, continued to insist on "faith in the Great Spirit," which could unite people from different tribes in a pan-Indian movement.[25] Not religious beliefs per se but the language of religion proved essential to their populist coalitions.

Religious discourse has long occupied a distinctive place in U.S. public culture, and it will likely hold that place well into the future. Learning to use religious discourse to bring people together is among the chief tasks of any populist leader. The time has come to stop thinking of religion as a conversation stopper and to start thinking of it as the source of some of the most powerful and potent symbolic resources in modern society.[26]

Five: The Value of Common Enemies

Religious discourse can bring people together, as I just suggested, but that does not mean an end to division. People regularly join together by opposing something else, which means a common enemy may be not only useful but also necessary. Far too often in the twentieth and twenty-first centuries, ordinary people have united against the elites, including academics, intellectuals, and experts. Or at least they have seen themselves as wholly distinct from or opposed to the elites, however accurate or inaccurate those perceptions are. While scholars retain some esteem for their insights and contributions, the rhetoric of scholars being out-of-touch, aloof, overpaid liberal elites is increasingly widespread, reinforcing the apparent divide between "the people" and academics and enhancing populism's anti-intellectual reputation.[27]

Intellectual populism offers insight on how to overcome the division between scholars and the people, but doing so hinges on a careful, strategic handling of the common enemy. To reconnect with the masses, scholars should seize the idea that intellectuals are aloof and disconnected from everyday life, and they should reaffirm that idea. Strange as it may sound, reinforcing perceptions that scholarship is out of touch may be the best way to engage the masses in intellectual affairs.

That is what Thomas Davidson did to great effect. Davidson was a philosopher dedicated to enriching, broadening, and democratizing philosophical conversations. To get the Breadwinners interested in philosophy, he defined his opposition as philosophy itself—or rather, philosophy as it was typically carried out in academic settings. In Davidson's discourse, philosophical business as usual was the nefarious force that created the need for a philosophical resurgence among the people. "Philosophy since Kant left it," he told the Breadwinners in 1898, "has rather gone backwards than forwards, wandering off either into a crude materialism or an empty, merely formal idealism. At present it has come almost to a standstill, ashamed to go back openly to the absurdities of the old theology and afraid to go forward to pure science destitute of theology. It is in a sore strait, and this largely owing to the fact that its professors mostly occupy paid positions in unemancipated colleges and universities."[28] The appeal was strategically brilliant. To get ordinary people interested in philosophy—people whom professional philosophy in universities had passed over—Davidson denounced the philosophical status quo, thereby offering his listeners a foray into the subject of philosophy. As he wondered aloud later in his lectures, "Somewhere there must be found a small devoted band of men and women of fearless character, clear philosophic insight, and mighty spiritual love, who, living a divine life in their relations to each other, shall labor, with all the strength that is in them, to lift their fellows into the same divine life."[29] By voicing this idea, Davidson invited the Breadwinners to "labor" with one another in a new, fearless, philosophical community. Once again, critiquing the established order (in this case, professional philosophy) was an effective way to generate interest and participation in the area on which the established order was built (in this case, philosophy itself).

What this means for scholars today is that we ought to critique and oppose the established academic order that "the people" supposedly oppose. Many people mistrust intellectualism, but we can use that to our advantage. By deriding what they scorn, we can realign ourselves with the masses and animate intellectual conversations about the subjects we study. When we as academics denounce academic culture as out of touch and elitist, we create an opening for ordinary people to join us in a new intellectual movement. Making the academy a common enemy invites people with similar frustrations into an equivalential chain that can broaden, diversify, and democratize the very discussions the academy advances.

Six: The Malleability of Populist Discourse

The reason we can oppose academic culture at one level and energize inquiry at another level is because of the malleability of populist discourse, even in the pursuit of knowledge. Writers such as Michael Kazin have long insisted that populism is a flexible discourse that can be deployed in a variety of political situations and contexts.[30] The preceding chapters have demonstrated how flexible it can be in intellectual situations and contexts. Populist discourse can critique religion while simultaneously facilitating religious discussion. It can denounce medicine while affirming a science of healing. It can deride philosophy to promote philosophy. It can chastise education to revitalize education. It can denounce America to bolster the first Americans.

Likewise, scholars today can use intellectual populism for their own purposes. Even though populism has an anti-intellectual reputation, it remains a tool for intellectual engagement. It moves and inspires across demographics and situations—in the lecture halls of white America, the tenements of the Lower East Side, the African American churches of the South, and the Indian reservations of the West. Because of this malleability, we can adapt it to our present situations. But we must remember that intellectual populism requires eloquence and commitment. It requires an appreciation of speech, discussion, deliberation, and public engagement. The thinkers discussed in this book generally failed to create the change they wanted—at least in terms of the utopias they proffered. The religious status quo only got stronger after Ingersoll's assault. The medical establishment went on to world-changing discoveries and advancements, despite Eddy's efforts. Academic philosophy paid little attention to people like the Breadwinners after Davidson passed away. In the South, of course, problems for African Americans remained horrific, despite everything Washington did. Similar horrors plagued the

American Indian population, despite Zitkala-Ša's tireless work. They envisioned a utopian future that never came to pass. Yet their eloquence still mattered. It mattered to the people who attended their lectures. It mattered to the people who had long felt displaced by the establishment. It mattered because it gave ordinary individuals a sense of agency in the pursuit of knowledge. Intellectual populism can make a difference, even if it doesn't change the world.

Intellectual populism won't start a revolution today, but its malleable discourse can foster the spaces and generate the energy needed to change people's attitudes, beliefs, and commitments. Populist frustrations exist and will continue to exist. If we don't engage those frustrations, other rhetors will—and they may do so at our peril. But if we hope to create a broader, more diverse, increasingly pluralistic intellectual community, we can borrow the symbolic tools of populist resistance and build coalitions of thought better attuned to the needs of the people.

Notes

Introduction

1. Joshua Zeitz, "Historians Have Long Thought Populism Was a Good Thing. Are They Wrong?," *Politico*, January 14, 2018, https://www.politico.com/magazine/story/2018/01/14/trump-populism-history-216320.
2. Jennifer Rubin, "Populism Is No Way to Govern, and Trump Is Proving It," *Washington Post*, January 19, 2018, https://www.washingtonpost.com/blogs/right-turn/wp/2018/01/19/populism-is-no-way-to-govern-and-trump-is-proving-it/.
3. Evan McMullin, "Trump's Rise Proves How Dangerous Populism Is for Democracy," *NBCNews.com*, October 11, 2017, https://www.nbcnews.com/think/opinion/trump-s-rise-proves-populism-democracy-s-greatest-threat-ncna809521.
4. Jan-Werner Müller, *What Is Populism?* (Philadelphia: University of Pennsylvania Press, 2016).
5. Barry Eichengreen, *The Populist Temptation: Economic Grievance and Political Reaction in the Modern Era* (Oxford: Oxford University Press, 2018).

6. Yascha Mounk, *The People vs. Democracy: Why Our Freedom Is in Danger and How to Save It* (Cambridge, MA: Harvard University Press, 2018).
7. William Galston, *Anti-pluralism: The Populist Threat to Liberal Democracy* (New Haven, CT: Yale University Press, 2018), 79.
8. Galston, *Anti-pluralism*, 128.
9. Galston, *Anti-pluralism*, 101.
10. Richard Hofstadter, *Anti-intellectualism in American Life* (New York: Vintage Books, 1963), 154–155, 151, 404–412.
11. For perspectives on Hofstadter's account of populism, see Robert D. Johnston, "'The Age of Reform': A Defense of Richard Hofstadter Fifty Years On," *Journal of the Gilded Age and Progressive Era* 6 (2007): 127–137; and Gillis Harp, "Hofstadter's 'The Age of Reform' and the Crucible of the Fifties," *Journal of the Gilded Age and Progressive Era* 6 (2007): 139–148.
12. Kenneth Minogue, "Populism as a Political Movement," in *Populism: Its Meaning and National Characteristics*, ed. Ghita Ionescu and Ernest Gellner (London: Macmillan, 1969), 208–209.
13. Colleen J. Shogan, "Anti-intellectualism in the Modern Presidency: A Republican Populism," *Perspectives on Politics* 5 (2007): 296.
14. John Lukacs, *Democracy and Populism: Fear and Hatred* (New Haven, CT: Yale University Press, 2005), 60–61.
15. Aaron Lecklider, "The Real Victims of Anti-intellectualism," *Chronicle of Higher Education*, September 20, 2017, https://www.chronicle.com/article/The-Real-Victims-of/241101.
16. See Laura Grattan, *Populism's Power: Radical Grassroots Democracy in America* (New York: Oxford University Press, 2016); Benjamin Moffitt, *The Global Rise of Populism: Performance, Political Style, and Representation* (Stanford, CA: Stanford University Press, 2016), esp. ch. 8; and Jason Frank, "Populism and Praxis," in *The Oxford Handbook of Populism*, ed. Cristobal Rovira Kaltwasser, Paul Taggart, Paulina Ochoa Espejo, and Pierre Ostiguy (Oxford: Oxford University Press, 2017), 629–643.
17. See Charles Postel, *The Populist Vision* (Oxford: Oxford University Press, 2007).
18. For more on the ambiguity and usefulness of "the people" and its many permutations, see Michael Calvin McGee, "In Search of 'the

People': A Rhetorical Alternative," *Quarterly Journal of Speech* 61 (1975): 236–249; Maurice Charland, "Constitutive Rhetoric: The Case of the *Peuple Québécois*," *Quarterly Journal of Speech* 73 (1987): 133–150; and Vanessa B. Beasley, *You, the People: American National Identity in Presidential Rhetoric* (College Station: Texas A&M University Press, 2004).

19. Paul Stob, *William James and the Art of Popular Statement* (East Lansing: Michigan State University Press, 2013).
20. I borrow the phrase "thinking together" from Angela G. Ray and Paul Stob, eds., *Thinking Together: Lecturing, Learning, and Difference in the Long Nineteenth Century* (State College: Pennsylvania State University Press, 2018).
21. Postel, *The Populist Vision*, 22.
22. See Michael Kazin, *The Populist Persuasion: An American History* (New York: Basic Books, 1995).
23. Postel, *The Populist Vision*, 4.
24. Robert C. McMath, *American Populism: A Social History, 1877-1898* (New York: Hill and Wang, 1993), 44, 8.
25. Postel, *The Populist Vision*, 36.
26. See McMath, *American Populism*, 50–82; and Postel, *The Populist Vision*, 45–67.
27. Grattan, *Populism's Power*, 71.
28. For an overview, see Frank, "Populism and Praxis," 638–640.
29. Postel, *The Populist Vision*, 4.
30. McMath, *American Populism*, 135, 146.
31. See Kazin, *The Populist Persuasion*, 42.
32. Quoted in Postel, *The Populist Vision*, 161.
33. McMath, *American Populism*, 52.
34. Donnelly quoted in Kazin, *The Populist Persuasion*, 29.
35. Donnelly quoted in Kazin, *The Populist Persuasion*, 29.
36. McMath, *American Populism*, 52.
37. Rhys H. Williams and Susan M. Alexander, "Religious Rhetoric in American Populism: Civil Religion as Movement Ideology," *Journal for the Scientific Study of Religion* 33 (1994): 5.
38. Kazin, *The Populist Persuasion*, 27–46.

39. Postel, *The Populist Vision*, 103–133.
40. Richard Hofstadter, *The Age of Reform: From Bryan to F. D. R.* (New York: Vintage, 1955), 62.
41. See McMath, *American Populism*, 180–211.
42. Kazin, *The Populist Persuasion*, 45.
43. See Ronald P. Formisano, *For the People: American Populist Movements from the Revolution to the 1850s* (Chapel Hill: University of North Carolina Press, 2008).
44. For more on Huey Long, Charles Coughlin, and the legacy of populism, see Alan Brinkley, *Voices of Protest: Huey Long, Father Coughlin, and the Great Depression* (New York: Vintage Books, 1982), 143–168.
45. See Joseph Lowndes, "From Founding Violence to Political Hegemony: The Conservative Populism of George Wallace," in *Populism and the Mirror of Democracy*, ed. Francisco Panizza (London: Verso, 2005), 144–171.
46. See Linda Schulte-Sasse, "Meet Ross Perot: The Lasting Legacy of Capraesque Populism," *Cultural Critique* 25 (1993): 92–93.
47. Adrian Kuzminski, *Fixing the System: A History of Populism, Ancient and Modern* (New York: Continuum, 2008), 4.
48. Cristobal Rovira Kaltwasser, Paul Taggart, Paulina Ochoa Espejo, and Pierre Ostiguy, "Populism: An Overview of the Concept and State of the Art," in Kaltwasser et al., *Oxford Handbook of Populism*, 7–8.
49. Moffitt, *Global Rise of Populism*, 38, 43–45.
50. See Cas Mudde, "Populism: An Ideational Approach," 27–47; Kurt Weyland, "Populism: A Political Strategic Approach," 48–72; and Pierre Ostiguy, "Populism: A Socio-cultural Approach," 73–97, all in Kaltwasser et al., *Oxford Handbook of Populism*; and Moffitt, *Global Rise of Populism*.
51. Kazin, *The Populist Persuasion*, 3, 1.
52. Kazin, *The Populist Persuasion*, 12.
53. Kazin, *The Populist Persuasion*, 13, 15, 16.
54. Kazin, *The Populist Persuasion*, 6–7.
55. Howard S. Erlich, "Populist Rhetoric Reassessed: A Paradox," *Quarterly Journal of Speech* 63 (1977): 140–151.
56. Erlich, "Populist Rhetoric Reassessed," 147–148.
57. Ronald Lee, "The New Populist Campaign for Economic Democracy: A

Rhetorical Exploration," *Quarterly Journal of Speech* 72 (1986): 274–289.

58. Lee, "New Populist Campaign," 285.
59. Lloyd Rohler, "Conservative Appeals to the People: George Wallace's Populist Rhetoric," *Southern Communication Journal* 64 (1999): 316–322.
60. Rohler, "Conservative Appeals," 317.
61. Michael J. Lee, "The Populist Chameleon: The People's Party, Huey Long, George Wallace, and the Populist Argumentative Frame," *Quarterly Journal of Speech* 92 (2006): 358, 359, 360, 362.
62. Ernesto Laclau, *On Populist Reason* (London: Verso, 2007), 74–77.
63. Laclau, *On Populist Reason*, 81, 108, 16–20, 117–123.
64. An excellent account of how knowledge proceeds through people, struggles, and coalitions is Randall Collins, *The Sociology of Philosophies: A Global Theory of Intellectual Change* (Cambridge, MA: Belknap Press of Harvard University Press, 1998).
65. For more on ideographs, see Michael Calvin McGee, "The 'Ideograph': A Link between Rhetoric and Ideology," *Quarterly Journal of Speech* 66 (1980): 1–16.
66. Grattan, *Populism's Power*, 47.
67. For more on the deliberative potential of populism, see Frank, "Populism and Praxis," 629–643.
68. Arabella Lyon, *Deliberative Acts: Democracy, Rhetoric, and Rights* (State College: Pennsylvania State University Press, 2013), 15.
69. Christian Kock and Lisa S. Villadsen, "Introduction: Citizenship as a Rhetorical Practice," in *Rhetorical Citizenship and Public Deliberation*, ed. Christian Kock and Lisa S. Villadsen (State College: Pennsylvania State University Press, 2012), 13.
70. For more on these grassroots cultures of discussion and argumentation, see Roderick P. Hart, *Civic Hope: How Ordinary Americans Keep Democracy Alive* (Cambridge: Cambridge University Press, 2018).
71. James P. McDaniel and Bruce E. Gronbeck, "Through the Looking Glass and Back: Democratic Theory, Rhetoric, and Barbiegate," in *The Prettier Doll: Rhetoric, Discourse, and Ordinary Democracy*, ed. Karen Tracy, James P. McDaniel, and Bruce E. Gronbeck (Tuscaloosa: University of Alabama Press, 2007), 35.

72. See Karen Tracy, *Challenges of Ordinary Democracy: A Case Study in Deliberation and Dissent* (State College: Pennsylvania State University Press, 2010); and Robert Asen, *Democracy, Deliberation, and Education* (State College: Pennsylvania State University Press, 2015).
73. Robert Hariman, "Amateur Hour: Knowing What to Love in Ordinary Democracy," in Tracy, McDaniel, and Gronbeck, *The Prettier Doll*, 222.
74. For a compelling comparison between the Gilded Age of the nineteenth century and the gilded age of today, see Cecelia Tichi, *Civic Passions: Seven Who Launched Progressive America (and What They Teach Us)* (Chapel Hill: University of North Carolina Press, 2009), esp. the introduction.
75. For an excellent overview, see Charles W. Calhoun, introduction to *The Gilded Age: Perspectives on the Origins of Modern America*, 2nd ed., ed. Charles W. Calhoun (Lanham, MD: Rowman & Littlefield, 2007).
76. Alan Trachtenberg, *The Incorporation of America: Culture and Society in the Gilded Age* (New York: Hill and Wang, 1982), 54.
77. Robert H. Wiebe, *The Search for Order, 1877-1920* (New York: Hill and Wang, 1967).
78. H. Wayne Morgan, "Toward National Unity," in *The Gilded Age*, rev. ed., ed. H. Wayne Morgan (Syracuse: Syracuse University Press, 1970), 11.
79. Walter Licht, *Industrializing America: The Nineteenth Century* (Baltimore: Johns Hopkins University Press, 1995), 186.
80. See Eric Arnesen, "American Workers and the Labor Movement in the Late Nineteenth Century," in *The Gilded Age*, 39–61.
81. See Dennis Cashman, *America in the Gilded Age: From the Death of Lincoln to the Rise of Theodore Roosevelt*, 3rd ed. (New York: New York University Press, 1993), 73–99.
82. See Cashman, *America in the Gilded Age*, 36–72.
83. Trachtenberg, *The Incorporation of America*, 72.
84. Burton J. Bledstein, *The Culture of Professionalism: The Middle Class and the Development of Higher Education in America* (New York: Norton, 1978), 88.
85. Magali Sarfatti Larson, *The Rise of Professionalism: A Sociological Analysis* (Berkeley: University of California Press, 1977), xvi–xvii.
86. Roger L. Geiger, *To Advance Knowledge: The Growth of American Research Universities, 1900-1940* (New York: Oxford University Press, 1986), 1.

87. Geiger, *To Advance Knowledge*, 20.
88. See Bruce A. Kimball, *The "True Professional Ideal" in America: A History* (Cambridge, MA: Blackwell, 1992), 205–212; Thomas Bender, *Intellect and Public Life: Essays on the Social History of Academic Intellectuals in the United States* (Baltimore: Johns Hopkins University Press, 1993), 49–77; and Gregory Clark and S. Michael Halloran, eds., *Oratorical Culture in Nineteenth-Century America: Transformations in the Theory and Practice of Rhetoric* (Carbondale: Southern Illinois University Press, 1993).
89. Thomas L. Haskell, introduction to *The Authority of Experts: Studies in History and Theory*, ed. Thomas L. Haskell (Bloomington: Indiana University Press, 1984), xii.
90. Larson, *The Rise of Professionalism*, 4.
91. For details, see Larson, *The Rise of Professionalism*, 104–135.
92. See Kimball, *True Professional Ideal*, 243–251.
93. Larson, *The Rise of Professionalism*, 135.
94. Bledstein, *The Culture of Professionalism*, 90. Also see Bender, *Intellect and Public Life*, 43–44.
95. Larson, *The Rise of Professionalism*, 208–244.
96. For a classic account, see Joseph F. Kett, *The Pursuit of Knowledge under Difficulties: From Self-Improvement to Adult Education in America, 1750-1990* (Stanford, CA: Stanford University Press, 1994).
97. Andrew C. Rieser, *The Chautauqua Moment: Protestants, Progressives, and the Culture of Modern Liberalism* (New York: Columbia University Press, 2003), 84–85. Also see Andrew Chamberlin Rieser, "Secularization Reconsidered: Chautauqua and the De-Christianization of Middle-Class Authority, 1880–1920," in *The Middling Sorts: Explorations in the History of the American Middle Class*, ed. Burton J. Bledstein and Robert D. Johnston (New York: Routledge, 2001), 136–150.
98. Frederick J. Antczak, *Thought and Character: The Rhetoric of Democratic Education* (Ames: Iowa State University Press, 1985), 56.
99. For an excellent overview of early lecture culture, see Granville Ganter, "Women's Entrepreneurial Lecturing in the Early National Period," in Ray and Stob, *Thinking Together*, 41–55.
100. Carl Bode, *The American Lyceum: Town Meeting of the Mind* (Carbondale:

Southern Illinois University Press, 1968), 7.

101. Donald M. Scott, "The Popular Lecture and the Creation of a Public in Mid-Nineteenth-Century America," *Journal of American History* 66 (1980): 797.

102. James Perrin Warren, *Culture of Eloquence: Oratory and Reform in Antebellum America* (University Park: Pennsylvania State University Press, 1999).

103. For more on the active, reciprocal role that audiences played, see Warren, *Culture of Eloquence*, 16. For a nineteenth-century account of active audiences, see Josiah Holland, "The Popular Lecture," *Atlantic Monthly* 15 (1865): 363.

104. Clark and Halloran, introduction to *Oratorical Culture*, 8.

105. In general, see Clark and Halloran, afterword to *Oratorical Culture*, 247–250.

106. See Angela G. Ray, *The Lyceum and Public Culture in the Nineteenth-Century United States* (East Lansing: Michigan State University Press, 2005), 3–8.

107. Edward T. Channing, *Lectures Read to the Seniors in Harvard College* (Boston: Ticknor and Fields, 1856), 17.

108. For an excellent study of insight, academic spaces, and supposed boundaries of inquiry, see Francesca Bordogna, *William James at the Boundaries: Philosophy, Science, and the Geography of Knowledge* (Chicago: University of Chicago Press, 2008).

109. See Bledstein, *The Culture of Professionalism*, especially 46–79.

110. For an overview, see Lewis Perry, *Intellectual Life in America: A History* (Chicago: University of Chicago Press, 1989), 281–291.

111. Ray, *Lyceum and Public Culture*, 13–47.

112. For two case studies on this point, see Sara E. Lampert, "The 'Perfect Delight' of Dramatic Reading: Gertrude Kellogg and the Post–Civil War Lyceum," in Ray and Stob, *Thinking Together*, 130–149; and E. Douglas Bomberger, "Talking Music: Amy Fay and the Origins of the Lecture Recital," in Ray and Stob, *Thinking Together*, 150–168.

113. Ray, *Lyceum and Public Culture*, 3.

114. For an overview of the waning intellectual reputation of popular lectures and lyceum performances, see Thomas Augst, "Humanist Enterprise in the Marketplace of Culture," in *The Cosmopolitan Lyceum: Lecture Culture*

and the Globe in Nineteenth-Century America, ed. Tom F. Wright (Amherst: University of Massachusetts Press, 2013), 223–240.

115. For more on counterpublics, see Michael Warner, *Publics and Counterpublics* (New York: Zone Books, 2002), esp. 64–124.
116. As several scholars have pointed out, "Native American" is no more accurate a descriptor than "Indian." Kimberly Wieser, for instance, explains the point this way: "Indigenous people in the United States and Canada prefer to be referred to by their tribally specific names for their people, preferably in their own language, while some term must be used to address the ideas we as Indigenous peoples often share in common." In the United States, she continues, many Indigenous people "prefer 'American Indian' or 'Indian,' . . . not only because 'Indian' is the general term most people grew up with, but also because it is the word used in article 1, section 8 of the U.S. Constitution and is the word in which all legal rights are vested." See Kimberly G. Wieser, *Back to the Blanket: Recovered Rhetorics and Literacies in American Indian Studies* (Norman: University of Oklahoma Press, 2017), 199(n7).

Chapter One. Robert Ingersoll's Religious Resistance

1. "Ingersoll on Ministers," *New York Sun*, February 25, 1895, 1.
2. Alexander Clark to Robert Ingersoll, December 14, 1877, Box 1, Folder 7, Robert Green Ingersoll Papers, Abraham Lincoln Presidential Library.
3. Fred W. E. Shrivell to Robert Ingersoll, February 15, 1887, Papers of Robert G. Ingersoll, Library of Congress, Microfilm Edition, Reel 18.
4. A. H. Byington to Robert Ingersoll, November 8, 1888, Papers of Robert G. Ingersoll, Library of Congress, Microfilm Edition, Reel 18.
5. Ernesto Laclau, *On Populist Reason* (London: Verso, 2005), 74–77.
6. Susan Jacoby, *The Great Agnostic: Robert Ingersoll and American Freethought* (New Haven, CT: Yale University Press, 2013), 5, 59, 38.
7. Information on Ingersoll's life has been gleaned from the following biographies: C. H. Cramer, *Royal Bob: The Life of Robert G. Ingersoll* (New York: Bobbs-Merrill, 1952); David D. Anderson, *Robert Ingersoll* (New York: Twayne Publishers, 1972); Orvin Larson, *American Infidel: Robert G. Ingersoll* (Madison, WI: Freedom From Religion Foundation, 1993); and

Frank Smith, *Robert G. Ingersoll: A Life* (Buffalo, NY: Prometheus Books, 1990).

8. See, for example, *Lowell Daily Citizen*, January 12, 1877. Also see Smith, *Robert G. Ingersoll*, 45–46.
9. Quoted in Cramer, *Royal Bob*, 207.
10. As the *Chicago Inter-Ocean* put it, Ingersoll "has no superior as a stump orator in the universe." *Chicago Inter-Ocean*, July 7, 1876, 2. For more on Ingersoll's orations for Republican candidates, see Paul Stob, "Sacred Symbols, Public Memory, and the Great Agnostic: Robert Ingersoll Remembers the Civil War," *Rhetoric & Public Affairs* 19, no. 2 (2016): 275–306.
11. Quoted in Larson, *American Infidel*, 119.
12. For early praise of the nominating speech, see "Ingersoll on Blaine," *Chicago Inter-Ocean*, June 19, 1876, 3. For more coverage, see Smith, *Robert G. Ingersoll*, 104–108.
13. See, for example, Cramer, *Royal Bob*, 13–17.
14. For an 1876 discussion of Ingersoll's prominence prior to the Blaine speech, see the *Milwaukee Daily Sentinel*, September 19, 1876, 4.
15. Cramer, *Royal Bob*, 97.
16. For discussion of Ingersoll's most extensive lecture tour, see Smith, *Robert G. Ingersoll*, 227–233. Also see Cramer, *Royal Bob*, 96–100.
17. For this and other lecture schedules, see "Miscellany," Box 34, Robert Green Ingersoll Papers, Library of Congress, Microfilm Edition, Reel 23.
18. Cramer, *Royal Bob*, 96.
19. For just one example of Farrell insisting on ticket prices, see C. P. Farrell to W. H. Rapley, December 27, 1892, Oversize BV 28, Letters of Mr. & Mrs. Clinton P. Farrell & Family, Abraham Lincoln Presidential Library.
20. See, for example, C. P. Farrell to Col. W. M. Morton, March 2, 1893, Oversize BV 28, Letters of Mr. & Mrs. Clinton P. Farrell & Family, Abraham Lincoln Presidential Library. Also see C. P. Farrell to Edwin Knowles, November 17, 1893, Oversize BV 28, Letters of Mr. & Mrs. Clinton P. Farrell & Family, Abraham Lincoln Presidential Library. Toward the end of Ingersoll's career, after his reputation had soared and he had proven his ability to draw massive crowds, the terms of his

lectures became 80 percent for Ingersoll and 20 percent for the house. See "Col. Ingersoll's Lectures, 1896," Box 11, Folder 6, Robert Green Ingersoll Papers, Abraham Lincoln Presidential Library.

21. See Cramer, *Royal Bob*, 118.
22. Quoted in "Col. Ingersoll," in *Complete Lectures of Col. R. G Ingersoll* ([Chicago?]: Published for the Trade, [1886?]), 5–6. This volume, which I reference frequently in this chapter, contains over two dozen texts paginated nonconsecutively. Each lecture, speech, or interview begins with page 1. As a result, my citations refer to the pagination within each lecture. Many library catalogs list it as being published in Chicago in 1886, but the book itself does not include a city or date.
23. Robert Ingersoll to Eva Ingersoll, February 21, 1878, Box 21, Folder 3, Robert G. Ingersoll Papers, Abraham Lincoln Presidential Library.
24. Robert Ingersoll to Eva Ingersoll, November 21, 1878, Box 21, Folder 3, Robert G. Ingersoll Papers, Abraham Lincoln Presidential Library.
25. See, for example, "In Brief," *The Congregationalist*, August 18, 1880, 4; "No Proof in Negation," *North American*, April 29, 1881; and "The Infidel Ingersoll," *Raleigh News and Observer*, May 14, 1881.
26. For example, see "The Great Infidel," *Cleveland Herald*, June 27, 1884, 8.
27. For a warning against a forthcoming Ingersoll lecture, see "Some Mistakes of Ingersoll," *Rocky Mountain News*, July 26, 1879, 2.
28. See, for example, the verbatim transcript of Ingersoll's lecture "Ghosts," in *Complete Lectures*, 1.
29. For instance, see "About Town," *Daily Inter-Ocean*, September 20, 1880, 8. For other instances, see Cramer, *Royal Bob*, 120–121.
30. See "Ingersoll on Politics," *St. Louis Globe-Democrat*, February 2, 1880, 3.
31. "Looking Towards God," *Milwaukee Daily Sentinel*, February 23, 1880, 8.
32. For a host of replies to an Ingersoll visit, and a response to that visit by a local clergyman, see "Briggs—Ingersoll," *Galveston News*, May 23, 1880, 2. Also see "Dr. Palmer on Bob Ingersoll," *Galveston News*, May 30, 1880, 2.
33. Susan Jacoby, *Freethinkers: A History of American Secularism* (New York: Metropolitan Books, 2004), 149–185.
34. See Jacoby, *Freethinkers*, 154–156.
35. See Charles Postel, "Murder on the Brazos: The Religious Context of

the Populist Revolt," *Journal of the Gilded Age and Progressive Era* 15 (2016): 197–219.

36. For an overview of the growth of religion during this time period, see Sydney E. Ahlstrom, *A Religious History of the American People*, 2nd ed. (New Haven, CT: Yale University Press, 2004), 715–748. For an 1894 report on how Ingersoll's lectures were not, in fact, leading Americans away from religion, see "Ingersoll and the Churches," *Daily Inter Ocean*, February 7, 1894, 6.
37. Edward J. Blum, *Reforging the White Republic: Race, Religion, and American Nationalism, 1865–1898* (Baton Rouge: Louisiana State University Press, 2005), 9.
38. See Kristin Schwain, *Signs of Grace: Religion and American Art in the Gilded Age* (Ithaca, NY: Cornell University Press, 2008).
39. In general, see Blum, *Reforging the White Republic.*
40. See Ahlstrom, *Religious History*, 698–714. Also see Edwin S. Gaustad and Leigh E. Schmidt, *The Religious History of America*, rev. ed. (San Francisco: HarperSanFrancisco, 2002), 217–219.
41. For an overview, see Ahlstrom, *Religious History*, 743–748. Also see Gaustad and Schmidt, *Religious History of America*, 222–225.
42. For coverage of Ingersoll and Moody, see Smith, *Robert G. Ingersoll*, 378–379. For coverage of Ingersoll and Sunday, see Cramer, *Royal Bob*, 98–99. For a newspaper interview with Moody in which he chides Ingersoll, see "Moody's Mission," *Chicago Inter-Ocean*, October 28, 1879, 2.
43. Gaustad and Schmidt, *Religious History of America*, 209.
44. Gary Dorrien, *The Making of American Liberal Theology: Imagining Progressive Religion, 1805–1900* (Louisville, KY: Westminster John Knox Press, 2001), 179.
45. Peter J. Thuesen, *In Discordance with the Scriptures: American Protestant Battles over Translating the Bible* (New York: Oxford University Press, 1999), 10.
46. In general, see William R. Hutchinson, *The Modernist Impulse in American Protestantism* (Cambridge, MA: Harvard University Press, 1976).
47. See, for example, the conclusion to Ingersoll's lecture "Some Mistakes of Moses," in *The Works of Robert G. Ingersoll*, vol. 2: *Lectures* (New York: Dresden Publishing, 1901), 251–252.

48. When these rumors about Ingersoll's supposed immorality circulated, several newspapers investigated the claims, found them specious, and printed stories setting the record straight. See, for example, "Robert Ingersoll," *Milwaukee Daily Sentinel*, July 13, 1880; "Robert Ingersoll," *Atchison Globe*, July 10, 1880; and "Col. Robert Ingersoll and His Family," *Lynchburg Virginian*, July 10, 1880.
49. Hutchinson, *Modernist Impulse*, 57.
50. Hutchinson, *Modernist Impulse*, 72–74.
51. Hutchinson, *Modernist Impulse*, 95.
52. "Skulls," for example, was mostly an excerpt of "The Liberty of Man, Woman, and Child."
53. The best example of Ingersoll revising a lecture for publication concerns "Some Mistakes of Moses," which spans over 250 pages in the Dresden edition. Ingersoll would have had to lecture for well over four hours to deliver that much material, and there are no records of Ingersoll speaking for more than three hours on any particular occasion.
54. For example, the Robert G. Ingersoll Papers contains a complete, handwritten copy of "Myth and Miracle," which spans 170 pages, due to the length of Ingersoll's lectures and to the fact that he left plenty of white space on his long-hand pages. See "Myth and Miracle," Box 14, Folder 5, Robert G. Ingersoll Papers, Abraham Lincoln Presidential Library.
55. The typeset version of "Myth and Miracle" matches the handwritten copy discussed above, though the typeset version spans only sixty-three pages. Given the number of words on the page, Ingersoll would have been able to deliver that much content in approximately two hours.
56. See Cramer, *Royal Bob*, 27.
57. Robert Ingersoll, "Individuality," in *Complete Lectures*, 6.
58. Ingersoll, "Individuality," 7.
59. Robert Ingersoll, "Gods," in *Complete Lectures*, 10.
60. Robert Ingersoll, "Heretics and Heresies," in *Lectures of Col. R. G. Ingersoll, Latest* (Chicago: Rhodes & McClure, 1898), 758.
61. Robert Ingersoll, "Ghosts," in *Complete Lectures*, 11–12.
62. Robert Ingersoll, "Some Reasons Why," in *Complete Lectures*, 3–4.

63. Robert Ingersoll, "Orthodoxy," in *Complete Lectures*, 7.
64. Robert Ingersoll, "Liberty of Man, Woman, and Child," in *Complete Lectures*, 484.
65. Robert Ingersoll, "The Great Infidels," in *Complete Lectures*, 2.
66. Ingersoll, "Liberty of Man," 3.
67. Robert Ingersoll, "What Must We Do to Be Saved?" Box 31, Robert Green Ingersoll Papers, Library of Congress, Microfilm Edition, Reel 22.
68. As Angela Ray has noted, "white Protestant middling classes" were the most stalwart supporters of lecture culture in the nineteenth century (Angela Ray, "Making History by Analogy: Frederick Douglass Remembers William the Silent," in *Exploring Argumentative Contexts*, ed. Frans H. van Eemeren and Bart Garseen [Amsterdam: John Benjamins Publishing, 2012], 100). When Ingersoll lectured in small to medium sized cities, particularly in the nation's heartland, it is reasonable to assume that white Protestants of some variety made up the bulk of the audience.
69. Elizabeth Fenton, *Religious Liberties: Anti-Catholicism and Liberal Democracy in Nineteenth-Century U.S. Literature and Culture* (Oxford: Oxford University Press, 2011), 4.
70. Fenton, *Religious Liberties*, 5.
71. Ingersoll, "Ghosts," 13.
72. Ingersoll, "Ghosts," 14.
73. Robert Ingersoll, "Foundations of Faith," Box 28, Robert Green Ingersoll Papers, Library of Congress, Microfilm Edition, Reel 20.
74. Ingersoll, "Individuality," 6.
75. Ingersoll, "What Must We Do?"
76. Susan M. Griffin, *Anti-Catholicism and Nineteenth-Century Fiction* (Cambridge: Cambridge University Press, 2004), 17.
77. See Raymond L. Fischer, "Ingersoll on the Lecture Platform," *Central States Speech Journal* 22 (1971): 123–126; Ralph L. Towne and Frederick Speckeen, "Robert Green Ingersoll: A Case Study of Free Speech," *Today's Speech* 10, no. 4 (1962): 10–29; Lionel Crocker, "Robert Green Ingersoll's Influence on American Oratory," *Quarterly Journal of Speech* 24, no. 2 (1938): 299–312; J. Vernon Jensen, "Robert G. Ingersoll: 'True

Believer' Unbeliever," *Central States Speech Journal* 35 (1984): 105–112; and J. Vernon Jensen, "The Rhetorical Strategy of Thomas H. Huxley and Robert G. Ingersoll: Agnostics and Roadblock Removers," *Speech Monographs* 32 (1965): 59–68.

78. Ingersoll, "Heretics and Heresies," 760.
79. Ingersoll, "What Must We Do?"
80. Ingersoll, "Ghosts," 1.
81. Robert Ingersoll, "The Devil," Box 28, Robert Green Ingersoll Papers, Library of Congress, Microfilm Edition, Reel 20.
82. Ingersoll, "The Great Infidels," 4.
83. Ingersoll, "Individuality," 7.
84. Robert Ingersoll, "The Truth," Box 31, Robert Green Ingersoll Papers, Library of Congress, Microfilm Edition, Reel 22.
85. Ingersoll, "Liberty of Man," 3.
86. Ingersoll, "The Truth."
87. Ingersoll, "Liberty of Man," 498.
88. Ingersoll, "The Great Infidels," 7.
89. Ingersoll, "Individuality," 3.
90. Robert Ingersoll, "How to Reform Mankind," Box 28, Robert Green Ingersoll Papers, Library of Congress, Microfilm Edition, Reel 20.
91. Ingersoll, "The Ghosts," 2.
92. Michael Calvin McGee, "The 'Ideograph': A Link between Rhetoric and Ideology," *Quarterly Journal of Speech* 66, no. 1 (1980): 1–16.
93. "Mr. Ingersoll as an Orator," *Milwaukee Sentinel*, April 30, 1877, 4.
94. Benjamin Moffitt, *The Global Rise of Populism: Performance, Political Style, and Representation* (Stanford, CA: Stanford University Press, 2016), ch. 4.
95. Ingersoll, "What Must We Do?," 2; and Ingersoll, "Liberty of Man," 495.
96. Ingersoll, "The Ghosts," 2.
97. Ingersoll, "Liberty of Man," 8. For a similar anecdote, see "Gods," 3.
98. Ingersoll, "Orthodoxy," 10.
99. Ingersoll, "Some Reasons Why," 7.
100. Kenneth Burke, *Permanence and Chance: An Anatomy of Purpose*, 3rd ed. (Berkeley: University of California Press, 1984), 74, 90, 119.
101. See Émile Durkheim, *The Elementary Forms of Religious Life*, trans. Karen E.

Fields (New York: Free Press, 1995), 33–44.

102. See Ingersoll, "Gods," 2; and Ingersoll, "Blasphemy," in *Complete Lectures*, 4.
103. Ingersoll, "Heretics and Heresies," 769.
104. Ingersoll, "Some Mistakes of Moses."
105. Ingersoll, "Some Reasons Why," 7; Ingersoll, "Individuality," 3; Ingersoll, "Gods," 1.
106. Ingersoll, "Liberty of Man," 4–6.
107. Ingersoll, "The Great Infidels," 8.
108. Ingersoll, "Heretics and Heresies," 781.
109. Ingersoll, "The Truth."
110. Ingersoll, "Gods," 3.
111. Ingersoll, "The Devil," 35.
112. See, for instance, Ingersoll, "Liberty of Man," 3.
113. Ingersoll, "Some Mistakes of Moses."
114. Ingersoll, "Some Mistakes of Moses."
115. Ingersoll, "What Must We Do?"
116. Ingersoll, "What Must We Do?"
117. Ingersoll, "What Must We Do?"
118. Ingersoll, "What Must We Do?"
119. Ingersoll, "Gods," 2.
120. Mark A. Noll, *Between Faith and Criticism: Evangelicals, Scholarship, and the Bible in America* (San Francisco: Harper & Row, 1986), 11.
121. Alan Richardson, "The Rise of Modern Biblical Scholarship and Recent Discussion of the Authority of the Bible," in *The Cambridge History of the Bible: The West from the Reformation to the Present Day*, ed. S. L. Greenslade (Cambridge: Cambridge University Press, 1963), 301.
122. Ingersoll, "Liberty of Man," 524.
123. Ingersoll, "The Gods," 15.
124. Ingersoll, "Individuality," 8.
125. Ingersoll, "Some Reasons Why," 8.
126. See "Sermon on Ingersoll," *Milwaukee Sentinel*, December 29, 1895, 10; and "Our Morning Sermon," *Denver Daily News*, December 29, 1895, 18.
127. "Our Morning Sermon," *Denver Daily News*, December 29, 1895, 18.

128. "Our Morning Sermon," *Denver Daily News*, December 29, 1895, 18.
129. Julia Clask to Robert Ingersoll, November 28, 1877, Box 1, Folder 7, Robert Green Ingersoll Papers, Abraham Lincoln Presidential Library.
130. D. C. Sowers to Robert Green Ingersoll, February 6, 1878, Box 1, Folder 8, Robert Green Ingersoll Papers, Abraham Lincoln Presidential Library.
131. F. L. Brown to Robert Ingersoll, May 8, 1882, Box 2, Folder 1, Robert Green Ingersoll Papers, Abraham Lincoln Presidential Library.
132. Alsop Leffingwell to Robert Ingersoll, January 9, 1894, Papers of Robert Green Ingersoll, Library of Congress, Microfilm Edition, Reel 18.
133. James Vernon to Robert Ingersoll, December 16, 1895, Papers of Robert Green Ingersoll, Library of Congress, Microfilm Edition, Reel 18.
134. See, for example, Arthur R. Pierce to Robert Ingersoll, December 3, 1895, Papers of Robert Green Ingersoll, Library of Congress, Microfilm Edition, Reel 18.

Chapter Two. Mary Baker Eddy's Divine Healing Science

1. C. S. Harris, untitled testimony, *Christian Science Journal* 19 (September 1901): 376–378.
2. Elma E. Williams, untitled testimony, *Christian Science Journal* 19 (November 1901): 507–509.
3. Louise Reich, untitled testimony, *Christian Science Journal* 19 (February 1902): 714.
4. David G. Moir, untitled testimony, *Christian Science Journal* 21 (February 1904): 691–693.
5. See Gage Chapel and Richard Jensen, "Synthesizing Jamesian Pragmatism and Platonic Idealism in Nineteenth-Century America: The Discourse of Mary Baker Eddy's Christian Science," *Journal of Communication and Religion* 23 (2000): 96. For other estimates, see Rennie B. Schoepflin, *Christian Science on Trial: Religious Healing in America* (Baltimore: Johns Hopkins University Press, 2003), 53.
6. Gillian Gill, *Mary Baker Eddy* (Cambridge, MA: Perseus Books, 1998), 295–296.
7. For an overview, see Gill, *Mary Baker Eddy*, 450–463.
8. Rosemary R. Hicks, "Religion and Remedies Reunited: Rethinking

Christian Science," *Journal of Feminist Studies in Religion* 20 (2004): 57.

9. For a description of the venue and a discussion of the sermon, see Jean Angela McDonald, "Mary Baker Eddy at the Podium: The Founder of the Christian Science Church" (master's thesis, University of Minnesota, 1969), 73–76.
10. Gill, *Mary Baker Eddy*, 270.
11. Robert Peel, *Mary Baker Eddy: The Years of Authority* (New York: Holt, Rinehart and Winston, 1977), 73. The other sermon published from this time period was "Christian Healing." While "The People's God" predated "Christian Healing" in terms of oral delivery, "Christian Healing" was published in 1880, while "The People's God" did not appear until 1883.
12. Mary Baker Eddy, *The People's God* (Cambridge, MA: John Wilson and Son, 1883), 3. Box 89, Folder: Writings–The People's God, Mary Baker Eddy Library, Boston, MA.
13. Eddy, *The People's God*, 4.
14. Eddy, *The People's God*, 4.
15. Eddy, *The People's God*, 5, 6, 11, 12.
16. Eddy, *The People's God*, 5, 9.
17. Eddy, *The People's God*, 7, 8, 10, 9.
18. Eddy, *The People's God*, 10, 8, 6.
19. Eddy, *The People's God*, 13.
20. For more on Eddy's motherly persona, see Gail Parker, "Mary Baker Eddy and Sentimental Womanhood," *New England Quarterly* 43 (1970): 3–18.
21. For examples, see Chapel and Jensen, "Synthesizing Jamesian Pragmatism," 108; Jean A. McDonald, "Mary Baker Eddy and the Nineteenth-Century 'Public' Woman: A Feminist Reappraisal," *Journal of Feminist Studies in Religion* 2 (1986): 89–111; Kimber Charles Pearce, "Rhetorical Polysemy in Mary Baker Eddy's 'Christian Science in Tremont Temple,'" *Journal of Communication and Religion* 23 (2000): 80; Beth Rapp Young, "Defending Child Medical Neglect: Christian Science Persuasive Rhetoric," *Rhetoric Review* 20, nos. 3–4 (2001): 273.
22. Paul Starr, *The Social Transformation of American Medicine: The Rise of a Sovereign Profession and the Making of a Vast Industry* (New York: Basic Books, 1982), 32.

23. John Duffy, *From Humors to Medical Science: A History of American Medicine*, 2nd ed. (Urbana: University of Illinois Press, 1993), 47.
24. Duffy, *From Humors to Medical Science*, 47.
25. John S. Haller Jr., *American Medicine in Transition, 1840–1910* (Urbana: University of Illinois Press, 1981), 160.
26. As late as 1900, in fact, midwives helped deliver half the babies born in the United States. See Charlotte G. Borst, *Catching Babies: The Professionalization of Childbirth, 1870–1920* (Cambridge, MA: Harvard University Press, 1995), 1.
27. See Borst, *Catching Babies*, 15. Also see Deborah Kuhn McGregor, *From Midwives to Medicine: The Birth of American Gynecology* (New Brunswick, NJ: Rutgers University Press, 1998).
28. For details of the disparate power structures in nineteenth-century medicine, especially in hospital medical care, see Charles E. Rosenberg, "And Heal the Sick: The Hospital and the Patient in the 19th Century America," *Journal of Social History* 10 (1977): 428–447.
29. W. F. Bynum, *Science and the Practice of Medicine in the Nineteenth Century* (Cambridge: Cambridge University Press, 1994), 115.
30. Haller, *American Medicine in Transition*, 201–202.
31. For an overview of the divisions within the medical community, see Starr, *Social Transformation*, 79–144.
32. Erwin H. Ackerknecht, *A Short History of Medicine*, rev. ed. (Baltimore: Johns Hopkins University Press, 1982), 194.
33. Starr, *The Social Transformation of American Medicine*, 136, 4.
34. Quoted in Haller, *American Medicine in Transition*, 155–156.
35. See Diane Price Herndl, *Invalid Women: Figuring Feminine Illness in American Fiction and Culture, 1840–1940* (Chapel Hill: University of North Carolina Press, 1993), 110–112.
36. Martha H. Verbrugge, *Able-Bodied Womanhood: Personal Health and Social Change in Nineteenth-Century Boston* (New York: Oxford University Press, 1988), 102.
37. Patricia Vertinsky, *The Eternally Wounded Woman: Women, Doctors, and Exercise in the Late Nineteenth Century* (Manchester: Manchester University Press, 1990), 69–70, 58.

38. For discussion of some of the horrific treatments, see Herndl, *Invalid Women*, 29; and Ann Douglas Wood, "'The Fashionable Diseases': Women's Complaints and Their Treatment in Nineteenth-Century America," *Journal of Interdisciplinary History* 4 (1973): 25–52. For a critique of Wood's interpretation, see Regina Markell Morantz, "The Perils of Feminist History," *Journal of Interdisciplinary History* 4 (1974): 649–660. For the role of arsenic at the time, see Haller, *American Medicine in Transition*, 90–98.
39. In an early circular advertising her professional services, Eddy wrote in the royal "we" about her ability to help women with childbirth: "We have a certificate from the most celebrated and skillful Obstetrician and Surgeon in Massachusetts, stating our qualification to teach Obstetrics. And what is better, our system prevents the suffering that has attended accouchment, and with the great auxiliary of Mind, obviates the use of medicine." See "Circular," Box 86, Folder: Writings—Lectures and Addresses, Mary Baker Eddy Library, Boston, MA. Also see Gill, *Mary Baker Eddy*, 285.
40. To Eddy, healing comes through Divine Mind, not the human mind or mortal mind. She saw "mind cure" as nothing more than occultism. See Mary Baker Eddy, *Science and Health with Key to the Scriptures* (Boston: Christian Science Publishing Society, 1906), 167. For further explanation of this aspect of Christian Science theology, see Stephen Gottschalk, *The Emergence of Christian Science in American Religious Life* (Berkeley: University of California Press, 1973), 138–143.
41. Verbrugge, *Able-Bodied Womanhood*, 5.
42. Robert Peel's two-volume biography remains the authoritative treatment. Robert Peel, *Mary Baker Eddy: The Years of Discovery* (New York: Holt, Rinehart and Winston, 1966); and Peel, *The Years of Authority*. Another excellent treatment is Gill, *Mary Baker Eddy*.
43. Decades after her initial treatments, Eddy's relationship with Quimby would spark a number of debates and lawsuits, as some argued that Eddy simply ripped off Quimby's ideas and rebranded them as Christian Science. These accusations of intellectual plagiarism eventually died off, though Eddy's philosophy overlapped with Quimby's system at certain

key points. See Gill, *Mary Baker Eddy*, 119–121.

44. Quoted in Peel, *The Years of Discovery*, 195.
45. Peel, *The Years of Discovery*, 195.
46. Mary Baker Eddy, *Miscellaneous Writings, 1883–1896* (Boston: Trustees Under the Will of Mary Baker G. Eddy, 1896), 24.
47. Peel, *The Years of Discovery*, 196.
48. Mary Baker Eddy, *Retrospection and Introspections* (Boston: Joseph Armstrong, 1906), 39.
49. See, for example, David Heywood, *Divine Revelation and Human Learning: A Christian Theory of Knowledge* (Aldershot, England: Ashgate, 2004), 13; Rolfe King, *Obstacles to Divine Revelation: God and the Reorientation of Human Reason* (London: Continuum, 2008), 232; and Ormond Rush, *The Eyes of Faith: The Sense of the Faithful and the Church's Reception of Revelation* (Washington, DC: Catholic University of America Press, 2009), 11.
50. See, for example, Benjamin D. Sommer, "Revelation at Sinai in the Hebrew Bible and in Jewish Theology," *Journal of Religion* 79 (1999): 449–450; Asma Afsaruddin, "Revelation in the Qur'ān," in *Communicating the Word: Revelation, Translation, and Interpretation in Christianity and Islam*, ed. David Marshall (Washington, DC: Georgetown University Press, 2011), 53; and Ross Woodman, *Revelation and Knowledge: Romanticism and Religious Faith* (Toronto: University of Toronto Press, 2011), 217–218.
51. Gottschalk, *Emergence of Christian Science*, 26.
52. Mary Baker Glover [Eddy], *Science and Health* (Boston: Christian Scientist Publishing Company, 1875), 3–4.
53. Gottschalk, *Emergence of Christian Science*, 54.
54. Gottschalk, *Emergence of Christian Science*, 83.
55. Gottschalk, *Emergence of Christian Science*, 64–67.
56. Gottschalk, *Emergence of Christian Science*, 64.
57. Gottschalk, *Emergence of Christian Science*, 92, 147.
58. See Gill, *Mary Baker Eddy*, 288.
59. Gottschalk, *Emergence of Christian Science*, 148–149, 130.
60. Chapel and Jensen, "Synthesizing Jamesian Pragmatism," 97.
61. Chapel and Jensen, "Synthesizing Jamesian Pragmatism," 112–113.
62. James himself even visited a Christian Science practitioner for a period

of time to work on his health. For more on his visits and his defense of Christian Science, see Robert D. Richardson, *William James in the Maelstrom of American Modernism* (Boston: Houghton Mifflin, 2006), 275–276, 394–398.

63. Gottschalk, *Emergence of Christian Science*, 281.
64. Quoted in Peel, *The Years of Authority*, 158.
65. See, for example, Gill, *Mary Baker Eddy*, 321.
66. See Schoepflin, *Christian Science on Trial*, 113.
67. Quoted in Schoepflin, *Christian Science on Trial*, 121.
68. See Schoepflin, *Christian Science on Trial*, 82–85, 179–184.
69. Schoepflin, *Christian Science on Trial*, 184–190.
70. Schoepflin, *Christian Science on Trial*, 146–150, 164, 190.
71. See Gill, *Mary Baker Eddy*, 281–291.
72. As Gottschalk summarizes, it was in 1898 that Eddy "created the agencies through which The Mother Church fulfilled its more positive function of providing the channels for the propagation of her teaching." Gottschalk, *Emergence of Christian Science*, 188.
73. "Church Rule," *Christian Science Journal* 15 (February 1898): 666.
74. For just two examples of Eddy and her associates working out the details of the board, see "Board of Lectureship," *Christian Science Journal* 15 (March 1898): 774; and "The Board of Lectureship," *Christian Science Journal* 16 (July 1898): 272.
75. "As to the Lectureship," *Christian Science Sentinel* 2 (March 2, 1899): 5.
76. See "International Board of Lectureship," Box 213, Folder: The First Church of Christ Scientist—Lectures and Board of Lectureship, Mary Baker Eddy Library, Boston, MA.
77. Edward Kimball to "The Churches in Milwaukee," May 16, 1898, Box 150, Folder: Kimball, Edward A. (1845–1909), Papers 1896–1907, Mary Baker Eddy Library, Boston, MA.
78. See Jean A. McDonald, "Mary Baker Eddy and the Nineteenth-Century 'Public' Woman: A Feminist Reappraisal," *Journal of Feminist Studies in Religion* 2 (1986): 107.
79. Edward Kimball to Mary E. Smith, April 28, 1898, Box 150, Folder: Kimball, Edward A. (1845–1909), Papers 1896–1907, Mary Baker Eddy

Library, Boston, MA.

80. Irving Tomlinson to Members of the Board of Lectureship, December 22, 1899, Box 213, Folder: The First Church of Christ Scientist—Lectures and Board of Lectureship, Mary Baker Eddy Library, Boston, MA.
81. Irving C. Tomlinson undated letter, Box 219, Folder: Tomlinson, Irving C. (ca. 1860–1944), Lecture Data, Mary Baker Eddy Library, Boston, MA.
82. For an example, see the news clippings related to William McCracken, Box 4, Folder: 531536, S-29, Committee on Publication Clipping File Collection, Mary Baker Eddy Library, Boston, MA.
83. Irving C. Tomlinson, "1000 Word Report," Box 219, Folder: Tomlinson, Irving C. (ca. 1860–1944), Lecture Data, Mary Baker Eddy Library, Boston, MA.
84. "The Christian Science Board of Lectureship, Historical Record," Box 213, Folder: The First Church of Christ Scientist—Lectures and Board of Lectureship—Historical Record, Mary Baker Eddy Library, Boston, MA.
85. See, for example, "A Tribute to Mrs. Sue Harper Mims by Her Students," Box 174 A, Folder: Mims, Sue Harper (d. 1913), Mary Baker Eddy Library, Boston, MA. Also see "Reminiscences of Annie M. Knott," Box 37, Folder 10, Mary Baker Eddy Library, Boston, MA.
86. See Schoepflin, *Christian Science on Trial*, 34.
87. The list comes from a memo dated April 18, 1927. The memo concerns Bicknell Young, an early lecturer, and the advice he received from Kimball, who had supposedly gotten the prescribed topics directly from Eddy. The memo exists in Box 213, Folder: The First Church of Christ Scientist—Lectures and Board of Lectureship, Post 1910, Mary Baker Eddy Library, Boston, MA.
88. The recipient of the letter is unclear, but the letter is dated June 22, 1899. Box 213, Folder: The First Church of Christ Scientist—Lectures and Board of Lectureship, 1898–1910, Mary Baker Eddy Library, Boston, MA.
89. See the letter from Irving Tomlinson to the entire Board of Lectureship, July 22, 1919, Box 213, Folder: The First Church of Christ Scientist—Lectures and Board of Lectureship, Post 1910, Mary Baker Eddy Library,

Boston, MA. For another letter on how to discuss the discoverer of Christian Science, see Mary Baker Eddy to Septimus J. Hanna, October 13, 1902, Box 213, Folder: The First Church of Christ Scientist—Lectures and Board of Lectureship, 1898–1910, Mary Baker Eddy Library, Boston, MA.

90. See "Church By-Law," *Christian Science Journal* 19 (March 1902): 742. For more, see Box 219, Folder: Tomlinson, Irving C. (ca. 1860–1944), Published/Printed Items, Mary Baker Eddy Library, Boston, MA.
91. "Aims to Enlighten," *Portland Oregonian*, March 26, 1905. For similar coverage, see "Kimball's Lecture," *San Jose News*, April 10, 1905.
92. "Disease Is Not Real," *St. Paul Globe*, November 3, 1902.
93. "Free Lecture on Christian Science," *Riverside Enterprise*, November 26, 1904.
94. "Christian Science Lecture," *Wausau (Wisc.) Daily News*, May 4, 1905.
95. See, for example, untitled article, *Milton (Mass.) News*, April 10, 1903; "A C. S. Lecture," *The Inter Lake* (Kalispell, Montana), February 17, 1905.
96. For two examples, see "Disturbed by Toughs," *Worcester Telegram*, January 25, 1909; and "Christian Science and Physical Force," *Belfast (Ireland) Northern Whig*, November 8, 1907.
97. George Tomkins, "Christian Science and Bible Science Alphabet," *Supplement Washington News Letter*, December 14, 1898.
98. Frank H. Leonard, "Christian Science," *Needham Chronicle*, October 23, 1909.
99. "Immense Crowd: Christian Scientists Meet in Music Hall," *Boston Journal*, April 6, 1899.
100. Clarence Eaton, "On Christian Science," *Everett Republican*, n.d.
101. Sue Harper Mims, "Among the Clouds," Box 530775, Folder: Lecture Publication—Mims, Sue Harper—Among the Clouds, Mary Baker Eddy Library, Boston, MA.
102. For just some examples, see Eddy, *Science and Health*, 108, 113, 128, 219, 546.
103. "Grave Not the Goal," *Peoria Herald-Transcript*, November 14, 1904.
104. "Christian Science, the Science of Salvation," *Milwaukee Daily News*, October 11, 1909.

105. "Christian Science: Its Work and Scope," *Supplement to the Christian Science Sentinel* 3, no. 25 (1900): 401.
106. "Christian Science: Its Claims," *Concord Evening Monitor*, March 30, 1899, Box 220, Subject File, Mary Baker Eddy Library, Boston, MA.
107. "Dr. Fluno's Able Lecture," *Supplement to the New Bern Journal*, January 1909, Box 531511, Folder 254157, Committee on Publication Clipping File, Mary Baker Eddy Library, Boston, MA.
108. "Lecture on Christian Science," *Cambridge Chronicle*, October 17, 1908, Box 531511, Folder 254157, Committee on Publication Clipping File, Mary Baker Eddy Library, Boston, MA.
109. "Lecture at Christian Science Church," *Des Moines Capital*, December 4, 1907, Box 531511, Folder 253697, Committee on Publication Clipping File, Mary Baker Eddy Library, Boston, MA.
110. "The Panacea for the World's Unrest," *Worcester Evening Gazette*, January 18, 1901.
111. "Christian Science, the Law of Spirit," *Atlanta Constitution*, December 17, 1901.
112. An excellent example of how deductive, syllogistic arguments from uncontroversial major premises function can be found in Susan B. Anthony's 1872 voting rights speech, which is analyzed adroitly in Karlyn Kohrs Campbell, *Man Cannot Speak for Her*, vol. 1: *A Critical Study of Early Feminist Rhetoric* (New York: Greenwood Press, 1989), 105–119.
113. See David E. Shi, *Facing Facts: Realism in American Thought and Culture, 1850-1920* (Oxford: Oxford University Press, 1995), especially 66–78.
114. For more on the importance of supporting the minor premise in arguments like this one, see Stephen E. Lucas, "Justifying America: The Declaration of Independence as a Rhetorical Document," in *American Rhetoric: Context and Criticism*, ed. Thomas W. Benson (Carbondale: Southern Illinois University Press, 1989), 67–130.
115. "On Christian Science," *Everett Republican*, n.d.
116. "Christian Science and Its Message," *Daily Patriot* (Concord, NH), October 17, 1904.
117. "Christian Science and the Bible Science Alphabet," *Supplement Washington News Letter*, December 14, 1898.

118. For a couple of those exceptions, see "Answers to Mr. Peabody," *La Crosse Leader-Press*, January 7, 1910, Box 531511, Folder 253697, Committee on Publication Clipping File, Mary Baker Eddy Library, Boston, MA; and "Grave Not the Goal," *Peoria Herald-Transcript*, November 14, 1904, Box 531536, Folder 254591, Committee on Publication Clipping File, Mary Baker Eddy Library, Boston, MA.
119. See Schoepflin, *Christian Science on Trial*, 113–137.
120. Eddy, *Science and Health*, 600–700.
121. For more on science and popular culture—including lecture culture—in the nineteenth century, see Aileen Fyfe and Bernard Lightman, eds., *Science in the Marketplace: Nineteenth-Century Sites and Experiences* (Chicago: University of Chicago Press, 2007).
122. "Christian Science and Its Message," *Daily Patriot*, October 17, 1904.
123. "Christian Science and Its Message," *Daily Patriot*, October 17, 1904.
124. "Judge Hanna," *New Hampshire Patriot*, October 22, 1908.
125. "On Christian Science," *Everett Republican*, n.d.
126. "Lecture on Christian Science," *Cambridge Chronicle*, October 17, 1908.
127. For more on arguing through experience, see Paul Stob, "Pragmatism, Experience, and William James's Politics of Blindness," *Philosophy and Rhetoric* 44 (2011): 227–249.
128. For a good critique of experience as evidence, see Mari Boor Tonn, "Taking Conversation, Dialogue, and Therapy Public," *Rhetoric & Public Affairs* 8 (2005): 405–430. Also see Joan W. Scott, "The Evidence of Experience," *Critical Inquiry* 17 (1991): 773–797.
129. William James, *The Varieties of Religious Experience* (Cambridge, MA: Harvard University Press, 1985), 66.
130. James, *Varieties of Religious Experience*, 66–67.
131. Lecture by Edward A. Kimball, December 2, 1906, Box 530775, Folder 519941, Published Lecture File, Mary Baker Eddy Library, Boston, MA.
132. "Christian Science," *Reading (Mass.) Chronicle*, Box 531536, Folder 254583, Committee on Publication Clipping File, Mary Baker Eddy Library, Boston, MA.
133. "Lecture on Christian Science," *Cambridge Chronicle*, October 17, 1908.
134. "Grave Not the Goal," *Peoria Herald-Transcript*, November 14, 1904.

135. For instance, see Michael Lee's characterization of the populist promises offered by the People's Party leaders as well as Huey Long and George Wallace. Michael J. Lee, "The Populist Chameleon: The People's Party, Huey Long, George Wallace, and the Populist Argumentative Frame," *Quarterly Journal of Speech* 92, no. 4 (2006): 355–378.
136. "On Christian Science," *Everett Republican*, n.d.
137. "The Spiritual Dominion of Man through Scientific Christianity," *Grand Rapids Chronicle*, May 5, 1904.
138. "Seventh Free Lecture on Christian Science," *Needham Chronicle*, October 23, 1909.
139. "'Christian Science as Religion of Progress' Is Theme of M'Crackan," *Denver Post*, Box 531511, Folder 253697, Committee on Publication Clipping File, Mary Baker Eddy Library, Boston, MA.

Chapter Three. Thomas Davidson's Push for Philosophical Community

1. John Louis Recchiuti, *Civic Engagement: Social Science and Progressive-Era Reform in New York City* (Philadelphia: University of Pennsylvania Press, 2007), 12.
2. Quoted in Recchiuti, *Civic Engagement*, 67.
3. Steven L. Piott, *Daily Life in the Progressive Era* (Santa Barbara, CA: Greenwood, 2011), 68.
4. Thomas Davidson, "The Problems Set by the Nineteenth Century to the Twentieth," Box 27, Thomas Davidson Papers, Sterling Memorial Library, Yale University.
5. The term famously comes from Benedict Anderson, *Imagined Communities: Reflections on the Origin and Spread of Nationalism*, rev. ed. (London: Verso, 1991).
6. Doreen Massey, *Space, Place, and Gender* (Minneapolis: University of Minnesota Press, 1994), 23.
7. For an excellent overview of the relationship between space and rhetoric in ancient Athens, see James Fredal, *Rhetorical Action in Ancient Athens: Persuasive Artistry from Solon to Demosthenes* (Carbondale: Southern Illinois University Press, 2006).

8. Jane S. Sutton, "Space in Tropes, an Opaque but Visible Relationship," *Review of Communication* 12 (2012): 32. In general, see Debra Hawhee, *Moving Bodies: Kenneth Burke at the Edges of Language* (Columbia: University of South Carolina Press, 2009).
9. See, for example, Timothy Barney, "Power Lines: The Rhetoric of Maps as Social Change in the Post-Cold War Landscape," *Quarterly Journal of Speech* 95 (2009): 412–434; Thomas R. Dunn, "Remembering 'A Great Fag': Visualizing Public Memory and the Construction of Queer Space," *Quarterly Journal of Speech* 97 (2011): 435–460; and John Lynch, "Prepare to Believe: The Creation Museum as Embodied Conversion Narrative," *Rhetoric & Public Affairs* 16 (2013): 1–28.
10. For example, see Paul Stob, "Lonely Courage, Commemorative Confrontation, and Communal Therapy: William James Remembers the Massachusetts 54th," *Quarterly Journal of Speech* 98 (2012): 249–271.
11. See Elizabethada A. Wright, "Rhetorical Spaces in Memorial Places: The Cemetery as a Rhetorical Memory Place/Space," *Rhetoric Society Quarterly* 35 (2005): 51–81.
12. Roxanne Mountford, "On Gender and Rhetorical Space," *Rhetoric Society Quarterly* 30 (2001): 58.
13. For an excellent example, see Carly S. Woods, *Debating Women: Gender, Education, and Spaces for Argument, 1835-1945* (East Lansing: Michigan State University Press, 2018).
14. Robert J. Topinka, "Resisting the Fixity of Suburban Space: The Walker as Rhetorician," *Rhetoric Society Quarterly* 42 (2012): 68.
15. Douglas Reichert Powell, *Critical Regionalism: Connecting Politics and Culture in the American Landscape* (Chapel Hill: University of North Carolina Press, 2007), 14.
16. Dave Tell, "The Meanings of Kansas: Rhetoric, Regions, and Counter Regions," *Rhetoric Society Quarterly* 42 (2012): 215.
17. Tell, "The Meanings of Kansas," 222.
18. Jenny Rice, "From Architectonic to Tectonics: Introducing Regional Rhetorics," *Rhetoric Society Quarterly* 42 (2012): 204.
19. Tell, "The Meanings of Kansas," 229.
20. The concept of the geography of knowledge emerged from the work of

the historian of science David Livingston. See David N. Livingston, "The History of Science and the History of Geography: Interactions and Implications," *History of Science* 22 (1984): 271–302; and David N. Livingston, "The Spaces of Knowledge: Contributions towards a Historical Geography of Science," *Environment and Planning D: Society and Space* 13 (1995): 5–34.

21. Diarmid A. Finnegan, "The Spatial Turn: Geographical Approaches in the History of Science," *Journal of the History of Biology* 41 (2008): 383.
22. For an excellent case study of this theme, see Francesca Bordogna, *William James at the Boundaries: Philosophy, Science, and the Geography of Knowledge* (Chicago: University of Chicago Press, 2008).
23. David N. Livingston, *Putting Science in Its Place: Geographies of Scientific Knowledge* (Chicago: University of Chicago Press, 2003), 7.
24. Livingston, *Putting Science in Its Place*, 14.
25. Simon Naylor, "Introduction: Historical Geographies of Science—Places, Contexts, Cartographies," *British Journal for the History of Science* 38 (2005): 6.
26. Thomas F. Gieryn, *Cultural Boundaries of Science: Credibility on the Line* (Chicago: University of Chicago Press, 1999), 4–5.
27. See Amy Kittelstrom, *The Religion of Democracy: Seven Liberals and the American Moral Tradition* (New York: Penguin, 2015), 221.
28. Tom Andersen, "Glenmore," *Adirondack Life*, March/April 1982, 20.
29. William Angus Knight, ed., *Memorials of Thomas Davidson: The Wandering Scholar* (Boston: Ginn and Company, 1907), 13.
30. See Leslie Butler, *Critical Americans: Victorian Intellectuals and Transatlantic Liberal Reform* (Chapel Hill: University of North Carolina, 2007).
31. Knight, *Memorials of Thomas Davidson*, ix. Also see William James, "Thomas Davidson: Individualist," in *Essays, Comments, and Reviews: The Works of William James* (Cambridge: Harvard University Press, 1987), 86–97.
32. For a good overview of Davidson's teaching career, see W. H. G. Armytage, "Thomas Davidson, Anglo-American Educator," *History of Education Journal* 2 (1951): 75–79.
33. James Good, "The Value of Thomas Davidson," *Transactions of the Charles S. Peirce Society* 40 (2004): 290.

34. Thomas Davidson, "Autobiographical Sketch," *Journal of the History of Ideas* 18 (1957): 532.
35. Good, "Value of Thomas Davidson," 293.
36. See Denis Brian, *Pulitzer: A Life* (New York: John Wiley and Sons, 2001), 23–25.
37. Good, "Value of Thomas Davidson," 293.
38. Good, "Value of Thomas Davidson," 293.
39. Thomas Davidson, "The Ideal Training of the American Boy," *The Forum* 27 (July 1894): 573, 578, 580.
40. For a good discussion of how William James tried and failed to get Davidson a position teaching Greek at Harvard, see "Professor William James's Reminiscences," in Knight, *Memorials of Thomas Davidson*, 111–113.
41. Good, "Value of Thomas Davidson," 295.
42. Knight, *Memorials of Thomas Davidson*, 16.
43. Knight, *Memorials of Thomas Davidson*, 19.
44. Thomas Davidson, "Organization of the New Fellowship," in *Memorials of Thomas Davidson*, 22.
45. Davidson, "Organization of the New Fellowship," 23.
46. Davidson, "Organization of the New Fellowship," 25.
47. For an overview, see Richard Francis, *Transcendental Utopias: Individual and Community at Brook Farm, Fruitlands, and Walden* (Ithaca, NY: Cornell University Press, 1997).
48. For more on the early Fabian Society, see Edward R. Pease, *The History of the Fabian Society* (New York: E. P. Dutton, 1916).
49. Pease, *History of the Fabian Society*, 26.
50. Quoted in *Memorials of Thomas Davidson*, 26, 27.
51. "The Fellowship of the New Life," Box 24, Thomas Davidson Papers, Sterling Memorial Library, Yale University.
52. "The Fellowship of the New Life," Box 30, Thomas Davidson Papers, Sterling Memorial Library, Yale University.
53. "The Fellowship of the New Life," Box 30, Thomas Davidson Papers, Sterling Memorial Library, Yale University.
54. "The Fellowship of the New Life," Box 24, Thomas Davidson Papers, Sterling Memorial Library, Yale University.

55. Bruce Kuklick, *The Rise of American Philosophy: Cambridge, Massachusetts, 1860–1930* (New Haven, CT: Yale University Press, 1977), 58.
56. Joseph F. Kett, *The Pursuit of Knowledge under Difficulties: From Self-Improvement to Adult Education in America, 1750–1990* (Stanford, CA: Stanford University Press, 1994), 167.
57. Quoted in Austin Warren, "The Concord School of Philosophy," *New England Quarterly* 2 (1929): 202.
58. Bruce Ronda, "The Concord School of Philosophy and the Legacy of Transcendentalism," *New England Quarterly* 82 (2009): 587.
59. For an extensive list of lecturers and topics over the years at the Concord school, see Warren, "Concord School of Philosophy," 199–233. Davidson saved many of the school's programs, which are now preserved in Box 32, Thomas Davidson Papers, Sterling Memorial Library, Yale University.
60. See Warren, "Concord School of Philosophy," 220.
61. Ronda, "Concord School of Philosophy," 607.
62. See "Farmington Lectures on Philosophy and Art," Box 32, Thomas Davidson Papers, Sterling Memorial Library, Yale University.
63. "St. Cloud Lectures on Ancient Philosophy and Art," Box 32, Thomas Davidson Papers, Sterling Memorial Library, Yale University.
64. "Farmington Lectures on Philosophy and Art," Box 32, Thomas Davidson Papers, Sterling Memorial Library, Yale University.
65. "Farmington Lectures on Philosophy and Ethics, 1889," Box 32, Thomas Davidson Papers, Sterling Memorial Library, Yale University.
66. "Farmington Lectures on Philosophy and Ethics, 1889," and "Farmington Lectures on Philosophy and Ethics, 1890," Box 32, Thomas Davidson Papers, Sterling Memorial Library, Yale University.
67. See Andersen, "Glenmore," 19.
68. Mary Foster, "Recollections of Glenmore," in *Memorials of Thomas Davidson*, 64.
69. Quoted in Andersen, "Glenmore," 49. Also see "Glenmore School for the Culture Sciences, Season 1892," Box 32, Thomas Davidson Papers, Sterling Memorial Library, Yale University.
70. Andersen, "Glenmore," 21.
71. Foster, "Recollections of Glenmore," 64.

72. Andersen, "Glenmore," 21.
73. Andersen, "Glenmore," 22.
74. Foster, "Recollections of Glenmore," 65.
75. Robert H. Wiebe, *Search for Order, 1877–1920* (New York: Hill and Wang, 1967), 33–75.
76. Foster, "Recollections of Glenmore," 65.
77. "Glenmore School for the Culture Sciences, Season 1893," Box 32, Thomas Davidson Papers, Sterling Memorial Library, Yale University.
78. "Glenmore School for the Culture Sciences, Season 1892, 1893, 1894," Box 32, Thomas Davidson Papers, Sterling Memorial Library, Yale University.
79. Foster, "Recollections of Glenmore," 72.
80. Foster, "Recollections of Glenmore," 72.
81. Thomas Davidson, "Rousseau, and Education According to Nature," in *Memorials of Thomas Davidson*, 152.
82. See Knight's headnote to "Rousseau, and Education According to Nature," 152.
83. Davidson, "Rousseau, and Education According to Nature," 160.
84. Davidson, "Rousseau, and Education According to Nature," 160, 163, 164.
85. Davidson, "Rousseau, and Education According to Nature," 168.
86. Davidson, "Rousseau, and Education According to Nature," 169.
87. Davidson, "Rousseau, and Education According to Nature," 172.
88. See Gail Bederman, *Manliness and Civilization: A Cultural History of Gender and Race in the United States, 1880–1917* (Chicago: University of Chicago Press, 1995).
89. For Davidson's telling of this history, Thomas Davidson, *The Education of the Wage-Earners*, ed. Charles M. Bakewell (Boston: Ginn and Company, 1904), 96–97.
90. Daniel Burnstein, *Next to Godliness: Confronting Dirt and Despair in Progressive Era New York City* (Urbana: University of Illinois Press, 2010), 56.
91. See Melvyn Dubofsky, *When Workers Organize: New York City in the Progressive Era* (Amherst: University of Massachusetts Press, 1968), 10–12.
92. Quoted in Dubofsky, *When Workers Organize*, 20.

93. See James Gilbert, *Designing the Industrial State: The Intellectual Pursuit of Collectivism in America, 1800–1940* (Chicago: Quadrangle Books, 1972), ch. 4.
94. David A. Zonderman, *Uneasy Allies: Working for Labor Reform in Nineteenth-Century Boston* (Amherst: University of Massachusetts Press, 2011), ch. 6.
95. In general, see Allen F. Davis, *Spearheads for Reform: The Social Settlements and the Progressive Movement, 1890–1914* (New York: Oxford University Press, 1967).
96. Adam Bellow, *The Educational Alliance: A Centennial Celebration* (New York: Educational Alliance, 1990), 35–43.
97. Morris R. Cohen, *A Dreamer's Journey* (Boston: Beacon Press, 1949), 98.
98. See application of M. H. Newman to the Thomas Davidson Society, Box 32, Thomas Davidson Papers, Sterling Memorial Library, Yale University.
99. Application of Bertha Ryshpen to the Thomas Davidson Society, Box 32, Thomas Davidson Papers, Sterling Memorial Library, Yale University.
100. Application of Jacob Greenberg to the Thomas Davidson Society, Box 32, Thomas Davidson Papers, Sterling Memorial Library, Yale University.
101. Davidson, *Education of the Wage-Earners*, 96–97.
102. Cohen, *A Dreamer's Journey*, 103.
103. Davidson, *Education of the Wage-Earners*, 97.
104. Thomas Davidson, "The Problems Set by the Nineteenth Century to the Twentieth," Box 27, Thomas Davidson Papers, Sterling Memorial Library, Yale University. All subsequent citations of this document refer to this handwritten, inconsistently paginated manuscript, which Davidson used at the lectern to deliver these lectures. As a result, the following analysis relies exclusively on this text, but I do not provide subsequent footnotes, which would be redundant, nor page numbers, which are either confusing or unavailable.
105. In general, see Dubofsky, *When Workers Organize*, 1–27.
106. A footnote written by Davidson after the lecture revealed the details of this exchange.
107. Davidson, *Education of the Wage-Earners*, 101. Also see Leonora Cohen Rosenfield, *Portrait of a Philosopher: Morris R. Cohen in Life and Letters* (New York: Harcourt, Brace & World, 1962), 49.
108. Davidson, *Education of the Wage-Earners*, 101.

109. Davidson, *Education of the Wage-Earners*, 106.
110. Davidson, *Education of the Wage-Earners*, 107.
111. Davidson, *Education of the Wage-Earners*, 105, 104, 108–109, 108.
112. The surviving demographic information from the group comes from the Thomas Davidson Society, which was organized by members of the early class after Davidson's death. The ages of the students have been adjusted from the available records to reflect when they were in Davidson's class. For the information contained in this paragraph, see the records of the Thomas Davidson Society, Box 32, Thomas Davidson Papers, Sterling Memorial Library, Yale University.
113. For these and other reflections on Davidson from students, see the applications to thc Thomas Davidson Society, Box 32, Thomas Davidson Papers, Sterling Memorial Library, Yale University.
114. For various references to the visiting speakers during the summer months, see Davidson, *Education of the Wage-Earners*, 124–172.
115. Davidson, *Education of the Wage-Earners*, 113.
116. Davidson, *Education of the Wage-Earners*, 124, 127, 130, 135, 140, 141, 146, 157.
117. Davidson, *Education of the Wage-Earners*, 124–125, 126, 158, 168.
118. Davidson, *Education of the Wage-Earners*, 133–134, 137.
119. Davidson, *Education of the Wage-Earners*, 159.
120. Davidson, *Education of the Wage-Earners*, 171.
121. Davidson, *Education of the Wage-Earners*, 154, 150, 157, 160–161.
122. Davidson, *Education of the Wage-Earners*, 127.
123. See Cohen, *A Dreamer's Journey*, 105–109; and Rosenfield, *Portrait of a Philosopher*, 50–53.
124. Davidson, *Education of the Wage-Earners*, 136.
125. Davidson, *Education of the Wage-Earners*, 140.
126. Davidson, *Education of the Wage-Earners*, 156.
127. For details on the increase in numbers because of Davidson's influence, see Rosenfield, *Portrait of a Philosopher*, 54–56.
128. See Charles M. Bakewell, "The Vitality of the Ideal," in *Education of the Wage-Earners*, 216–217.
129. Davidson, *Education of the Wage-Earners*, 181–183.
130. Cohen, *A Dreamer's Journey*, 121.

Chapter Four. Booker T. Washington's Reclamation of Work

1. Booker T. Washington, "To the Editor of the *Southern Workman*," July 14, 1881, in *The Booker T. Washington Papers*, ed. Louis R. Harlan, vol. 2, *1860–89* (Urbana: University of Illinois Press, 1972), 140.
2. Washington, "To the Editor of the *Southern Workman*," 141.
3. Booker T. Washington, "A Speech before the Alabama State Teachers' Association," April 7, 1882, in *Booker T. Washington Papers*, 2:192, 194.
4. Booker T. Washington, "Extracts from Three Addresses Delivered in Louisiana," April 13–16, 1915, *The Booker T. Washington Papers*, ed. Louis R. Harlan and Raymond W. Smock, vol. 13, *1914–15* (Urbana: University of Illinois Press, 1984), 263.
5. For some examples, see F. Anderson, "Dignity of Labor," *Evangelical Magazine and Gospel Advocate* 13 (October 28, 1842): 337; William Lusk Crandal, *Talks with the People of New York* (Albany, NY: C. Van Benthuysen, 1853), 36–39; and Newman Hall, "The Dignity of Labor," in *The Columbian Speaker* (Boston, MA: Lee and Shepard, 1875), 71–72.
6. See Charles Postel, *The Populist Vision* (Oxford: Oxford University Press, 2007), ch. 6.
7. W. E. B. DuBois, *The Souls of Black Folks: Essays and Sketches*, 5th ed. (Chicago: A. C. McClurg, 1904), 50.
8. Pero Gaglo Dagbovie, "Exploring a Century of Historical Scholarship on Booker T. Washington," *Journal of African American History* 92, no. 2 (2007): 246, 253–256. Also see Rebecca Carroll, ed., *Uncle Tom or New Negro? African Americans Reflect on Booker T. Washington and "Up from Slavery" 100 Years Later* (New York: Harlem Moon, 2006).
9. David H. Jackson Jr., *Booker T. Washington and the Struggle against White Supremacy: The Southern Educational Tours, 1908–1912* (New York: Palgrave Macmillan, 2008); and Robert J. Norrell, *Up from History: The Life of Booker T. Washington* (Cambridge, MA: Belknap Press of Harvard University Press, 2009).
10. Kirt Wilson, "The Racial Contexts of Public Address: Interpreting Violence during the Reconstruction Era," in *The Handbook of Rhetoric and Public Address*, ed. Shawn J. Parry-Giles and J. Michael Hogan (Malden, MA: Wiley-Blackwell, 2010), 215.

11. Mia Bay, *The White Image in the Black Mind: African-American Ideas about White People, 1830–1925* (New York: Oxford University Press, 2000), 188.
12. Riché Richardson, *Black Masculinity and the U.S. South: From Uncle Tom to Gangsta* (Athens: University of Georgia Press, 2007), 14.
13. See Jay Watson, *Reading for the Body: The Recalcitrant Materiality of Southern Fiction, 1893–1985* (Athens: University of Georgia Press, 2012), 16.
14. Richardson, *Black Masculinity*, 52, 230, 232.
15. Jennifer Putzi, *Identifying Marks: Race, Gender, and the Marked Body in Nineteenth-Century America* (Athens: University of Georgia Press, 2006), 9, 118.
16. For an overview of how the push for strength and success in the Gilded Age played out in literary culture, see Judy Hilkey, *Character Is Capital: Success Manuals and Manhood in Gilded Age America* (Chapel Hill: University of North Carolina Press, 1997), 74–85.
17. Alan Trachtenberg, *The Incorporation of America: Culture and Society in the Gilded Age* (New York: Hill and Wang, 1982), 112, 115.
18. The definitive biography of Washington's life remains Louis Harlan's two-volume project rich with primary documentation: Louis R. Harlan, *Booker T. Washington: The Making of a Black Leader, 1856–1901* (London: Oxford University Press, 1972); Louis R. Harlan, *Booker T. Washington: The Wizard of Tuskegee, 1901–1915* (New York: Oxford University Press, 1983). For a more recent biography, see Norrell, *Up from History*.
19. Norrell, *Up from History*, 35.
20. For details on Washington's training in rhetoric, see Norrell, *Up from History*, 27–37.
21. Andrew A. King, "Booker T. Washington and the Myth of Heroic Materialism," *Quarterly Journal of Speech* 60, no. 3 (1974): 324.
22. See, for example, Robert L. Heath, "A Time for Silence: Booker T. Washington in Atlanta," *Quarterly Journal of Speech* 64, no. 4 (1978): 392; and Bradford J. Vivian, "Up from Memory: Epideictic Forgetting in Booker T. Washington's Cotton States Exposition Address," *Philosophy & Rhetoric* 45, no. 2 (2012): 192.
23. In general, see Departmental File, 1897–1915, Booker T. Washington Papers, Manuscript Division, Library of Congress.
24. For example, on February 26, 1914, Washington sent a letter to J. H.

Palmer instructing him to tell all the heads of Tuskegee departments not to rely on outside labor, even if it was easier and cheaper to do so, but to rely on student labor for projects across campus. Some of the departments had gotten in the habit of hiring outside laborers because working with students was too cumbersome. Washington was dismayed with this tendency. "We understand fully," he wrote, "that it is more difficult to work student labor than outside labor, but if we are patient and painstaking with the students, they will more than repay us for the effort put into their training." The point was ultimately that everyone had to work harder if the race was going to advance. See Booker T. Washington to J. H. Palmer, February 26, 1914, Departmental File, Booker T. Washington Papers, Manuscript Division, Library of Congress.

25. See Nathan Hunt to Emmett Scott, July 25, 1904, Departmental File, Booker T. Washington Papers, Manuscript Division, Library of Congress.
26. Charles Fearing to Emmett Scott, January 8, 1912, Departmental File, Booker T. Washington Papers, Manuscript Division, Library of Congress.
27. Charles W. Wood to Charles Fearing, February 22, 1912, Departmental File, Booker T. Washington Papers, Manuscript Division, Library of Congress.
28. C. W. Wood to Booker T. Washington, October 12, 1912, Departmental File, Booker T. Washington Papers, Manuscript Division, Library of Congress.
29. Broadside, Supplemental File, Booker T. Washington Papers, Manuscript Division, Library of Congress.
30. Supplemental File, Booker T. Washington Papers, Manuscript Division, Library of Congress.
31. Supplemental File, Booker T. Washington Papers, Manuscript Division, Library of Congress.
32. For an example of the form of bequest, see Circular, Supplemental File, Booker T. Washington Papers, Manuscript Division, Library of Congress. For more on the importance of these circulars and donation

cards to Washington's campaign, see Nathan Hunt to Emmett Scott, August 7, 1912, Departmental File, Booker T. Washington Papers, Manuscript Division, Library of Congress; Nathan Hunt to Emmett Scott, October 17, 1912, Departmental File, Booker T. Washington Papers, Manuscript Division, Library of Congress; Nathan Hunt to Charles Fearing, November 21, 1912, Departmental File, Booker T. Washington Papers, Manuscript Division, Library of Congress; Charles Fearing to Nathan Hunt, January 29, 1914, Departmental File, Booker T. Washington Papers, Manuscript Division, Library of Congress.

33. "Pointing the Way to Negro Progress," *Daily Picayune*, November 11, 1899, 7.
34. "Booker T. Washington Delivers Two Fine Addresses to the Delight of His Hearers," *The Freeman* (Indianapolis), April 27, 1904, 1.
35. "Booker Washington at Cawker City," *Topeka Plaindealer*, August 3, 1906, 1.
36. See, for instance, "Extracts from Address of Booker T. Washington, Arlington St. Church, December 7," no year given, Box 115, Folder 3, Papers of Booker T. Washington, Tuskegee University Archives. Also see Booker T. Washington, "A Commencement Address in Washington, D.C.," June 16, 1905, in *The Booker T. Washington Papers*, ed. Louis R. Harlan and Raymond W. Smock, vol. 8, *1904–6* (Urbana: University of Illinois Press, 1979), 307.
37. In general, see Michael Kazin, *The Populist Persuasion: An American History* (New York: Basic Books, 1995), 13–15.
38. Booker T. Washington, "First Joint Commencement," Armstrong Manual Training School, 1905, Speech, Article, Book File, Booker T. Washington Papers, Manuscript Division, Library of Congress.
39. See, for instance, "Extracts from Address of Booker T. Washington, Arlington St. Church, December 7," no year given, Box 115, Folder 3, Papers of Booker T. Washington, Tuskegee University Archives.
40. Booker T. Washington, "A Speech before the New York Congregational Club," in *The Booker T. Washington Papers*, ed. Louis R. Harlan, vol. 3, *1889–95* (Urbana: University of Illinois Press, 1974), 282.
41. Washington, "A Commencement Address in Washington, D. C.," in *Booker T. Washington Papers*, 8:308.

42. "Extracts from Address of Booker T. Washington Before the Society for the Promotion of Industrial Education, Spelman Seminary, Atlanta, Ga., November 20, 1908," bound speeches volume, Papers of Booker T. Washington, Tuskegee University Archives.
43. For an overview of "producerism" in the populist sociopolitical tradition, see Laura Grattan, *Populism's Power: Radical Grassroots Democracy in America* (Oxford: Oxford University Press, 2016), 59–61. Also see Robert C. McMath Jr., *American Populism: A Social History, 1877-1898* (New York: Hill and Wang, 1993), 73.
44. "Extracts from Address of Booker T. Washington before the High School, Springfield, Mass., Mar. 17, 1899," Box 113, Folder 15, Papers of Booker T. Washington, Tuskegee University Archives.
45. "Extracts from Address Delivered by Booker T. Washington at the Annual Fair and Convocation of the Farmers' Improvement Society, October 11, 1900," Box 114, Folder 6, Papers of Booker T. Washington, Tuskegee University Archives.
46. "Extracts from address of Booker T. Washington before the Colored Methodist Episcopal Church General Conference, Nashville, Tenn., May 15th, 1902," bound speeches volume, Papers of Booker T. Washington, Tuskegee University Archives.
47. "Extracts from the Address of Booker T. Washington at the Opening of the Ohio State Colored Educational and Industrial Exposition, Columbus, Ohio, Saturday Afternoon, August 15, 1906," Box 116, Folder 25, Papers of Booker T. Washington, Tuskegee University Archives.
48. "Delivered at Carnegie Hall, New York City, Tuesday Evening, February 23rd, 1909," bound speeches volume, Papers of Booker T. Washington, Tuskegee University Archives.
49. "Extracts from Address of Booker T. Washington at Unitarian Club, Wednesday Evening, February 14, 1900," Box 114, Folder 18, Papers of Booker T. Washington, Tuskegee University Archives.
50. "Extracts from the Address of Booker T. Washington at the New Old South Church, Sunday Evening, December 16, 1900," Box 114, Folder 5, Papers of Booker T. Washington, Tuskegee University Archives.
51. "Extracts from Address Delivered by Booker T. Washington at the

Annual Fair and Convocation of the Farmers' Improvement Society, October 11, 1900," Box 114, Folder 6, Papers of Booker T. Washington, Tuskegee University Archives.

52. "What Co-Operation Can Accomplish. Delivered before the Negro Organization Society, Norfolk, Virginia, November 12, 1914," Box 118A, Folder 10, Papers of Booker T. Washington, Tuskegee University Archives.
53. "Extracts from Address of Booker T. Washington at a Banquet, in Cambridge, Mass., Given by Colored Young Men's Forum and Boston Negro Business League, Monday Eve., October 3, 1904," bound speeches volume, Papers of Booker T. Washington, Tuskegee University Archives.
54. See Hilary J. Moss, *Schooling Citizens: The Struggle for African American Education in Antebellum America* (Chicago: University of Chicago Press, 2009).
55. See James D. Anderson, *The Education of Blacks in the South, 1860–1935* (Chapel Hill: University of North Carolina Press, 2014), esp. ch. 1.
56. See William Preston Vaughn, *Schools for All: The Blacks and Public Education in the South, 1865–1877* (Lexington: University Press of Kentucky, 2015), esp. ch. 1.
57. Vaughn, *Schools for All*, 30.
58. "Extracts from Address of Booker T. Washington Before the Colored Methodist Episcopal Church General Conference, Nashville, Tenn. May 15th, 1902," bound speeches volume, Papers of Booker T. Washington, Tuskegee University Archives.
59. "Address Before the State University of New York, June 28, 1898," Box 118A, Folder 2, Papers of Booker T. Washington, Tuskegee University Archives.
60. Untitled address in Alabama, 1899, Box 114, Folder 2, Papers of Booker T. Washington, Tuskegee University Archives.
61. Booker T. Washington, "An Abraham Lincoln Memorial Address in Philadelphia," February 14, 1899, in *The Booker T. Washington Papers*, vol. 5, *1899–1900*, ed. Louis R. Harlan and Raymond W. Smock (Urbana: University of Illinois Press, 1976), 37–38.
62. "Extracts from Address of Booker T. Washington at Farmers' National Congress, Fort Worth, Texas, December 6th, 1898," Box 114, Folder 18,

Papers of Booker T. Washington, Tuskegee University Archives.

63. "Dr. Booker T. Washington's Lecture at Metropolitan A.M.E. Church (Rev. O.J.W. Scott, D.D., Pastor), On Friday Evening, March 18, 1904," Box 115, Folder 7, Papers of Booker T. Washington, Tuskegee University Archives.
64. See, for example, William James, *Pragmatism: The Works of William James* (Cambridge, MA: Harvard University Press, 1975), 17–18. For Dewey's thinking in this regard, see John Dewey, *Democracy and Education, 1916: The Middle Works, 1899–1924*, vol. 9, ed. Jo Ann Boydston (Carbondale: Southern Illinois University Press, 1985), esp. ch. 23.
65. Booker T. Washington, "An Address at the Metropolitan A.M.E. Church," May 22, 1900, in *Booker T. Washington Papers*, 5:532.
66. Washington was not alone in his warnings about city life. For an excellent case study, see Leslie J. Harris, "Rhetorical Mobilities and the City: The White Slavery Controversy and Racialized Protection of Women in the U.S.," *Quarterly Journal of Speech* 104, no. 1 (2018): 22–46.
67. "Extracts from Speech Delivered by Booker T. Washington, Before A. M. E. General Conference, May 23, 1900, Columbus, Ohio," Box 115, Folder 23, Papers of Booker T. Washington, Tuskegee University Archives.
68. "Report of the Meeting Held in the Interest of the Manassas Industrial School, on the Evening of February 14th, 1906, at the First Congregational Church, Washington, D. C.," Box 116, Folder 19, Papers of Booker T. Washington, Tuskegee University Archives.
69. "Part of the Address by Booker T. Washington at a Meeting for Colored Men, Old Ship Church, Montgomery, Ala., Jan. 17, 1909," Box 118A, Folder 14, Papers of Booker T. Washington, Tuskegee University Archives.
70. "The Care of Dependent Children, New Willard Hotel, Washington, D. C., January 25th, 1912," Box 118, Folder 4, Papers of Booker T. Washington, Tuskegee University Archives.
71. Untitled speech in Alabama, 1899, Box 114, Folder 2, Papers of Booker T. Washington, Tuskegee University Archives.
72. "Extracts from Address of Booker T. Washington Before the Society for the Promotion of Industrial Education, Spelman Seminary, Atlanta,

Ga., November 20, 1908," bound speeches volume, Papers of Booker T. Washington, Tuskegee University Archives.

73. "Extracts from address of Booker T. Washington at the New Old South Church, Sunday Evening, December 14, 1902," bound speeches volume, Papers of Booker T. Washington, Tuskegee University Archives.
74. In general, see B. Edward McClellan, *Moral Education in America: Schools and the Shaping of Character from Colonial Times to the Present* (New York: Teachers College Press, 1999); and William J. Reese, *America's Public Schools: From the Common School to "No Child Left Behind"* (Baltimore: Johns Hopkins University Press, 2005).
75. "Extracts from an Address Delivered by Booker T. Washington at a Banquet Given in His Honor by the Business Men's League of Chicago, Ill., on the Evening of April 5th, 1904," bound speeches volume, Papers of Booker T. Washington, Tuskegee University Archives.
76. "Extracts from Address of Booker T. Washington at Olivet Baptist Church, 27th & Dearborn St., Chicago, April 5, 1907," bound speeches volume, Papers of Booker T. Washington, Tuskegee University Archives.
77. "Extracts from Address Delivered at Steubenville, Ohio, Tuesday Afternoon, Sept. 5, 1911," Box 118A, Folder 6, Papers of Booker T. Washington, Tuskegee University Archives.
78. "Dr. Booker T. Washington's Lecture at Metropolitan A.M.E. Church (Rev. O.J.W. Scott, D.D., Pastor), On Friday Evening, March 18, 1904," Box 115, Folder 7, Papers of Booker T. Washington, Tuskegee University Archives.
79. "Address of Booker T. Washington, Delivered at Witherspoon Hall, Philadelphia, March 19th, 1900," Box 114, Folder 21, Papers of Booker T. Washington, Tuskegee University Archives.
80. "Report of the Meeting Held in the Interest of the Manassas Industrial School, on the Evening of February 14th, 1906, at the First Congregational Church, Washington, D. C.," Box 116, Folder 19, Papers of Booker T. Washington, Tuskegee University Archives.
81. "Address of Booker T. Washington, Prin., Tuskegee Normal and Industrial Institute, Tuskegee, Ala., Before the Union League Club, Brooklyn, Feb. 12, 1896," Box 113, Folder 6, Papers of Booker T.

Washington, Tuskegee University Archives.

82. "Extracts from Address of Booker T. Washington Before the High School, Springfield, Mass., Mar. 17, 1899," Box 114, Folder 15, Papers of Booker T. Washington, Tuskegee University Archives.
83. "Extracts from Address of Booker T. Washington, delivered in Augusta, Ga., January 2, 1905," Box 116, Folder 3, Papers of Booker T. Washington, Tuskegee University Archives.
84. "Address of Booker T. Washington, President National Negro Business League, Convention Hall, Muskogee, Oklahoma, August 19, 1914," Box 118A, Folder 16, Papers of Booker T. Washington, Tuskegee University Archives.
85. "Delivered at the Conservation Congress, Knoxville, Tennessee, Oct. 14, 1913," Box 118A, Folder 7, Papers of Booker T. Washington, Tuskegee University Archives.
86. Catalogue of the Tuskegee State Normal School at Tuskegee, Alabama, for the Academic Year 1881–82, Papers of Booker T. Washington, Tuskegee University Archives.
87. Catalogue of the Tuskegee State Normal School at Tuskegee, Alabama, for the Academic Year 1881–82, Papers of Booker T. Washington, Tuskegee University Archives.
88. Booker T. Washington, *Working with the Hands* (New York: Doubleday, Page, 1904), 40–41.
89. Washington, *Working with the Hands*, 32.
90. Catalogue of the Tuskegee State Normal School at Tuskegee, Alabama, for the Academic Year 1886–1887, Papers of Booker T. Washington, Tuskegee University Archives.
91. Catalogue of the Tuskegee State Normal School at Tuskegee, Alabama, for the Academic Year 1886–1887, Papers of Booker T. Washington, Tuskegee University Archives.
92. Twenty-Second Annual Catalogue of the Tuskegee Normal and Industrial Institute, Tuskegee, Alabama, 1902–1903, Papers of Booker T. Washington, Tuskegee University Archives.
93. Twenty-Second Annual Catalogue of the Tuskegee Normal and Industrial Institute, Tuskegee, Alabama, 1902–1903, Papers of Booker T.

Washington, Tuskegee University Archives.

94. Washington, *Working with the Hands*, 71–72.
95. Washington, *Working with the Hands*, 45, 50.
96. Washington, *Working with the Hands*, 56, 58.
97. Twenty-Second Annual Catalogue of the Tuskegee Normal and Industrial Institute, Tuskegee, Alabama, 1902–1903, Papers of Booker T. Washington, Tuskegee University Archives.
98. Washington, *Working with the Hands*, 187, 188.
99. Evelyn Brooks Higginbotham, *Righteous Discontent: The Women's Movement in the Black Baptist Church, 1880–1920* (Cambridge, MA: Harvard University Press, 1994), 14.
100. Patricia Hill Collins, *Black Sexual Politics: African Americans, Gender, and the New Racism* (New York: Routledge, 2004), 72.
101. Farah Jasmine Griffin, "Black Feminists and Du Bois: Respectability, Protection, and Beyond," *Annals of the American Academy of Political and Social Science* 568 (2000): 34.
102. Higginbotham, *Righteous Discontent*, 193; and Griffin, "Black Feminists and Du Bois," 34.
103. E. Frances White, *Dark Continent of Our Bodies: Black Feminism and the Politics of Respectability* (Philadelphia: Temple University Press, 2001), 36–37. Also see Michelle Smith, "Affect and Respectability Politics," *Theory and Event* 17, no. 3 Supplement (2014): n.p.
104. See Fredrick C. Harris, "The Rise of Respectability Politics," *Dissent* 61 (2014): 34, 37.
105. See Kevin K. Gaines, *Uplifting the Race: Black Leadership, Politics, and Culture in the Twentieth Century* (Chapel Hill: University of North Carolina Press, 1996), 22–24.
106. Kirt H. Wilson, "The Racial Politics of Imitation in the Nineteenth Century," *Quarterly Journal of Speech* 89, no. 2 (2003): 89, 102.
107. Washington, *Working with the Hands*, 79–80.
108. Washington, *Working with the Hands*, 80.
109. Ellen Weiss, *Robert R. Taylor and Tuskegee: An African American Architect Designs for Booker T. Washington* (Montgomery, AL: New South Books, 2012), 25.
110. Weiss, *Robert R. Taylor and Tuskegee*, 53–56, 60–63.

111. Weiss, *Robert R. Taylor and Tuskegee*, xix, 21.
112. Washington, *Working with the Hands*, 135.
113. Washington, *Working with the Hands*, 138.
114. For anecdotes of ownership through the Negro Conference, see Washington, *Working with the Hands*, 140–146.
115. For an overview of the creation and work of the National Negro Business League, see Harlan, *Making of a Black Leader*, 266–271.
116. Emmett Scott, *The Tuskegee Negro Conferences* (Tuskegee, AL: Tuskegee Institute Press, 1904), 12.
117. Weiss, *Robert R. Taylor and Tuskegee*, 72.
118. The Tuskegee University Archives has made many of these bulletins available online: http://archive.tuskegee.edu/archive/handle/123456789/170/browse?type=dateissued.
119. Washington, *Working with the Hands*, 119–129.
120. See Felix James, "The Tuskegee Institute Movable School, 1906–1923," *Agricultural History* 45, no. 3 (1971): 202.
121. Booker T. Washington, "A Farmers' College on Wheels," in *The Papers of Booker T. Washington*, vol. 9, *1906–8*, ed. Louis R. Harlan and Raymond Smock (Urbana: University of Chicago Press, 1980), 176, 177.
122. Washington, "Farmers' College on Wheels," 178.
123. Washington, "Farmers' College on Wheels," 180, 178–179.
124. James, "The Tuskegee Institute Movable School, 1906–1923," 206.
125. The published reports are housed at the Tuskegee University Archives. See the bound manuscript pages catalogued as *Tuskegee Alumni*, 2A1.012 Copy 1–3. Although the volumes are titled as "Copy 1," "Copy 2," and "Copy 3," each contains unique profiles.
126. All accounts in this paragraph come from *Tuskegee Alumni*, 2A1.012 Copy 1.
127. *Tuskegee Alumni*, 2A1.012 Copy 3, 40.
128. *Tuskegee Alumni*, 2A1.012 Copy 2, 23.
129. The above accounts come from *Tuskegee Alumni*, 2A1.012 Copy 2.

Chapter Five. Zitkala-Ša's Pan-Indian Intellectual Populism

1. For the full version of this story, see Zitkala-Ša, "The School Days of an Indian Girl," *Atlantic Monthly* 85, no. 508 (February 1900): 189.

2. Throughout this chapter I use the words "American Indian," "Indian," and "Native" interchangeably. As scholars have pointed out, "Native American" is no more accurate a descriptor than "Indian." Kimberly Wieser, for instance, explains: "Indigenous people in the United States and Canada prefer to be referred to by their tribally specific names for their people, preferably in their own language, while some term must be used to address the ideas we as Indigenous peoples often share in common." In the United States, she continues, many Indigenous people "prefer 'American Indian' or 'Indian,' . . . not only because 'Indian' is the general term most people grew up with, but also because it is the word used in article 1, section 8 of the U.S. Constitution and is the word in which all legal rights are vested." See Kimberly G. Wieser, *Back to the Blanket: Recovered Rhetorics and Literacies in American Indian Studies* (Norman: University of Oklahoma Press, 2017), 199(n7).
3. As John Sanchez and Mary E. Stuckey explain, dislocation from white and Indian society was common for those who passed through boarding schools for Native children. See "From Boarding Schools to the Multicultural Classroom: The Intercultural Politics of Education, Assimilation, and American Indians," *Teacher Education Quarterly* 26, no. 3 (1999): 86.
4. Zitkala-Ša, "An Indian Teacher among Indians," *Atlantic Monthly* 85, no. 509 (March 1900): 385–386.
5. Richard Morris, "Educating Savages," *Quarterly Journal of Speech* 83 (1997): 155.
6. Jason Edward Black, "Remembrances of Removal: Native Resistance to Allotment and the Unmasking of Paternal Benevolence," *Southern Communication Journal* 72 (2007): 185–203.
7. Morris, "Educating Savages," 162.
8. See Kiara M. Vigil, *Indigenous Intellectuals: Sovereignty, Citizenship, and the American Imagination, 1880–1930* (Cambridge: Cambridge University Press, 2015), esp. 1–23.
9. For more on performing Indianness at the time, see Lucy Maddox, *Citizen Indians: Native American Intellectuals, Race, and Reform* (Ithaca, NY: Cornell University Press, 2005).

10. Maddox, *Citizen Indians*, 7.
11. Frederick E. Hoxie, introduction to *Talking Back to Civilization: Indian Voices from the Progressive Era* (Boston: Bedford / St. Martin's, 2001), 5.
12. See Mary E. Stuckey and John M. Murphy, "By Any Other Name: Rhetorical Colonialism in North America," *American Indian Culture and Research Journal* 25, no. 4 (2001): 76–81.
13. See Brian W. Dippie, *The Vanishing American: White Attitudes and U.S. Indian Policy* (Middletown, CT: Wesleyan University Press, 1982), 3–11.
14. Mary E. Stuckey, *Defining Americans: The Presidency and National Identity* (Lawrence: University Press of Kansas, 2004), 35.
15. Dippie, *The Vanishing American*, 56.
16. Dippie, *The Vanishing American*, 56–57.
17. Stuckey, *Defining Americans*, 54.
18. For discussion of land and citizenship in U.S.-Indian relations prior to the Dawes Act, see Jason Edward Black, "Native Resistive Rhetoric and the Decolonization of American Indian Removal Discourse," *Quarterly Journal of Speech* 95, no. 1 (2009): 66–88, esp. 72–73.
19. Russell Thornton, *American Indians Holocaust and Survival: A Population History since 1492* (Norman: University of Oklahoma Press, 1987), 123.
20. Jason Edward Black, *American Indians and the Rhetoric of Removal and Allotment* (Jackson: University Press of Mississippi, 2015), 85.
21. David Wallace Adams, *Education for Extinction: American Indians and the Boarding School Experience, 1875-1928* (Lawrence: University Press of Kansas, 1995), 29, 31.
22. Adams, *Education for Extinction*, 39–42, 48.
23. The phrase comes from a speech that Pratt delivered in 1892. See Richard H. Pratt, "The Advantages of Mingling Indians with Whites," in *Americanizing the American Indians: Writings by the "Friends of the Indian," 1880-1900*, ed. Francis Paul Prucha (Cambridge, MA: Harvard University Press, 1973), 260–271.
24. Adams, *Education for Extinction*, 57–59.
25. See Anthony F. C. Wallace, *Jefferson and the Indians: The Tragic Fate of the First Americans* (Cambridge, MA: Belknap Press of Harvard University Press, 1999).

26. See Dippie, *The Vanishing American*, 12–31.
27. Stuckey, *Defining Americans*, 43.
28. Dippie, *The Vanishing American*, 223.
29. For a thorough examination of population figures, see Thornton, *American Indian Holocaust and Survival.*
30. See Hoxie, introduction to *Talking Back to Civilization*, 26.
31. Hoxie, introduction to *Talking Back to Civilization*, 25.
32. Robert Allen Warrior, *Tribal Secrets: Recovering American Indian Intellectual Traditions* (Minneapolis: University of Minnesota Press, 1995), 4, 13–14.
33. Maddox, *Citizen Indians*, 168.
34. Vigil, *Indigenous Intellectuals*, 171.
35. Jessica Enoch, *Reconfiguring Rhetorical Education: Women Teaching African American, Native American, and Chicano/a Students, 1865–1911* (Carbondale: Southern Illinois University Press, 2008), 75.
36. For an overview of her work with Pratt, see Tadeusz Lewandowski, *Red Bird, Red Power: The Life and Legacy of Zitkala-Ša* (Norman: University of Oklahoma Press, 2016), 68–69.
37. "Zitkala-Ša," *Marion Daily Star*, May 8, 1900.
38. "A Bright Sioux Maiden," *New Haven News*, April 19, 1900.
39. "A Talented Sioux Girl," *Le Mars Sentinel*, May 31, 1900.
40. See Lewandowski, *Red Bird, Red Power*, 45–48.
41. "Historian of the Sioux," *Barre Evening Telegram*, November 10, 1900.
42. See Zitkala-Ša, "The Trial Path," *Harper's Monthly Magazine* 103 (June 1901): 741–744; Zitkala-Ša, "A Warrior's Daughter," *Everybody's Magazine* 6 (April 1902): 132–140; Zitkala-Ša, "Why I Am a Pagan," *Atlantic Monthly* 90 (December 1902): 801–803.
43. Zitkala-Ša, *Old Indian Legends* (Boston: Ginn, 1901).
44. Lewandowski, *Red Bird, Red Power*, 66.
45. Jace Weaver, *That the People Might Live: Native Literatures and Native American Community* (New York: Oxford University Press, 1997), xiii.
46. See Lewandowski, *Red Bird, Red Power*, 65–77, 102–108.
47. Gertrude Bonnin, "A Year's Experience in Community Service Work among the Ute Tribe of Indians," *American Indian Magazine* 4 (October/November 1916): 307, 308.

48. Bonnin, "Year's Experience in Community Service Work," 308.
49. Bonnin, "Year's Experience in Community Service Work," 309–310.
50. Bonnin, "Year's Experience in Community Service Work," 310.
51. Bonnin, "Year's Experience in Community Service Work," 310.
52. See Warrior, *Tribal Secrets*, 9–10.
53. See Lewandowski, *Red Bird, Red Power*, 89.
54. Lewandowski, *Red Bird, Red Power*, 91.
55. Zitkala-Ša, "The Menace of Peyote," in *American Indian Stories, Legends, and Other Writings*, ed. Cathy N. Davidson and Ada Norris (New York: Penguin, 2003), 239.
56. Zitkala-Ša, "The Menace of Peyote," 240.
57. Zitkala-Ša, "The Menace of Peyote," 241.
58. See Jason Edward Black, "Native Authenticity, Rhetorical Circulation, and Neocolonial Decay: The Case of Chief Seattle's Controversial Speech," *Rhetoric & Public Affairs* 15, no. 4 (2012): 635–646.
59. See Vigil, *Indigenous Intellectuals*, 188–189.
60. "Women's Party Idea Condemned," *Salt Lake Tribune*, June 16, 1921.
61. See Leslie A. Hahner, *To Become an American: Immigrants and Americanization Campaigns of the Early Twentieth Century* (East Lansing: Michigan State University Press, 2017).
62. Gertrude Bonnin, chronology of major activities, 1876–1929, Box 1, Folder 1, MSS 1704, Gertrude and Raymond Bonnin Collection, L. Tom Perry Special Collections, Brigham Young University; "Club Women to Work for Indian Welfare," *Fayetteville Daily Democrat*, August 9, 1921.
63. Gertrude Bonnin, "Brief History of Activities in Behalf of the American Indian, 1902–1932," Box 1, Folder 1, MSS 1704, Gertrude and Raymond Bonnin Collection, L. Tom Perry Special Collections, Brigham Young University.
64. Bonnin, chronology of major activities, 1876–1929, Box 1, Folder 1, MSS 1704, Gertrude and Raymond Bonnin Collection, L. Tom Perry Special Collections, Brigham Young University.
65. Lewandowski, *Red Bird, Red Power*, 151.
66. See, for instance, Black, "Native Resistive Rhetoric," 71–72.
67. For details on what happened to Bonnin's papers, see Register of the

Gertrude and Raymond Bonnin Collection, 1926–1938, MSS1704, L. Tom Perry Special Collections, Brigham Young University. Available online at http://files.lib.byu.edu/ead/XML/MSS1704.xml.

68. Vigil, *Indigenous Intellectuals*, 203.
69. Women orators had long had to negotiate newspaper coverage of their appearance, femininity, and arguments. See, for example, Angela Ray, *The Lyceum and Public Culture in the Nineteenth-Century United States* (East Lansing: Michigan State University Press, 2005), 143–156; and Sara E. Lampert, "The 'Perfect Delight' of Dramatic Reading: Gertrude Kellogg and the Post–Civil War Lyceum," in *Thinking Together: Lecturing, Learning, and Difference in the Long Nineteenth Century*, ed. Angela G. Ray and Paul Stob (State College: Pennsylvania State University Press, 2018), 130–149.
70. "The Club Federation," *Oak Park Oak Leaves*, February 4, 1922.
71. "River Forest Women," *Oak Park Oak Leaves*, November 21, 1925.
72. "Reciprocity Day," *Oak Park Oak Parker*, February 6, 1925.
73. "Urges Full Citizenship for Indians," *Anaconda Standard*, March 27, 1918.
74. "Indian to Address Club," *Canton Sunday News*, June 10, 1923.
75. Davidson and Norris, introduction to *American Indian Stories*, xxiii.
76. James Mooney, a white ethnologist who worked for the Smithsonian Institute and championed the use of peyote among Native tribes, attacked Zitkala-Ša in his congressional testimony about peyote. Referring to a recent article about her that included a publicity picture, Mooney lambasted her outfit: "The dress is a woman's dress from some southern tribe, as shown by the long fringes; the belt is a Navajo man's belt; the fan is a peyote man's fan, carried only by men, usually in the peyote ceremony." Quoted in Lewandowski, *Red Bird, Red Power*, 141.
77. Arietta Wimer Towne, "The Sixth District," *Oak Parker*, February 20, 1925.
78. Davidson and Norris, introduction to *American Indian Stories*, xxiii.
79. See "Host to Wounded Men," *Washington Post*, March 28, 1920; and "Club Women to Work for Indian Welfare," *Fayetteville Daily Democrat*, August 9, 1921.
80. "Citizenship for Red Men Urged by the Woman's Club," *Atlanta Constitution*, November 15, 1921.
81. "Indian Princess Is Historian," *Los Angeles Times*, September 22, 1925.

82. "Red Bird, First Americans Queen, Pleads Cause of 'Vanishing Race,'" *Bismarck Tribune*, June 11, 1928.
83. "Lecturer Will Speak on Indian Problems," *Daily Palo Alto*, November 7, 1922.
84. "The Indian's Eleventh Hour," *Bismarck Tribune*, June 11, 1928.
85. "Famous Sioux Indian Woman Seeks Out Money Outposts of Her Rapidly Dying Race," *San Francisco Chronicle*, September 8, 1922.
86. "Plays Fitting Roles in Navy League Pageant," *Dubuque Times-Journal*, March 14, 1920.
87. Lewandowski, *Red Bird, Red Power*, 136. Also see Davidson and Norris, introduction to *American Indian Stories*, xiv.
88. See Benjamin Moffitt, *The Global Rise of Populism: Performance, Political Style, and Representation* (Stanford, CA: Stanford University Press, 2016), esp. ch. 4.
89. Frederic J. Haskin, "Furthers Indian Welfare," *Los Angeles Times*, April 3, 1926.
90. "Zitkala-Ša Brings Indians' Needs before Women's Forum," *Christian Science Monitor*, April 22, 1926.
91. "Zitkala-Ša the Red Bird of the Sioux," *New York Tribune*, September 23, 1906.
92. "Indian Princess to Speak at Woman's Club," *Canton Daily News*, February 3, 1924.
93. "River Forest Women," *Oak Park Oak Leaves*, November 14, 1925.
94. "Lecturer Will Speak on Indian Problems," *Daily Palo Alto*, November 7, 1922.
95. "Should He Forget?" *Bradford Era*, January 18, 1930.
96. "The Oratorical Contest," *Earlhamite*, March 1896, 183.
97. For coverage of these orations, see "The Oratorical Contest," 183–185.
98. Lewandowski, *Red Bird, Red Power*, 3.
99. See Dexter Fisher, "Zitkala-Ša: The Evolution of a Writer," *American Indian Quarterly* 5, no. 3 (1979): 232–233; Deborah Welch, "Zitkala-Ša: An American Indian Leader, 1876–1938" (PhD dissertation, University of Wyoming, 1985), 11; Betty Louise Bell, "If This Is Paganism," in *Native Religious Identity*, ed. Jace Weaver (Maryknoll, NY: Orbis, 1998), 63.

100. Lewandowski, *Red Bird, Red Power*, 208, n. 53.
101. "Side by Side," *American Indian Stories*, 222.
102. "Side by Side," 223.
103. "Side by Side," 223.
104. "Side by Side," 224, 225.
105. "Side by Side," 224.
106. "Side by Side," 225.
107. "Side by Side," 226.
108. "Side by Side," 226.
109. For an excellent overview of sovereignty in Indian communities, see Joanne Barker, ed., *Sovereignty Matters: Locations of Contestation and Possibility in Indigenous Struggles for Self-Determination* (Lincoln: University of Nebraska Press, 2005).
110. "The Oratorical Contest," 185.
111. "Cheers for the Indian Maiden," *Indianapolis News;* reprinted in *The Earlhamite*, 187.
112. "The Oratorical Contest," 185.
113. The opera was a success overall, and it attracted the kind of attention to which Zitkala-Ša had grown accustomed. Newspapers across the country marveled that an Indian girl could in fact write an opera. For an overview of the opera, see Lewandowski, *Red Bird, Red Power*, 78–88.
114. Maddox, *Citizen Indians*, 16.
115. Maddox, *Citizen Indians*, 9.
116. Lewandowski, *Red Bird, Red Power*, 105.
117. Quoted in Lewandowski, *Red Bird, Red Power*, 118.
118. For more on the history of the term "back to the blanket," see Wieser, *Back to the Blanket*, especially the introduction.
119. Lewandowski, *Red Bird, Red Power*, 119–122.
120. See Lewandowski, *Red Bird, Red Power*, 153–156.
121. For extensive coverage of the convention, including primary documents, see "Annual Convention," *American Indian* 7, no. 3 (Fall 1919): 145–180.
122. Lewandowski, *Red Bird, Red Power*, 154.
123. Lewandowski, *Red Bird, Red Power*, 156.
124. "Address by Mrs. Gertrude Bonnin," *American Indian* 7, no. 3 (Fall 1919):

153, 154.

125. "Address by Mrs. Gertrude Bonnin," 154.
126. "Address by Mrs. Gertrude Bonnin," 154.
127. "Address by Mrs. Gertrude Bonnin," 154.
128. "Address by Mrs. Gertrude Bonnin," 154.
129. "Address by Mrs. Gertrude Bonnin," 154–155.
130. "Address by Mrs. Gertrude Bonnin," 155.
131. "Address by Mrs. Gertrude Bonnin," 156.
132. See Lewandowski, *Red Bird, Red Power*, 154–155.
133. Lewandowski, *Red Bird, Red Power*, 156.
134. For an excellent study of this horrible situation, see David Grann, *Killers of the Flower Moon: The Osage Murders and the Birth of the FBI* (New York: Doubleday, 2017).
135. Gertrude Bonnin, Charles H. Fabens, and Matthew K. Sniffen, *Oklahoma's Poor Rich Indians: An Orgy of Graft and Exploitation of the Five Civilized Tribes—Legalized Robbery* (Philadelphia: Office of the Indian Rights Association, 1924).
136. Lewandowski, *Red Bird, Red Power*, 163–172.
137. Lewandowski, *Red Bird, Red Power*, 176.
138. For an excellent overview, see Dippie, *The Vanishing American*, 297–321.
139. See Lewandowski, *Red Bird, Red Power*, 181–182.
140. For more on the founding of the IRA, see William T. Hagan, *The Indian Rights Association: The Herbert Welsh Years, 1882–1904* (Tucson: University of Arizona Press, 1985).
141. Gertrude Bonnin, "American Indian Problem: Address Before the Indian Rights Association to Discuss the Report 'Problem of Indian Administration' by the Institute for Government Research," MSS1704, Box 1, Folder 5, Gertrude Bonnin Collection, Brigham Young University, Provo, Utah.
142. Bonnin, "American Indian Problem," 1.
143. Bonnin, "American Indian Problem," 1.
144. Bonnin, "American Indian Problem," 2.
145. For a series of case students around this theme, see Cecelia Tichi, *Civic Passions: Seven Who Launched Progressive America (and What They Teach Us)*

(Chapel Hill: University of North Carolina Press, 2009).

146. Again, see Black, *American Indians*, 85.
147. Bonnin, "American Indian Problem," 3.
148. Bonnin, "American Indian Problem," 2–3.
149. Bonnin, "American Indian Problem," 6.
150. Bonnin, "American Indian Problem," 8, 11.
151. Bonnin, "American Indian Problem," 4.
152. Bonnin, "American Indian Problem," 8.
153. Bonnin, "American Indian Problem," 11.
154. Bonnin, "American Indian Problem," 4–5.
155. Bonnin, "American Indian Problem," 9.
156. Bonnin, "American Indian Problem," 14.
157. Lewandowski, *Red Bird, Red Power*, 187.

Conclusion

1. Chad Wellmon, *Organizing Enlightenment: Information Overload and the Invention of the Modern Research University* (Baltimore: Johns Hopkins University Press, 2015).
2. Kevin Carey, *The End of College: Creating the Future of Learning and the University of Everywhere* (New York: Riverhead Books, 2015), 5.
3. Carey, *The End of College*, 6.
4. Ryan Craig, *College Disrupted: The Great Unbundling of Higher Education* (New York: Palgrave Macmillan, 2015), 103–108.
5. Richard A. DeMillo, *Revolution in Higher Education: How a Small Band of Innovators Will Make College Accessible and Affordable* (Cambridge, MA: MIT Press, 2015), 7, 14.
6. For similar predictions of revolution, see William J. Bennett and David Wilezol, *Is College Worth It?* (Nashville, TN: Thomas Nelson, 2013); Jeffrey J. Sellingo, *College (Un)Bound: The Future of Higher Education and What It Means for Students* (Las Vegas, NV: Amazon Publishing, 2013); Rebecca Chopp, Susan Frost, and Daniel H. Weiss, eds., *Remaking College: Innovation and the Liberal Arts* (Baltimore: Johns Hopkins University Press, 2014); William Deresiewicz, *Excellent Sheep: The Miseducaton of the American Elite and the Way to a Meaningful Life* (New York: Free Press, 2014); Michael W. Kirst and

Mitchell L. Stevens, eds., *Remaking College: The Changing Ecology of Higher Education* (Stanford, CA: Stanford University Press, 2015); Richard Susskind and Daniel Susskind, *The Future of the Professions: How Technology Will Transform the Work of Human Experts* (Oxford: Oxford University Press, 2015).

7. See Lewis Perry, *Intellectual Life in America: A History* (Chicago: University of Chicago Press, 1989), 433–448.
8. Neuroscientists refer to this phenomenon as "interpersonal brain synchronization." See Honghong Tang, Xiaoqin Mai, Shun Wang, Chaozhe Zhu, Frank Krueger, and Chao Liu, "Interpersonal Brain Synchronization in the Right Temporo-Parietal Junction during Face-to-Face Economic Exchange," *Social Cognitive and Affective Neuroscience* 11, no. 1 (2016): 23–32; and Molly J. Henry, Daniel J. Cameron, Dana Swarbick, Dan Bosnyak, Laurel Trainor, and Jessica Grahn, "Live Music Increases Intersubject Synchronization of Audience Members' Brain Rhythms," presented at the 2018 Cognitive Neuroscience Symposium, online at https://www.cogneurosociety.org/mycns/?page=invited_symposia#4.
9. "Ingersoll on Ministers," *New York Sun*, February 25, 1895, 1.
10. See Paul Stob, "Black Hands Push Back: Reconsidering the Rhetoric of Booker T. Washington," *Quarterly Journal of Speech* 104, no. 2 (2018): 145–165.
11. Quoted in Booker T. Washington, *Up from Slavery*, in *The Booker T. Washington Papers*, vol. 1: *The Autobiographical Writings*, ed. Louis R. Harlan (Urbana: University of Illinois Press, 1972), 342.
12. Thomas Davidson, "The Problems Set by the Nineteenth Century to the Twentieth," Box 27, Thomas Davidson Papers, Sterling Memorial Library, Yale University.
13. See "International Board of Lectureship," Box 213, Folder: The First Church of Christ Scientist—Lectures and Board of Lectureship, Mary Baker Eddy Library, Boston, MA.
14. Edward Kimball to "The Churches in Milwaukee," May 16, 1898, Box 150, Folder: Kimball, Edward A. (1845–1909), Papers 1896–1907, Mary Baker Eddy Library, Boston, MA.
15. "Extracts from Address of Booker T. Washington before the High

School, Springfield, Mass., Mar. 17, 1899," Box 113, Folder 15, Papers of Booker T. Washington, Tuskegee University Archives.

16. "Extracts from address of Booker T. Washington before the Colored Methodist Episcopal Church General Conference, Nashville, Tenn., May 15th, 1902," bound speeches volume, Papers of Booker T. Washington, Tuskegee University Archives.
17. For more, see Kimberly G. Wieser, *Back to the Blanket: Recovered Rhetorics and Literacies in American Indian Studies* (Norman: University of Oklahoma Press, 2017).
18. Gertrude Bonnin, "A Year's Experience in Community Service Work among the Ute Tribe of Indians," *American Indian Magazine* 4 (October/November 1916): 307.
19. William James, *Pragmatism: The Works of William James* (Cambridge, MA: Harvard University Press, 1975), 10.
20. Robert Ingersoll, "The Devil," Box 28, Robert Green Ingersoll Papers, Library of Congress, Microfilm Edition, Reel 20; Robert Ingersoll, "Gods," in *Complete Lectures of Col. R. G Ingersoll* ([Chicago?]: Published for the Trade, [1886?]), 2; Robert Ingersoll, "Blasphemy," in *Complete Lectures*, 4; and Robert Ingersoll, "Foundations of Faith," Box 28, Robert Green Ingersoll Papers, Library of Congress, Microfilm Edition, Reel 20.
21. Robert Ingersoll, "The Truth," Box 31, Robert Green Ingersoll Papers, Library of Congress, Microfilm Edition, Reel 22.
22. For more, see Paul Stob, "Sacred Symbols, Public Memory, and the Great Agnostic: Robert Ingersoll Remembers the Civil War," *Rhetoric and Public Affairs* 19, no. 2 (2016): 275–306.
23. Thomas Davidson, *The Education of the Wage-Earners*, ed. Charles M. Bakewell (Boston: Ginn, 1904), 181–183.
24. See Robert J. Norrell, *Up from History: The Life of Booker T. Washington* (Cambridge, MA: Belknap Press of Harvard University Press, 2009), 104–106.
25. "Address by Mrs. Gertrude Bonnin," *American Indian* 7, no. 3 (Fall 1919): 154.
26. I borrow the phrase "religion as a conversation stopper" from Richard Rorty, "Religion as Conversation-Stopper," in *Philosophy and Social Hope*

(London: Penguin, 1999), 168–174.

27. The number of news stories in the wake of 2016 political turmoil between academics and the people is simply too numerous to list here. But for a few examples, see Ron Grossman, "Brexit, Donald Trump Show How Elite Lost Touch with Workaday Voices," *Chicago Tribune*, June 26, 2016, https://www.chicagotribune.com/news/opinion/commentary/ct-brexit-trump-grossman-0630-20160629-story.html; Charles Camosy, "Trump Won Because College-Educated Americans Are Out of Touch," *Washington Post*, November 9, 2016, https://www.washingtonpost.com/posteverything/wp/2016/11/09/trump-won-because-college-educated-americans-are-out-of-touch/?utm_term=.a09b2720d1b5; Roland Merullo, "What Liberal Academics Don't Get," *Chronicle of Higher Education*, November 20, 2016, https://www.chronicle.com/article/What-Liberal-Academics-Don-t/238428; James Bartholomew, "What Explains the Idiocy of the Liberal Elite? It's Their Education," *The Spectator*, January 7, 2017, https://www.spectator.co.uk/2017/01/what-explains-the-idiocy-of-the-liberal-elite-its-their-education/.
28. Davidson, *Education of the Wage-Earners*, 36.
29. Davidson, *Education of the Wage-Earners*, 47–48.
30. Michael Kazin, *The Populist Persuasion: An American History* (New York: Basic Books, 1995).

Bibliography

Archival Collections

Booker T. Washington Papers. Manuscript Division. Library of Congress, Washington, DC.

Gertrude and Raymond Bonnin Collection. L. Tom Perry Special Collections. Brigham Young University, Provo, UT.

Mary Baker Eddy Collection. Mary Baker Eddy Library, Boston, MA.

Organizational Records of The First Church of Christ, Scientist. Mary Baker Eddy Library, Boston, MA.

Papers of Booker T. Washington. Tuskegee University Archives, Tuskegee, AL.

Robert Green Ingersoll Papers. Abraham Lincoln Presidential Library, Springfield, IL.

Robert Green Ingersoll Papers. Manuscript Division. Library of Congress, Washington, DC.

Thomas Davidson Papers. Sterling Memorial Library. Yale University, New Haven, CT.

Lectures and Speeches

Buskirk, Clarence. "Grave Not the Goal." *Peoria Herald-Transcript*, November 14, 1904. Mary Baker Eddy Library.

Davidson, Thomas. "The Problems Set by the Nineteenth Century to the Twentieth." Thomas Davidson Papers. Sterling Memorial Library, Yale University.

——. "Rousseau, and Education According to Nature." In *Memorials of Thomas Davidson: The Wandering Scholar*, edited by William Angus Knight, 152–172. Boston: Ginn, 1907.

Eaton, Clarence. "On Christian Science." *Everett Republican*, n.d. Mary Baker Eddy Library.

Eddy, Mary Baker. *The People's God.* Cambridge, MA: John Wilson and Son, 1883. Mary Baker Eddy Library.

Fluno, Francis. "Dr. Fluno's Able Lecture." *Supplement to the New Bern Journal*, January 1909. Committee on Publication Clipping File. Mary Baker Eddy Library.

Hanna, Septimus. "Judge Hanna." *New Hampshire Patriot*, October 22, 1908. Mary Baker Eddy Library.

Hering, Hermann. "Christian Science, the Science of Salvation." *Milwaukee Daily News*, October 11, 1909. Mary Baker Eddy Library.

Ingersoll, Robert. "Blasphemy." In *Complete Lectures of Col. R. G Ingersoll.* [Chicago?]: Published for the Trade, [1886?].

——. "The Devil." Robert Green Ingersoll Papers. Library of Congress, Microfilm Edition.

——. "Foundations of Faith." Robert Green Ingersoll Papers. Library of Congress, Microfilm Edition.

——. "Ghosts." In *Complete Lectures of Col. R. G Ingersoll.* [Chicago?]: Published for the Trade, [1886?].

——. "Gods." In *Complete Lectures of Col. R. G Ingersoll.* [Chicago?]: Published for the Trade, [1886?].

——. "The Great Infidels." In *Complete Lectures of Col. R. G Ingersoll.* [Chicago?]: Published for the Trade, [1886?].

——. "Heretics and Heresies." In *Lectures of Col. R. G. Ingersoll, Latest.* Chicago: Rhodes & McClure, 1898.

———. "How to Reform Mankind." Robert Green Ingersoll Papers. Library of Congress, Microfilm Edition.

———. "Individuality." In *Complete Lectures of Col. R. G Ingersoll.* [Chicago?]: Published for the Trade, [1886?].

———. "Liberty of Man, Woman, and Child." In *Complete Lectures of Col. R. G Ingersoll.* [Chicago?]: Published for the Trade, [1886?].

———. "Myth and Miracle." Robert G. Ingersoll Papers. Abraham Lincoln Presidential Library.

———. "Orthodoxy." In *Complete Lectures of Col. R. G Ingersoll.* [Chicago?]: Published for the Trade, [1886?].

———. "Some Mistakes of Moses." In *The Works of Robert G. Ingersoll.* Vol. 2, *Lectures.* New York: Dresden Publishing, 1901.

———. "Some Reasons Why." In *Complete Lectures of Col. R. G Ingersoll.* [Chicago?]: Published for the Trade, [1886?].

———. "The Truth." Robert Green Ingersoll Papers. Library of Congress, Microfilm Edition.

———. "What Must We Do to Be Saved?" Robert Green Ingersoll Papers. Library of Congress, Microfilm Edition.

Kimball, Edward A. Untitled Lecture. December 2, 1906. Published Lecture File. Mary Baker Eddy Library.

Knapp, Bliss. "Lecture on Christian Science." *Cambridge Chronicle*, October 17, 1908. Committee on Publication Clipping File. Mary Baker Eddy Library.

Leonard, Frank H. "Christian Science." *Needham Chronicle*, October 23, 1909. Mary Baker Eddy Library.

McCracken, William. "'Christian Science as Religion of Progress' Is Theme of M'Crackan." *Denver Post*, n.d. Committee on Publication Clipping File. Mary Baker Eddy Library.

McKenzie, William. "Christian Science." *Reading (Mass.) Chronicle.* Committee on Publication Clipping File. Mary Baker Eddy Library.

———. "The Panacea for the World's Unrest." *Worcester Evening Gazette*, January 18, 1901. Mary Baker Eddy Library.

Norton, Carol. "Christian Science: Its Work and Scope." *Supplement to the Christian Science Sentinel* 3, no. 25 (1900): 401–404. Mary Baker Eddy Library.

Linscott, John. "Christian Science, the Law of Spirit." *Atlanta Constitution*, December 17, 1901. Mary Baker Eddy Library.

Tomkins, George. "Christian Science and Bible Science Alphabet." *Supplement Washington News Letter*, December 14, 1898. Mary Baker Eddy Library.

Tomlinson, Irving. "Immense Crowd: Christian Scientists Meet in Music Hall." *Boston Journal*, April 6, 1899. Mary Baker Eddy Library.

Washington, Booker T. "An Abraham Lincoln Memorial Address in Philadelphia," February 14, 1899. In *The Booker T. Washington Papers*, vol. 5, *1899–1900*, edited by Louis R. Harlan and Raymond W. Smock, 32–38. Urbana: University of Illinois Press, 1976.

———. "An Address at the Metropolitan A.M.E. Church," May 22, 1900. In *The Booker T. Washington Papers*, vol. 5, *1899–1900*, edited by Louis R. Harlan and Raymond W. Smock, 527–540. Urbana: University of Illinois Press, 1976.

———. "Address Before the State University of New York, June 28, 1898." Papers of Booker T. Washington. Tuskegee University Archives.

———. "Address of Booker T. Washington, Delivered at Witherspoon Hall, Philadelphia, March 19th, 1900." Papers of Booker T. Washington. Tuskegee University Archives.

———. "Address of Booker T. Washington, President National Negro Business League, Convention Hall, Muskogee, Oklahoma, August 19, 1914." Papers of Booker T. Washington. Tuskegee University Archives.

———. "The Care of Dependent Children, New Willard Hotel, Washington, D. C., January 25th, 1912." Papers of Booker T. Washington. Tuskegee University Archives.

———. "A Commencement Address in Washington, D.C.," June 16, 1905. In *The Booker T. Washington Papers*, vol. 8, *1904–6*, edited by Louis R. Harlan and Raymond W. Smock, 304–317. Urbana: University of Illinois Press, 1979.

———. "Delivered at Carnegie Hall, New York City, Tuesday Evening, February 23rd, 1909." Papers of Booker T. Washington. Tuskegee University Archives.

———. "Delivered at the Conservation Congress, Knoxville, Tennessee, Oct. 14, 1913." Papers of Booker T. Washington. Tuskegee University Archives.

———. "Dr. Booker T. Washington's Lecture at Metropolitan A.M.E. Church

(Rev. O.J.W. Scott, D.D., Pastor), On Friday Evening, March 18, 1904." Papers of Booker T. Washington. Tuskegee University Archives.

———. "Extracts from Address Delivered at Steubenville, Ohio, Tuesday Afternoon, Sept. 5, 1911." Papers of Booker T. Washington. Tuskegee University Archives.

———. "Extracts from Address Delivered by Booker T. Washington at the Annual Fair and Convocation of the Farmers' Improvement Society, October 11, 1900." Papers of Booker T. Washington. Tuskegee University Archives.

———. "Extracts from Address of Booker T. Washington, Arlington St. Church, December 7," n.d. Papers of Booker T. Washington. Tuskegee University Archives.

———. "Extracts from Address of Booker T. Washington at a Banquet, in Cambridge, Mass., Given by Colored Young Men's Forum and Boston Negro Business League, Monday Eve., October 3, 1904." Papers of Booker T. Washington. Tuskegee University Archives.

———. "Extracts from Address of Booker T. Washington at Farmers' National Congress, Fort Worth, Texas, December 6th, 1898." Papers of Booker T. Washington. Tuskegee University Archives.

———. "Extracts from Address of Booker T. Washington at Olivet Baptist Church, 27th & Dearborn St., Chicago, April 5, 1907." Papers of Booker T. Washington. Tuskegee University Archives.

———. "Extracts from Address of Booker T. Washington at Unitarian Club, Wednesday Evening, February 14, 1900." Papers of Booker T. Washington. Tuskegee University Archives.

———. "Extracts from Address of Booker T. Washington before the Colored Methodist Episcopal Church General Conference, Nashville, Tenn., May 15th, 1902." Papers of Booker T. Washington. Tuskegee University Archives.

———. "Extracts from Address of Booker T. Washington before the High School, Springfield, Mass., Mar. 17, 1899." Papers of Booker T. Washington. Tuskegee University Archives.

———. "Extracts from Address of Booker T. Washington before the Society for the Promotion of Industrial Education, Spelman Seminary, Atlanta,

Ga., November 20, 1908." Papers of Booker T. Washington. Tuskegee University Archives.
——. "Extracts from Address of Booker T. Washington, delivered in Augusta, Ga., January 2, 1905." Papers of Booker T. Washington. Tuskegee University Archives.
——. "Extracts from an Address Delivered by Booker T. Washington at a Banquet Given in His Honor by the Business Men's League of Chicago, Ill., on the Evening of April 5th, 1904." Papers of Booker T. Washington. Tuskegee University Archives.
——. "Extracts from Speech Delivered by Booker T. Washington, Before A. M. E. General Conference, May 23, 1900, Columbus, Ohio." Papers of Booker T. Washington. Tuskegee University Archives.
——. "Extracts from the Address of Booker T. Washington at the New Old South Church, Sunday Evening, December 16, 1900." Papers of Booker T. Washington. Tuskegee University Archives.
——. "Extracts from the Address of Booker T. Washington at the Opening of the Ohio State Colored Educational and Industrial Exposition, Columbus, Ohio, Saturday Afternoon, August 15, 1906." Papers of Booker T. Washington. Tuskegee University Archives.
——. "Extracts from Three Addresses Delivered in Louisiana," April 13–16, 1915. In *The Booker T. Washington Papers*, vol. 13, *1914–1915*, edited Louis R. Harlan and Raymond W. Smock, 262–270. Urbana: University of Illinois Press, 1984.
——. "First Joint Commencement," Armstrong Manual Training School, 1905. Booker T. Washington Papers. Manuscript Division, Library of Congress.
——. "Part of the Address by Booker T. Washington at a Meeting for Colored Men, Old Ship Church, Montgomery, Ala., Jan. 17, 1909." Papers of Booker T. Washington. Tuskegee University Archives.
——. "Report of the Meeting Held in the Interest of the Manassas Industrial School, on the Evening of February 14th, 1906, at the First Congregational Church, Washington, D.C." Papers of Booker T. Washington. Tuskegee University Archives.
——. "A Speech before the Alabama State Teachers' Association." April 7,

1882. In *The Booker T. Washington Papers*, vol. 2, *1860–89*, edited by Louis R. Harlan, 191–194. Urbana: University of Illinois Press, 1972.

——. "A Speech before the New York Congregational Club." In *The Booker T. Washington Papers*, vol. 3, *1889–95*, edited Louis R. Harlan, 279–287. Urbana: University of Illinois Press, 1974.

——. Untitled address in Alabama, 1899. Papers of Booker T. Washington. Tuskegee University Archives.

——. "What Co-Operation Can Accomplish. Delivered before the Negro Organization Society, Norfolk, Virginia, November 12, 1914." Papers of Booker T. Washington. Tuskegee University Archives.

Young, Bicknell. "Christian Science and Its Message." *Daily Patriot* (Concord, NH), October 17, 1904. Mary Baker Eddy Library.

——. "Lecture at Christian Science Church." *Des Moines Capital*, December 4, 1907. Committee on Publication Clipping File. Mary Baker Eddy Library.

Zitkala-Ša. "Address by Mrs. Gertrude Bonnin." *American Indian* 7, no. 3 (Fall 1919): 153–157.

——. "American Indian Problem: Address Before the Indian Rights Association to Discuss the Report 'Problem of Indian Administration' by the Institute for Government Research." Gertrude Bonnin Collection. Brigham Young University.

——. "Side by Side." In *American Indian Stories, Legends, and Other Writings*, edited by Cathy N. Davidson and Ada Norris, 222–226. New York: Penguin, 2003.

Books, Articles, and Other

Ackerknecht, Erwin H. *A Short History of Medicine.* Rev. ed. Baltimore: Johns Hopkins University Press, 1982.

Adams, David Wallace. *Education for Extinction: American Indians and the Boarding School Experience, 1875-1928.* Lawrence: University Press of Kansas, 1995.

Afsaruddin, Asma. "Revelation in the Qur'ān." In *Communicating the Word: Revelation, Translation, and Interpretation in Christianity and Islam*, edited by David Marshall, 44–55. Washington, DC: Georgetown University Press, 2011.

Ahlstrom, Sydney E. *A Religious History of the American People.* 2nd ed. New Haven, CT: Yale University Press, 2004.

Andersen, Tom. "Glenmore." *Adirondack Life*, March/April 1982, 19–22, 48–49.

Anderson, Benedict. *Imagined Communities: Reflections on the Origin and Spread of Nationalism.* Rev. ed. London: Verso, 1991.

Anderson, David D. *Robert Ingersoll.* New York: Twayne Publishers, 1972.

Anderson, F. "Dignity of Labor." *Evangelical Magazine and Gospel Advocate* 13 (October 28, 1842): 337.

Anderson, James D. *The Education of Blacks in the South, 1860–1935.* Chapel Hill: University of North Carolina Press, 2014.

"Annual Convention." *American Indian* 7, no. 3 (Fall 1919): 145–180.

Antczak, Frederick J. *Thought and Character: The Rhetoric of Democratic Education.* Ames: Iowa State University Press, 1985.

Armytage, W. H. G. "Thomas Davidson, Anglo-American Educator." *History of Education Journal* 2 (1951): 75–79.

Arnesen, Eric. "American Workers and the Labor Movement in the Late Nineteenth Century." In *The Gilded Age*, rev. ed., edited by H. Wayne Morgan, 39–61. Syracuse: Syracuse University Press, 1970.

Asen, Robert. *Democracy, Deliberation, and Education.* State College: Pennsylvania State University, 2015.

Augst, Thomas. "Humanist Enterprise in the Marketplace of Culture." In *The Cosmopolitan Lyceum: Lecture Culture and the Globe in Nineteenth-Century America*, edited by Tom F. Wright, 223–240. Amherst: University of Massachusetts Press, 2013.

Bakewell, Charles M. "The Vitality of the Ideal." In *The Education of the Wage-Earners*, edited by Charles M. Bakewell, 216–239. Boston: Ginn, 1904.

Barker, Joanne, ed. *Sovereignty Matters: Locations of Contestation and Possibility in Indigenous Struggles for Self-Determination.* Lincoln: University of Nebraska Press, 2005.

Barney, Timothy. "Power Lines: The Rhetoric of Maps as Social Change in the Post–Cold War Landscape." *Quarterly Journal of Speech* 95, no. 4 (2009): 412–434.

Bartholomew, James. "What Explains the Idiocy of the Liberal Elite? It's Their Education." *The Spectator*, January 7, 2017, https://www.spectator.

co.uk/2017/01/what-explains-the-idiocy-of-the-liberal-elite-its-their-education/.

Bay, Mia. *The White Image in the Black Mind: African-American Ideas about White People, 1830-1925.* New York: Oxford University Press, 2000.

Beasley, Vanessa B. *You, the People: American National Identity in Presidential Rhetoric.* College Station: Texas A&M University Press, 2004.

Bederman, Gail. *Manliness and Civilization: A Cultural History of Gender and Race in the United States, 1880-1917.* Chicago: University of Chicago Press, 1995.

Bell, Betty Louise. "If This Is Paganism." In *Native Religious Identity*, edited by Jace Weaver, 61–68. Maryknoll, NY: Orbis, 1998.

Bellow, Adam. *The Educational Alliance: A Centennial Celebration.* New York: Educational Alliance, 1990.

Bender, Thomas. *Intellect and Public Life: Essays on the Social History of Academic Intellectuals in the United States.* Baltimore: Johns Hopkins University Press, 1993.

Bennett, William J., and David Wilezol. *Is College Worth It?* Nashville, TN: Thomas Nelson, 2013.

Biel, Steven. *Independent Intellectuals in the United States, 1910-1945.* New York: New York University Press, 1992.

Black, Jason Edward. *American Indians and the Rhetoric of Removal and Allotment.* Jackson: University Press of Mississippi, 2015.

——. "Native Authenticity, Rhetorical Circulation, and Neocolonial Decay: The Case of Chief Seattle's Controversial Speech." *Rhetoric & Public Affairs* 15, no. 4 (2012): 635–646.

——. "Native Resistive Rhetoric and the Decolonization of American Indian Removal Discourse." *Quarterly Journal of Speech* 95, no. 1 (2009): 66–88.

——. "Remembrances of Removal: Native Resistance to Allotment and the Unmasking of Paternal Benevolence." *Southern Communication Journal* 72, no. 2 (2007): 185–203.

Bledstein, Burton J. *The Culture of Professionalism: The Middle Class and the Development of Higher Education in America.* New York: Norton, 1978.

Blum, Edward J. *Reforging the White Republic: Race, Religion, and American Nationalism, 1865-1898.* Baton Rouge: Louisiana State University Press, 2005.

Bode, Carl. *The American Lyceum: Town Meeting of the Mind.* Carbondale: Southern

Illinois University Press, 1968.

Bomberger, E. Douglas. "Talking Music: Amy Fay and the Origins of the Lecture Recital." In *Thinking Together: Lecturing, Learning, and Difference in the Long Nineteenth Century*, edited by Angela G. Ray and Paul Stob, 150–168. State College: Pennsylvania State University Press, 2018.

Bonnin, Gertrude. "Statement of Gertrude Bonnin." In *Peyote: Hearings before a Subcommittee of the Committee on Indian Affairs of the House of Representatives on H. R. 2614*. Washington, DC: Government Printing Office, 1918.

———. "A Year's Experience in Community Service Work among the Ute Tribe of Indians." *American Indian Magazine* 4 (October/November 1916): 307–310.

Bonnin, Gertrude, Charles H. Fabens, and Matthew K. Sniffen. *Oklahoma's Poor Rich Indians: An Orgy of Graft and Exploitation of the Five Civilized Tribes—Legalized Robbery*. Philadelphia: Office of the Indian Rights Association, 1924.

Bordogna, Francesca. *William James at the Boundaries: Philosophy, Science, and the Geography of Knowledge*. Chicago: University of Chicago Press, 2008.

Borst, Charlotte G. *Catching Babies: The Professionalization of Childbirth, 1870–1920*. Cambridge, MA: Harvard University Press, 1995.

Bradbury, Kelly Susan. *Reimagining Popular Notions of American Intellectualism: Literacy, Education, and Class*. Carbondale: Southern Illinois University Press, 2016.

Brian, Denis. *Pulitzer: A Life*. New York: John Wiley and Sons, 2001.

Brinkley, Alan. *Voices of Protest: Huey Long, Father Coughlin, and the Great Depression*. New York: Vintage Books, 1982.

Burke, Kenneth. *Permanence and Chance: An Anatomy of Purpose*. 3rd ed. Berkeley: University of California Press, 1984.

Burnstein, Daniel. *Next to Godliness: Confronting Dirt and Despair in Progressive Era New York City*. Urbana: University of Illinois Press, 2010.

Butler, Leslie. *Critical Americans: Victorian Intellectuals and Transatlantic Liberal Reform*. Chapel Hill: University of North Carolina Press, 2007.

Bynum, W. F. *Science and the Practice of Medicine in the Nineteenth Century*. Cambridge: Cambridge University Press, 1994.

Calhoun, Charles W., ed. *The Gilded Age: Perspectives on the Origins of Modern America*. 2nd ed. Lanham, MD: Rowman & Littlefield, 2007.

Camosy, Charles. "Trump Won Because College-Educated Americans Are Out of Touch." *Washington Post*, November 9, 2016, https://www.washingtonpost.com/posteverything/wp/2016/11/09/trump-won-because-college-educated-americans-are-out-of-touch/?utm_term=.a09b2720d1b5.

Campbell, Karlyn Kohrs. *Man Cannot Speak for Her*. Vol 1: *A Critical Study of Early Feminist Rhetoric.* New York: Greenwood Press, 1989.

Carey, Kevin. *The End of College: Creating the Future of Learning and the University of Everywhere.* New York: Riverhead Books, 2015.

Carroll, Rebecca, ed. *Uncle Tom or New Negro? African Americans Reflect on Booker T. Washington and "Up from Slavery" 100 Years Later.* New York: Harlem Moon, 2006.

Cashman, Dennis. *America in the Gilded Age: From the Death of Lincoln to the Rise of Theodore Roosevelt.* 3rd ed. New York: New York University Press, 1993.

Channing, Edward T. *Lectures Read to the Seniors in Harvard College.* Boston: Ticknor and Fields, 1856.

Chapel, Gage, and Richard Jensen. "Synthesizing Jamesian Pragmatism and Platonic Idealism in Nineteenth-Century America: The Discourse of Mary Baker Eddy's Christian Science." *Journal of Communication and Religion* 23, no. 2 (2000): 95–122.

Charland, Maurice. "Constitutive Rhetoric: The Case of the Peuple Québécois." *Quarterly Journal of Speech* 73, no. 2 (1987): 133–150.

Chopp, Rebecca, Susan Frost, and Daniel H. Weiss, eds. *Remaking College: Innovation and the Liberal Arts.* Baltimore: Johns Hopkins University Press, 2014.

Clark, Gregory, and S. Michael Halloran, eds. *Oratorical Culture in Nineteenth-Century America: Transformations in the Theory and Practice of Rhetoric.* Carbondale: Southern Illinois University Press, 1993.

Cohen, Morris R. *A Dreamer's Journey.* Boston: Beacon Press, 1949.

Collins, Patricia Hill. *Black Sexual Politics: African Americans, Gender, and the New Racism.* New York: Routledge, 2004.

Collins, Randall. *The Sociology of Philosophies: A Global Theory of Intellectual Change.* Cambridge, MA: Belknap Press of Harvard University Press, 1998.

Craig, Ryan. *College Disrupted: The Great Unbundling of Higher Education.* New York:

Palgrave Macmillan, 2015.

Cramer, C. H. *Royal Bob: The Life of Robert G. Ingersoll.* New York: Bobbs-Merrill, 1952.

Crandal, William Lusk. *Talks with the People of New York.* Albany, NY: C. Van Benthuysen, 1853.

Crocker, Lionel. "Robert Green Ingersoll's Influence on American Oratory." *Quarterly Journal of Speech* 24, no. 2 (1938): 299–312.

Crosby, Richard Benjamin. "'Which is the Wisest Course?': Political Power and Prophetic Agency in Nineteenth-Century Mormon Rhetoric." *Journal of Communication and Religion* 34, no. 1 (2011): 1–23.

Dagbovie, Pero Gaglo. "Exploring a Century of Historical Scholarship on Booker T. Washington." *Journal of African American History* 92, no. 2 (2007): 239–264.

Davidson, Cathy N., and Ada Norris, eds. *American Indian Stories, Legends, and Other Writings.* New York: Penguin, 2003.

Davidson, Thomas. "Autobiographical Sketch." *Journal of the History of Ideas* 18, no. 4 (1957): 531–536.

——. *The Education of the Wage-Earners.* Edited by Charles M. Bakewell. Boston: Ginn, 1904.

——. "The Ideal Training of the American Boy." *The Forum* 27 (July 1894): 571–581.

——. "Organization of the New Fellowship." In *Memorials of Thomas Davidson: The Wandering Scholar,* edited by William Angus Knight, 48–54. Boston: Ginn, 1907.

Davis, Allen F. *Spearheads for Reform: The Social Settlements and the Progressive Movement, 1890–1914.* New York: Oxford University Press, 1967.

DeMillo, Richard A. *Revolution in Higher Education: How a Small Band of Innovators Will Make College Accessible and Affordable.* Cambridge, MA: MIT Press, 2015.

Deresiewicz, William. *Excellent Sheep: The Miseducaton of the American Elite and the Way to a Meaningful Life.* New York: Free Press, 2014.

Dewey, John. *Democracy and Education, 1916: The Middle Works, 1899–1924.* Vol. 9. Edited by Jo Ann Boydston. Carbondale: Southern Illinois University Press, 1985.

Dippie, Brian W. *The Vanishing American: White Attitudes and U.S. Indian Policy.*

Middletown, CT: Wesleyan University press, 1982.

Dixon, Joseph K. *The Vanishing Race: The Last Great Indian Council.* New York: Double Day, Page, 1913.

Dorrien, Gary. *The Making of American Liberal Theology: Imagining Progressive Religion, 1805-1900.* Louisville, KY: Westminster John Knox Press, 2001.

Dubofsky, Melvyn. *When Workers Organize: New York City in the Progressive Era.* Amherst: University of Massachusetts Press, 1968.

DuBois, W. E. B. *The Souls of Black Folks: Essays and Sketches.* 5th ed. Chicago: A. C. McClurg, 1904.

Duffy, John. *From Humors to Medical Science: A History of American Medicine.* 2nd ed. Urbana: University of Illinois Press, 1993.

Dunn, Thomas R. "Remembering 'A Great Fag': Visualizing Public Memory and the Construction of Queer Space." *Quarterly Journal of Speech* 97, no. 4 (2011): 435–460.

Durkheim, Émile. *The Elementary Forms of Religious Life.* Translated by Karen E. Fields. New York: Free Press, 1995.

Eddy, Mary Baker. *Miscellaneous Writings, 1883–1896.* Boston: Trustees Under the Will of Mary Baker G. Eddy, 1896.

——. *Retrospection and Introspections.* Boston: Joseph Armstrong, 1906.

——. *Science and Health.* Boston: Christian Scientist Publishing Company, 1875.

——. *Science and Health with Key to the Scriptures.* Boston: Christian Science Publishing Society, 1906.

Eichengreen, Barry. *The Populist Temptation: Economic Grievance and Political Reaction in the Modern Era.* Oxford: Oxford University Press, 2018.

Enoch, Jessica. *Reconfiguring Rhetorical Education: Women Teaching African American, Native American, and Chicano/a Students, 1865-1911.* Carbondale: Southern Illinois University Press, 2008.

Erlich, Howard S. "Populist Rhetoric Reassessed: A Paradox." *Quarterly Journal of Speech* 63, no. 2 (1977): 140–151.

Fenton, Elizabeth. *Religious Liberties: Anti-Catholicism and Liberal Democracy in Nineteenth-Century U.S. Literature and Culture.* Oxford: Oxford University Press, 2011.

Finnegan, Diarmid A. "The Spatial Turn: Geographical Approaches in the History of Science." *Journal of the History of Biology* 41, no. 2 (2008): 369–388.

Fischer, Raymond L. "Ingersoll on the Lecture Platform." *Central States Speech Journal* 22, no. 2 (1971): 123–126.

Fisher, Dexter. "Zitkala-Ša: The Evolution of a Writer." *American Indian Quarterly* 5, no. 3 (1979): 229–338.

Formisano, Ronald P. *For The People: American Populist Movements from the Revolution to the 1850s*. Chapel Hill: University of North Carolina Press, 2008.

Foster, Mary. "Recollections of Glenmore." In *Memorials of Thomas Davidson: The Wandering Scholar,* edited by William Angus Knight, 63–73. Boston: Ginn, 1907.

Francis, Richard. *Transcendental Utopias: Individual and Community at Brook Farm, Fruitlands, and Walden*. Ithaca, NY: Cornell University Press, 1997.

Frank, Jason. "Populism and Praxis." In *The Oxford Handbook of Populism*, edited by Cristobal Rovira Kaltwasser, Paul Taggart, Paulina Ochoa Espejo, and Pierre Ostiguy, 629–643. Oxford: Oxford University Press, 2017.

Fredal, James. *Rhetorical Action in Ancient Athens: Persuasive Artistry from Solon to Demosthenes*. Carbondale: Southern Illinois University Press, 2006.

Fyfe, Aileen, and Bernard Lightman, eds. *Science in the Marketplace: Nineteenth-Century Sites and Experiences*. Chicago: University of Chicago Press, 2007.

Gaines, Kevin K. *Uplifting the Race: Black Leadership, Politics, and Culture in the Twentieth Century*. Chapel Hill: University of North Carolina Press, 1996.

Galston, William. *Anti-pluralism: The Populist Threat to Liberal Democracy*. New Haven, CT: Yale University Press, 2018.

Ganter, Granville. "Women's Entrepreneurial Lecturing in the Early National Period." In *Thinking Together: Lecturing, Learning, and Difference in the Long Nineteenth Century,* edited by Angela G. Ray and Paul Stob, 41–55. State College: Pennsylvania State University Press, 2018.

Gaustad, Edwin S., and Leigh E. Schmidt. *The Religious History of America*. Rev. ed. San Francisco: HarperSanFrancisco, 2002.

Gehrke, Pat J. *The Ethics and Politics of Speech: Communication and Rhetoric in the Twentieth Century*. Carbondale: Southern Illinois University Press, 2009.

Geiger, Roger L. *To Advance Knowledge: The Growth of American Research Universities, 1900–1940*. New York: Oxford University Press, 1986.

Gieryn, Thomas F. *Cultural Boundaries of Science: Credibility on the Line*. Chicago: University of Chicago Press, 1999.

Gilbert, James. *Designing the Industrial State: The Intellectual Pursuit of Collectivism in America, 1800–1940.* Chicago: Quadrangle Books, 1972.

Gill, Gillian. *Mary Baker Eddy.* Cambridge, MA: Perseus Books, 1998.

Good, James. "The Value of Thomas Davidson." *Transactions of the Charles S. Peirce Society* 40, no. 2 (2004): 289–318.

Gottschalk, Stephen. *The Emergence of Christian Science in American Religious Life.* Berkeley: University of California Press, 1973.

Grann, David. *Killers of the Flower Moon: The Osage Murders and the Birth of the FBI.* New York: Doubleday, 2017.

Grattan, Laura. *Populism's Power: Radical Grassroots Democracy in America.* New York: Oxford University Press, 2016.

Griffin, Farah Jasmine. "Black Feminists and Du Bois: Respectability, Protection, and Beyond." *Annals of the American Academy of Political and Social Science* 568 (2000): 28–40.

Griffin, Susan M. *Anti-Catholicism and Nineteenth-Century Fiction.* Cambridge: Cambridge University Press, 2004.

Grossman, Ron. "Brexit, Donald Trump Show How Elite Lost Touch with Workaday Voices." *Chicago Tribune*, June 26, 2016, https://www.chicagotribune.com/news/opinion/commentary/ct-brexit-trump-grossman-0630-20160629-story.html.

Hagan, William T. *The Indian Rights Association: The Herbert Welsh Years, 1882–1904.* Tucson: University of Arizona Press, 1985.

Hahner, Leslie A. *To Become an American: Immigrants and Americanization Campaigns of the Early Twentieth Century.* East Lansing: Michigan State University Press, 2017.

Hariman, Robert. "Amateur Hour: Knowing What to Love in Ordinary Democracy." In *The Prettier Doll: Rhetoric, Discourse, and Ordinary Democracy*, edited by Karen Tracy, James P. McDaniel, and Bruce E. Gronbeck, 218–249. Tuscaloosa: University of Alabama Press, 2007.

Hall, Newman. "The Dignity of Labor." In *The Columbian Speaker*, 71–72. Boston: Lee and Shepard, 1875.

Haller, John S. *American Medicine in Transition, 1840–1910.* Urbana: University of Illinois Press, 1981.

Harlan, Louis R. *Booker T. Washington: The Making of a Black Leader, 1856–1901.*

London: Oxford University Press, 1972.

——. *Booker T. Washington: The Wizard of Tuskegee, 1901–1915.* New York: Oxford University Press, 1983.

Harlan, Louis R., and Raymond W. Smock, eds. *The Booker T. Washington Papers.* 14 vols. Urbana: University of Illinois Press, 1972–1989.

Harp, Gillis. "Hofstadter's 'The Age of Reform' and the Crucible of the Fifties." *Journal of the Gilded Age and Progressive Era* 6 (2007): 139–148.

Harris, Fredrick C. "The Rise of Respectability Politics." *Dissent* 61, no. 1 (2014): 33–37.

Harris, Leslie J. "Rhetorical Mobilities and the City: The White Slavery Controversy and Racialized Protection of Women in the U.S." *Quarterly Journal of Speech* 104, no. 1 (2018): 22–46.

Hart, Roderick P. *Civic Hope: How Ordinary Americans Keep Democracy Alive.* Cambridge: Cambridge University Press, 2018.

Haskell, Thomas L., ed. *The Authority of Experts: Studies in History and Theory.* Bloomington: Indiana University Press, 1984.

Hawhee, Debra. *Moving Bodies: Kenneth Burke at the Edges of Language.* Columbia: University of South Carolina Press, 2009.

Heath, Robert L. "A Time for Silence: Booker T. Washington in Atlanta." *Quarterly Journal of Speech* 64, no. 4 (1978): 385–399.

Henry, Molly J., Daniel J. Cameron, Dana Swarbick, Dan Bosnyak, Laurel Trainor, Jessica Grahn. "Live Music Increases Intersubject Synchronization of Audience Members' Brain Rhythms." 2018 Cognitive Neuroscience Symposium. https://www.cogneurosociety.org/mycns/?page=invited_symposia#4.

Herndl, Diane Price. *Invalid Women: Figuring Feminine Illness in American Fiction and Culture, 1840–1940.* Chapel Hill: University of North Carolina Press, 1993.

Heywood, David. *Divine Revelation and Human Learning: A Christian Theory of Knowledge.* Aldershot, England: Ashgate, 2004.

Hicks, Rosemary R. "Religion and Remedies Reunited: Rethinking Christian Science." *Journal of Feminist Studies in Religion* 20, no. 2 (2004): 25–58.

Higginbotham, Evelyn Brooks. *Righteous Discontent: The Women's Movement in the Black Baptist Church, 1880–1920.* Cambridge, MA: Harvard University Press, 1994.

Hilkey, Judy. *Character Is Capital: Success Manuals and Manhood in Gilded Age America.* Chapel Hill: University of North Carolina Press, 1997.

Hofstadter, Richard. *The Age of Reform: From Bryan to F. D. R.* New York: Vintage, 1955.

———. *Anti-intellectualism in American Life.* New York: Vintage Books, 1963.

Holland, Josiah. "The Popular Lecture." *Atlantic Monthly* 15 (1865): 362–371.

Hoxie, Frederick E., ed. *Talking Back to Civilization: Indian Voices from the Progressive Era.* Boston: Bedford / St. Martin's, 2001.

Hutchinson, William R. *The Modernist Impulse in American Protestantism.* Cambridge, MA: Harvard University Press, 1976.

Jackson, David H. *Booker T. Washington and the Struggle against White Supremacy: The Southern Educational Tours, 1908–1912.* New York: Palgrave Macmillan, 2008.

Jacoby, Russell. *The Last Intellectuals: American Culture in the Age of Academe.* New York: Noonday Press, 1987.

Jacoby, Susan. *Freethinkers: A History of American Secularism.* New York: Metropolitan Books, 2004.

———. *The Great Agnostic: Robert Ingersoll and American Freethought.* New Haven, CT: Yale University Press, 2013.

James, Felix. "The Tuskegee Institute Movable School, 1906–1923." *Agricultural History* 45, no. 3 (1971): 201–209.

James, William. *Pragmatism: The Works of William James.* Cambridge, MA: Harvard University Press, 1975.

———. "Thomas Davidson: Individualist." *Essays, Comments, and Reviews: The Works of William James*, 86–97. Cambridge: Harvard University Press, 1987.

———. *The Varieties of Religious Experience: The Works of William James.* Cambridge, MA: Harvard University Press, 1985.

Jensen, J. Vernon. "The Rhetorical Strategy of Thomas H. Huxley and Robert G. Ingersoll: Agnostics and Roadblock Removers." *Speech Monographs* 32, no. 1 (1965): 59–68.

———. "Robert G. Ingersoll: 'True Believer' Unbeliever." *Central States Speech Journal* 35, no. 2 (1984): 105–112.

Johnson, Nan. "The Popularization of Nineteenth Century Rhetoric: Elocution and the Private Learner." In *Oratorical Culture in Nineteenth-Century America*, edited by Gregory Clark and S. Michael Halloran, 139–157. Carbondale:

Southern Illinois University Press, 1993.

Johnston, Robert D. "'The Age of Reform': A Defense of Richard Hofstadter Fifty Years On." *Journal of the Gilded Age and Progressive Era* 6 (2007): 127–137.

Kaltwasser, Cristobal Rovira, Paul Taggart, Paulina Ochoa Espejo, and Pierre Ostiguy. "Populism: An Overview of the Concept and State of the Art." In *The Oxford Handbook of Populism*, edited by Cristobal Rovira Kaltwasser, Paul Taggart, Paulina Ochoa Espejo, and Pierre Ostiguy, 1–26. Oxford: Oxford University Press, 2017.

Kaplan, Edward K. "Heschel as Philosopher: Phenomenology and the Rhetoric of Revelation." *Modern Judaism* 21, no. 1 (2001): 1–14.

Kazin, Michael. *The Populist Persuasion: An American History*. New York: Basic Books, 1995.

Kett, Joseph F. *The Pursuit of Knowledge under Difficulties: From Self-Improvement to Adult Education in America, 1750–1990*. Stanford, CA: Stanford University Press, 1994.

Kimball, Bruce A. *The "True Professional Ideal" in America: A History*. Cambridge, MA: Blackwell, 1992.

King, Andrew A. "Booker T. Washington and the Myth of Heroic Materialism." *Quarterly Journal of Speech* 60, no. 3 (1974): 323–327.

King, Rolfe. *Obstacles to Divine Revelation: God and the Reorientation of Human Reason*. London: Continuum, 2008.

Kirst, Michael W., and Mitchell L. Stevens, eds. *Remaking College: The Changing Ecology of Higher Education*. Stanford, CA: Stanford University Press, 2015.

Kittelstrom, Amy. *The Religion of Democracy: Seven Liberals and the American Moral Tradition*. New York: Penguin, 2015.

Knight, William Angus, ed. *Memorials of Thomas Davidson: The Wandering Scholar*. Boston: Ginn, 1907.

Kock, Christian, and Lisa S. Villadsen. "Introduction: Citizenship as a Rhetorical Practice." In *Rhetorical Citizenship and Public Deliberation*, edited by Christian Kock and Lisa S. Villadsen, 1–12. State College: Pennsylvania State University Press, 2012.

Kuklick, Bruce. *The Rise of American Philosophy: Cambridge, Massachusetts, 1860–1930*. New Haven, CT: Yale University Press, 1977.

Kuzminski, Adrian. *Fixing the System: A History of Populism, Ancient and Modern*. New

York: Continuum, 2008.

Laclau, Ernesto. *On Populist Reason*. London: Verso, 2007.

———. *Politics and Ideology in Marxist Theory: Capitalism, Fascism, Populism*. London: New Left Books, 1977.

Lampert, Sara E. "The 'Perfect Delight' of Dramatic Reading: Gertrude Kellogg and the Post–Civil War Lyceum." In *Thinking Together: Lecturing, Learning, and Difference in the Long Nineteenth Century*, edited by Angela G. Ray and Paul Stob, 130–149. State College: Pennsylvania State University Press, 2018.

Larson, Magali Sarfatti. *The Rise of Professionalism: A Sociological Analysis*. Berkeley: University of California Press, 1977.

Larson, Orvin. *American Infidel: Robert G. Ingersoll*. Madison, WI: Freedom From Religion Foundation, 1993.

Lecklider, Aaron. "The Real Victims of Anti-intellectualism." *Chronicle of Higher Education*, September 20, 2017, https://www.chronicle.com/article/The-Real-Victims-of/241101.

Lee, Michael J. "The Populist Chameleon: The People's Party, Huey Long, George Wallace, and the Populist Argumentative Frame." *Quarterly Journal of Speech* 92, no. 4 (2006): 355–378.

Lee, Ronald. "The New Populist Campaign for Economic Democracy: A Rhetorical Exploration." *Quarterly Journal of Speech* 72, no. 3 (1986): 274–289.

Lewandowski, Tadeusz. *Red Bird, Red Power: The Life and Legacy of Zitkala-Ša*. Norman: University of Oklahoma Press, 2016.

Licht, Walter. *Industrializing America: The Nineteenth Century*. Baltimore: Johns Hopkins University Press, 1995.

Livingston, David N. "The History of Science and the History of Geography: Interactions and Implications." *History of Science* 22, no. 3 (1984): 271–302.

———. *Putting Science in Its Place: Geographies of Scientific Knowledge*. Chicago: University of Chicago Press, 2003.

———. "The Spaces of Knowledge: Contributions towards a Historical Geography of Science." *Environment and Planning D: Society and Space* 13, no. 1 (1995): 5–34.

Lowndes, Joseph. "From Founding Violence to Political Hegemony: The

Conservative Populism of George Wallace." In *Populism and the Mirror of Democracy*, edited by Francisco Panizza, 144–171. London: Verso, 2005.

Lucas, Stephen E. "Justifying America: The Declaration of Independence as a Rhetorical Document." In *American Rhetoric: Context and Criticism*, edited by Thomas W. Benson, 67–130. Carbondale: Southern Illinois University Press, 1989.

Lukacs, John. *Democracy and Populism: Fear and Hatred*. New Haven, CT: Yale University Press, 2005.

Lynch, John. "Prepare to Believe: The Creation Museum as Embodied Conversion Narrative." *Rhetoric & Public Affairs* 16, no. 1 (2013): 1–28.

Lyon, Arabella. *Deliberative Acts: Democracy, Rhetoric, and Rights*. State College: Pennsylvania State University Press, 2013.

Maddox, Lucy. *Citizen Indians: Native American Intellectuals, Race, and Reform*. Ithaca, NY: Cornell University Press, 2005.

Madigan, Daniel A. "Particularity, Universality, and Finality: Insights from the Gospel of John." In *Communicating the Word: Revelation, Translation, and Interpretation in Christianity and Islam*, edited by David Marshall, 14–25. Washington, DC: Georgetown University Press, 2011.

Mailloux, Steven. "Thinking in Public with Rhetoric." *Philosophy & Rhetoric* 39, no. 2 (2006): 140–146.

Massey, Doreen. *Space, Place, and Gender*. Minneapolis: University of Minnesota Press, 1994.

McClellan, B. Edward. *Moral Education in America: Schools and the Shaping of Character from Colonial Times to the Present*. New York: Teachers College Press, 1999.

McDaniel, James P., and Bruce E. Gronbeck. "Through the Looking Glass and Back: Democratic Theory, Rhetoric, and Barbiegate." In *The Prettier Doll: Rhetoric, Discourse, and Ordinary Democracy*, edited by Karen Tracy, James P. McDaniel, and Bruce E. Gronbeck, 22–44. Tuscaloosa: University of Alabama Press, 2007.

McDonald, Jean A. "Mary Baker Eddy and the Nineteenth-Century 'Public' Woman: A Feminist Reappraisal." *Journal of Feminist Studies in Religion* 2, no. 1 (1986): 89–111.

———. "Mary Baker Eddy at the Podium: The Founder of the Christian Science Church." Master's thesis, University of Minnesota, 1969.

McGee, Michael Calvin. "The 'Ideograph': A Link between Rhetoric and Ideology." *Quarterly Journal of Speech* 66, no. 1 (1980): 1–16.

———. "In Search of 'the People': A Rhetorical Alternative." *Quarterly Journal of Speech* 61, no. 3 (1975): 236–249.

McGregor, Deborah Kuhn. *From Midwives to Medicine: The Birth of American Gynecology*. New Brunswick, NJ: Rutgers University Press, 1998.

McMath, Robert C. *American Populism: A Social History, 1877-1898*. New York: Hill and Wang, 1993.

McMullin, Evan. "Trump's Rise Proves How Dangerous Populism Is for Democracy." *NBCNews.com*, October 11, 2017, https://www.nbcnews.com/think/opinion/trump-s-rise-proves-populism-democracy-s-greatest-threat-ncna809521.

Merullo, Roland. "What Liberal Academics Don't Get." *Chronicle of Higher Education*, November 20, 2016, https://www.chronicle.com/article/What-Liberal-Academics-Don-t/238428.

Minogue, Kenneth. "Populism as a Political Movement." In *Populism: Its Meaning and National Characteristics*, edited by Ghita Ionescu and Ernest Gellner, 197–211. London: Macmillan, 1969.

Moffitt, Benjamin. *The Global Rise of Populism: Performance, Political Style, and Representation*. Stanford, CA: Stanford University Press, 2016.

Morantz, Regina Markell. "The Perils of Feminist History." *Journal of Interdisciplinary History* 4, no. 4 (1974): 649–660.

Morgan, H. Wayne. "Toward National Unity." In *The Gilded Age*, rev. ed., edited by H. Wayne Morgan, 1–12. Syracuse: Syracuse University Press, 1970.

Morris, Richard. "Educating Savages." *Quarterly Journal of Speech* 83, no. 2 (1997): 152–171.

Moss, Hilary J. *Schooling Citizens: The Struggle for African American Education in Antebellum America*. Chicago: University of Chicago Press, 2009.

Mounk, Yascha. *The People vs. Democracy: Why Our Freedom Is in Danger and How to Save It*. Cambridge, MA: Harvard University Press, 2018.

Mountford, Roxanne. "On Gender and Rhetorical Space." *Rhetoric Society Quarterly* 30, no. 1 (2001): 41–71.

Mudde, Cas. "Populism: An Ideational Approach." In *The Oxford Handbook of Populism*, edited by Cristobal Rovira Kaltwasser, Paul Taggart, Paulina

Ochoa Espejo, and Pierre Ostiguy, 27–47. Oxford: Oxford University Press, 2017.

Müller, Jan-Werner. *What Is Populism?* Philadelphia: University of Pennsylvania Press, 2016.

Naylor, Simon. "Introduction: Historical Geographies of Science—Places, Contexts, Cartographies." *British Journal for the History of Science* 38, no. 1 (2005): 1–12.

Noll, Mark A. *Between Faith and Criticism: Evangelicals, Scholarship, and the Bible in America.* San Francisco: Harper & Row, 1986.

Norrell, Robert J. *Up from History: The Life of Booker T. Washington.* Cambridge, MA: Belknap Press of Harvard University Press, 2009.

Ostiguy, Pierre. "Populism: A Socio-cultural Approach." In *The Oxford Handbook of Populism*, edited by Cristobal Rovira Kaltwasser, Paul Taggart, Paulina Ochoa Espejo, and Pierre Ostiguy, 73–97. Oxford: Oxford University Press, 2017.

Parker, Gail. "Mary Baker Eddy and Sentimental Womanhood." *New England Quarterly* 43, no. 1 (1970): 3–18.

Pearce, Kimber Charles. "Rhetorical Polysemy in Mary Baker Eddy's 'Christian Science in Tremont Temple.'" *Journal of Communication and Religion* 23, no. 2 (2000): 73–94.

Pease, Edward R. *The History of the Fabian Society.* New York: E. P. Dutton, 1916.

Peel, Robert. *Mary Baker Eddy: The Years of Authority.* New York: Holt, Rinehart and Winston, 1977.

———. *Mary Baker Eddy: The Years of Discovery.* New York: Holt, Rinehart and Winston, 1966.

Perry, Lewis. *Intellectual Life in America: A History.* Chicago: University of Chicago Press, 1989.

Piott, Steven L. *Daily Life in the Progressive Era.* Santa Barbara, CA: Greenwood, 2011.

Postel, Charles. "Murder on the Brazos: The Religious Context of the Populist Revolt." *Journal of the Gilded Age and Progressive Era* 15 (2016): 197–219.

———. *The Populist Vision.* Oxford: Oxford University Press, 2007.

Powell, Douglas Reichert. *Critical Regionalism: Connecting Politics and Culture in the American Landscape.* Chapel Hill: University of North Carolina Press, 2007.

Pratt, Richard H. "The Advantages of Mingling Indians with Whites." In *Americanizing the American Indians: Writings by the "Friends of the Indian," 1880–1900*, edited by Francis Paul Prucha, 260–271. Cambridge, MA: Harvard University Press, 1973.

Putzi, Jennifer. *Identifying Marks: Race, Gender, and the Marked Body in Nineteenth-Century America.* Athens: University of Georgia Press, 2006.

Ray, Angela G. *The Lyceum and Public Culture in the Nineteenth-Century United States.* East Lansing: Michigan State University Press, 2005.

——. "Making History by Analogy: Frederick Douglass Remembers William the Silent." In *Exploring Argumentative Contexts*, edited by Frans H. van Eemeren and Bart Garseen, 95–114. Amsterdam: John Benjamins Publishing, 2012.

Ray, Angela G., and Paul Stob, eds. *Thinking Together: Lecturing, Learning, and Difference in the Long Nineteenth Century.* State College: Pennsylvania State University Press, 2018.

Recchiuti, John Louis. *Civic Engagement: Social Science and Progressive-Era Reform in New York City.* Philadelphia: University of Pennsylvania Press, 2007.

Reese, William J. *America's Public Schools: From the Common School to "No Child Left Behind."* Baltimore: Johns Hopkins University Press, 2005.

Reyes, Oscar. "Skinhead Conservatism: A Failed Populist Project." In *Populism and the Mirror of Democracy*, edited by Francisco Panizza, 99–117. London: Verso, 2005.

Rice, Jenny. "From Architectonic to Tectonics: Introducing Regional Rhetorics." *Rhetoric Society Quarterly* 42, no. 3 (2012): 201–213.

Richardson, Alan. "The Rise of Modern Biblical Scholarship and Recent Discussion of the Authority of the Bible." In *The Cambridge History of the Bible: The West from the Reformation to the Present Day*, edited by S. L. Greenslade, 38–93. Cambridge: Cambridge University Press, 1963.

Richardson, Riché. *Black Masculinity and the U.S. South: From Uncle Tom to Gangsta.* Athens: University of Georgia Press, 2007.

Richardson, Robert D. *William James in the Maelstrom of American Modernism.* Boston: Houghton Mifflin, 2006.

Rieser, Andrew C. *The Chautauqua Moment: Protestants, Progressives, and the Culture of Modern Liberalism.* New York: Columbia University Press, 2003.

———. "Secularization Reconsidered: Chautauqua and the De-Christianization of Middle-Class Authority, 1880–1920." In *The Middling Sorts: Explorations in the History of the American Middle Class*, edited by Burton J. Bledstein and Robert D. Johnston, 136–150. New York, NY: Routledge, 2001.

Rohler, Lloyd. "Conservative Appeals to the People: George Wallace's Populist Rhetoric." *Southern Communication Journal* 64, no. 4 (1999): 316–322.

Ronda, Bruce. "The Concord School of Philosophy and the Legacy of Transcendentalism." *New England Quarterly* 82, no. 4 (2009): 575–607.

Rorty, Richard. *Philosophy and Social Hope.* London: Penguin, 1999.

Rosenberg, Charles E. "And Heal the Sick: The Hospital and the Patient in the 19th Century America." *Journal of Social History* 10 (1977): 428–447.

Rosenfield, Leonora Cohen. *Portrait of a Philosopher: Morris R. Cohen in Life and Letters.* New York: Harcourt, Brace & World, 1962.

Rubin, Jennifer. "Populism Is No Way to Govern, and Trump Is Proving It." *Washington Post*, January 19, 2018, https://www.washingtonpost.com/blogs/right-turn/wp/2018/01/19/populism-is-no-way-to-govern-and-trump-is-proving-it/.

Rush, Ormond. *The Eyes of Faith: The Sense of the Faithful and the Church's Reception of Revelation.* Washington, DC: Catholic University of America Press, 2009.

Sanchez, John, and Mary E. Stuckey. "From Boarding Schools to the Multicultural Classroom: The Intercultural Politics of Education, Assimilation, and American Indians." *Teacher Education Quarterly* 26, no. 3 (1999): 83–96.

Schoepflin, Rennie B. *Christian Science on Trial: Religious Healing in America.* Baltimore: Johns Hopkins University Press, 2003.

Schulte-Sasse, Linda. "Meet Ross Perot: The Lasting Legacy of Capraesque Populism." *Cultural Critique* 25 (1993): 91–119.

Schwain, Kristin. *Signs of Grace: Religion and American Art in the Gilded Age.* Ithaca, NY: Cornell University Press, 2008.

Scott, Donald M. "The Popular Lecture and the Creation of a Public in Mid-Nineteenth-Century America." *Journal of American History* 66, no. 4 (1980): 791–809.

Scott, Emmett. *The Tuskegee Negro Conferences.* Tuskegee, AL: Tuskegee Institute Press, 1904.

Scott, Joan W. "The Evidence of Experience." *Critical Inquiry* 17, no. 4 (1991): 773–797.

Sellingo, Jeffrey J. *College (Un)Bound: The Future of Higher Education and What It Means for Students.* Las Vegas, NV: Amazon Publishing, 2013.

Shi, David E. *Facing Facts: Realism in American Thought and Culture, 1850–1920.* Oxford: Oxford University Press, 1995.

Shogan, Colleen J. "Anti-intellectualism in the Modern Presidency: A Republican Populism." *Perspectives on Politics* 5, no. 2 (2007): 295–303.

Smith, Frank. *Robert G. Ingersoll: A Life.* Buffalo, NY: Prometheus Books, 1990.

Smith, Michelle. "Affect and Respectability Politics." *Theory and Event* 17, no. 3 *Supplement* (2014): n.p.

Sommer, Benjamin D. "Revelation at Sinai in the Hebrew Bible and in Jewish Theology." *Journal of Religion* 79, no. 3 (1999): 422–451.

Starr, Paul. *The Social Transformation of American Medicine: The Rise of a Sovereign Profession and the Making of a Vast Industry.* New York: Basic Books, 1982.

Stob, Paul. "Black Hands Push Back: Reconsidering the Rhetoric of Booker T. Washington." *Quarterly Journal of Speech* 104, no. 2 (2018): 145–165.

———. "Lonely Courage, Commemorative Confrontation, and Communal Therapy: William James Remembers the Massachusetts 54th." *Quarterly Journal of Speech* 98, no. 3 (2012): 249–271.

———. "Pragmatism, Experience, and William James's Politics of Blindness." *Philosophy and Rhetoric* 44, no. 3 (2011): 227–249.

———. "Sacred Symbols, Public Memory, and the Great Agnostic: Robert Ingersoll Remembers the Civil War." *Rhetoric & Public Affairs* 19, no. 2 (2016): 275–306.

———. *William James and the Art of Popular Statement.* East Lansing: Michigan State University Press, 2013.

Stuckey, Mary E. *Defining Americans: The Presidency and National Identity.* Lawrence: University Press of Kansas, 2004.

Stuckey, Mary E., and John M. Murphy. "By Any Other Name: Rhetorical Colonialism in North America." *American Indian Culture and Research Journal* 25, no. 4 (2001): 76–81.

Susskind, Richard, and Daniel Susskind. *The Future of the Professions: How Technology Will Transform the Work of Human Experts.* Oxford: Oxford

University Press, 2015.

Sutton, Jane S. "Space in Tropes, an Opaque but Visible Relationship." *Review of Communication* 12, no. 1 (2012): 30–43.

Tang, Honghong, Xiaoqin Mai, Shun Wang, Chaozhe Zhu, Frank Krueger, and Chao Liu. "Interpersonal Brain Synchronization in the Right Temporo-Parietal Junction during Face-to-Face Economic Exchange." *Social Cognitive and Affective Neuroscience* 11, no. 1 (2016): 23–32.

Tell, Dave. "The Meanings of Kansas: Rhetoric, Regions, and Counter Regions." *Rhetoric Society Quarterly* 42, no. 3 (2012): 214–232.

Terrill, Robert. "Irony, Silence, and Time: Frederick Douglass on the Fifth of July." *Quarterly Journal of Speech* 89, no. 3 (2003): 216–234.

Thornton, Russell. *American Indians Holocaust and Survival: A Population History since 1492.* Norman: University of Oklahoma Press, 1987.

Thuesen, Peter J. *In Discordance with the Scriptures: American Protestant Battles over Translating the Bible.* New York: Oxford University Press, 1999.

Tichi, Cecelia. *Civic Passions: Seven Who Launched Progressive America (and What They Teach Us).* Chapel Hill: University of North Carolina Press, 2009.

Tonn, Mari Boor. "Taking Conversation, Dialogue, and Therapy Public." *Rhetoric & Public Affairs* 8, no. 3 (2005): 405–430.

Topinka, Robert J. "Resisting the Fixity of Suburban Space: The Walker as Rhetorician." *Rhetoric Society Quarterly* 42, no. 1 (2012): 65–84.

Towne, Ralph L., and Frederick Speckeen. "Robert Green Ingersoll: A Case Study of Free Speech." *Today's Speech* 10, no. 4 (1962): 10–29.

Trachtenberg, Alan. *The Incorporation of America: Culture and Society in the Gilded Age.* New York: Hill and Wang, 1982.

Tracy, Karen. *Challenges of Ordinary Democracy: A Case Study in Deliberation and Dissent.* State College: Pennsylvania State University, 2010.

Vaughn, William Preston. *Schools for All: The Blacks and Public Education in the South, 1865-1877.* Lexington: University Press of Kentucky, 2015.

Verbrugge, Martha H. *Able-Bodied Womanhood: Personal Health and Social Change in Nineteenth-Century Boston.* New York: Oxford University Press, 1988.

Vertinsky, Patricia. *The Eternally Wounded Woman: Women, Doctors, and Exercise in the Late Nineteenth Century.* Manchester: Manchester University Press, 1990.

Vigil, Kiara M. *Indigenous Intellectuals: Sovereignty, Citizenship, and the American*

Imagination, 1880–1930. Cambridge: Cambridge University Press, 2015.

Vivian, Bradford J. "Up from Memory: Epideictic Forgetting in Booker T. Washington's Cotton States Exposition Address." *Philosophy & Rhetoric* 45, no. 2 (2012): 189–212.

Wallace, Anthony F. C. *Jefferson and the Indians: The Tragic Fate of the First Americans.* Cambridge, MA: Belknap Press of Harvard University Press, 1999.

Walsh, Lynda. "The Rhetoric of Oracles." *Rhetoric Society Quarterly* 33, no. 3 (2003): 55–78.

Warner, Michael. *Publics and Counterpublics.* New York: Zone Books, 2002.

Warren, Austin. "The Concord School of Philosophy." *New England Quarterly* 2, no. 2 (1929): 199–233.

Warren, James Perrin. *Culture of Eloquence: Oratory and Reform in Antebellum America.* University Park: Pennsylvania State University Press, 1999.

Warrior, Robert Allen. *Tribal Secrets: Recovering American Indian Intellectual Traditions.* Minneapolis: University of Minnesota Press, 1995.

Washington, Booker T. "A Farmers' College on Wheels." In *The Papers of Booker T. Washington*, vol. 9, *1906–8*, edited by Louis R. Harlan and Raymond Smock, 175–180. Urbana: University of Illinois Press, 1980.

———. *Up from Slavery.* In *The Booker T. Washington Papers*, vol. 1: *The Autobiographical Writings*, edited by Louis R. Harlan. Urbana: University of Illinois Press, 1972.

———. *Working with the Hands.* New York: Doubleday, Page, 1904.

Watson, Jay. *Reading for the Body: The Recalcitrant Materiality of Southern Fiction, 1893–1985.* Athens: University of Georgia Press, 2012.

Weaver, Jace. *That the People Might Live: Native Literatures and Native American Community.* New York: Oxford University Press, 1997.

Weiss, Ellen. *Robert R. Taylor and Tuskegee: An African American Architect Designs for Booker T. Washington.* Montgomery, AL: New South Books, 2012.

Welch, Deborah. "Zitkala-Ša: An American Indian Leader, 1876–1938." PhD dissertation, University of Wyoming, 1985.

Wellmon, Chad. *Organizing Enlightenment: Information Overload and the Invention of the Modern Research University.* Baltimore: Johns Hopkins University Press, 2015.

Weyland, Kurt. "Populism: A Political Strategic Approach." In *The Oxford*

Handbook of Populism, edited by Cristobal Rovira Kaltwasser, Paul Taggart, Paulina Ochoa Espejo, and Pierre Ostiguy, 48–72. Oxford: Oxford University Press, 2017.

White, E. Frances. *Dark Continent of Our Bodies: Black Feminism and the Politics of Respectability*. Philadelphia: Temple University Press, 2001.

Wiebe, Robert H. *The Search for Order, 1877-1920*. New York: Hill and Wang, 1967.

Wieser, Kimberly G. *Back to the Blanket: Recovered Rhetorics and Literacies in American Indian Studies*. Norman: University of Oklahoma Press, 2017.

Williams, Rhys H., and Susan M. Alexander. "Religious Rhetoric in American Populism: Civil Religion as Movement Ideology." *Journal for the Scientific Study of Religion* 33, no. 1 (1994): 1–15.

Wilson, Kirt. "The Racial Contexts of Public Address: Interpreting Violence during the Reconstruction Era." In *The Handbook of Rhetoric and Public Address*, edited by Shawn J. Parry-Giles and J. Michael Hogan, 203–228. Malden, MA: Wiley-Blackwell, 2010.

———. "The Racial Politics of Imitation in the Nineteenth Century." *Quarterly Journal of Speech* 89, no. 2 (2003): 89–108.

Wood, Ann Douglas. "'The Fashionable Diseases': Women's Complaints and Their Treatment in Nineteenth-Century America." *Journal of Interdisciplinary History* 4, no. 1 (1973): 25–52.

Woodman, Ross. *Revelation and Knowledge: Romanticism and Religious Faith*. Toronto: University of Toronto Press, 2011.

Woods, Carly S. *Debating Women: Gender, Education, and Spaces for Argument, 1835-1945*. East Lansing: Michigan State University Press, 2018.

Wright, Elizabethada A. "Rhetorical Spaces in Memorial Places: The Cemetery as a Rhetorical Memory Place/Space." *Rhetoric Society Quarterly* 35, no. 4 (2005): 51–81.

Young, Beth Rapp. "Defending Child Medical Neglect: Christian Science Persuasive Rhetoric." *Rhetoric Review* 20, nos. 3–4 (2001): 268–292.

Zeitz, Joshua. "Historians Have Long Thought Populism Was a Good Thing. Are They Wrong?" *Politico*, January 14, 2018, https://www.politico.com/magazine/story/2018/01/14/trump-populism-history-216320.

Zitkala-Ša. "An Indian Teacher among Indians." *Atlantic Monthly* 85, no. 509 (March 1900): 381–387.

———. "The Menace of Peyote." In *American Indian Stories, Legends, and Other Writings*, edited by Cathy N. Davidson and Ada Norris, 239–241. New York: Penguin, 2003.

———. *Old Indian Legends*. Boston: Ginn, 1901.

———. "The School Days of an Indian Girl." *Atlantic Monthly* 85, no. 508 (February 1900): 185–194.

———. "The Trial Path." *Harper's Monthly Magazine* 103 (June 1901): 741–744.

———. "A Warrior's Daughter." *Everybody's Magazine* 6 (April 1902): 132–140.

———. "Why I Am a Pagan." *Atlantic Monthly* 90 (December 1902): 801–803.

Zonderman, David A. *Uneasy Allies: Working for Labor Reform in Nineteenth-Century Boston*. Amherst: University of Massachusetts Press, 2011.

Index

C